The Faces of
the Goddess

Contents

The Faces
of
the Goddess

Lotte Motz

New York   Oxford
OXFORD UNIVERSITY PRESS
1997

To My Daughter

"You come of the Lord Adam and the Lady Eve," said Aslan. "And that is both honour enough to erect the head of the poorest beggar, and shame enough to bow the shoulders of the greatest emperor on earth. Be content."
—C. S. Lewis, *Prince Caspian*

Oxford University Press

Oxford   New York
Athens   Auckland   Bangkok   Bogotá
Buenos Aires   Calcutta   Cape Town   Dar es Salaam   Delhi
Florence   Hong Kong   Istanbul   Karachi
Kuala Lumpur   Madras   Madrid   Melbourne
Mexico City   Nairobi   Paris   Singapore
Taipei   Tokyo   Toronto

and associated companies in
Berlin   Ibadan

Published by Oxford University Press, Inc.
198 Madison Avenue, New York, New York 10016

Library of Congress Cataloging-in-Publication Data
Motz, Lotte.
    The faces of the goddess /
    Lotte Motz.
        p.   cm.   Includes bibligraphical references.
    ISBN 0–19–508967–7
    1.   Mother goddesses.
    2.   Femininity of God.
    I. Title.
BL325.M6M68   1997   291.2'114—dc20   95–41494

9   8   7   6   5   4   3   2   1

Printed in the United States of America
on acid-free paper

Acknowledgments

Writing this book has been a deeply satisfying intellectual adventure, and I wish to thank those who helped and guided me in this experience. Professor horkild Jacobsen, Professor Walther Burkert, Professor Åke Hultkrantz, and Professor Joseph Kitagawa not only provided insight and inspiration through their work, but also read the pertinent chapters of my study and offered corrections and suggestions.

The inspired editorial advice of Professor James E. Preston allowed me to clarify my argument and to enrich the study with an added dimension.

I received comments and advice from the late Lisbeth Gombrich of Oxford, from Judith Hanson of Hong Kong, from Professor Edgar C. Polomé of Texas, from Professor Anatoly Liberman of Minnesota, Dr. Nigel Warburton of Oxford, and especially from my daughter, Anna.

I owe much to my late husband, Hans, who traveled with me on this journey, though he was a man of science, and from whose trenchant comments I could no longer profit while writing the last three chapters of this book.

I also wish to express my appreciation of the assistance rendered by Cynthia Read and the staff of Oxford University Press, New York.

I further wish to acknowledge with gratitude the unfailing interest and support of my brother, Herbert.

I am much indebted to the Ashmolean Library of Oxford, its splendid collections and its helpful staff. I also wish to thank Stephanie Warburton for her help in compiling the index.

L.M.
Oxford 1996

Introduction

I N discussion and reconstructions of archaic religions the figure of a divine mother has been given an important place. A number of books were devoted to this deity in the past—for example, Erich Neumann's *The Great Mother*, E. O. James's *The Cult of the Mother Goddess*, Robert Briffault's *The Mothers*—and were still written in recent time—such as Marija Gimbutas's *The Language of the Goddess* and Elinor Gadon's *The Once and Future Goddess*. These scholars invariably draw the image of a universal, archetypal, time-transcending being in whose womb all life has generated. She received her exaltation through the awe and wonder inspired by the powers of her fertile womb. The writers invariably include in their explorations divinities who did not bear a child and do not bear the title mother. Motherhood is also attributed to the mute forms of prehistory. Widely divergent qualities and creatures, belonging to various cultures, are held to be expressive of the many shapes of one single divinity. One gains the impression that the scholars set out on their endeavor with an already fixed belief in the existence of a primordial, maternal, all-encompassing, and sovereign deity.

In this study, I examine evidence that might point to the presence of the godhead, without holding a preconceived belief in her existence, and attempt to delineate, if possible, her dimensions. I have chosen several deities, all of importance in their respective religions, who might be variant forms of the great maternal being: Demeter of Greece, who reclaimed her child from death; Cybele of Anatolia, who bore the title Magna Mater; Amaterasu of Japan, the ancestress of the emperor; Mother Saule of Latvia, goddess of the sun; Sedna of the Eskimo, who engendered the fish and mammals of the sea; Nintur of Mesopotamia, who created the first human; and Mexican divinities who were ancestral to and protective of their tribes. I also examine the impact of the

1

vision of the goddess on a religious movement of our time, and I present birth helpers and nursing deities.

The divinities were selected on the basis of their qualities, not on their provenance in certain geographic regions. A comprehensive study of deities throughout the world is hardly possible and was never intended. Some regions, such as India, Egypt, and the provinces of Celtic occupation, might yield interesting information, and the American Shawnee female deity might be examined; these cultures had to be omitted because of space limitations. Since a concept cannot be divorced from its setting, the religious and social environment of a goddess is briefly delineated before she is described.

In order to trace a figure to its basic form, one must try to understand the world in which it developed. Almost inevitably, we interpret the evidence we receive through modern eyes. At a time when nature and not humanity is threatened (humans are threatened by other humans), it is difficult to relive the terror, awe, and admiration aroused by the elemental powers and the ferocity of beasts, and to visualize the religious experiences that arose from these emotions.

The difference of thought between modern and early peoples may be illuminated by the spontaneous utterance of an Eskimo (who belonged to an archaic form of society) on first beholding the city of New York. The statement was reported by Knud Rasmussen: "We who always believed that nature is the greatest and most inscrutable of all powers, now stand in a landscape of mountains and deep canyons, and all this created by the hand of men. . . . Nature is great, but are not men greater?" It is clear that the Eskimo came from a world in which humanity's potential strength and achievement had not yet unfolded, much like the universe of fishermen and hunters where the early forms of religion had come into existence.

In the arctic and subarctic regions, people lived, until very recently, at the edge of existence, as they had done during the millennia of the Paleolithic era. Urbanization never reached the region, though pastoralism and even some agriculture was adopted in various parts. Here archaic forms of religious life persisted through the ages. Karl Jettmar, an archaeologist, thus observes: "In no other place has the fateful impact of the harshness of existence been so profoundly experienced and clearly rendered and the interrelation between man and beast so deeply felt." Here also the mystical adventure of shamanism found its full expression.

Studying the spiritual universe of the northern people surely offers a way of retrieving some of the religious experiences of the past. I therefore include a brief description of the northern areas of Asia and Europe, which extend from Lapland to the Bering Strait, and of their beliefs. These are well documented and are largely homogeneous. Here we encounter the following basic groups of deities:

1. The supernatural owners of nature and its beasts. These are of importance to hunting communities, for they control the supply of game.

2. The sanctified elements of men's environment—the earth, the sky, the rivers. These rose to the fore in agricultural surroundings, where attention is centered on the earth's fertility and the rain-giving sky.
3. Ancestral and tribal spirits that are special to a family.
4. Goddesses who are especially concerned with the needs of women.
5. A more remote, high god who dwells in heaven. I did not find an all-embracing, sovereign, cosmic mother.

The goddesses of this study indeed show their derivation from one or more of the basic groups of North Eurasian belief, though naturally they acquired new attributes in their development within a complex society. The evaluation of the later forms of godhead yields the following conclusions:

1. They are of varied origin and have not descended from a single being.
2. They derive their significance from the phenomenon that they rule or represent—the earth, the sun, the tribal group—and not from their motherhood.
3. They bear the stamp of their social and religious environment.
4. Not the birth giver but the birth helper is of great importance.

These conclusions do not point to the existence of a sovereign, primeval mother who gave birth to all.

The following considerations may be added to the empirical evidence: early people did not seek the source of happenings within an organ of the human body. It was the arrow of an elf that brought pain to back or knee, the visit of a muse through which a poem was composed, the harassment of an incubus that brought the plague of evil dreams. Therefore, the ultimate source of creativity did not, in archaic thought, issue from a human womb, nor was a great cosmic divinity modeled on a human woman. Menaced by many dangers and snatching survival from the jaws of starvation, people would not visualize the ruler of the universe in the form of an ultimately loving mother.

The image of a sovereign force in the shape of a human mother must have evolved at a time when man and his condition had moved to the center of the stage. The vision of the ruler of all life as a nurturing and basically loving being belongs to an age of some ease and comfort. The separation from nature, the bewildering complexity of a more modern society, and a longing for a lost simplicity might have awakened the idea of a single all-embracing power as a symbol of an underlying unity. The concept of the Great Mother belongs to an age of complexity and change, not to the time of grim struggle for survival. The modern scholars' delineations of the archetype, in which divergent forms are said, without cogent reasons, to represent a single being, appear to be quests rather than explorations, expressions of a desire to find a primordial monotheistic faith—*Urmonotheismus*.

In a study of mother goddesses, one must also consider the exact meaning of the noun "mother." Sometimes this title is affixed to beings who show no maternal qualities. Psychological explanations have been offered for this phenomenon. One must realize, however, that the noun "mother" does not always point to a genetrix in a biological or even a figurative way. The goddess Cybele bears the title Mother of the Gods, yet she is not stationed within a family. According to one myth, *she* was fathered by Zeus. She is also called the Mountain Mother; yet she has not brought forth a mountain, while according to one myth, *she* was engendered by a rock.

The nouns of family relationships may simply denote status, age, and sex. French *fille* and Latvian *meita* may mean "daughter" or "young woman"; Latvian *māte* means "mother" and also "goddess." If we know that the title mother can have the sense of "lady," "goddess," and "queen," we need not construct a complex explanation when we find it in conjunction with a clearly nonmaternal creature.

By divesting myself of traditional notions concerning language and divinities, I believe I have gained new and valid views of the ancient forces.

The Great Mother

T HE concept of an all-embracing maternal divinity, a Great Mother, ruling religious life, manifest in the earliest symbolic expressions, and enduring and unfolding through the ages in an infinite variety of forms,
has been widely recognized by scholars of various disciplines. Her earliest
epiphany has been discerned in statuettes of ivory or stone that were found
in dwelling places of the Upper Paleolithic Aurignac–Solutrean cultures, dating
back as far as 30,000 B.C.E. The artifacts were unearthed in such widely separated places as Austria, Russia, and Spain, yet show a certain homogeneity
in certain aspects of the body. Frequently, the woman is of great obesity, with
sagging breasts, protruding stomach, and enormous haunches, though slim
and stylized versions have also been encountered. Since the woman's form is
suggestive of the state of pregnancy, she has been regarded as a power of
fecundity who gives expression to the deeply felt mystery of birth and generation.[1] In his book on the Great Mother, Erich Neumann states that "the
unshapely figures of the Great Mother are representations of the pregnant
goddess of fertility who was looked upon throughout the world as goddess of
pregnancy and childbearing, and who, as a cult object not only of women, but
also of men, represents the archetypal symbol of fertility."[2]

With the advent of agriculture in the Mediterranean regions (9000–7000
B.C.E.), the number of female statuettes did not decrease, and many hundreds
were retrieved in Anatolia, Crete, and Egypt from the houses, graves, and
sanctuaries of a farming population. Some stylistic similarity between the
hunters' and the farmers' artifacts indicates an awareness of the same principle
that, as it is believed, had given solace and sustenance in earlier ages. M.E.L.
Mallowan, the excavator of Arpachiyah, concluded that "fertility worship connected with a 'mother goddess' cult must indeed be one of the oldest and
longest surviving religions of the ancient world."[3]

The same life-shaping force is said to have acquired its fullest realization in Minoan Crete. Here "the Minoan Goddess was depicted in clay and porcelain as the Earth-Mother, the Mountain-Mother, the Mistress of trees and the Lady of wild beasts."[4] W.K.C Guthrie understands that the *Potnia* (Lady) was the earth in all its aspects, the universal mother goddess, mother of fruits, mother and mistress of animals, and had the king and his palace under her special protection.[5] We would thus find in this culture the first evidence of the infinite variety of forms that belong with the image of the maternal divinity.

She had received, it is said, her new significance with the agriculturalists' new mastery over their environment, since the miracle of vegetative growth was assimilated to the mystery of the fertile womb. Mircea Eliade thus asserts, "The sacrality of sexual life, and first of all of feminine sexuality, became inseparable from the miraculous enigma of creation. . . . A complex symbolism . . . associates woman and sexuality with lunar rhythm, with the earth (assimilated to the womb), and what must be called: the 'mystery of vegetation.' "[6] Since women participated more fully in tilling the soil than in hunting savage beasts and may even have invented agriculture, a matriarchal society may have arisen, in which it is only natural that the mother goddess, now seen in the image of the fruitful earth, the Earth Goddess, should have acquired yet another powerful dimension. Thus "it is not surprising that in the religious thought of a farming culture the great earth-goddess is conceived as a Supreme Being, and more especially as a Supreme Creator."[7]

Pointing to a vast assemblage of artifacts, Marija Gimbutas affirms that a vital agricultural society had also flourished in southeastern Europe; it had found its beginnings in about 7000 B.C.E. and was named by her the Culture of Old Europe. She discerned in her analysis of the archaeological remains, beneath the many forms, the contours of a Great Mother, a "Great Goddess of Life, Death and Regeneration in anthropomorphic form . . . a supreme Creator who creates from her own substance" and who represents "the primary Goddess of the Old European Pantheon."[8] And we would understand that the function and attributes of the mother goddess multiplied with the increasing complexity of social organization; still nurturing the wild creatures of the forest, she would now rule domesticated beasts and the seed placed in the soil.

Written documents indeed furnish testimony to the power of feminine divinities in the Aegean and Middle Eastern areas and the regions of the Indus Valley. It is believed that such goddesses as Artemis, Anat, Ishtar-Inanna, and Hera represent the various manifestations of the great primordial force. She is so diversified that she may show herself in virginal as well as maternal form, as maiden or as mother, as protector of the hearth and of the beasts of untamed nature, as life-giving or as life-taking. In the last aspect, she is named Mother Terrible. Figurines found in the Zhob Valley of Beluchistan present grotesque and frightening features, totally different from any other sculpture of prehistory, and seem to be the "grim embodiment of the mother goddess who is also the guardian of the dead, an underworld deity, concerned alike with the crops and the seed-corn buried beneath the earth."[9]

It is also held by some that with the establishment of patriarchal communities and states, the great goddess suffered an eclipse, pressed, as she now was, into the framework of a male-dominated order. The Greek Hera, once a sovereign ruler and a queen, submitted to the yoke of marriage and bowed, though not graciously, to her male master, the lord and king of earth and heaven. The change took place, in the view of Joseph Campbell, at the end of the Bronze and the beginning of the Iron Age when nomadic warrior races overran and conquered the ancient city-states.[10]

It is true, conversely, that people would continue to revere Demeter, who brings the harvest, and Artemis, who guides the young. And in the last pre-Christian millennium, when humans sought to obtain, in newly arising cults, through public or through secret ceremonies, a vision of eternity and a promise of salvation, the goddess was accorded a yet greater glory when she was the ruler of such a cult. The mystery religions spread beyond their point of origin, and such goddesses as Cybele, Isis, and Atargatis became the mothers of spiritual regeneration in many lands. When in the second century C.E. Lucius of the Golden Ass met the goddess Isis of many names, she described herself as the mother of nature, the mistress of all elements, the queen of the underworld, and the highest of the gods of heaven.[11] It would seem that the ancient goddess had regained her glory.

The reason for the awe and wonder inspired by the woman goddess, and her formation into the origin and fount of life, presumably lies in the fact that in very early ages men were unaware of their share in procreation so that woman was seen as the sole actor in the drama of the miracle of birth. Thus the goddess had no male partner in her earliest epiphanies; later, a young god, a son, or a lover was adjoined, and even later, a patriarchal spouse.[12]

These are some of the main and widely held ideas concerning the divinity. Let us now consider the claims more closely, especially with a view to what we have gained in knowledge concerning the beliefs and thought patterns of societies in various stages of cultural development.

Since men, above all, wish to sustain and propagate their kind, it is believed that the "Venus" statuettes of the Paleolithic, their reproductive organs fully exposed, were meant to bestow the blessing of fecundity on women. Found in the habitations of mammoth and reindeer hunters of the Solutrean and Aurignac, the artifacts were often lying closely beside the hearth where frequently a niche in the wall was also discovered. Franz Hančar concludes in his careful study of the Siberian evidence that the images had originally been stationed in the niche and had indeed been objects of religious reverence.[13] Since they appear in the context of hunting cultures, we may look to the attitudes and beliefs of modern hunting communities to gain an indication of the nature of the superhuman woman.

When we regard the beliefs of modern hunting and herding peoples of northern Eurasia, we note that their attitude toward the "mystery of the fertile womb" is far from reverent. In these regions, the climate of emotion is so deeply affected by a fear of women's biological functions, menstruation, pregnancy, and parturition that numerous rules and prohibitions were created to counteract the potential danger.

To avoid defilement, the houses of the northern peoples are divided into men's and women's parts, the former "pure" and "sacred," the latter "polluted" and "profane."[14] In some areas, such as Finland and Karelia, the most sacred space lies in the corner formed by the back and left walls of the dwelling; in other regions, such as Lapland, the sanctified area extends along the back wall of the habitation. In the "pure," or men's, part, the household gods reside, and here is stored the gear for hunting; here religious ceremonies are conducted, and here the dead are placed before removal from the dwelling. Here the shaman's drum is kept, and here the men prepare the meat of beasts that they have killed in hunting; whereas in their part, the women are allowed to cook the meat of domesticated animals.[15] Even in the homes of farmers who had accepted Christianity, some old names for both the men's and women's parts have persisted as a vestige of the earlier rules and prohibitions. The articles of the new faith and new way of life—images of Christian saints, consecrated candles, the sheaf of harvest celebrations—are still kept in the space sanctified by the earlier tradition.

The boundary between the areas of the hunters' dwellings may be marked off by a stone, the "women's stone"; by a pillar, the "Siimsi pillar"; or by a log.[16] Women, children, and strangers are, under no circumstances, allowed to cross the line. Among the Siberian Samoyeds, a woman who wishes to walk from one side of the hearth to the other must retrace her steps through her own area; among the tribe of the Yakuts, she is not permitted to cross the beam of light that issues from the fireplace in the men's part of the room.

A second door leads in Saami (Lapp) dwellings from the men's section to the place behind the tent. The men must go through this door when they leave for their hunting expeditions and when they return with the slain beasts. Through this door also the dead are carried to their final resting places, for in all these offices it is essential that a man not pass through the entrance that is also used by women.[17] This second door is also taken when men visit the family sanctuary in the forest, taking care not to wear a garment that has touched the garment of a woman.

Gustav Ränk finds clear evidence of past existence of a second door among most dwellings of the hunters and herders of Eurasia. Since such a door is no longer present, a window or an opening created especially for the purpose serves as a way of entrance or departure for those who must not be defiled.[18] Numinous significance adheres also to the space behind the tent, out of bounds for women. Here the men cut up the bodies of the hunted beasts; here may also stand the sacred sled, crowded with the puppets that are revered as household gods. Sometimes sacrifices are conducted in the hallowed space.

At the time of giving birth, women are not tolerated even in their portion of the habitation. In some places, a special tent is at times erected to house a woman in her travail; in others, she may have to find a space in the open. The women of the Samoyeds bed down on the pile of firewood near the tent, as do the women of the Yenisei.[19]

These examples may suffice to indicate the depth of fear and anxiety engendered among hunters of a wide-ranging area by the dynamics of female biology. It may be argued that we cannot draw conclusions from the beliefs of modern nations to the beliefs of prehistoric times. But we know that some continuity prevails in the spiritual life of ancient and modern hunters. Shamanism, a still extant phenomenon, appears to have been practiced in the Paleolithic. Admiration and reverence of the world of animals finds expression among modern hunters, as it did in prehistoric caves. Modern Eskimo draw images that are reminiscent of the rock drawings of ancient Scandinavia. Archaeological finds indicate a division between men's and women's sections in Paleolithic dwelling sites.[20]

The belief in the polluting effect of parturition has left its imprint among a wide range of cultures. The woman of the Herero of South Africa leaves her husband's dwelling to give birth behind her mother's hut. With the Kotas of the Nigerian hills, the laboring mother withdraws to the place to which she must also retire at the time of menstruation. Among the Indians of the Uaupes Valley of Brazil, the woman stays, but all the household goods are taken from the home so that they will not be defiled by the uncleanliness of bringing forth a child.[21]

The women of the Israelites were unclean for forty-two days after bearing a son and for sixty-six days after bearing a daughter. At the end of this period, a ceremony in the temple cleansed the mother so that she could once again resume her place in the community. A ceremony of purification was also performed before the Christian woman was again received in church (*ordo a purificandam mulierem post partum*). In Germany, as late as the eighteenth century, she was buried outside the cemetery in unhallowed ground, if she died before she could thus be "churched." It also was believed that the "unchurched" woman would cause the grass on which she walked to wither or the house to burn that she entered; therefore, she was confined to her habitation before her cleansing.[22] Among the Nambikwara Indians of Brazil, both husband and wife must leave their group for several months and return only when the child is able to eat solid food.[23]

The belief that the act of childbearing brings ritual impurity left its imprint on so large a number of peoples (only a few of the many instances have been cited) that we may consider it a possibly universal feature. Realizing this, we must be puzzled by Erich Neumann's assertion: "The earliest sacred precinct of the primordial age was probably that in which women gave birth."[24] If we consider how simple societies, especially those of hunting cultures, feel and felt toward the act of childbearing, we would not find it easy to believe that the Paleolithic figurines were shown in the state of pregnancy. It seems unlikely that the image of a woman with child, thus in a condition of ritual

Figure 1. Paleolithic figurine
from Willendorf, Austria.
Limestone.

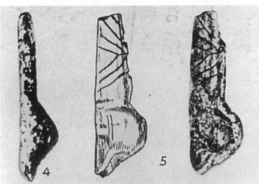

Figure 2. Stylized Aurignac
figurines from Mezin, Siberia.

impurity, even if she was a goddess, would be placed in a prominent position
in the habitation.

We note that most statuettes show no clear evidence of pregnancy. The
woman's belly bulges, but her thighs and buttocks, not organs of reproduction,
are proportionate in size (Figure 1). Stylized versions, centering on the buttocks, indicate this part of the body as the focus of significance (Figure 2).
Nor need long sagging breasts point to the state of pregnancy. The Wild

Women of the German forests are sometimes envisioned with long sagging breasts, as is the Vu-murt, a water spirit of the Udmurts, a Finnic culture.[25] These creatures are not considered to be the carriers of unborn children. The most natural way to symbolize motherhood is to show a mother with her child. The Virgin Mary, a truly maternal figure, is rarely seen without her son.[26] Children with or without their mothers are absent from Paleolithic imagery. This fact does not point to the high value supposedly accorded to the fertility of women.

In recent scholarship, the relation of the statuettes to human fecundity has been questioned. Franz Hančar believes that they represent the "clan mother," the tutelary spirit of the family or tribe. Karl Narr, Alexander Marshack, and James Preston think that a complex set of forces is symbolized by the artifacts, some relating to functions of the female body but others to such concerns as sustenance or protection from the many dangers of a mammoth-hunter's life.[27]

It is true that in agricultural societies the extreme fear of women and their functions greatly receded. In peasant communities, even of northern Eurasia, women have a share in the sacred life of their group and seek through their own celebrations a state of safety and prosperity.[28] The farmers of the Middle East molded, among other female figurines, some who hold a child; and these allow us to assume that here we meet a maternal deity or a votary desiring the fulfillment of motherhood.[29] The number of such figurines, however, is so small that it can in no way affirm the widespread worship of a universal mother.

Peter Ucko studied and analyzed several hundred sculptures attributed to predynastic Egypt, Neolithic Crete, the Greek mainland, and the Middle East; he found that only six of these show a woman with a child.[30] The others may appear in diverse forms, with arms beneath their breasts or at their sides, in seated, standing, or squatting positions, as male or female or sexless creatures (though the female form predominates), with or without facial features, sometimes holding an animal, corpulent or slim, steatopygic or flat-bottomed. On the basis of his detailed analysis of the artifacts and their archaeological context, Ucko considers it unlikely that the figurines of any complement served the same single purpose, that they represented the same aspect of one single individual, or that the majority of the figurines from any complement embodied the same aspect of a deity. He thus finds no evidence for the cultic reverence of a universal mother goddess.[31]

Marija Gimbutas, who asserts that a Goddess of Birth, Death, and Regeneration was worshipped in Old Europe, finds strong support for her claim in some clay figures of the Balkans of about 6000 B.C.E. These include a mother with an infant in her arms; however, none of them possessess a wholly human form. The head of a bear or of some other mammal or bird rests upon a body of somewhat human shape, and the infant, in its turn, shows the features of a bear or bird. It is not clear why a "bear mother" suckling her "bear child" should embody a force that gives fertility to human women.

Gimbutas believes that the maternal solicitude of an actual bear mother so impressed the Neolithic farmers of the region that they adopted her as the symbol of maternal love. Here Gimbutas surely brings modern, anthropocentric thinking to the task of deciphering the relics of an ancient belief. She fails to realize the measure of reverence and awe accorded by archaic societies to the animals into whose realm they had penetrated, and the deep sense of guilt when men killed, as they must in order to survive, their animal gods and masters.[32] Bear worship, especially, is attested through the ages for the provinces of Europe.[33] The Bear Mother, who may be the source of death or of glorious triumph to the hunter, is infinitely superior to a human mother. She would be revered because of her own awesome might and not as the symbol of a human emotion.

It is also held that the imagery of Minoan art points to the existence of a great primordial mother. Female forms abound in this imagery; seal and signet engravings, above all, show slim-waisted women, full-bosomed and bare-breasted, clothed in long flouncing skirts, in various activities. The woman may be stationed between beasts or seated beneath a tree, dancing in ecstatic motion, traveling in a boat, holding or receiving flowers, or surrounded by adoring votaries or priests. Here too it is assumed that a single godhead is presented in her various epiphanies. She is thus the mountain mother, the snake goddess of chthonic aspect, and the Lady of flowering plants, preserving beneath her various shapes the unchanging reality of the Great Mother.[34]

We may ask once more why the various activities depicted in the scenes should be ascribed to one all-embracing being. The gods of later pantheons do not wantonly change their attributes; we recognize Thor by his hammer, Athena by her owl, Apollo by his lyre, and the Hittite Teshup by his thunderbolt. Why should, just in Minoan art, a flowering tree, a spear, or a snake symbolize the aspects of a single godhead, and why a maternal figure? It is true that the women look extremely similar to one another, but this similarity arises through stylistic convention, and what is believed to be the goddess can hardly be distinguished through her appearance from her votaries. Surely they are not various aspects of a single creature. Let us also note that the women of Minoan imagery are not depicted in a state of pregnancy or, with some exceptions, with a child (Figure 3).

As the artifacts of prehistory indicate a worship of female forces, so the written documents of the Middle Eastern regions more fully name and describe a number of female deities of great splendor, and some goddesses are clearly designated and shown as mothers, such as Ninmah, Ninhursag, or Nintur of Sumero-Akkadian tradition. While these maternal figures play a role in the myths of creation they seem to have diminished before the greater glory of more dazzling divinities—the Great Goddesses Anat of the Canaanites, Inanna-Ishtar of Mesopotamia, Astarte, and Atargatis of the Syrians. These show much resemblance to one another: They are, with only some individual variations, imperious, sexually aggressive, warlike, violent and tempestuous, protective of certain chosen beings, able to grant kingship, order, or prosperity;

they may be brought into relation with seasonal ritual and the mourning for a young divinity. They are not portrayed as mothers.[35]

The important goddesses of the Greek pantheon—Hera, Athena, Artemis, and Aphrodite—have separated from the All Mother of Minoan times, according to E. O. James, and developed on the Greek mainland their different individualities.[36] While the separateness of these beings clearly emerged, the maternal aspect surely vanished, for Athena and Artemis are virginal; Aphrodite is involved in matters of erotic love; Hera brought forth some children but functions, above all, as a wife and queen. Though these goddesses are concerned with various areas of women's lives and assist in childbirth or protect the young, the core and heart of their being is not in the dominion over death, birth, and fecundity.

The Greek pantheon does contain, however, some deeply caring mothers, and the act of giving birth is brought dramatically before our eyes, as in the cases of Leto and Rhea. Thetis deeply feels and tries to heal the anguish of her son Achilles. None of these figures exhibit any sovereignty. The time of approaching birth represents a period of crisis in the lives of Rhea and Leto, the latter searching in despair for a place that would accept her in her travail, the former hiding in the shelter of a cave to protect her newborn child from death. Thetis must plead with Zeus to obtain new armor for Achilles.[37]

More power is accorded to another mother goddess of the Greeks: Demeter, who lost her beloved daughter, the "slender-ankled" Persephone, through rape. The most important mother figure of her tradition, she was unable to prevent her daughter's violation. Demeter herself was raped by Zeus and had in this union conceived her child. While she wandered in sorrow, searching for her vanished daughter, she was ravished by the god Poseidon of the sea. Obviously the theme of rape looms large in the stories surrounding the divinity, and the helpless acceptance of male violence accords ill with the image of a great and sovereign deity. Nor can Demeter recall, through her own might, her child from the regions of the dead. She cannot then be the supreme mistress over life and death which the great maternal power is envisioned.[38]

With the rising popularity of the mystery religions in the last pre-Christian millennium, the divine ruler of such a cult would attain a new and exalted stature. After the cult of Cybele, the Phrygian mountain mother, was brought to Rome in the midst of the Carthaginian crisis, she was revered as one who had bestowed a fruitful harvest and also the defeat of the Carthaginian forces. She became in time an almost universal goddess.[39] And Isis absorbed in her travel from Egypt so many qualities that she grew into an all-embracing power, among other things a "parent of nature, protectress of sailors, comforter of those in distress, kindler of the fire of the sun." And she was adored as "Isis of the many names." She herself declares, as told by Apuleius, that the Phrygians call her the mother of the gods, the Athenians Minerva, the Cyprians Venus, the Cretans Dyotinna, the Sicilians Proserpina, others Juno, Bellona, Hecate, or the goddess Rhamnusa, but the Egyptians call her by her right name, the queen Isis.[40]

The deities of the mystery religions truly attained the attributes of universal divinities who embrace and rule all aspects of human lives, but we must note that these beings stand at the end of a development. Having grown and fused with others through the ages, reshaped by poets, philosophers, and priests, intellectualized and spiritualized, belonging to the end of paganism, they cannot be one with the primary and enduring archetypal form that, so it is claimed, was present in men's souls as Great Mother from the earliest moments of their journey on the planet earth. It may also be of some interest to note that in the tales entwined around Cybele, whose cult was spread through many regions, the themes of monstrous birth and castration predominate. These hardly accord with one who, in her essence, should still be a fountainhead of life, fecundity, and regeneration.[41]

The figures that were briefly described here, all brought forward as epiphanies of the Great Mother, cannot, from the evidence we actually have, be understood as the embodiment of a great, universal, primeval maternal force. Those that are mothers are not sovereign, those that are sovereign are not mothers, and a sovereign and maternal goddess such as Isis is not primordial.

Some scholars, such as E. O. James, assume that men were not aware, in very early times, of their function in the process of conception and believed that woman alone was able to bring forth a living being. Thus the powers of creativity were allotted to a goddess. It has been pointed out, however, that myth does not necessarily parallel a terrestrial reality, and no natural cause is needed to account for a phenomenon. It is true that in some instances a creative act is pictured in the image of a human birth. Thus the Titans of the Greeks, representing aspects of the landscape, were, according to Hesiod's *Theogony,* brought forth through the embrace of Gaia and Ouranos, and the Sumerian goddess Ki gave birth to Enlil—the air. Yet the act of engendering new growth is set in motion more often by nonbiological activity.

A meeting of fire and ice created the first living form on earth in Old Norse tradition, and the shaping of the landscape was achieved through the slaughter of a giant. Through Yahweh's word the universe came into existence, and he made the first man from clay. The Finnish magician Väinämöinen "sang" a bird into a tree, and the Egyptian Khnum formed men and women on his potter's wheel. Food plants originated in American tales because parts of a man's or a woman's body had been buried in the earth. Birds fly through the air when the goddess Tomam of the Siberian Khets shakes her sleeves, and the sea filled with seals when the severed fingers of Sedna of the Eskimo fell into the waves.

According to the *Edda,* the feet of a male giant begot a son with one another, and Zeus gave birth to Dionysus and Athena. Children are, in modern German folklore, brought by the stork from ponds and wells, and the goddess Aphrodite rose from the sea. The examples could be greatly multiplied; even so, they suffice to show that in myth the wonder of generation is not tied to the process by which a battered bundle issues from a woman's womb. Men who might be ignorant of the workings of conception need not necessarily attribute the creative power to the woman; the Arunta of Australia believe that their girls are fecundated by an ancestral spirit.[42]

Since it is said that men in early time did not relate pregnancy and birth to the commerce between men and women, some scholars believe that the archetypal mother did not have a consort. However, the records do not present this self-sufficient being. It is true that the Babylonian Tiamat created offspring by herself (monsters to fight against Marduk), but other children she conceived through lying with her husband Apsû. The Greek Gaia bore without the act of love the ocean and the sky, but she had more children through Ouranos's embraces. In both cases the events are narrated within the same account, and it is impossible to say whether an older version of the tale had been joined to a later and which of the two would present the more archaic form.

It was noted earlier that in myth a man as well as a woman is able to create a child. When the severed phallus of Ouranos sank into the sea, the goddess Aphrodite was begotten. The ocean being masculine in Greek tradition, two male elements combined to bring forth the most seductive of all deities. The demiurge of the theology of Heliopolis engendered the first pair of gods, Schu and Tefnut, from the semen he had obtained through masturbation, and only a later source gave him a spouse.[43] In the rock drawings of archaic Scandinavia, which depict few women, men are frequently shown with erect phallus, often of enormous size (Figure 4). We do not know the thought that caused the drawing of these symbols of male potency, but we can be sure that significance was accorded to the organ of male sexual power. The animals carved into the rock are rarely fitted with the male productive member, and it almost seems as if it were the phallus that marked the human from the beast (Figures 5 and 6).[44] We may agree at this point that in archaic thought, miraculous action seems to be more important than the observed processes of biology.

It has also been assumed that the status of the woman goddess changed with the coming of a patriarchal order. Jane Ellen Harrison understands that the bonding of the matriarchal group was that of the mother with her son, as exemplified by Rhea who gave birth to Zeus (though a goddess who must hide in a cave to escape the murderous rage of the child's father cannot easily be seen as example of sovereign womanhood); in later times the son eclipsed the mother (Semele and Dionysus), and finally the son ruled, as did Zeus, with supreme authority over sky and earth. And he was determined to suppress the ancient figure. Harrison thus states: "Zeus the Father will have no great Earthgoddess, Mother and Maid, in his man-fashioned Olympus . . . so he remakes it; woman who was the inspirer, becomes the temptress. She who made all things, gods and mortals alike, becomes their plaything, their slave, dowered only with physical beauty and with a slave's tricks and blandishments."[45] We know, however, that a goddess of great potency can evolve in the midst of a patriarchal order, as did Inanna-Ishtar. The goddess Sedna dominates the religious emotions of the Eskimo, with whom women were of low account.

Figure 3. Gold ring of Isopata near Knossos (Minoan), about 1500 B.C.E.

Figure 4. Rock drawing from Fossum, Tanum, Bohuslän, Scandinavian Bronze Age.

Figure 5. Rock drawing from Bohuslän, Scandinavian Bronze Age.

Figure 6. Rock drawing from Nordland, Arctic Stone Age.

The cult of Isis flourished in the midst of a patriarchal society, and churches dedicated to the Virgin Mary rose in the patriarchal Middle Ages. A recent study shows that the number (i.e., importance) of female deities in a given group bears no relation to the status of the human women.[46]

The existence of a one-time matriarchal society has not been substantiated. The theory, advanced by Bachofen, was based on legendary and mythical matter that, according to him, had preserved the relics of a historic past. No other evidence has been brought forth. The idea that at one stage of development women held the rule in society is not accepted in modern anthropology.

It has also been asserted that the goddess clasped her own son in her embrace, while in later ages she submitted to the ardor of a domineering spouse.[47] Yet in the cited myths the woman's lover is not her son. It is also held that a young god was joined to the woman goddess when men began to understand that the universal mother, not being able to bring forth in parthenogenesis, needed a virile partner to achieve her maternity. Yet in the instances brought forward (Baal, Attis, Tammus, Adonis), the woman is not fecundated by the man.[48] We may also observe that the examples that are to delineate the form of a universal being are taken from a limited geographic region.

The ideas regarding the role of the Great Mother are to a large extent based on the assumption that she could bestow fertility on women, and that since men wished to continue life on earth, women's fecundity was a much desired blessing. A brief glance at ancient and present rites shows that few are conducted to promote a woman's reproductive powers. Many customs, on the other hand, seek to assure a sufficiency of food.[49] Toasts were drunk at Yule time in Norse tradition to secure the abundance of the crops; offerings are given to Dame Perchta of the Alps so that the grain might grow and the beasts might prosper; celebrations are conducted throughout Japan at crucial moments of the agricultural year—the times of sowing, transplanting, and reaping the new rice. The practices that are to endow women with fertility are of a private nature, performed by nubile girls or barren women, at wedding feasts, or in female mysteries of which we have no knowledge.[50] Modern nations living at the subsistence level, as some Indians of Brazil or the Bushmen of Africa, curtail the number of their offspring by abortion or infanticide.[51] We gain the impression that, as in our time, in the majority of cases the begetting of children was achieved with little effort, whereas the problem of their sustenance was heartrending and perennial. Historical nations have perished not because their women lacked reproductive powers but rather because of war, persecution, or economic plight.

We may also note that we do not find in myths of divine conception the awe and wonder inspired by the mystery of the fertile womb. When a woman is embraced, in violence or love, pregnancy and birth follow as normal and expected consequence and not as a mysterious or miraculous event. The interest of the tale is focused on the way in which the act of "love" was achieved. Zeus assumed the form of Alkmene's husband so that he might hold her in his arms, and their son was Hercules. Odin used potent charms on the woman Rindr so that he might gain a son; the wise smith Velent overcame a girl with "beer" and she bore a valiant hero. The god Enlil of Mesopotamian myth saw his own daughter bathing in a river and he took her maidenhood; through this and following unions she bore several gods.[52]

The goddess is viewed—by James and Gimbutas, for example—as the mistress of life, death and regeneration, yet her function as deity of death has not been substantiated or defined. If she were the mistress of the underworld, she would not need to search in sorrow for a departed child or lover, nor would she herself be threatened by extinction, as was Ishtar in her descent to the infernal regions. It is true that the goddess herself may bring death to humans, but any divinity may exercise this power.

Let me restate that a primordial sovereign goddess of fecundity is not present in our extant evidence. She has been reconstructed from archaeological remains that may be interpreted in various ways. Her true form is never seen, for it was supposedly achieved in a vanished age of mother-right that, in turn, is utterly hypothetical. Nor are the notions of fertility and motherhood imbued with the glory which they hold in our time.

The persistence of the concept among scholars in spite of the absence of any real evidence, their occasional changing of actual facts to preserve the image of the goddess, must in itself constitute a kind of faith. The same phenomenon has been observed by Olof Petterson regarding a very similar configuration—a universally worshipped Mother Earth.[53] At some time in intellectual history there must have occurred an exaltation of motherhood, coupled, so it would seem, with a degradation of sexual desire and fulfillment.

The desire to establish a maternal being may be illustrated by the scholarly interpretations of some archaeological remains. In sculptures, reliefs, or engravings of the Neolithic, one encounters a recurrent image: a woman with widely separated legs, exposing her pudenda. It is shown in relief on a vase of the early sixth millennium of Sarvaš in northern Yugoslavia and appears in various forms and executions from Thessaly and Macedonia to northern Hungary.[54] While the relief of Sarvaš is realistic, with facial features and carefully drawn vulvar region, other images are often schematized. Gimbutas understands that a fully schematized version of parted legs and pubic triangle resembling the letter M had become the shorthand symbol, the ideogram of the Great Goddess of the region. A woman parting her legs in nakedness recurs also among Middle Eastern artifacts, as in a clay figure of Hacilar in Anatolia, on cylinder seals from Mesopotamia (Figures 7 and 8), and in schematized form on the walls of shrines in Çatal Hüyük.[55] A small terra-cotta sculpture of Hellenistic times shows the goddess Isis with parted legs, seated on a boar (Figure 9). Although the swollen belly of pregnancy and the emerging child are missing, the images are related to the act of childbearing, and Gimbutas designates the figure as "Life-giving Goddess."[56]

Egyptian women were delivered of their children while squatting over the birth brick (or bricks), called Meshkenet, as shown by the temple carving in Figure 10; a birth brick is also mentioned in an Akkadian text.[57] One would assume that this brick might be present, at least sometimes, in Middle Eastern portrayals of birth. Neumann believes that the act of parturition is symbolized even where the woman hovers over the reclining figure of a man (see Figure 8). We know, however, that a goddess of vibrant sexuality had emerged in the Middle East, exemplified by Inanna-Ishtar, a patroness of harlots, who will give the kingship of the land to the one by whose "fair hands" her "loins were pressed" and who had laid his hands on her "pure vulva."[58] And a Middle Eastern queen is frank in the desire for her husband's love, which she expresses in poetry:

> . . . the place where, could you but do
> your sweet thing to me,

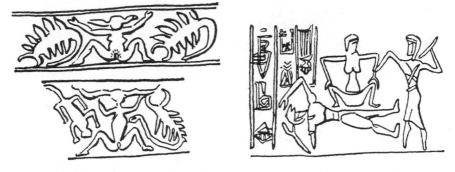

Figure 7. (*Left*) Cylinder seal from Ur, Babylonia. Figure 8. (*Right*) Cylinder seal from Lagash, Babylonia.

Figure 9. (*Left*) Terra-cotta sculpture of Isis, Hellenistic period. Figure 10. (*Right*) Carving of Egyptian women squatting over the birth brick in the temple of Kom Ombo, Ptolemaic period, after 203 B.C.E.

> where, could you but—
> like honey—
> put in your sweetness.[59]

A goddess who lifts her garment and shows her nakedness in a less aggressive fashion is also pictured on a cylinder seal of the Euphrates Valley. While the baring of the vulva in the artifacts here described strongly suggests erotic encounter, it may also be of magical significance; the belief that magic power issues from a woman's genitals is expressed in many lands. Without the

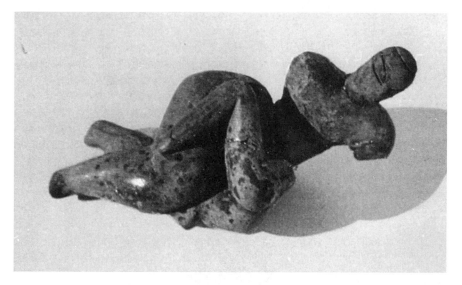

Figure 11. Statuette of a reclining woman and smaller figure from Hacilar VI, no. 528.

outward signs of pregnancy and the presence of a child, the images are not of parturition.

The proportions of an illustration in Mellaart's book on Hacilar are actually altered so that a maternal rather than an erotic being is presented. A sculpture from level VI of Hacilar shows the massive form of a reclining woman over whose thigh a slightly smaller and much slimmer figure has placed his leg while his right hand clasps the woman's waist (Figures 11 and 12). The upper portion of his body is broken off above the waist, and his other (right) leg seems to enter between the woman's thighs. In a drawing the sculpture is restructured to show a woman with a child on her lap. The artist changed the proportions between the woman's and the torso's thighs and buttocks, and he altered the position of the actors so that they no longer would recline. In showing a smaller, less muscular male figure and an upright rather than a reclining woman, the artist succeeded in removing the erotic aura from the artifact.[60] The drawing and not the photograph is printed in another of Mellaart's books and this drawing points to the presence of a mother goddess (Figure 13).[61]

The interpretations of ancient artifacts cited here seem to indicate that modern scholars find it difficult to view the existence of a faith in which motherhood held little glamor while sexual encounter might have its share of sanctity and a Mary Magdalene might be more highly honored than the Virgin Mary. Not all scholars have accepted the theories concerning the goddess. Walter Burkert and Thorkild Jacobsen do not discuss her in the presentation

Figure 12. Photographs
showing two views of the
statuette from Hacilar VI,
no. 528.

of their special fields (Greek and Mesopotamian). The archaeologist Andrew
Fleming finds that a belief in a universal being is not basic, as is frequently
assumed, to the building of megalithic monuments, and he understands that
the unquestioning acceptance of such a divinity has seriously impeded scientific study of the rituals implied by the structures. "The mother-goddess,"
he declares, "has detained us for too long; let us disengage ourselves from her
embrace."[62]

Yet even Wolfgang Helck, who affirms that eroticism rather than maternal
love marks the nature of Great Goddesses such as Ishtar or Cybele, believes
also without investigation in the existence of a great maternal form. Paul
Friedrich finds little of maternity in Hera or Athena, yet he states unques-
tioningly that "a generalized, loving, nurturing, strong mother figure is so
widespread in the myths of the world as to verge on being an empirically
universal archetype."[63] A close examination reveals, however, that the experiences, emotions, and qualities of sovereign motherhood are attributed without due cause to a number of numinous forces, practically to every feminine
divinity; if a goddess is virginal, warlike, or desirous of men's castration, she
is regarded as just another form of the all-embracing being; if she is cowed
or violated, she is held to have suffered the imprint of a patriarchal order.

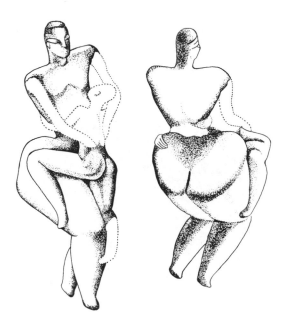

Figure 13. An artist's line
drawing of the statuette from
Hacilar VI, no. 528.

The yearning for a maternal power is strong in modern time; it is expressed by Joseph Campbell, who speaks of "the lovely world of a paradise neither lost nor regained, but ever present in the bosom of the goddess mother in whose being we have our death, as well as our life without fear."[64] The image of the goddess has attained new value and attention in recent years; it stimulated and awakened strong emotions—hence the growth of new religious movements that see the vision of the goddess as their central inspiration.

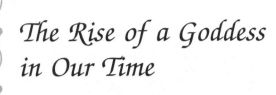

The Rise of a Goddess
in Our Time

A religious phenomenon has emerged in our time that is especially vital among feminists in England and the United States. A figure, designated as the Goddess, has been extolled in numerous books that describe her form and function (and the manner of her worship, as it had existed in ancient times), and that also proclaim her return. The Goddess has been instrumental to the creation of study groups, to circles and communities of a new cult, and she has also given rise to questions among those who remained within the frame of their traditional religions. No structural dogma has as yet evolved, but there is a general consensus concerning the nature of the Goddess that amounts to an unofficial theology.

THE CREED OF THE GODDESS RELIGION

Worship of the Goddess, so it is asserted, reaches back to the dawn of human existence; at that time she was the sole all-encompassing deity in which earth and all its creatures had originated, as formulated by Marija Gimbutas: "[I]t was the sovereign mystery and creative power of the female as the source of life that developed into the first religious experiences. The Great Mother Goddess who gives birth to all creation out of the holy darkness of her womb became the metaphor for nature herself."[1] This view is founded on the presence of female figurines in stone, ivory, or clay, all nude, some slender, some obese, that were excavated in great numbers from Paleolithic sites from Siberia to the Pyrenees. It is believed that the Goddess presided over the rituals of the cave, and thus her image might be carved into the rock near a cave, as in Laussel in the Dordogne: "Such a figure presided over the masked shamanic dances and the circles of communion with all animals, all life in which blood-woman-moon-bison-birth-magic—the cycle of life are analogized in a continuous resonance."[2] The placement of the figure of Laussel near the entrance of a cave is held to be significant, since the cave mouth symbolizes the entrance to the womb.[3]

The shaping of the female figure and figurines continued in the Neolithic period. The artifacts are spread throughout the Mediterranean regions but extend farther, more sparsely, toward India, toward eastern Europe and the Megalithic West. They were discovered in shrines, in graves, or in private dwellings. Thus it is assumed, especially in the Goddess cults, that her worship had not lessened, that it had intensified. It is also held that women had invented agriculture and so: "A strong link was forged connecting women as the cultivators of grain, to grain as the bounty of the Goddess, and to bread as the staff of life. Ovens, grain storage bins, and grinding stones became essential ritual furnishings of Goddess shrines."[4]

High levels of civilization were attained as early as the seventh millennium B.C.E. in the towns of Çatal Hüyük and Hacilar in western Anatolia. Excavated by James Mellaart, these offer dramatic insights into the life of their inhabitants. Numbers of workshops testify to high achievements in craftsmanship, and numbers of shrines to a flowering of religious life. Here too the female form predominates: Sculpted women, seated or standing, are frequently seen with feline beasts and holding and fondling young animals. Images of vultures swooping down upon their victims are interpreted as the Goddess in her death-bringing form; bulls' heads placed beneath the figure of a female are believed to be her sons.[5]

The Goddess worshippers thus adduce more evidence from these early centers of urban life for the all-powerful and all-encompassing presence of the Goddess. They assume that she was served by priestesses and that she ruled over a matrilocal society in which women held high social status: "[R]eligions in which the most powerful or sole deity is female tend to reflect a social order in which descent is matrilineal (traced through the mother) and domicile is likewise matrilocal."[6]

It is asserted in the Goddess creed that Neolithic towns were not fortified by defences, that there was no warrior equipment in the finds, and that only peaceful scenes were rendered in Neolithic art.[7] The Goddess, therefore, governed a peaceful society that was free from hierarchical structures.[8] And the leading group of women did not dominate the group of men: "[T]he primacy of the Goddess—and with this the centrality of the values symbolized by the nurturing and regenerative powers incarnated in the female body—does not justify the inference that women here dominated men."[9]

It is also thought that at the time of Goddess supremacy, emphasis was placed on union and interaction of all things rather than on strife and competition: "The operating principle of the ancient beliefs was the analogy between macrocosm and microcosm. What was true of the earth body was also true of the bodies of all creatures on earth."[10] The principles of harmony and peace were also said to be evident in Neolithic art:

> [T]his theme of the unity of all things in nature, as personified by the Goddess seems to permeate Neolithic art, for here the supreme power governing the universe is a divine Mother who gives her people life, provides them with material and spiritual nurturance, and who even in death can be counted on to take her children back into her cosmic womb.[11]

In agrarian Neolithic society, people would thus live in harmony with the natural environment:

> The main theme of Old European goddess symbolism is the cyclic mystery of birth, death and the renewal of life, involving not only human life but all life on earth. . . . Her energy is manifest in springs and wells, in the moon, sun and earth, and all animals and plants. She is the Giver of Life, the Wielder of Death, Regeneratrix and Earth Fertility Goddess, rising and dying with the plants.[12]

According to the creed, the religion of the Goddess suffered a decline in a slow process that possibly began in the third millennium B.C.E. The regions of southeastern Europe and the Middle East in which her cult had flourished were attacked and invaded by Indo-European and Semitic tribes, respectively, and these pastoralists, who raised horses or goats and camels, introduced their warlike ethos and they brought their warrior gods. In their homelands, the Syro-Arabian desert and the Russian plain, they had supposedly developed a patriarchal form of society; their ruling gods dwelled in heaven and commanded the terror of the thunderstorm. These divinities now wielded powers over life and death: "[T]he life-creating and death-wielding functions belonged to the principal male gods who also rode horses and brandished weapons. . . . This religion was oriented toward the rotating sun and other sky phenomena such as thunder and lightning."[13]

It is asserted that in the newly established hierarchy, the Goddess was relegated to become the wife or mother of the ruling male.[14] The ancient deity was bereft of her strength and glory: "The mother goddess, whether as Cybele, Ceres or Tellus Mater, who once was mother of the gods and soil as plants, fruit and golden grain, gradually became a 'mere personification of the earth' . . . eventually she was identified with the negative principle of materiality."[15]

In the desire to tarnish the image of the Goddess, it is further believed, men assimilated her at times with dark, evil forces, with the monster that must be defeated by the champion of light: "In many of these myths . . . the female is symbolized as a serpent or dragon, most often associated with darkness and evil."[16] The ancient ritual in which the blood of animals was shed to fertilize the soil was blended with the ruthless killing of the enemy in wars of conquest to sustain the life of the community.[17]

Yet, it is held, the vibrant force of the Goddess could not be eradicated; she lived on in folk religion; she may also be recognized in the great figures of a patriarchal pantheon—such as Artemis, Ishtar, or Shekinah. Joseph Campbell thus observes:

> And we are going to find throughout the following history of the orthodox patriarchal systems of the West, that the power of the goddess-mother of the world, whom we have seen defamed, abused, insulted, and overthrown by her sons, is to remain as an everpresent threat to their castle of reason.[18]

The fabric of life, however, the creed asserts, had been deeply altered with the coming of the patriarchal system. While the moral order of the Goddess culture was based on interchangeability and alternation of the elements that make up the world, on a basic unity and harmony between life and death, man and nature, the new view recognized an opposition between forces, conflicts that were to be resolved by conquest and by the power of the sword:[19]

> In the older mother myths and rites the light and the dark aspects of the mixed thing that is life had been honored equally and together; whereas in the latter male-oriented patriarchal myths, all that is good and noble was attributed to the new, heroic master gods, leaving to the native nature powers only the character of darkness—to which also a negative moral judgment was now attached.[20]

And naturally the state of woman was lowered; a class of priests arose to supplant the priestesses. Women were treated as servants or chattel by the Aryan tribes; they could be sold into slavery by their male kinfolk in the Babylonian kingdom.[21]

The mode of life introduced by the patriarchal pastoralists remained and molded human existence through the Iron Ages into our time. It was essentially a warriors' view: "[I]t was heroic, combative, and aggressive, since the emphasis was on victory in battle and acquisition through conquest."[22] There also was, in the view of the Goddess followers, a development of a new confidence and self-awareness, a new emphasis on excellence and valor. Such an ethos is expressed in Homer's *Iliad* and it has remained in strength through the centuries, for the Goddess has not yet returned in full honor and the main official religions of the world are still dominated by a patriarchal god.

THE HISTORICAL VALIDITY OF THE GODDESS RELIGION AND ITS CREED

The claims concerning the glory and decline of the Goddess cannot be substantiated. Many of the assertions are speculative. Documentation is sparse; references are frequently limited to authors who share the vision. Evidence is often garbled or misrepresented. While it is not necessary to correct all misinformation and impossible to argue against a speculative statement, it is easy and, in my view, desirable to refute some of the assumptions on which the

Figure 14. (*Left*) A painting of a part-man, part stag creature in the cave of Trois Frères, Ariège. Figure 15. (*Right*) An engraving of a horned and cloven-foot creature in the cave of Trois Frères, Ariège.

lofty building is constructed. I now present arguments against four widely held assumptions.

Assumption 1.   Female Images Brought to Light by Archaeology Show that Woman Inspired the Primordial Religious Experience. Male images are as widespread in time and space as the female figures. A form, partly man, partly stag, is portrayed in the cave of Trois Frères in Ariège (Figure 14), and a horned and cloven-footed creature can be seen in the same cave of the Dordogne (Figure 15). Marija Gimbutas dismisses these pictures as merely those of "Guardians of Nature," not realizing that the guardian and owner of the wilderness, who provides the hunter with his quarry, is frequently the highest god of a hunting community. If we recall that horned and antlered gods received worship in historic times, such as Celtic Cernunnos (Figure 16) or Greek Pan, we may recognize an early form of this kind of deity in the Paleolithic caves.

Figure 16. A segment of the cauldron of Guindestrup, a Celtic work, second to first century B.C.E.

A group of phallic men was painted in red color onto a cave wall in the Trondelag of northern Norway (Figure 17); it is attributed, as are the contents of the cave, to the so-called Arctic Stone Age.[23] Male figures are seen in rock engravings of Europe that extend from the arctic North to Italy and Spain and, in time, from the Stone Age to the last pre-Christian centuries (Figure 18).[24]

Men, their phalli huge and erect, appear in vast numbers in the rock drawings of southern Scandinavia, which are dated to the Bronze Age (Figures 4, 5, 19 21). They are active in many ways: wielding spears, lifting axes, dancing or leaping, leading a plow, or holding a woman in embrace. Many of the figures are portrayed with the ears or the tails of animals, and we do not know if we see gods with animal characteristics or men in animal disguise. It is clear, however, that much emphasis is placed on the virility of men.[25]

Advocates of the Goddess point to the predominance of female figures in the shrines of Çatal Hüyük. We know, however, that the halls are also thronged with the heads or the images of bulls. It is obvious that a bull would signify the qualities of male potency and strength. We also know that the weather god, a mighty ruler, was worshipped in the shape of a bull in archaic Anatolian religion. The pre-Hittite (Hattic) weather god bears the name Taru—related to the Greek *tauros* and the Celtic *tarvos:* bull.[26] A bull standing on a pedestal is pictured on a vase, as a recipient of sacrifice; the "Song of the Bull" is sung in the rituals of Nerik, a town that was dedicated to the weather god. The Hittite King Hattusilis I reports that he had seized a silver bull from the town of Zalpa and placed it in the temple of Hatti.[27]

When the animal epiphany of the god gave way to his human image, he retained a bull, or bulls, as his sons or companions.[28] Seals of the second

Figure 17. Phallic men on the eastern wall of a cave near Leka, Trondelag, Norway, Arctic Stone Age.

Figure 18. (*Left*) Rock drawing in Zalavrouga, near the White Sea, northern Russia. Figure 19. (*Right*) Rock drawing from Bohuslän, Sweden.

Figure 20. Rock drawing from Östfold, Scandinavia.

Figure 21. Rock drawing from Bohuslän, Scandinavia.

Figure 22. Minoan painted jars depicting bulls' heads.

millennium portray the god standing on a bull, leading it by a nose ring, his helmet fitted with bulls' horns, and also holding the emblems of thunder and lightning in his hands.[29] Canaanite tradition retained the vestiges of the bull shape of the god in the myth in which Baal, the weather god, mates with Anat in the form of a bull.[30] The god El is frequently addressed as Bull-god.[31] The weather god was worshipped in ancient times because of his powers to send the nourishing rains. We thus find that the gift of fruitfulness is related to a male and not to a female being.

It has been assumed that a bull's head placed beneath the sculpture of a goddess in an Anatolian shrine is that of the son to whom she has just given birth.[32] Aside from the fact that the two artifacts are not structurally related, I know no myth of this tradition in which a goddess has given birth to a bull.

It has also been suggested that the bull's head represents the uterus with the attached fallopian tubes.[33] One may ask why the faithful did not worship the uterus in its own form if it was a sacred object. One may also wonder what grotesque sense of whimsy prompted them to decorate a hallowed symbol with the snout, horns, and eyes of a bull.

Female figures of great grace and beauty predominate also in the imagery of Minoan Crete; hence Minoan Crete is held to be a place where goddess worship was more fully expressed and more faithfully retained than in other regions. Here also bulls' horns and heads are ubiquitous, sometimes set upon an altar as the "horns of consecration" (Figure 22). Again, we may assume that a potent male force was worshipped beside potent female powers.[34]

The images of horned beasts (bisons) were drawn in large numbers onto the walls in a cave of Altamira in northern Spain. If we are permitted to spin a thread from the "Venus" figurines of Paleolithic times to Middle Eastern sculptures and to the Great Lady of beasts and men, then we are permitted to spin a thread from the horned beasts of Altamira to the horned bulls of Çatal Hüyük and to the mighty weather god. There exists, in fact, a pictorial continuity from the cloven-footed, horned creature of Trois Frères to the horn-helmeted Anatolian weather god, the cloven-footed, horned Pan of Greece, and even to the cloven-footed, horned devil of modern folklore. There is no visual resemblance, on the other hand, between the bulging forms of the Paleolithic and the Great Goddesses of historic times. These are often shown with beasts, a stag or lion; the Mistress of Animals was not prefigured in the archaic sites (Figures 23, 24). We may assume that male and female godheads were worshipped in the most distant past, but that the woman had earlier gained her human form.

Assumption 2. Semitic and Indo-European Tribes Invaded the Regions of Goddess Worship. They Introduced their own Armed Warrior Gods and Suppressed the Native Forces to Install a Patriarchal System. Baring and Cashford thus assert: "Wherever sky gods—of lightning, thunder, fire, air and storm—are found together with the mace, the battle-axe and the glorification of the warrior, we are in the presence of the Indo-European (Aryan) and Semitic inheritance."[35]

It is true that Indo-European and Semitic languages came to prevail in wide areas of the world during the last pre-Christian millennia, and it is reasonable to assume that they were brought by conquering invaders. It is widely believed that warlike tribes overcame the settled farming population and that they introduced their heroic and celestial gods. Little was known until the last decades about the subjugated inhabitants. At present, however, a vast array of documents and texts has been amassed, dialects (e.g., Hittite, Ugaritic, Akkadian, and Sumerian) have been deciphered, and the cultures of the earlier settlers have been explored.

Even a superficial glance at the sources reveals that a celestial warrior god had developed among the agriculturalists and had not been brought by the

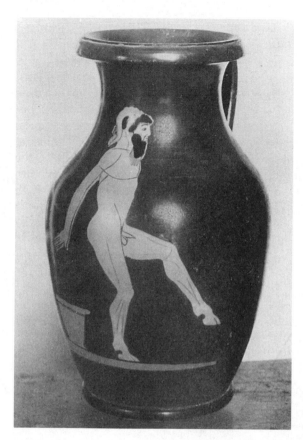

Figure 23. The god Pan on an Attic vase of the fifth century B.C.E.

Figure 24. Robin Goodfellow. Illustration of a horned devil from a seventeenth-century ballad.

foreign forces. He is a god of storms and lightning, and he wields a mace, an axe, a club against his enemy; he is usually the ruler of his pantheon. We shall now briefly survey the form and function of the armed god of storms.

Pre-Sumerian culture developed in the southern marshlands of present day Iraq and spread to the northern regions. Here the first irrigation channels were cut into the soil and here the first monumental buildings were constructed. The area was conquered by the Semitic Akkadians and the conquest was consolidated under King Sargon at about 2300 B.C.E. Sumerian preconquest tradition already knew the god Ninurta/Ningirsu—the power of the thunderstorm. A seal of the middle of the third millennium shows him with his bow, typifying lightning, and his lion, typifying the roar of thunder.[36] With his arms he defeated the stormbird, a lion-headed eagle, who held the powers of office of the untamed waters in his claws. And Ninurta hitched the vanquished creature to his chariot of war.[37] His martial powers are celebrated in a Sumerian hymn:

> Lord Ninurta, when thou approachest the enemy
> thou makest him into grass . . . [38]

The god was taken over into Akkadian myth. We thus find that the god of the subjugated population was taken and accepted by the conquerors.[39]

We have already encountered the weather god in his bull-shaped epiphany in the Neolithic shrines of Çatal Hüyük. In historic times the towns of Canaanite and Anatolian settlement each revered its own human weather god, who might be named after his locality (such as Lord of Maraš or Lord of Sapuna).[40] In his human shape the god would be armed in various ways: with an axe, a club, a spear, a trident.[41] Sometimes he might stride across the mountains and sometimes he might be stationed in a chariot.[42] We noted that the human god retained vestiges of his earlier animal appearance; hence we cannot doubt his origin. The figure of the human god of storms belonged already to the Hattic pantheon, hewn into the rock of Alaça Hüyük and engraved on Cappodocian seals.[43] And we cannot doubt that his form had existed before the Indo-European Hittites invaded Anatolia.

His name frequently links him to a mountain. It seems that in most archaic times his closest attachment was with the mountain, where the wild bull roams. In an agricultural community his power over storms and rains came to the fore. When cities and city-states were founded, he became the ruler of the town. In this form he was often endowed with royal qualities, described through his title as giver of justice, victory, or help in need.

Thus a multitude of weather gods was in existence, and these might fuse or travel or be taken by the conqueror of a town into his own divine family.[44] It is difficult to trace the journeys of the multiplaced divinity. It is, however, clear that the warlike deity of lightning and thunder had not been brought by an outside force, for he had developed in the agricultural regions. It is natural for a weather god to gain great importance among a farming population. Farmers, looking to the skies for the life-restoring rains, apparently did not spend much time in contemplating the "holy darkness of the womb."

The conquering invaders altogether accepted native religion, just as they accepted the native arts of building and of growing grain. The Sumerian goddess Inanna blended with the Akkadian (Semitic) Ishtar; both descended to the lower regions and returned to the world of men. Both delighted in the carnage of battle; in a hymn Inanna rejoices in her warlike powers:

> When I stand in the (front) line of battle
> I am the leader of all the lands,
> when I stand in the opening of battle,
> I am the quiver ready to hand.

And Ishtar of Arbella was the Assyrian goddess of war.[45] Both goddesses held the beloved Dumuzi in their embrace. The deeds of Gilgamesh, King of Uruk, were celebrated in Sumerian and Akkadian poetry.[46] The Hittites lost their Indo-European gods and adopted the gods of the towns they conquered to gain the benefits that the local gods might give. They, themselves, spoke of the "thousand gods of Hatti land."[47] Before their arrival, a state religion had been created, welded by priests from local and imported deities, and a family that was headed by a king and queen had originated.[48] This family was taken over by the Indo-European Hittites and worshipped in official rites. It was ruled by King Teshup, a weather god, and Queen Hebat, a goddess of the sun.

One invading Indo-European tribe did destroy native culture. A seminomadic Balkan people, the later Phrygians, entered Hittite territory at about 1200 B.C.E. They defeated the settled inhabitants, torched the villages and towns, and devastated the countryside. For centuries they continued their pastoral existence, until they established the Phrygian state. They adored a godhead of a different kind in orgiastic celebrations; she was the Mountain Mother of many names, a Great Goddess, who became the "Phrygian Goddess" or the Magna Mater of the Romans.[49]

Hence we may observe that a Great Goddess ruled a ruthless pastoral people while a god of storms and thunder was already present in the Neolithic urban culture of Çatal Hüyük. If we know that, with the exception of the Phrygians, the invaders accepted the native forces and also worshipped the heroic native god of the thunderstorm, then we cannot support the article of faith of Goddess religion by which the Great Goddess was defeated and debased. There clearly was no introduction of warrior gods and warrior values, no imposition of a patriarchal system, and no humiliation of the Goddess.

Assumption 3. In Male-dominated Religions the Goddess was at Times Assimilated to a Serpent, Personification of Evil and Darkness, to be Slain by the Male Champion of Light. It is true that Tiamat, vanquished by Marduk, and Medusa, slain by Perseus, were drawn as female creatures. Usually, however, the adversary of the divinity is male, such as Hrungnir (Germanic), Ullikummi (Hittite) or Typhoeus (Greek).[50] In his exhaustive study of tales of the "monster combat," Fontenrose notes that the fight may also be twofold, against a male as well as against a female enemy. The male, however, is the main opponent.[51]

Sex and gender are not important features of the adversary. He is monstrous and nonhuman; he symbolizes the chaotic void as a constant threat to cosmic order. The battle is between humans and nature—beasts, mountain ranges, and the sea—the man-made tool against claw and fang.

There is no evidence to show that female deities were willfully subjugated or suppressed. When a male god rules the world and when a male divinity pursues and rapes a nymph, myth merely records the facts of life on earth: that realms are usually governed by kings, and that men rape women. Conversely, female deities are often vital in a "patriarchal" pantheon. Anat of Canaan rules the battle and Demeter of Greece rules the produce of the earth.

It is true that divine women are absent from the Hebrew texts; but Yahweh in his "jealousy" does not tolerate any rival deity. The battle against the Canaanite *baalim* (male gods) is conducted more fiercely than the fight against the *asheroth* (female deities).[52]

Assumption 4. Peace Prevailed in Neolithic Society when the Goddess Ruled Religion and the Women were of High Estate. The walls of the town of Jericho, built in 7000 B.C.E. were sunk into a ditch; they reached a width of about 5 feet and a height of 13 feet. Surely they were erected against a formidable foe.[53]

For an example that a country may go to war even if it is beholden to a sovereign goddess, one may consider modern Japan. Here the powerful Amaterasu, goddess of the sun and ancestress of the emperor, did not prevent her nation from its venture of aggressive expansion in the first part of our century. As for the state of women in Japan, we know that it is lower than that of women of western "patriarchal" systems of religion.

In the faith of some tribes of the Eskimo, the goddess Sedna rules supremely as provider of the staff of life, the fish and seals of the sea, and as mistress of the underworld beneath the waves. Yet a woman has few rights in this society; she is not protected by law from her husband's violence.[54]

Let us state at this point that the evidence has shattered two pillars of the Goddess religion: that her worship preceded the worship of male gods and that there was a clash between a male-dominated and a female-dominated faith in which the Goddess was deposed. If these two pillars crumble, surely the building must collapse, as did the temple of the Philistines.

THE NEW RELIGIONS

While the historical claims for the existence of the Goddess cannot be substantiated, we cannot deny her power to evoke a genuine religious experience. Women who had grown up in a Christian or Jewish environment were not satisfied with a doctrine and a faith that was hierarchial, dominated by a male god, administered by male officials, and replete with notions of male supremacy. While some female theologians tried to influence their religious systems from within, some saw no happier recourse than to break away. They searched for a creed that would fulfill their desire for a closer involvement in the practices and for a stronger bonding with other believers, satisfy their longing for a greater harmony with nature, and also respond to their own psychic needs.

In the late 1960s the Women's Spirituality Movement came into existence, also known as Wicca, the Witches of the West, the Craft, Goddess Worship. The name Wicca, Witches, was chosen because it was believed that the witches, persecuted by the Church in the Middle Ages, had preserved and transmitted the ancient prepatriarchal tradition of the Goddess which was now to be restored.[55]

The rituals are flexible and spontaneous; though led by a priestess, the members are encouraged to participate as equals in a shared experience. Celebrations may be set to coincide with the festival times of pre-Christian faith, such as Halloween or Yule. They may also be related to the phases of the moon.[56] Often they take place in the open, in a grove or valley, for a greater union with nature is desired.

By casting a magic circle, the members believe to have created a sacred space, a microcosm in which their laws, the laws of the Goddess, are valid. By reenacting an event, the women may heal the wounds inflicted by a harsh society. They may recall the tale of Amaterasu, the Japanese deity of the sun, and her emergence from a cave, or the return of the maiden Persephone to her mother's arms. They may celebrate the phases of a woman's life or the rebirth of the seasons. They may wish to restore pride in a woman's biological functions or console her in bereavement.[57] The inspiration is drawn from the Goddess of many names and of many forms: "The Goddess is the means by which we know that our universe is sacred, through which we have the experience of the sacred. We have to live so that our lives come into harmony with the sacred. The invocation of her image is the cry to consciousness."[58]

The various groups or covens might develop their own traditions, but drawing a circle, dancing, chanting, lighting candles, and physical contact are standard features.[59] The members of the circles are often active in the social issues of our time, taking stands against injustice, racial discrimination, destruction of the environment, the threat of war. They understand the Goddess to be the means of healing the wounds of their own souls as well as the wounds inflicted on the earth.

The vision of the Goddess has also had a vivifying impact on women's art. By contemplating the prehistoric forms of female divinity, artists discovered new dimensions and a new awareness of the female body:

> The prehistoric goddess figure was an icon, a symbol of spiritual tradition.
> Encoded in her physical form were values inherent in the Goddess culture.
> The iconography of the sacred female focused on those parts of a woman's

body that had to do with the renewal of life. Nudity was sacred, not seductive.[60]

Artists, such as Georgia O'Keeffe and Louise Bourgeois, found their inspiration in the awakening of images and emotions that came to life through the perception and contemplation of the Goddess.[61]

Goddess religion thus serves many women as a potent means in the fulfillment of their needs, in restoring pride and self-esteem, as a valiant ally in their fight against perceived or actual injustice, as stated by Elinor Gadon: "The Goddess has reappeared in our midst in the late twentieth century as a symbol of the healing that is necessary for our survival, a transference of consciousness that holds promise for the renewal of our culture."[62]

Since the historical basis of the concepts that surround the Goddess cannot be established, one might suspect that her religion was created to fit the requirements of modern women at a time of shifting values, as assumed, for instance, by Mary Lefkowitz.[63] The fervor with which the concept is upheld surely testifies to its religious validity. The Great Mother who nourishes the body and the soul truly belongs to the faith of modern time.[64]

chapter 3

Reverence of Nature: Northern Eurasia

T
O gain insight into the spiritual universe in which the goddesses of this study found their earliest manifestations, we must turn to cultures that retained not only archaic ways of subsistence but also archaic modes of thought and religion. Such cultures exist, or existed until recently, in the arctic and subboreal belts where urbanization or even farming had not entered or prevailed. The European and Asiatic portions of this region, named North Eurasia, have been well explored and the mode of life of their inhabitants well documented; it was found that a homogeneous cultural unit had been formed.[1] In this chapter the beliefs of the North Eurasian peoples will briefly be presented in exploring the environment of very early forms of divinity and in examining to what extent the figures of more complex societies can be traced to the archaic gods.

North Eurasia is vast; it stretches across two continents from the Atlantic Ocean to the Bering Strait and reaches from the shores of the northern seas to a latitude of fifty-five degrees. It was the last region to be freed from the glacial cap of the Ice Age, and it was settled thereafter by many peoples who varied widely in race and speech. The millennia of shared existence and shared techniques in the battle for survival, however, created a body of common traditions and beliefs.

The climate was a vital force in shaping social structure. The briefness of the summer season did not foster the development of agriculture, and the bounty of living creatures in water, air, and forests encouraged the settlers to rely on the archaic techniques of hunting and fishing that had served their ancestors through the ages.

When agriculture did develop in some places in the Christian era, hunting and fishing continued as important sources of subsistence; in the absence of urban centers or a growing priesthood, the ancient forms of faith were not displaced.[2] Hence a deep reservoir of early beliefs was retained, of the kind held by peoples through the ages when they had lived as hunters, herders, or fishermen.

Through the study of the North Eurasian sources, we learn of the deep awe of men, tiny specks in the landscape, before the powers of nature, and their reverence of the all-important and mighty beasts; we can watch the stages by which an element of the environment grows into an anthropomorphic divinity; we meet goddesses who tend, above all, to women's needs; and we encounter clearly the various uses of the noun "mother." I now present a few examples of these phenomena.

HUMILITY BEFORE THE PHYSICAL ENVIRONMENT

Deeply distrustful of their powers of achievement, people do not seek salvation in the human sphere. Their main religious functionary, the shaman, travels to the world beyond to obtain a blessing.[3] He must also shed his human rationality and obtain a state of superhuman frenzy; he is helped by animal familiars, for human strength is not sufficient to the task.[4]

Beasts, altogether, hold important offices in the cosmic order. In a widespread myth, the world was formed when a bird brought some mud from the bottom of the sea.[5] Beasts may create storms and winds. And the highest god of the Ainus is a bear.[6]

The bear is the most sacred of all creatures, so holy that in some places his name must not be pronounced. When this noblest of all beings is killed, countless ceremonies are enacted to assuage the guilt of the human hunters. The bear is brought to the village where he is received in joy and reverence; the slayers try to overcome their shame and guilt in the rousing celebration of the "bear wedding" or "bear feast." Seated in the place of honor, the beast is the Lord of the festivity.[7] Throughout, the fiction is maintained that the bear is still alive, or that he himself had willed his death.

Things growing in the soil likewise receive respect and honor. When a hunter must take shelter for the night, he asks permission of a tree to lie beneath its branches, and he gives thanks in the morning for his peaceful rest.[8] In advanced societies humans are sure of their ability to construct a place of sanctity in stone or brick to create a dwelling for a god. The northern nations, on the other hand, seek the godhead in his own habitation, a sacred mountain or a sacred lake (Figure 25).[9] In this location men are forever only humble and tolerated guests. And the chief symbols of their faith are sacred trees or sacred pillars that form not a hallowed place on earth but a pathway to the superhuman realms.

As the sacred sites are not usually marked off from the rest of nature, so

Figure 25. A worshipper prays near a sacred stone. One may notice the absence of any enclosure.

the boundaries between a creature and the world around him are not fixed. Several souls inhabit the human body, and while this body lies in trance or sleep, one or more of these may leave its dwelling. The person's "double," or protective spirit, has arisen in the phenomenon of the "wandering soul."[10]

The evidence cited here shows not only men's feelings of inferiority but also an absence of firm demarcations between the various areas of life. The holy sites are not marked off from the rest of nature, or the settlements from the forest. The soul is not confined by the boundaries of the body; in the shaman's journey, the wall between the human and the superhuman realms is transcended; when the soul of a dead is brought back to life, the clear division between life and death is broken. In denying the bear's death at the "bear feast," reality is not separated from imagination.

THE NUMINOUS POWERS

In the life of most northern peoples a god of heaven directs the course of the world. He may represent an ordering and guiding principle, related to atmospheric elements, and he achieves prominence in agricultural communities. Often though he is remote and withdrawn.[11] Other powers, however, are more closely interwoven in daily life. These may be roughly divided into four classes: rulers of localities and living creatures, deified elements of the surroundings, ancestral tutelary spirits, and goddesses of women.

Owners of Places and Beasts

These are of special importance to fishermen and hunters. It is believed that every portion of the landscape and every beast of the forest is beholden to a power that is both its master and its representative.[12] The Guardians of Nature are visualized as humans but may be fitted with aspects of the phenomenon that they rule. The Guardian of the walrus among the Chuckchee is equipped with walrus tusks, and a Master of Fish may appear in the form of a pike.[13] Great power is wielded by these forces, for they may cause well-being or starvation by sending or withholding the creatures in their care. The Lord of the Mountain of the Nivchi (Giliaks) decides when an animal is to fall to the hunter's weapon, and the Lady of the Sea fills the nets of fishermen with fish.[14]

The spaces of human settlements are also owned and populated by the superhuman. A spirit lives beneath the roof, the hearth, and the threshhold of the Estonian dwelling.[15] The Old Woman of the Earth resides beneath the earth on which the Samoyeds have built their tent.[16] And we may note that it is not the human but the spirit that owns and rules the human habitation.

Animated and Deified Elements

Yet another set of powers grew from the elements of men's surroundings. The North Eurasian peoples live in a fully animated world where every entity—the sky, the earth, the sickle, or the fire—possesses a conscience, voice, and will. Those phenomena that are important to human welfare (such as the earth in farming communities) would be endowed with religious significance, and frequently they are given human features so that some appear eventually as men and women.[17] Yet even in their human form they may retain some basic qualities. The Lady Wind of the Mordvins is thus addressed in prayer:

> In the spring when the new seed is sprouting
> then blow gently; when you see a blue cloud,
> drive it before you above our grain. When
> the ears of corn are full, blow softly. . . ."[18]

And the Lady Water is implored:

> [Y]ou who give drink to many . . . give mercy
> to the poor, from the silver flow of your
> water, from the golden reeds, bending in
> the breezes. . . . [19]

It appears that among farmers, who depend on inanimate entities, on earth, rain, and growing plants, an animated element has risen to cultic stature; whereas in communities of hunters, which survive on living beings, the Lords and Guardians of Nature loom large in religious thought.[20] It has been observed by Uno Harva that in farming villages the animated elements are exalted, while the Lords and Guardians of the place may sink to become ill-tempered, mischievous, or fully evil.[21]

Among farmers, honor and adoration are centered on the earth, the waters, and the rain-giving sky. And these receive the sacrifice of butter, milk, or slaughtered beasts.[22] Lakes and rivers, which bestow the blessedness of moisture, attained special significance. Offerings are tossed into certain wells and rivers so that these might send the needed rains.[23]

The belief arose, and this is of significance in a study of maternal beings, that the liquid of a river or a well, which promotes the growth of vegetation, can extend its life-giving powers over men and beasts. Through this assumption, Lady Water achieved an important place in the customs and rituals of marriage among some Finno-Ugric groups.[24] Thus the newly wedded Mokshan bride goes to the river with the gift of a living chicken, bread, and pancakes; and a prayer is addressed to the water by an older woman:

> Little Mother, you are clean, cleanse
> this girl from sickness and from evil;
> let her bear often and successfully.[25]

The Family Protectors

Every family is protected by a set of guardian spirits that are inherited from the father by the son, and these promote the welfare and safety of the group. They are portrayed in concrete form, carved from the tree of a sacred site or stone broken from a sacred mountain, or shaped of metal, bone, or cloth.[26] The images are placed in the most sacred part of the dwelling, hung from a tree, or set into a sled behind the house. The spirits may also be adored in nature sanctuaries, on certain islands or mountaintops.[27] Among the Saamis, they are embodied by strange, natural stone formations, the *seide*, and play a central role in religion. Here every family has its sacred mountain, sacred lake, or sacred site.[28]

These guardians may extend their caring from a family to a tribe. They are sometimes named after the region they protect, such as the Old Man of the Ob or the god of the Pelym River.[29] We encounter among these spirits human heroes who had lived in ancient times. The Nivchi (Giliaks) believe that a man who had died a certain death joined the retinue of the Lord of the Mountain and became the special protector of his family.[30]

Goddesses of Women

The women of the family are excluded from the worship of the tutelary spirits of a patrilineal tribe. For divine protection at times of crisis and in the tasks of daily life, women must turn to a different sort of deity. A bride brings her own idols from her parental dwelling and places them in her own section of the house. They will give her succor in her special needs and tasks: during menstruation or childbirth, while tending to the young or to domestic beasts, for these are in the charge of women. The women's separate deities also guard the right to privacy of the women's rituals, and they frequently set the fate of the newborn child.[31]

Though the discussion of the main godheads presented here is necessarily superficial and schematic, it still serves to reveal and illuminate their kinship with goddesses of complex and literate societies so that these might be considered to have developed from the basic forms. Artemis of Greece, designated as Mistress of Wild Beasts, ranges through the countryside in pursuit and protection of the wild game of the forest. She is surely the counterpart of the Guardian of Nature of the North Eurasian communities. The fair-haired Greek Demeter is vital to the growth of grain. We may recognize in her the qualities of a Mistress of the Fields, the personification of the cultivated land who bestows the harvest. Amaterasu, symbol of the nation of Japan, is ancestral to the imperial family and akin to the ancestral tribal spirits of a family or clan. The Greek Eileithyia is indispensable as helper in the birth of the human child and thus parallels the role of the spirits especially charged with the concerns of menstruation, pregnancy, and parturition.

We have not met in the northern cultures a sovereign goddess who rose to greatness through the power of her womb; however, we do encounter maternal spirits and female godheads bearing the title "mother." In examining the role and nature of these beings, I have found them to exist in several forms: the Animal Mother of a shaman; the ancestress of a family or race; ruler or representative of a phenomenon; and the relative of a god.

MATERNAL DIVINITIES

The Animal Mother

The visionary gifts of the shaman's calling can be attained only by a being who was nourished in childhood by an animal. This creature may be a bird with an iron beak, a spotted blue bull, an elk, a reindeer, or some unidentifiable beast. It is designated as Animal Mother (Yiä-il) among the Buriats and Dolgans,[32] and appears three times before her fosterling: at his birth, at reaching manhood, and at death. According to one informant, this being embodies "the shaman's visionary power which is able to penetrate both the past and the future."[33] The presence of the Animal Mother indicates once again men's feelings of inferiority, showing that a purely human heritage does not suffice to obtain true wisdom or spiritual growth.

The Ancestress

The Chukchee tell the story of a dog who married a young woman; she kicked his mother, a bitch, and struck the puppies who were his brothers. He then took another, gentler woman to be his bride; she was tender with his relatives and she fed them with the dainties that she had brought from the wedding celebration. At night her husband changed into a handsome youth, the owner of many herds of reindeer. In this union many children were begotten, and they grew into a mighty tribe.[34]

According to another Chukchee narrative, the first pair on earth, a sister and a brother, fed on stones. The woman yearned for her brother's embraces, but she met rejection until she disguised herself and pretended to be another woman. In this encounter originated the human race. In a Mansi (Vogul) tale, the first man slept with the Lady of the Ruffle (a fish) and begot boys and girls (i.e., the first humans).

A girl living in the village of Niaksimvol in northeastern Siberia was wooed by a Nenets knight and by a man from the upper Ob. She married both successively and left them, having borne a daughter in each marriage. She became the ancestress of the Mansi people and was much adored as the Great Lady of the Kazym River. Her image was recently recovered from a ritual shed.[35]

Accounts in which the human race originates through pregnancy or birth (i.e., on a human model) are rare in North Eurasian tradition. In two of the tales we meet an ancestral animal, indicating once again the deep significance of beasts.

The "Mothers"

We encounter a large number of superhuman beings who are addressed and designated as mother—for example, *mōtsa-äma,* Forest Mother of the Livonians; *gudici-mumi,* Thunderstorm Mother of the Udmurts (Votiaks); *jumon-ava,* Mother of Jumo (a god) of the Mari (Cheremiss); *mastor-ava,* Earth Mother of the Mordvins; *Kaltaš-agke,* Mother of Kaltaša (a village) of the Mansi (Voguls).[36]

We must realize that "mother" designates a variety of forces. Some may be regarded as Owners and Guardians of beasts: When Tomam, Mother Tom of the Khets, stations herself near the Yenisei River in spring and shakes her sleeves, birds emerge to flutter through the breezes; they return to her in the autumn when she again moves her arms.[37] A "mother" may also be the spirit owner of a place of human habitation: Such a spirit is the Earth Mother of the Nentsi (Yurak Samoyeds) who dwells in the earth beneath the tent.[38]

The title "mother" is also given to animated elements of men's surroundings. In these instances the original phenomenon is frequently perceptible in the creature. The Sun Mother of the Mari (Cheremiss) "rises in the sky" and "burns the earth."[39] The Corn Mother of the Mordvins is "sown in the dawn, reaped at dusk, poured into a rich man's granary at night, made into small beer at Easter and into pastry at Christmastime."[40]

Sometimes the title "mother" is bestowed because the spirit is related to a god: *jumon-awa,* Mother of Jumo, the sky god of the Mari (Cheremiss); and *ški-ava,* Mother of Škaj, the god of heaven of the Mordvins.[41] The title is also conjoined, though rarely, with an abstract concept, as in *šotsĕn-awa,* Mother of Growth among the Mari.[42]

The Religious Stature of the "Mothers." As spirit Owner and Guardian of nature, human habitations, or beasts, the "mother" is given the respect that is accorded to such beings. As mother of a divinity she is revered as the member of the family of gods. When the title has been conjoined with an animated element, we encounter various degrees of sanctity. Some spirits simply remain what they were: animated elements, such as the Eye-ball Mother of the Mari. Others, however, that play a part in well-being and prosperity have attained deep significance and are approached in prayer and adoration. Gifts for the Earth Mother are taken to sacrificial groves by the Mari, or set upon the soil itself; placing porridge on the ground, the farmers plead: "Eat, Earth, and let us grow grain."[43] Bread is spread with butter and tossed from the boat in fishing expeditions on the Ym River in Komi (Sirjan) territory, and prayers are addressed to the water: "Mother Vorik-va, carry us safely . . . protect us and give us many fish."[44]

When she is gracious, *büt-awa* of the Mari grants not only fish and rain but also fertility to beasts, fields, and human women.[45] The "silken-haired Water Lady" of the Mokshans cleanses flax from sickness, bleaches it to whiteness, and relieves the pain of women in travail.[46] We noted earlier that wells and rivers are held to be in close and beneficial contact with human reproduction. A newly wedded couple brings money, bread, salt, and cotton to the Water Mother of the Komi (Sirjans), praying: "During my wedded life, give me happiness, food and health, and grant me many sons and daughters."[47] A barren woman of the Erza goes to the river to ask forgiveness: "Water Mother, forgive me, perhaps I have offended you and therefore cannot bear any children."[48] Children are told among the Mokshans that "Water Mother brings the babies."[49]

Imaginative Embellishment of "Mothers." Some of the important "mothers" stimulated the imagination and were endowed with human form, human emotions, and adventures while simultaneously retaining the aspect of the element from which they grew. The Wind Mother of the Mordvins blows gently or blows fiercely, for she is the wind, but she also owns a manor house in heaven and is mother of twelve sons.[50] The Yukaghir throw beads into the river while they implore the River Mother to hold them safely on her surface (in her form as water) and to accept the gems as playthings for her children (in her human form).[51] The Corn Mother who is "sown in the morning and reaped at dusk" sings with the voice of a human woman. The Water Mother of the Mordvins, highly significant in her form as water, also became a many-colored, vital creature in tales where she climbs ashore to comb her hair, is accidentally caught by a fisherman, appears at the hour of noon before the villagers, or flees in deathly terror before the Christian cross.[52]

In some cases the "mother" seems to fuse within herself several kinds of spirits. The *vel-ava*, Village Mother of the Udmurts, is the protector of the village (tutelary force) and owner of the locality. The Earth Mother of the Samoyeds lives as a healing deity beneath the tent and is visited by the shaman when he wishes to cure a disease; she is the special godhead of the family, as well as the owner of the locality. Mother Kaltaš guards and guides a settlement of humans as its tutelary deity, and she is the spirit owner of the village Kaltaša of the Nentsi.

The Meaning of the Epithet "Mother." Sometimes we cannot tell whether a "mother" in human form originated in the Lord and Owner of a region or in an animated element. The Livonian Ocean Mother may be the animated ocean or its superhuman Owner.[53] The *büt-awa* of the Mari, an old woman, mixes mud into the water of her well in spring and honey in the autumn, and we cannot determine her derivation.[54] It may seem pedantic to wish to concern oneself about this distinction, but many cultures are aware of the origin and nature of the spirits. Sometimes the different nature of the two is indicated by their designations. Among the Udmurt (Votiaks) the noun *mumi* (mother) is applied only to animated elements, and the name *murt* (man, human) only to the spirit owner. Such use also prevails among the Mari (*awa* and *ia*), among the Permians, the Mordvins (*etsa* and *awa*), and among the Estonians. The epithet "mother" is, in these cases, clearly not bestowed on the basis of a specifically human quality.

We may be sure that the word "mother," employed in naming elements of no resemblance to a human woman, does not denote a creature who has given birth, and not even, metaphorically, a nourishing or protective being. The Cloud Mother or the Eye Mother are in no way protective or generative of the eye or the cloud, but are the eye or the cloud itself. When an animated element, such as the Water Mother of the Mordvins, is envisaged with her children, she received these in the course of becoming human and not in her quality of fruit-bearing woman.

We may agree that in the cases enumerated above, the name "mother" does not describe the bearer as a biological procreator. The word "mother" cannot be understood, moreover, in the sense of "mother of" or "nourishing, protective force of." The Water Mother is not the protector or nourisher of water, but of the soil, men, and beasts. The Corn Mother is not the nourisher, protector, or creator of rye or wheat, but is the grain itself. We may conclude that in these instances the word "mother" does not describe a function or relationship, but serves as a title of respect, meaning Our Lady. The name *ved-ava*, for instance, should not be translated as Water Mother, but as Lady Water or Dame Water, just as the name *mjer-iza* would be translated as Sir

Ocean or Lord Ocean. This conclusion is supported by the fact that the name "mother" alternates with other titles of reverence, such as Old Woman, Noble Lady, Mistress (*büt-ava* alternating with *büt-kawa*—"Old Woman" of the Mari).

The evidence is not quite so clear when we deal with a spirit-owner or guardian. The Forest Mother *vir-ava* might indeed be the protector of the forest, and the Fox Mother *keten-emu* of the Finns the protector or guardian of foxes. We may merely observe that the title "mother" occurs with much less frequency in the case of Guardians and Owners where it might indeed denote a "mother" in a metaphoric sense, and here it also alternates with other titles of respect, as in the case of *loddiš-aedne* (Bird Mother of the Saamis, also called *barbmo-akka,* Old Woman of the Birds) or with the Forest Mother or Forest Mistress of the Mokshans.[55] We may also note that the name Tomam of a goddess of the Khets (Yenisei), who generates and harbors birds and is thus their figurative mother, does not indicate this function, for it means Mother or Lady of the Tom River.

That the title "mother" of certain phenomena does not indicate a relationship, but rather a feeling of awe and respect before the deity, has been observed by Harva. He states in his treatise on the water spirits of the Finno-Ugric nations that the noun *aba* of *büt-aba* (Water Mother) is never anything but "a cultic epithet of the animated water."[56] He furthermore declares that the title *aba* is never carried by a spirit owner.

Karjalainen notes, in his discussion of the Ob-Ugrians, that they habitually address their honored spirits with the names of relatives (i.e., grandfather, son, father) as is also their custom with members of the human community. The name "mother" is borne by all older women of the village as a title of respect. He concludes that such a designation is "nothing more than a flattering and respectful epithet."[57]

The phenomenon may also be observed elsewhere. In Hungarian (closely related to Mansi [Vogul]), the words "little mother" and "little father" are terms of affection; the names "aunt" and "uncle" merely relate to age without expressing any personal emotion. Anthropologist Edmund Leach observes that kinship terms do not necessarily carry kinship meanings, but rather those of status, age, and sex.[58] The German noun *Frau* signifies the partner in a marriage (relation) and also a noblewoman (in earlier speech), as in *Unsere liebe Frau* for the Virgin Mary, and is used today as a title of address. Latvian *meita* means "daughter" and "young woman"; when Latvian folk poetry speaks of Saules (the sun) *meita,* it tells of the sun's daughter or of the young, virgin sun.

Let us note that the tutelary spirits of a family or tribe (*sjaddai, haehe, sietti*), among whom we might indeed encounter ancestral, nurturing, and protective beings, are not designated as "mothers" or "fathers." The Mari know the procreative force that lives in humans and beasts as *šotšen,* and not as "mother" or as "father"; however, this generative power is honored with the *title* "mother" so that we meet with Mother Fertility or Lady Fertility (*šotšen-*

awa). Only in those spirits, who became the wife or mother of a god in the course of his humanization, can the meaning of "one who has given birth," be attributed to the title "mother."

Summary

Let us summarize the complicated (though still simplified) classification by stating that the "mothers" pertain to the various groups that make up the spiritual vision of the North Eurasian peoples. "Mothers" may be Rulers and Guardians of nature (i.e., of a species or a geographic region) and are also found as guardians of human settlements. In this function they are imagined in the form of humans, more rarely in the form of animals, and sometimes fitted with features of their element. The greater category of "mothers" contains beings that personify entities of the environment—water, fire, earth, or human dwellings. These spirits may be of small significance, but may also reach a state of great sacredness if their office is of benefit to humans. Such figures often receive human features, and we meet them in various stages of their development into the full form of womanhood. In agricultural communities the animated element gained ascendance over the earlier spirit owner so that water itself, as source of blessing, dwarfed the importance of the Owner and Guardian of fish. The name "mother" frequently serves as a title of respect. A "mother" may also appear as the mistress of a household, and as a wife and mother when she or another godhead has acquired human form.

We have met many spirits designated as "mother," but hardly any maternal divinities. We may agree that the female deities do not receive their place in faith from the role or function of human mothers. Only the superhuman ancestress (not a goddess) achieves significance because she has given birth in the manner of the wives of men. Even here, in tales of descent, the beast form of the mother or her mate is stressed to impart the flash of sacrality to the event. The Animal Mother of the shaman is surely not shaped on a human model. Admittedly, those forces who acquired children or became the wife or mother of a god share the role of a human mother. In these cases, however, we deal only with reshaping external forms, with poetry and imagination, rather than with religious faith.

The basic and deep significance of feminine divinities stems from the various phenomena that they personify or rule. The goddess Tomam controls the departure and return of migratory birds which are vital to existence, and the Ocean Mother governs the supply of fish. Mother Earth offers the bounty of her fruit, and Lady Water the blessed moisture of her waves. Even when Lady Water bestows fertility on women, she does so in her form of the life-giving waters and the fruit-bringing rain, and not through the generative power of her womanhood. The concept of the Animal Mother of the shaman, in turn, indicates with great clarity that spiritual vision and transcendental nature, such as is needed by the shaman in his craft, cannot be imparted by a human mother.

It is in keeping with peoples' awe and dread before the world around them that the shock and wonder of the holy, the *mysterium tremendum* in which gods are created, would be awakened by nonhuman forces—the sky, the earth, the beasts of the forest and the sea. These powers might also affect the birth of children. As in North Eurasian tradition, the killing of the bear is not attributed to *human* strength, so the continuation of life through birth would not be attributed to the wonder of the *human* womb. Clearly, a goddess modeled on a mortal woman and celebrating a mortal woman's fruit-bearing power did not and could not have come into existence.

Since creative energy was not attributed to the process of human birth, the theme of conception and of birth did not enter northern myths of the creation of the world or of the origin of the human race. The world came into being, as earlier noted, because a bird brought mud from the bottom of the sea, or it was crafted by a beast, or also sometimes dropped from heaven, and a creator god would usually shape the first human from clay, grass, or the bones of a seal. It is characteristic of North Eurasian tradition that the soul was infused into man's lifeless body by yet another separate act.[59]

If we agree that the North Eurasian cultures retained aspects of the beliefs of early men, and if we agree that there was community of faith between the various cultures of prehistoric times, then the survey of North Eurasian religions has given us a base to which we may trace the godheads of complex societies. It has offered us a glimpse of a preanthropocentric universe and shown us how, through human imagination, an entity develops into human shape with human experiences and with a family—that is, we watch the creation of mythology. We have seen that no special reverence is rendered to the power of the womb, and no great mother goddess has arisen. On the other hand, we have noted that a stream of blessing issues from the family protectors who blend with the ancestral dead. We have also seen, and this is especially important to further explorations, that the title "mother" need not contain a kinship meaning. The study of North Eurasian cultures will enable us to understand the gods of complex societies in the light of the more archaic forms.

We must also realize, however, that in spite of men's humility before the powers of nature, they do not cease attempting to bend it to their will, to trap and kill the beasts of the forest and to fell its trees. In reshaping divinities into human form, in addressing them as friends and relatives with human titles, we would find evidence of the same tendency in the realm of religion and mythology.

While the creative aspect of bringing forth a child left little impact on religion, the fears and dangers attending the event formed a deep impression. Tutelary spirits, inherited from the woman's family, are committed to her needs at this time of existential crisis. These deities are also credited with breathing a soul into the unawakened form and with setting the course of fate. These goddesses, so intimately tied to feminine experiences, are discussed in the following section.

AKKAS—GODDESSES
OF SAAMI WOMEN

A careful study of the deities of women's lives was rendered by Gustav Ränk, who centered his attention on the spirits of the Saamis and placed them in the context of North Eurasian culture.[60] The Saamis (Lapps), who speak a Finno-Ugric language, are settled in the far North of Europe; they are divided into: the fishing Saamis of the Norwegian coast; the fishing and reindeer herding Saamis in the northern and central parts of the Kola Peninsula; the fishing Saamis on the shore of Lake Inari in Finland; the reindeer herding Mountain Saamis in Sweden, Norway, and Finland; and the Forest Saamis of Sweden's northern forests, who engage in fishing, hunting, and reindeer herding. A small minority exhibiting very archaic features in its religion lives by reindeer herding in the high mountains.[61]

The raising and herding of reindeer is at present the main source of sustenance for Saamis and was probably introduced through Swedish and Norwegian impact. It replaced an older hunting and fishing culture, but it did not eradicate or replace the religious forms of the earlier economy. This religion paralleled that of other arctic or subarctic nations, and thus we find among the Saamis, as elsewhere, the worship of the Lords and Owners of wild beasts, especially the bear, and of fish among the coastal dwellers, and of the spirits of the individual family or clan that coalesce in some ways with the ancestral dead.[62]

These godheads may be represented by strangely formed stones, the *seide*, and since the most vital concern of the group related at one time to a sufficiency of game, the *seide* appear in places that are especially suited to hunting or fishing. They are also seen on sites that are sacred to the individual village in the vicinity of the mountain where the ancestors are said to dwell.[63]

Since women had no share in hunting, were barred from ritual, and were not protected by the ancestral spirits of the new family, they were guarded by their own deities: the Madder-akka and her daughters Sar-akka, Jux-akka, and Ux-akka. The group appears in its entirety only among the Saamis of Norway and Sweden; only some of the members of the family are found in other segments of Saami culture.

The Function of the *Akkas*

Madder-akka receives the soul of the unborn child from the hunting god Leib-olmay, a celestial deity, and she plants it in the woman's womb. Her daughter Sar-akka causes flesh to grow around this soul, and she grants good delivery if she is honored with a sacrifice. Another daughter, Jux-akka, may change the girl into a boy, and she must also be given an offering. Ux-akka watches at the door, and in her turn accepts a gift and then protects the child from harm.[64]

According to another account, the soul is shaped by the important god Radien-atje, who sends it to Mader-atje, the husband of Madder-akka; this deity accepts the soul within himself, and encircling the sun, hands it over when he reaches the lowest beam. Madder-akka grows a body around the soul and passes it to Ux-akka if it is to become a boy and to Sar-akka if it is to become a girl. She then takes it back into herself and in time inserts it in the human woman. Such tales of complex activity in the formation of the child, in which celestial spirits participate, are told only by the Saamis of Norway and Sweden.

Besides partaking in the fashioning of children, Madder-akka may assist the woman in travail, and according to one author, she is of help in menstruation.[65] A report about the Finnish Saamis describes her only as a power of healing: "To the blind who worshipped her for seven years, she gave the light of his eyes, to the deaf his hearing; she showed the traveller his way."[66] She is also said to have the power to grant fertility to beasts and men.[67]

Like her mother, Sar-akka may ease the pangs of labor and may concern herself with women's menses. Sacrifices are rendered to her at such times, and men do not approach the menstruating women because they are frightened of the power of Sar-akka.[68] Sar-akka gained great importance among the Saamis and is invoked when children fall victim to diseases. When Christianity was accepted, water drunk in church ritual was named "Sar-akka's blood," just as bread was named "Leib-olmay's flesh."[69]

The name Ux-akka means "Door-akka"; she guards the door from the entrance of evil spirits and also aids the menstruating woman. In some myths she passes the child, prepared by Madder-akka and "warmed" by Sar-akka, to the future mother.[70] The noun *jux* has the meaning "bow," and Jux-akka is brought into relation with the small bow that is hung above the cot of the male child; according to some accounts, she especially guards the male infant and may change a girl into a boy.[71]

The Saami goddesses of women are thus engaged in two main offices: shaping the infant to be born, and tending as midwife, nurse, or healer to human needs. Gustav Ränk believes that the former is the higher function that was acquired by basically terrestrial spirits in the course of time. It is, however, not possible to know which aspect of the goddesses had preceeded the other, and the *akkas* might have acted in both matters from their earliest conception.

The Names

The noun *akka* has the meaning "old woman, mother, grandmother"; the form *madder* is etymologically identical with the Estonian and Finnish word *manner* (earth, ground); this in turn is related to a word meaning "earth floor, tent ground" among the Komi. In meaning, however, it conveys to modern Saamis the feeling of "ancestry, root, descent"; *madder* added to *akka* (grand mother) thus denotes a great-grandmother, and the noun *madder-aggja* means great-grandfather among the Swedish Saamis.[72]

The noun *madder* thus lost the sense of "ground, earth" and acquired the meaning "ancestral." This change may be explained by the fact that the dead were believed to dwell in the realm beneath the ground. The compound *madder-akka* developed further to accept also the meaning "midwife" among some segments of the Saami population.[73]

The compound *sar* of Sar-akka has been traced to the verb *saret* (to cleave); the syllable also occurs in the name of another divinity of childbirth, Sar-edna (*edni*—"mother"); Sar-akka is rendered as *skilequinde* (dividing woman) in a Swedish translation (i.e., the force that separates the mother from her child). Matches with cloven ends were placed in the porridge cooked in honor of Sar-akka after delivery, and on magic drums she is often depicted with a forked stick in her hand. We also know that the cutting of wood belongs to the rites of birth-giving.[74] The significance of the names Ux-akka (Door-akka) and Jux-akka (Bow-akka) has already been observed; it may merely be added that on magic drums Jux-akka may be depicted with a bow (Figure 26).[75]

The Location of the *Akkas*

The universe of Saami mythology is horizontally divided into layers that rest upon one another, each sphere ruled and inhabited by its special god. Radien, who is the mightiest, dwells in the highest of the spheres, and Jabmeakka and Rota reign over the lowest layer, the kingdom of the dead.

The god Madder-atje who hands the new soul to his wife Madder-akka, is stationed in the realm beneath the sky; as his wife, Madder-akka would thus be a celestial deity. Other accounts, however, place her beneath the ground, and it is said that libations were poured for her and her daughters onto the floor of the tent. It was earlier noted that *madder* has the meaning "earth, ground"; in depictions on magic drums the *akkas* are stationed with other terrestrial deities near the lower rim.[76] We thus meet with contradictory beliefs concerning the dwelling of the spirits. It has been observed that the myth of the complex creation of the child occurs only among the Swedish and Norwegian Saamis, and it is only here that we meet with a contradiction.

The terrestrial *akkas* are located, more precisely, near the door of the human dwelling. This station is obvious in the case of "Door-akka"; we also know that the porridge presented to Sar-akka stayed for three days in its place near the door, and on Christmas Eve libations for the goddess were poured onto the space before the entrance.[77]

The choice for the location of the spirits becomes evident when we consider the domestic arrangement of the Saami habitation. As with other North Eurasian cultures, it was divided into a man's part and a woman's part. The men's area, or *poshjo,* was located at the rear of the house; here was kept the hunting gear, and the booty of the chase prepared by the male members of the group. A special door at the rear, called the "bloody door" by the Kola Saami, was reserved for bringing in the game. Through this door men also left to worship at the sacred places.[78]

Figure 26. Magic drum with three akka-figures: no. 18 Jux-akka, No. 19 Sar-akka, No. 20 Madder-akka. [After the Naero-Manuscript (Manker).]

Women were not allowed in the *poshjo,* and a stone marked the boundary of the forbidden space. Their occupations were carried out in the front part of the dwelling, and in times of crisis they came even closer to the door. The child-bearing mother thus moved to the left side of the entrance. Högström observes that in their menses women would not only leave their accustomed sleeping places and bed down near the door, but would also eat their meals in isolation.[79]

The Derivation of the Godheads

Whereas the male grows and lives beneath the protective gaze of his ancestral deities, the bride receives no succor from the godheads of her husband's family and must bring her protectors from her father's house. It appears that of the *saivos* (ancestral forces) dwelling in a sacred mountain, a share was allotted to the departing bride to take with her as her heritage. If this derivation of the women's gods is to be accepted, then we must observe that they changed their functions. They served the needs of men as long as they resided in the ancestral mountain, and they attended the needs of women in their new abode. Ränk believes that a certain antagonism between the gods of men and the gods of women is rooted in their derivation from different clans.[80]

WOMEN'S GODDESSES AMONG OTHER NORTH EURASIAN NATIONS

The Saami *akkas* do not represent an isolated phenomenon, for kindred spirits may be encountered throughout the reaches of northern Eurasia among the reindeer hunters and nomads of the North, the cattle nomads of the Siberian steppes and forests, and the Turkish and Mongolian nomads of Central Asia.

The Nentsi (Yural Samoyeds), whose settlements extend from the arctic shores, between the Yenisei and the Barents Sea, to the forest zone, believe that the "earth carrying old woman," or "earth grandmother," has her residence beneath the earth and that she wears seven belts, a skirt, and a hat of earth. She sends the child into the world and determines the length of its life; therefore, birthmarks are called "the documents of the earth carrying old woman" among the Forest Nentsi. She is also active at the time of bringing forth the infant and is invoked in difficult deliveries. She is addressed as "earth-mother-opener" in magic songs of the Tundra Nentsi that were chanted to alleviate the throes of labor. She is also able to release the sick from their diseases.[81]

The father of the newborn sacrifices a reindeer to the goddess, smearing its blood on the lips of her image, a wooden idol, and she also receives a bowl of steaming flesh. The idol(s) had been carved by the girl's mother and then placed in the "woman's corner" in the new home. Since among the Nentsi childbirth was considered "the most sinful of all diseases," young girls, men, and their deities had to leave the dwelling at this time of crisis.[82]

The birth deities of the Chanti and Mansi (Ob-Ugrians) are frequently stationed in the spheres of heaven. Among the Irtysh Chanti, the god of the skies, Tūrem father, creates the infant with the assistance of his wife, Tūrem mother, and both control its fate and age. In Mansi (Vogul) belief the soul is shaped by Joli-Tārem, who is the sister of the celestial god. An especially popular goddess is Kaltaš-Agke, the wife or daughter of the deity of heaven, who implants the soul into the infant's body and writes its fate into a "golden book."[83] Vagneg-Īmi, of the Surgutian Chanti, who herself had borne seven sons, inserts the soul into the body and decrees its destiny.[84] These celestial and creative beings also extend their powers toward easing the agony of labor pain. Kaltaš-Agke is offered sacrifices by pregnant women, and Vagneg-Īmi is honored after the child has been brought forth.[85]

Ajysyt, a deity of manifold powers and qualities, appears among the Yakuts. She is in some accounts the daughter of the god of heaven, who carries the soul, shaped by her father, from the heights to the "middle world" to be born on earth; she may also determine the infant's fate. In addition, Ajysyt is a deity of horses (envisioned as male) and of cattle (envisioned as a female force). She may also grant fertility.[86] One report declares that the Ajysyt of humans dwells where the sun rises in summer, the Ajysyt of horses where the sun rises in winter, and the Ajysyt of cattle beneath the ground.[87]

The goddess must be personally present at the time of parturition, for without her attendance both mother and child would die. For three days afterward Ajysyt remains in the dwelling, from which men are banished in this span of time. Women would gather in the room of childbirth, sacrifice to Ajysyt, eat ritual meals in her honor, and praise the goddess for her help. After three days have passed, the midwife takes both the straw on which the new mother had been lying and the refuse of the birth to a tall tree in the forest. It is then that Ajysyt is thought to leave the house.[88]

The Tungus woman inherited a portion of her father's household deities in marriage; these spirits were named Malu and were given a new name—Nadzhil—after they changed their dwelling place. They guarded the health of the women of the household and protected them in labor, remaining separate from the household gods of men. The Nadzhil were mistrusted and feared as alien spirits and often held responsible for misfortune of the house. Their name means "my mother's relatives" in the language of the Manchurian Tungus.[89]

Among the Turkish peoples of the Altaic mountains, including the Mongols, the name of women's spirits is derived from one or two roots with the meaning "woman, wife, old woman, grandmother, ancestress." Such forces are the Emegender of the Teleuts, the Örekenner of the Shors, the Öreköndor of the Kumandines, and the Emegen of the Soyots. They might take the form of abstract beings, but they were also reproduced concretely as dolls stuffed with rags, as wooden puppets, or even as drawings on a piece of cloth. Their

Figure 27. Emegender idols of the Teleuts.

eyes were usually made of glass. The dolls were created in the bride's home by her female relatives before her marriage, and her brother would supply the cloth (Figure 27).[90]

Without such a puppet in the vicinity, the woman did not venture to give birth, since she believed that without it she might die and the child might be born without sight. The color of the baby's eyes would, in fact, be the same as those of the glass beads in the idol's face. Beyond their function at the time of birth, the deities might also act in another medical capacity: The Teleuts sought their help concerning eye and ear diseases, and the Shors turned to them when they feared the death of children or cattle.[91]

The images were kept separately from the idols of men and were placed near the door. A description of a tent of the Alarian Buriats notes sculpted figures at the right side of the door. These were especially devoted to the care of the young; some were to dangle them and attend to them in case of illness, some were female shamans who would help with their meals, and one image represented a celestial virgin, also a guardian of children.[92]

That the deities of women are of great power and potential harmfulness may be surmised from the precautions taken by the Ainus during childbirth. The men were banished for six days from the dwelling, and if one of them had to return for an urgent reason, he had to make his way through an entrance at the rear. If such an entrance was not in existence, the man would have to proceed through a window. The image of the deity of birth was placed near the door, and it received a sacrifice six days after the delivery when the dangerous period came to an end.[93]

Though we have noted some variations in the deities of this discussion, we have also noted many common features. The spirits aid in the birth of children and sometimes cattle; their role may include the shaping of the infant or its soul, planting it in a woman's womb, setting the fate of the newborn, healing diseases, or easing the course of menstruation.

The numina are visualized in concrete form, represented by manmade idols, and also as abstract forces. The latter may be members of a celestial family and have their dwelling place in heaven, but they may also live beneath the floor of the tent. The puppets find their station near the entrance in the woman's portion of the house and are brought by the new bride as her heritage. They remain alien spirits and do not mingle with the gods of men. Their power to protect the women may be matched by a power to guard the privacy of women's rituals, paralleling the exclusion of women from the rituals of men. And antagonism between the divinities of the two sexes may be observed.

Since the deities described are deeply involved with childbirth and motherhood and since they sometimes even shape the unborn child, it may be argued that they represent a variant form of the Great Sovereign Mother. The two configurations, however, spring from very different roots. The Great Mother was supposedly created in the reverence generated by the mystery of her fertile womb. The Goddesses of Birth, on the other hand, frequently are not mothers and are frequently too old to bear a child. They could not be symbols of fertile womanhood. They derive their power from their nature as tutelary forces that are inherited by the woman from her family; thus they represent the counterpart to the ancestral tutelary spirits of the men. Like their male analogues, they are shown in concrete form and stationed in a special section of the dwelling. Since the idols are brought by the bride to her husband's home, they exist in the context of a patrilineal succession. These deities are indeed of high significance, but this significance did not arise in celebration of the creative aspect of female fruitfulness, but in the fears that denied a woman even a share in the protection granted by the gods of men.

The survey of the women's goddesses of northern Eurasia has revealed an important connection: the new life is fostered and promoted by tutelary, ancestral spirits. As ancestral beings these belong, in some measure, to the world of the dead, as does the "earth carrying old woman" who dwells beneath the tent of the Nentsi. The gift of continued life thus springs from the sphere of the departed rather than from the human sphere. It seems as if the blessed influence of the ancestral world were needed to counteract the sins committed by the living body.

The Creativity of Suffering: The Eskimo

T HE territory of the Eskimo (Inuit) is sparsely settled. A population of about 100,000 dwells in an area that extends across the North American continent and reaches the Chukchee Peninsula of Siberia.[1] The most northern of the groups, the Polar Eskimo, lives at the edge of the inhabitable world. Some experts believe that the tribes had been pressed toward the North from a more southerly station of the continent.[2] Whatever their point of origin, they found their new homeland to be a place of harsh and cruel natural conditions that allowed them no more than a life of bare subsistence. In our time the region has been modernized, and Inuit culture has all but vanished. The following description is based on reports that were composed when Inuit tradition was still in flower.

The briefness of the summer season does not allow the growth of vegetation. Thus the Inuit (excepting the caribou hunters) were forced to rely for their nourishment on the products of the sea. Also, the waters of the arctic seas are blocked by ice or ice fragments, preventing the importation of foreign materials or innovations.[3]

The means for existence of the Inuit were supplied by the fish and mammals of the ocean: Whales, walrus, and seals provided food, blubber for lamps, skins for clothing and tents, sinews for sewing thread, and ivory for needles.[4] Except for some berries in the summer, the diet consisted entirely of the meat, blood, entrails, and fat of animals. Starvation was an everpresent prospect because a delay in the arrival of the caribou or a snowstorm might easily lead to the death of some or many of the members of the group. Cannibalism at the time of great distress was not unknown.[5] Female children who were not pledged in marriage were routinely killed among the Netsilikniut Eskimo.[6] Old people committed suicide, for the community could not afford to feed those who did not bring in food by hunting. The death rate was highest among infants and young men in a place where even the healing herbs of folk medicine could not be applied to staunch a wound or cure diseases.

The heavy burden of their physical existence did not mark the character of the Eskimo, for they appeared as a merry rather than a brooding people.[7] It left, however, a lasting mark on Inuit religion.

INUIT RELIGION

The spiritual universe of the Eskimo was ruled by mighty and capricious forces who did not harbor feelings of benevolence for humans. They were deeply resentful of any slighting of their rules and punished the offender and the group with sickness and starvation. The attitude of people before these forces was one of humility, fear, and a deep sense of their own impotence and sinfulness. These emotions were voiced by a woman of the Caribou Eskimo:

> We fear the elements which we have to fight in their fury to wrest out food from land and sea. We fear cold and famine in our snow huts. We fear the sickness that is daily to be seen amongst us. . . . We fear the souls of the dead. . . . We fear the spirits of earth and air. . . . Therefore we hold by our customs and observe all the rules of tabu.[8]

Taboos

Inuit life was embedded in a web of rules and prohibitions, most of which centered on the handling of hunted and slain animals, the handling of the dead, and the biological functions of women. Among the Central Eskimo, the harpoon with which an animal was killed had to stand beside the lamp for the night so that the soul of the beast, still present in the weapon, would not suffer cold.[9] The Netsilik would not place a freshly killed seal on the igloo floor unless the floor was covered with fresh snow; sweet water was poured into the beast's mouth, and women were not allowed to do their sewing while the unflensed body was still present in the dwelling.[10]

Among the Caribou Eskimo, a woman who had given birth had to live alone for two months and could not eat meat for an entire year.[11] The Central Eskimo considered one of the greatest crimes to be concealment of the onset of menses or of an abortion. When someone perished, most of the possessions of the dead had to be destroyed; for three days, the others in the household were forbidden to cut their nails, comb their hair, work, or hunt.

These were only some of the rules to be obeyed to prevent the rise of deadly retribution.

Creative Value of Suffering

The Inuit imbued the painful and unavoidable experiences of their existence with religious value. Scarcity of possessions, for instance, which was endemic to life near the Arctic Ocean, was attenuated by the demand that property must be destroyed at the event of death or a miscarriage. Cold and hunger were often endured by the community, and it was through an added experience of cold and hunger that the shaman gained his superhuman powers. The prospect of drowning in the sea must have been everpresent in the mind of kayak hunters, and it was by drowning that Sedna, the Lady of the Sea, gained her dominion. A shaman explained his views to the explorer Rasmussen in this fashion:

> All true wisdom is only to be learned far from the dwellings of men, out in the great solitudes; and is only to be attained through suffering. Privation and suffering are the only things which can open the mind of men to those things which are hidden from others.[12]

In some tales certain forms of life originated in the intense anguish of a creature: A woman was deserted by her brothers and hated and ill-treated by her husband because she had not given birth. In despair she plunged into the sea and arose as a kind of seal, *Phoca leonina,* that swims, continually weeping, through the waves.[13] According to the myth of Sedna, whales, seals, and fish came into being after her father cut off her fingers with his knife.

Religious Life

The care of the spiritual life of the Eskimo lay above all with the man of visionary powers—the *angakoq*—who might approach the gods, because these could not be reached by ordinary men. He could intervene when a member of the community was threatened by disease, or when the group was threatened by starvation. He had attained his craft through an initiation that entailed great suffering. The future shaman of the Caribou Eskimo had to spend thirty days by himself in a snow hut; his fast was broken after fifteen days by a drink and after another fifteen days by another potion and a piece of meat.[14] In his solitude and anguish he then heard the voice of the great god of air and winds, and accepted in awe and trembling the mysterious force within himself.[15]

There were also some periodical feasts, such as the autumn rites of Sedna, the Lady of the Sea,[16] or the ceremony of seals' bladders held by the Alaskans in December. The bladders of the seals, caught in the preceding year, were returned with much ritual to the water, for it was believed that from these the slain animals were regenerated and would rise so that once again they might be caught.[17]

Superhuman Powers

As among other hunting nations the physical environment was infused with innumerable spirits. Every object, be it an arrow, a boat, a spoon, or a drill was thought to be in possession of a soul.[18] Similarly there was belief in the superhuman Lords and Owners of many elements: the *inua* of beasts, or parts of nature, and even of activities, such as the *inua* of sleep or of the desire to eat.[19]

Great Gods

Some of the *inua* achieved great significance. It is the Lord of the air, of storms and winds and weather who towered above the others. Named Sila, Hila among the Caribou Eskimo and Sla or Tla among the Alaskans, he was thus described by a shaman:

> A great spirit, supporting the world and weather and all life on earth, a spirit so mighty that his utterance to mankind is not through common words, but by storm and snow and rain and the fury of the sea; all the forces of nature that men fear. But he has also another way of utterance, by sunlight and calm of the sea, and little children innocently at play ... No one has seen Sila; his place of being is a mystery, in that he is at once among us and unspeakably far away.[20]

Another, less exalted though still important, divinity was the moon. He watched over the rites of hunting among the western and the rites of childbirth among the eastern Eskimo. A tall man, clad in the skins of a white bear (in East Greenland), he drove his sled or rowed his kayak, and was thought to be hunting whales when he was absent from the sky.[21]

The god had some erotic aspects. According to some tales from Greenland, he may come to earth to seduce and impregnate women, and in some regions of this area girls did not dare to drink water that was illuminated by the rays of the full moon, for this drink might cause conception of a child.[22] It was also thought that the moon's rays shining on a girl in her sleep would induce her menstruation.[23]

MATERNAL DEITIES

Important female deities with maternal aspects were indeed envisaged, especially among the eastern and Central Eskimo. A potent female deity was manifest in three main forms: as ancestress of mythical and human populations, as mistress of the animals of land and sea, and as ruler of the dead. The various figures merged to some extent and borrowed features from one another, so that in some tales the ancestress became the Lady of the Beasts, and even more frequently, the Lady of the Beasts was also shown as the Mistress of the Dead. We may be justified in treating the divinities as part of one configuration. Several names have been recorded among the various tribes, such as Arnarkuagsac (the old woman) in Greenland, or Nerrivik (food vessel) at Smith Sound. The name Sedna is usually employed by scholars in discussion of the goddess; in this study also, the name Sedna refers to the Great Lady of the Eskimo. Stories with minor variations were found in many places and are presented in Appendix A.

The Ancestress

The tales are of a young woman who, in most cases, did not wish to marry; hence she sometimes bore the name Uinigmuissitung (the one who does not want to have a husband). She was urged by her father, and eventually gave way, in spite of her protesting, to wed a creature in the form of a dog. In some tales he was her father's dog, transformed for the occasion into a man; in others he was a stranger from afar, or even a red and white stone changed into a dog with red and white fur.

The girl was soon impregnated and found herself, in all versions, with her brood of puppies on an island. She might have been sent there by her father because he could not bear the children's noise, or because she herself had fled before her marriage, or because her father had removed her while her lover was away. The dog husband grieved at the event; he devotedly sustained his wife and his children, and he swam across the water with provisions in a pair of boots tied around his neck or in a skin float. One day, however, stones placed in the container by the girl's father dragged him to the bottom of the sea. The girl, in revenge, incited her brood to devour the cruel man, and after they destroyed or merely mutilated him, she set them out to sea on the sole of a boot. In the ports of their arrival they became ancestral to various races: Europeans, Indians, or Eskimo, dwarfs or giants, or to the *adlets,* creatures half dog and half man. The girl herself might stay to starve on the island, or she might join her dead father beneath the waves.

The Mother of Sea Animals and Lady of the Sea

The life story of this woman began with a marriage to a nonhuman creature (Figure 28). A bird, a fulmar or petrel, had taken the young girl to be his bride to a distant place across the sea. She, however, was not happy in her new home, where she encountered the hardness of fish skins and not the softness of furs, the sparseness of fish food rather than the succulence of seals. She was therefore taken from her husband by her father, her brothers, or her grandfather. When the bird-husband discovered this act, he pursued the vessel of escape in rage, and by flapping his wings he created a storm at sea.

The boat filled with water, and when it was about to sink, the father tossed the woman to the waves. In terror she clung to the side of the craft, but her father chopped off all her fingers with his knife. In one variant (Cumberland Sound) he also pierced her eye. She sank into the ocean, though in one version

Figure 28. (*Left*) Mother of Sea Creatures. Drawing by the Eskimo Arnaqoq. Figure 29. (*Right*) Nuliayoq, creatress of land creatures. Drawing by the Eskimo Arnaqoq.

she was taken back after the storm abated. In a wonderful way the girl's agony gave birth to the beasts that sustain human life. Whale bones grew from her fingernails, whales from the first joints of her fingers, and ground whales from the stumps of her hands. She stayed at the bottom of the ocean and became the mistress of the sea and its creatures.

The figure of the Lady of the Sea occurs also in tales that do not present the girl's sad fate. An old woman dwelled at the bottom of the ocean in Greenland, and from the vessel into which the oil of her lamp had dripped, issued all creatures that swim through the waters. Aiviliayoq of the Iglulirmiut of Baffinland resided in a fine house in the sea, with much food, a dog without a tail, and her dwarflike father.

When the Lady of the Sea was angered the human group was faced with starvation, for she withheld the animals of her domain. Hence men were careful in their observation of her laws and followed the multitude of regulations concerning the treatment of slain beasts. Violation of the rules brought pain to the soul of the dead animal, pain that was felt by Sedna in her hands where the creatures had ultimately originated.

The breaking of taboos in relation to women's functions, the concealment of a miscarriage or the failure to announce menses, brought yet another kind of distress to Sedna. These sins fastened as parasites in her hair, which she could not comb because she had no fingers; they might also accumulate as dirt on other parts of her body.

It was the shaman's task to seek out and appease the goddess; for this purpose he embarked on a difficult and dangerous journey. Descending to the bottom of the ocean, he had to cross a bridge as thin as a "woman's knife," walk over a slippery and ever turning wheel, and face the fierce assaults of the guardian dogs and seals before Sedna's dwelling. When he met the goddess in her fury and her pain, he had to rid her of her pollution: comb her hair, free her of dirt, or sometimes fight with her until she was exhausted. If he succeeded, men on earth were saved from starving because she would once again send her creatures into the sea.

The Mistress of Land Animals

Since most Eskimo, as coastal dwellers, depended on the game of the ocean, the Mistress of Land Animals was of lesser importance than the Lady of the Sea (Figure 29). Among the Inland Eskimo, the goddess Pinga was named Mother of the Caribou and dwelled in heaven, and a woman named Nuliayoq generated all birds, foxes, caribou, and fish. According to the settlers near the Hudson Strait, reindeer were created from the fat of the belly of a female being. The people near the Davis Strait believed that a goddess transformed her boots into the form of reindeer and her breeches into that of walrus, and thus created beings for human benefit. The reindeer originally had tusks, and the walrus carried antlers—a very dangerous arrangement for the hunters because the walrus could upset a kayak with its antlers, and the reindeer could spear people with its tusks. Therefore the appendages were reversed.

The Mistress of the Dead

Sedna resided in a dwelling at the bottom of the sea in which her father might lie on a ledge and her dog might be stretched across the threshold. It was not a happy place, for here entered those who had sinned or had died of sickness (Davis Strait), or women who had prematurely given birth (Cumberland Sound). Some of these, though not the women, left to reside in a different "heaven" after they had been purified and healed. The dead in Sedna's realm were, according to the Central Eskimo, plagued and pinched by Sedna's father.

Some tales explain how Sedna came to be the Ruler of the Dead. According to a story from Baffinland, the earth opened after the dogs had gnawed off the hands and feet of Sedna's father, and it swallowed all—the woman, the father, and the dogs. She thus became the Mistress of the Underworld.

Cultic Observances

It was especially important to accord proper treatment to the beasts that arose from Sedna's hands, for they returned to their mother in the sea. After slaying one of these creatures, people were thus forbidden to scrape frost from windows, shake beds, take drippings from beneath a lamp, remove hair from skins, or work iron, stone, or wood for the period of time in which the animal's soul stayed with the body after it was physically killed. Women were not allowed to comb their hair, wash their faces, or dry their boots and stockings.[24]

Séances

Séances were performed at times of crisis when the goodwill of the goddess was to be restored. According to a description by Rasmussen, people assembled in the communal building from which the shaman would undertake his (supposed) journey to the nether regions. Lights were extinguished, clothes were loosened, and with closed eyes the group listened to the shaman's calls for his helping spirits. After these arrived, the magician's voice grew fainter as he left the human world, while the others, singing songs, waited for his return in the darkness of the séance hut. His voyage, as noted earlier, was fraught with many dangers, and after his arrival he had to soothe the wrath of the goddess by cleansing her from the pollution of human sins. When he returned to earth (awakened from his trance), he demanded a confession of violations from the members of his community; and they complied, calling out loudly and openly the names and ways of their transgressions.[25]

Among the Copper Eskimo, a rope was placed on the floor of the hut in such a way that it resembled the breathing hole of a seal. Magic songs lured the goddess to the spot. When she appeared, she was captured by the shaman and was not released until she promised to send her liberated beasts into the sea.[26]

Periodic Festivals

In autumn the Central Eskimo performed a ceremony in honor of the Lady. Here, too, a breathing hole was simulated on the floor of the dancing hut, and here also the Mistress of the Beasts was brought by magic to the mortal world. When her heavy breathing, which resembled the breathing of a seal, announced that she was near, two shamans placed themselves in a position to harpoon her. She fought fiercely to regain her freedom, and the shamans proudly showed their bloodstained weapons to prove their deed. On the next day of the festival, men raced shouting through the village, visiting individual houses and accepting gifts. Performances were held and games were played, and a rope-pulling contest between "summer" and "winter" people was arranged. The ceremonies ended with sexual encounters in which partners were chosen and exchanged.[27]

Near Cumberland Sound, as related by Franz Boas, the shaman followed Sedna with a knife, intending to cut her hand, for she was pleased to see her flowing blood. On the second day of the festival, Sedna's servant made her appearance: she was tall and heavy, in fact, a man in disguise, who carried a harpoon line and a harpoon.[28] In some communities men terrorized the villagers with their shouting and their simulated assaults.[29]

It is clear that we meet a complex deity in the Sedna figure.[30] As observed by Ivar Paulsen, she represents the Owner and Guardian of Sea Animals, the Owner of a locality (the ocean), a hunting goddess who supplies or withholds the game, a Mistress of the Underworld, and a godhead who gave of herself a vital element of human existence.[31] This type of deity often appears in the myths of agricultural nations and is frequently imagined as a woman. She is either killed or dies naturally, and in her body the most important food plants have originated. This being has been designated as a Dema-god. I would add to Sedna's picture that she occasionally merges with the ancestress of humans.

The tales of Sedna bear, as is to be expected, the imprint of the harshness that marked life on the arctic shores. Only utensils of the stark necessities of life are cited—a boat, a lamp, a knife, a pair of boots—and the stories do not afford a glimpse of objects of luxury or aesthetic pleasure. The images of agony and despair are everpresent: Sedna clasping in mortal terror the gunwale of the boat, watching the bloody stumps of her fingers as they disappear in the waves; Sedna writhing in fury and in pain, choked with dirt and unable to rid herself of the affliction; the dog-husband, anxious in his devotion, striving in vain to reach the ones he loves, who must perish through unmotivated cruelty. These scenes surely reflect the suffering and helplessness of mortals in the face of powers without mercy.

If we consider that the staff of life originated in Sedna's agony, that human and mythical races came into being after experiences of exposure, cruelty, and loss, then we are led to the deep-seated feature of the Inuit vision of existence already noted: that creativity is chiefly generated through suffering. We may recall the statement of a shaman: "All true wisdom is . . . only to be attained through suffering."[32]

The pups devouring a near-relative may point to the times of starvation and despair in which people turned to eating human flesh. The stories depict a way of life (though Inuit reality might have differed) without the soothing cover thrown by a more luxurious existence over the stark and basic emotions or experiences of hunger, terror, lust, or danger. The tales also show a life devoid of pleasure from material objects or adornments.

Sedna's ways are strangely passive in so powerful a figure. Married against her will, banished from her home, retaken by her father, thrown overboard and mutilated, bloodied by harpoons, helpless against the parasites and dirt sent by human sins, waiting for the shaman for release, her only action was to send her pups across the sea. Even her punishment was that of withholding rather than attacking, and she depended on others for her revenge.

Sedna's adventures mirror, in some ways, the events in the life of human women of her society: abduction, seduction, ill-treatment at the hands of men, dependence on male relatives for rescue (though many Inuit tales present a woman running off on her own from a bad marriage), and a temporary state of impurity. The afflictions were usually settled in Sedna's hair; taboos concerning their hair also had to be observed by human women during the time of their dangerous emanations. We may understand that in one of her forms Sedna is the type of the ritually unclean woman. In the scenarios of some myths and rituals the salvation of the community was thus accomplished by the release of a woman from her pollution.[33] In another of her aspects, when she was lured in the course of a séance to a breathing hole by magic songs, when she approached the opening while snorting like a seal, and when she was wounded by harpoons, she appears to be the prototype of a seal.[34]

In being married to an animal and giving birth to young dogs, she is expressive of the emotional closeness of hunting nations with the world of beasts. In the Sedna cycle the primary bonding is between a woman and her father, who between them ruled the sea and the kingdom of the dead, though for this companionship there was no model in the social setting of the Eskimo. Sedna was a sexually attractive creature desired by her respective husbands. We can only speculate concerning the psychological and social phenomena behind the incidents in which a girl's father pits himself against her husband and is successful in destroying the relationship.

A psychoanalytical interpretation of the Sedna stories was given by Géza Róheim, who points to the close, "incestuous" relationship between daughter and father, the "man with the knife," to Róheim obviously a castrating force. Róheim assumes that the dog-husband represents the father's sexuality; the incestuous relation between girl and "father" then is punished by himself.[35] Newell Wardle, on the other hand, suggests a seasonal base for the tales. In this view Sedna represents summer and the father wintertime. The bird-husband is the force of the wind, and the woman's stay in the dwelling of the wind coincides with the absence of the summer season. According to Wardle, spring and summer return with the return of Sedna. The old man's resting in Adlivum at the end of the tale is likened to the winter sleep of earth.[36] It is impossible to either disprove or prove the psychoanalytical interpretation; and it seems unlikely that the seasonal cycle, with its time for planting and harvesting so vital to agriculturalists, would be of great interest to the whale and seal hunters of the North.

John Fischer understands that in all tales concerning Sedna a dangerous situation is alleviated and relieved: food and offspring are created. In all the stories at least one person dies and some benefit is generated. The combination of her tales reveals the Eskimo view of life: death even of a loved one and a harmonious relationship with animals is necessary for Eskimo existence. By marrying a dog, Sedna establishes a bond with the world of animals; by sending her children across the sea, she creates links with other nations. Fischer sees her as a mediator between several sets of opposites: land and sea, Eskimo and other peoples, food and starvation, men and animals, life and death. And with some tribes she retained her power until very recent times.[37]

Birgitte Sonne believes that the Sedna tales originated when white whalers came to the Eskimo of Baffinland in the middle of the nineteenth century. Girls became mistresses of the whalers and were left with offspring that the girl's father had to sustain. This situation created, according to Sonne, the tale of Sedna and her puppies, supplied with food by Sedna's father. Sometimes when a whale was injured, it would die, and its body would be washed onto the beach. There it would attract the fulmars. Thus the image of the bird husband had arisen. Sonne also assumes that the interior of Sedna's house beneath the sea is symbolic of her womb, and that the entrance to her house represents the parturial canal; through this life goes out to the human world.[38]

Inuit tradition shares aspects with the traditions of the North Eurasian hunting cultures that were earlier described. In both we meet the themes of mating between beast and human and of the ancestral animal. In both, men's surroundings are vivid with innumerable spirits, and there is belief in Owners and Guardians of beasts and of localities who are crucial to survival. Inuit culture, however, has no counterpart to the ancestral tutelary numina of the family or tribe, neither those who promote the pursuits of men nor those who tend to the needs of women. These ancestral forces are of truly beneficial nature. It may be that the Eskimo could not envisage the existence of a fully beneficial god. Ancestral beings also blend with the landscape, dwelling in sacred mountains or beneath the earth; they have established a kinship of the family with its surroundings and thus legitimize the presence of its descendants. The Eskimo apparently did not have the confidence to make this claim.

In the terror-laden world of the Eskimo, the fears concerning women's functions were intensified to such a pitch that in Inuit belief a woman's ritual pollution could endanger the entire community. And the birth-giving woman had to face her agony alone without the solace of human or superhuman helpers, in a scenario that recalls the loneliness and suffering of a shaman's initiation. Both the continuation of life and the lifesaving powers of the shaman were thus attained in the fullness of afflictions. Surely the creative value of suffering was held more highly than the creative value of birth. Even the descent of races, which indeed arises from a sexual union and from parturition, was not wholly in the image of human propagation, for one of the ancestors was an animal.

We may note that the image of biological motherhood on a human model was altogether absent from Inuit mythology. In the climate of fear of Eskimo existence all human activity was viewed as a source of potential danger; and especially such life-affirming events as pregnancy and birth were seen as challenge to the stern and capricious masters of the universe. In no other environment covered in this study is motherhood held in such low esteem and enmeshed in such a multitude of sanctions. The breaking of any of the rules that surround the childbearing capacities of a woman would bring ruin to the entire community. No birth-helping spirits had arisen that might aid the woman in her need. The study of Inuit tradition and beliefs is valuable because it shows how in a culture at the edge of survival, the roles of birth-giving and of motherhood were envisaged.

chapter

5

The Lady of the Manor: Latvia

A N important female deity designated as Mother Sun appears in Latvian tradition. Another highly placed divinity bears the name Mother Laima; and a multitude of lesser spirits holds the title. This chapter traces the outlines of these goddess figures to determine whether they are related to a great maternal divinity.

The Latvians speak an Indo-European language that belongs, with Lithuanian and Prussian (now extinct), to the so-called Baltic language group. Politically, Latvia is classed together with Estonia and Lithuania as a Baltic state, all three, until recently, under Soviet domination. They are situated along the eastern shores of the Baltic Sea, whose waters had originated in the melting ice of the Quaternary period.

The sandy beaches of the Latvian coast give way to low-lying marshy plains and, further inland, to cultivated fields. Spruce and pine predominate among the trees. The land is dotted with hills and divided by large waterways that have been intensively employed as trade routes both in the past and in the present.[1] Speakers of an Indo-European language are believed to have entered at about 2000 B.C.E., and they encountered in the forests and the marshes a population of fishermen and hunters. The invaders established a chalcolithic culture, breeding pigs and cattle, reaping their harvests with stone sickles, and defending their homes with arms of stone.[2]

By the Bronze Age, Baltic culture had extended over a large area, reaching south to the basin of the lower Vistula. In the early centuries of the Christian era the lands rose to prominence because their geographic position was vital to transmitting trade between the South and both the northern and northeastern nations.[3]

Warfare seems to have been continuous between the Baltic people and their neighbors, until the wars were halted by the victory of the German religious order of the Teutonic Knights. At the end of the thirteenth century the Latvians submitted to the Christian forces.[4] They remained under foreign rule, dominated successively by Germany, Poland, Sweden, and Russia, and were granted their first season of independence between the two great wars of this century.

RELIGION

The German conquest changed the structure of Latvian society, supplanting the native aristocracy with German rulers and suppressing the status of the farmers.[5] Christianity thus came to the Latvians in the wake of bloodshed and defeat, associated in their minds with brutality and oppression. Native faith naturally became linked with national identity and the desire to preserve ancestral traditions. Under these circumstances much of the native creed remained alive, though it must have greatly altered in the thought and practice of an unlettered nation.

We gain insight into Latvian religion through church documents, but more so through the perusal of folklore and folk traditions. Thousands of legends, folksongs, proverbs, and riddles have been gathered by enthusiastic and often anonymous collectors. The *dainas* (short lyrical poems) have survived in great numbers and are especially valuable in their revelation of the emotional and spiritual universe of their creators. The old gods are also frequently presented in the songs.[6] The poems testify to the faith of deeply rooted farmers who were exposed to an alien creed. They also testify to the imaginative elaboration of the ancient forms.[7]

The Superhuman Powers

It appears that a multitude of divinities thronged the realm of Baltic faith. Thus a god exists who rules the heavens, another who governs the terrestrial expanse, and yet another who holds dominion over a host of minor divinities: one who gives fish, another who sends game, and yet another who offers sheep, cows, horses, and other animals.[8] An ancient chronicle relates that the natives of Baltic lands adore thunder, sun, moon, stars, and animals, down to the toad.[9] The ceremonies of the faith were conducted in sacred groves, at the shores of sacred waters, or beneath the branches of a sacred tree.[10] Like the holy places of nature, the places of human settlements were honored by the presence of the superhuman. The household gods might dwell beneath the hearth, under the threshold, or behind the stove, so that they might shed their blessing over the habitation.[11]

The Great Gods

A divine family dwells in heaven, its members interacting with one another in anger, love, affection, and strife in the way of human families. We learn about them through the songs, named *dainas,* and in the following brief description the number of the respective *daina* is given in parentheses.[12]

The family is ruled by Dievs, whose name has been traced to a root that also formed the names of Greek Zeus and Sanskrit Dyāus; he is thus related to other Indo-European gods.[13] He leads the good life of a prosperous farmer, rich in fields and livestock, and above all, in horses. He brews beer from the hops grown in his garden, which is the drink imbibed at festive gatherings (54040). He frequently leaves his celestial mansion to visit human settlements, where he shares the farmers' toil and feasts, fells their trees (33657), guards their horses (30074), and takes his place at the head of the table to drink his beer (33271).

The goddess Saule, her name meaning "sun," appears as both a celestial body and its anthropomorphic epiphany. Like Dievs she inhabits a magnificent estate in heaven; like him she travels down to earth, in a carriage drawn by horses which never sweat and never tire (J172). Mēness, the moon, is male and also dwells on the Mountain of the Sky. He appears at times as the suitor or husband of the Sun. Great significance is attached to Pērkons, a god of thunder, who is also known by such names as God of Thunder, Smith of Heaven, Father Pērkons, or Thunderer. A fighter, he may also extend his beneficial powers over the fruitfulness of fields. Bloody and unbloody sacrifices are rendered to Pērkons at harvest time, for his "growling" in the summer promoted fertility and growth:

> Because the god Pērkons in the summer
> has growled loudly in the sky
> we offer him a load of barley
> a half-load of hop and a load of rye.
> (28818)

Laima, a divinity of great importance, does not reside in the sky; she is frequently encountered in the bathhouse, where she helps the woman in travail. She also sets the fate of the newborn (1196), and her name became synonymous with "fate." We furthermore meet chthonic deities. Jumis, meaning "double ear of wheat," resides beneath the plowed field or in the room where the corn is stored. He is invoked at harvest festivals and is also the indwelling spirit of the reaped corn or flax. In a systematic study, Lena Neuland has drawn him as the force most closely allied to agricultural fertility. The chthonic goddess *zemes māte* (Mother Earth) receives the dead within her realm. In *dainas* addressed to her, she provides the eternal resting place:

> Rock me mother, hold me mother!
> Short is the time spent at your breast.

> Mother Earth will hold me longer,
> beneath her turf, a welcome guest.
> (J1209)

This short and simplified survey of the major figures of Latvian faith shows them to be expressive of the basic needs and wishes of a farming population: fruitful harvests and fertile livestock. The desire for individual happiness is articulated in poems to the goddess Laima—Dame Fortune. In the *dainas* of the gods, I did not encounter, on the whole, the themes of rape and incest, murderous assault, or erotic unions, so frequent in the myths of other nations. I also did not meet the "lewd and lecherous" songs noted by the preacher Einhorn, which were sung "all through the night" at the farmers' wedding feasts.[14]

Knowing that the raids of coastal Latvians struck terror into the hearts of Danes and Swedes, we must also be surprised at the absence of heroic ideals. It may be that such ideals had been held by a nobility that was vanquished and exterminated by the conquerors. It is therefore likely that the folk traditions mirror, on the whole, a faith which had developed after the loss of independence among people who had no priest or warrior class.

SAULES MĀTE: MOTHER SUN

Her name has been related to the Indo-European roots *sauel-, suuel-,* next to *suen-,* both meaning "sun."[15] The daughter(s) of this deity are named *Saules meita(s)*—Daughter(s) of the Sun. We must note, however, that the noun *meita* also means "young woman." In those poems where only one *meita* is cited, we are faced with an ambiguity: the tale might be of Saule's daughter or of the young, the Maiden Saule. In poems in which Saule stands beside her daughter(s), however, she is clearly visualized in her maternal form. In the following *daina* both mother and daughter are presented:

> Saule dressed her daughter
> in the green leaves of the willow tree.
> Green and silken is her garment,
> silver the hem below the knee. (J307)

Personification of the Sun

The phenomenon that has come to life in the deity is still very much in evidence; thus she rides across the sky in a carriage drawn by yellow horses:

> Three yellow horses draw Saule's carriage
> riding over land and seas;
> Oh dear, white goddess Saule
> Will you give me one of these? (J171)

Her journey may lead her to the ocean where she drowns so that only her crown is seen above the waves (J341), an image taken from the sun's apparent disappearance in the sea.[16] Where she spends the night, however, is not known, and several thoughts are voiced in the matter: that she rests in the middle of the ocean on a layer of green reeds (J212), or that she does not sleep at all, and rides nightly in a golden boat:

> Mēness asked the goddess Saule
> where she spent the night in sleep.
> As the goddess gave her answer
> she bitterly began to weep.
>
> I am not allowed to slumber
> amidst green birches I ride in the light.
> Upon the waves of the water
> I steer my golden boat at night. (J221)[17]

Saule's hanging her red silken garment in the wind brings the red glow to the evening sky:

> Do you know why in the evening
> our sky is turning red?
> Saule hangs her silken garment
> in the winds near her bed. (J202)

The flickering of the sun's rays on the tops and slopes of hills must have created the image of Saule's dance in golden slippers on a silver mountain (J155). It is in keeping with the aspect of the natural phenomenon that so many of her possessions are of gold: her shoes, scarf, belt, and the shuttle of her loom. Related to her station in the sky is her ability to see all things (J254), and to the power of her fire her compassion that sends warming rays to orphaned children:

> Where did the shivering orphan cry
> alone and out of sight?
> Only Saule knew who sent her
> the warming fire of her light. (J270)

Saule as Owner of an Estate

While the golden tools and garments belonging to Mother Sun may be interpreted as renderings of her appearance, they may also be interpreted as symbols of her wealth. Her garments are of silk and silver (J317), and she wears a silver crown or wreath (J152). Her estate contains golden hills and silken meadows (M65, p. 81). The labors of her household—the sweeping, scrubbing, washing of linen—are usually performed by Saule's daughters or her maids. She herself is visualized as she spins silken threads in the foliage of an apple tree (J227), gathers hay with a silver rake (J133), plants a garden of roses (J304), or plays the harp in the eastern wind (J164).[18]

Saule as a Mother

The goddess is a caring mother. She dresses her daughter in garments of green silk (J307), scolds one girl because she has not swept the floor and another because she has not scrubbed the table (J312). Recurrently, she marries off her daughter to the son of Mēness (J348), to the son of Dievs (J351, 352), or to yet other suitors:

> Clad with iron are the wheels;
> grey are the horses of the carriage.
> Saule gives her child away,
> gives away her child in marriage. (J350)

Saule also offers rich wedding presents while she herself rides in the festive train (J355).

Saule's Relations to Others

Saule has had erotic entanglements; thus it is said that she was a bride in those distant days when the world was created, or also that Mēness had taken the maiden's wreath from her tresses:

> Who has seen the goddess Saule
> when she was a maid and fair?
> Mēness saw her as a maiden
> and took the wreath from her hair. (J141)

There are some quarrels between Saule and the other gods. Once she hacked the moon to pieces because he had stolen the bride of another man (J301).[19] She shows gentleness and pity toward humans. Hence she may rise tardily to stay behind a mountain where she comforts orphaned children with her warmth (J274). Sometimes she is followed by a hundred waifs with bare feet:

> If you look behind you, Saule,
> what a sight your eyes will meet.
> A hundred small orphaned children
> follow you on their bare feet. (M p. 75)

Saule's Tears

Surprising in a goddess of the sun is the frequent shedding of tears. She may cry because her boat has sunk in the waters of the sea (J243, 1), because the wind has blown the leaves from a birch tree (J257), or because an apple has fallen to the ground:

> Weeping in the apple orchard
> Saule's tears are sad to see.
> She weeps because a golden apple
> Has fallen from the apple tree.

> Saule dearest,
> cease your sorrow;
> Of gold or silver or of copper
> another will be shaped tomorrow. (J243)

The goddess weeps in sadness over the departure of her daughter, regretting also the rich dowry given to the bride (J368). Her desperate sobbing echoes through the forest (J245), and she may drench two silken sheets with her bitter tears:

> The goddess Saule weeps in sorrow,
> rains of heaven calm her pain.
> Mother Saule drenched already
> two silken sheets with tears of rain. (J246)

The weeping of the deity apparently expresses the belief that the sun brings, besides daylight, the lash of rain.[20]

The Celestial Wedding

As the rousing celebration of the human wedding forms a high point in the life of Latvian farmers, so the wedding of the gods is of central importance to the dwellers of the sky. The woman, always Saule or her daughter, is here united with one of the male figures. Like the human bride, she is taken on her wedding day in a festive procession to her new home by members of her husband's family. They carry the bridal chest, heavy with her dowry, and chosen members of her family follow in the train.[21]

According to Latvian tradition gifts are presented by the bride to the members of her new family. In the divine celebration, where the train soars through the air, the gifts are rendered to the forest trees. Thus the oak may receive a belt of gold or a crown of silver (34039,2; 34929,10), the linden tree a scarf of wool (34039,3), and the small willow a golden garter (34039,1).

The present of a crown of gold or silver, or even of a flowering wreath, is never given in a human wedding; thus the image of this brightly glowing jewel bestowed on a tree must have its derivation in the natural phenomenon of the radiant sun.[22]

Saule is the only female force in the songs of the celestial wedding (the goddess Laima is mentioned once or twice in a subordinate position), and thus she embodies the forms of womanhood, that of young beauty in the maiden, and that of love and caring in her mother. She also embodies a farm woman of great wealth and simultaneously the golden star that illuminates the world.[23]

Cultic Importance

Whatever cultic significance Saule may have once possessed became entwined and embedded in the folk traditions. Even in modern times the young village girls would gather to perform dances in the warm nights of spring and early summer. Since the girls are designated as Sun Maidens, it is possible that the dances are performed in honor of the sun. It is also possible that the rousing feast of the solstice was at one time dedicated to the sun though it now bears the name of the Christian figure of St. John. The conspicuous part played by girls and women who proceed through the streets to distribute flowering wreaths and branches, the central importance of dancing around the flames, as well as the point in time, indicate an earlier, more specific linkage with the sun.[24] An old dictionary names the festival *saules währssums* the turning of the sun.

Composite Image

It is not possible to enumerate all the qualities and actions attributed through the centuries by folk imagination to the golden goddess. In her human form she is a stately farm wife and also a tender gentlewoman. When she engages in farm labor, she wields tools of gold and silver while the heavy work is usually done by her daughter or her maids. The frequent flowing of her tears and her generosity toward orphans accent her nature of a high-strung, emotional, and tender wellborn lady.

Saule has, in fact, become many things in her human form: a girl who loses her maidenhood and a mother who gives away her daughter, the proprietress of an estate and a creature who beds down in the wind, one who hacks the moon to pieces and one who weeps in helpless sorrow over an apple broken from a tree. Within the human woman we still clearly see the star that sheds its light across the mountaintops and travels across the heavens to the sea.

We do not find an impact of the goddess on the earth's fertility, and in contrast to the goddess Laima, she does not set the course of fate.[25] She symbolizes, on the other hand, in her beauty and splendor, her concerns and caring, her entanglements and petulance, the various forms of human womanhood. The *dainas,* devoted to the Mother or Maiden Sun, testify to a sensitivity of their composers to the natural surroundings, to green foliage rustling in the breezes, to the glow of sunset on the sea, or to the drizzling drops of rain. The impressions of nature were translated to appear in the image of the beautiful, compassionate, rich, and stately Lady Sun.

THE LATVIAN MOTHERS

The sources also indicate the presence of a large number of superhuman female beings who carry the name *māte* (mother). This finding agrees with the observation of Paul Einhorn, a seventeenth-century church official, who complained that the supposedly Christian inhabitants of Latvia would call in all of their endeavors on such spirits for assistance:

[T]hey call on Dahrsemate, the mother or goddess of the garden, when they work in the garden, on Laukemate, the goddess or mother of the fields, when they labor in the fields and they also thank her when the crops grow well; the hunters call on Meschemate, the mother or the goddess of the forests, and ask her to grant them luck in hunting.[26]

A closer look at the "mothers" shows them to belong to various categories. A *māte* may be the relative of a god, as in *Pērkons māte*. The term may be combined with the name of a river, as in *Daugava māte* (Mother Daugava); with a phenomenon of nature, as in *zemes māte* (Mother Earth), *meža māte* (Mother Forest), or *juras māte* (Mother Ocean); with a place of habitation, as in *pirts māte* (Mother Bathhouse); with an abstraction as in *gausa māte* (Mother of Blessing); or with an activity, as in *rīsǔ māte* (Mother of Spinning).[27]

We note a striking similarity between the Latvian "mothers" and those of the North Eurasian nations discussed in Chapter 3, and they may be classed in the same categories—that is, owners and guardians of nature, protective deities of dwelling places, personified objects or phenomena that might or might not receive cultic worship, personifications of abstract qualities, or the relatives of gods. The meaning of "biological mother" is conveyed only in the last category. Some of the spirits, such as Mother Drying Barn, Mother Forest, and Mother Fire, have their exact counterpart in the faith of the peoples of the North. We may therefore assume, as was done in the case of the latter, that the name "mother" of the Latvian spirits does not refer to aspects of maternity, but that it serves as a title of respect which is bestowed on female deities (the male title is often *kungs*). An eighteenth-century dictionary of Latvian speech translates the word *maat, mahte* as *Göttin* (goddess).[28]

COMPONENTS OF LATVIAN RELIGION

Latvian culture and tradition is derived from various roots. The country borders and belongs partially with the North Eurasian regions described in Chapter 3. It also participated historically in the experiences of a wider culture. Through trade and through empirical expansion, urban centers originated and a hierarchical society was created. The Christian Teutonic Knights who defeated this society introduced the feudal system. The North Eurasian heritage, however, remained very much in evidence into modern times.

The groves, wells, stones, and trees condemned in church documents as places of heathen worship find counterparts in the sacred sites of the arctic or subarctic cultures. The Latvians also share the belief that the portions of the landscape are governed by a ruler. As, for instance, brandy is poured into the ocean in Estonia to please the Ocean Mother, so bread and milk were tossed into the Latvian river Susseja to appease the waves.[29] Like other northern peoples the Latvians respect the numina of the household who rule and protect the farmstead and its buildings, for whom the names *mājas kungs, mājas gars, mājas dievs, zemes dievs* have been recorded.[30] Thus the spirit owner of the threshing barn, *rijas dievs,* resides behind the stove; here he receives food for his help in threshing grain.[31] He corresponds to *avyn-ava,* the Threshing Barn Mother of the Mordvins, the *rehe haldijas* of the Estonians, the *agun-kugaza* of the Mari. The many "mothers" of the various localities and occupations surely present a parallel to the "mothers" of the North Eurasian cultures, as goddesses of the animated elements which make up the universe. It is clear that the world of the Latvians is, like that of their northern neighbors, replete and vivid with the superhuman.

The High Gods of the divine family bear a different stamp. A divine pantheon develops through the efforts of poets or priests, from the many spirits of local faith when hunting, fishing, and farming villages become part of a larger group, an empire, kingdom, or state. Such formation undoubtedly occurred in the centuries of Baltic independence (or even earlier in the Indo-European past) before the word of Christ was brought by the conquerors' swords. During the time of subjugation the figures of the ancient faith were thrown back into the fold of folk belief, and the folk imagination of the Middle Ages and of modern times worked its way upon the deities. Concerning Latvian religion in general, we may observe that in the absence of independence that must be heroically defended and without the spiritual guidance of scholars or priests, people turned toward the good things of daily life: joy in material possessions, celebration of traditional festivities, and the beauty of their native land.

The goddess Saule probably originated in the native figure of the animated sun, and she blended with a goddess of the pantheon, possibly of Indo-European derivation. She received a daughter through poetic embellishment. Saule gained her stature and importance through the phenomenon that she embodies, the warmth and illumination, the life-bestowing power of the sun, and not through the generative aspect of her womanhood. In this she parallels important spirits of the northern nations, such as Mother Earth, providing grain, and Mother Water, providing fertilizing moisture. The presence of many "mothers" in Latvian faith may at first glance be interpreted as a special devotion to maternal principles. A closer look reveals, however, that these too have obvious counterparts in the North Eurasian numina to whom the title "mother" is given as an honorific epithet.

While the Latvians share in some ways in the vision of the settlers of the North, they have also moved toward a less restrictive, more stratified society. The hunters' heritage has receded and with it the many fears and sanctions that surround a woman's biological life. We may recall that through these fears goddesses were generated who were exclusively devoted to the needs of women. The Latvian pantheon contains a deity of this kind: Laima. As Latvian women were allowed to share the religious life of the community, so the woman's goddess, Laima, extended her dominion. As Dame Fortune, the Lady who sets fate, she was revered and sometimes cursed, and she retained her divine powers longer than the other gods during the centuries of Christianity.

LAIMA: GODDESS OF BIRTH AND FATE

The goddess Laima—Dame Fortune—is the most vital of the Latvian deities. Her name has been related to the verbs *likt* (to lay down), *lemt* (to determine), and *laist* (to let), and to the noun *laiduma* (to have caused).[32] Her function as a women's goddess and especially as a helper at the time of parturition is still very much in evidence.

Laima and the Birth of Children

The bathhouse held a place of ritual significance in Latvian tradition. Here diseases might be cured, and here, above all, women experienced the pain, fears, and joy of giving birth. Even if the delivery did not occur within the bathhouse, the new mother would be brought there afterward for the feast, named *pirtīžas* (*pirtis*—bathhouse). The noun *pirtīžas* has other meanings: it designates the ritual bath before parturition and the first bath of the child.[33] After the celebration of the bathhouse feast the Bathhouse Mother (*pirts māte*) or the goddess Laima might receive a gift. That the newborn child was also given the sacrament of baptism in church indicates the enduring coexistence of the native and the Christian traditions.[34]

Laima's presence in the bathhouse is so frequent an occurrence that the place is also designated as "Laima's bathhouse," as in the following *daina:*

> Some girls think it's heavy labor
> when corn and wheat they must grind:
> Yet a harder undertaking
> in Laima's bath-house they will find. (1229)

The path to the bathhouse, treaded by the young woman, receives much attention; it must be kept free from weeds (1076), and Laima herself might perform this task (1077). The path may be strewn with leaves of hops, for these are light and hence labor may be lightened (1106). Then Laima meets the expectant mother:

> Why so swift Mother Laima
> with linden twigs in your hand?
> To still the tears of the young bride
> who came last year to our land. (1101)

The goddess Laima may open up her braids to help in the delivery (1090); she will gird the girl with her own belt (1109) and spread a silken sheet beneath the body (1107).[35]

Already at her wedding the bride is admonished to offer gifts so that her pangs will be softened:

> Give a gift young woman
> no matter if it's dear,
> for the time of giving birth
> the time of pain is near. (25588)

The gift, offered before or after birth, may be a ring (1096), a garter of colored wool (1138), gloves or stockings (T6588), or the life of a beast:

> I caught and slaughtered a chicken
> with a crest of splendid size
> and gave it, to help me in my labor,
> to Mother Laima who is wise. (1140)[36]

Laima's link with pregnancy and birth may also be recognized from a *daina* which states that her room is filled with many tiny cradles (1872). Einhorn, a church official in Kurzeme, wrote in the seventeenth century: "Especially honored and invoked, above all by pregnant women and those in childbed, is Laima, who is *Fortuna* or the goddess of luck."[37]

Laima and the Conduct of Girls and Women

It seems that a girl must be very careful to guard her honor, for in the tightly knit community of the Latvian village it easily receives a stain. However, a girl of good conduct who has been slandered may be confident that Laima will avenge her:

> Laima, you yourself have honor,
> cleanse me of my stain.
> Thrust the one who uttered slander
> into a swamp of pain. (8298)

And one who guards her behavior may be sure of Laima's affection and support (8774). If, on the other hand, she strays from virtue, Laima's love will cease:

> Laima pleats a wreath of gold
> for her whose honor is not spoiled.
> She weaves a wreath of thorns and clover
> for one whose honor has been soiled. (6621,10)

And girls and women must be forever careful to please the mighty goddess, for she walks softly on the roofs to listen to their talk (1440).

Laima and a Girl's Marriage

Of great significance to a woman's happiness is the kind of marriage she enters and the kind of man with whom she shares her life.[38] In this area also Laima holds a role of great importance. She knows, for instance, who will be a girl's husband and is asked to reveal his identity (9313). She also has the power to select the proper partner:

> Goddess Laima, send as suitor
> an honest ploughman to my door.
> If you choose to send another
> I'll stay a maiden evermore. (9496)

The goddess may receive the plea to keep a widower away; his hand is heavy, for "it twice changed rings" (9738,9). Sometimes Laima herself arranges a wedding for one who is destitute (12032), at other times she joins the celebration (16095), and she is deeply grieved when a girl dies before she has been wedded (27741).

Laima as Goddess of Men's Fate

Laima's dimensions extend far beyond her caring for women's special needs, for she unswervingly and inexorably sets the course of human destiny:

> I fled by day and I fled by night,
> I tried to run and tried to tarry.
> The life which Laima shaped for me
> it was the life I had to carry. (9170)

Sometimes Laima is addressed in sadness and complaint about her arbitrary ways (9201); sometimes she arouses real anger and one man voices the wish that she would drown in the tears that he has shed (9189).[39] Dievs, the highest god, at times shares her office, and the two divinities discuss what destiny is to be accorded (27684); in such discussions conflicts may arise (9242), and occasionally Laima must subordinate her will (7733).[40]

Laima and Latvian Faith

It was observed that folk imagination held a great share in forming the main gods of Latvian mythology; the songs devoted to these forces may often be classed as folk poetry.[41] The songs of Laima, on the other hand, are addressed to her in pleading, hope, anger, confidence, or despair, and they would therefore represent the expression of a living faith.[42] It is not surprising that the name Laima so often interchanges with the name Māra (a variant of the Virgin Mary) that it is impossible to draw a clear dividing line between the two. At times the two sources of blessing stand side by side, as in a seventeenth-century court document: "Holy Mother of Jesus Christ, *Laimes māhte* (Mother Laima), help the sick."[43]

We meet in the Latvian environment the unusual phenomenon of a woman's goddess who has risen to a dominant position in belief. The presence of women is, to be sure, highly visible in Latvian ritual and myth. A wedding celebration, not a feat of war or the hunt, forms the central event in the life of the divinities. The songs and dances of women are prominent in the ritual festivities of the community. The *dainas* frequently express a woman's views. It may be that the strong presence of women in cultic matters has contributed to the stature of the woman's goddess Laima.

Laima's significance arises from her sovereignty over the destiny of men and women. She received this power because fate is determined at the time of birth; this power is also held by the birth-helping deities of the North Eurasian cultures. Laima does not inhabit the heavenly abode of Latvian divinities; she is deeply involved in terrestrial concerns. Her relation to the bathhouse, a place of women's rituals, recalls the station of the women's spirits of the North in the women's section of the habitation. We may agree that Laima belongs in kind with deities of the arctic cultures.

The great goddesses of Latvian tradition do not derive their significance from the awesome function of the fertile womb; Saule, the sun, rules the light of day, and Laima rules the fate of humans. In Latvian society, where the fertility of fields stands in the forefront of concern, no great goddess of the earth has developed, nor was the fruitful earth "assimilated" to the fruitful womb. Mother Earth—*zemes māte*—is chiefly the resting place of the departed, and girls do not go to Mother Earth to ask for children. Blessing of fields and livestock is sought from the creature who rules and dwells in the respective element. The growth of corn and flax is bestowed, above all, by Jumis, a male force. Protection of the household is received by the spirit of the dwelling. Laima, the goddess of birth and fate, Saule, the goddess of the sun, the numina of localities and of activities, all have their counterparts in North Eurasian tradition. Hence the inhabitants of Latvia share, with some alterations, the inheritance of the arctic North. Latvian tradition shows, furthermore, the noun *māte* (mother) in a clear meaning of "Goddess, Queen."

We may observe the difference of respect accorded to the process of birth within the various cultures. Whereas in Eskimo society it was held in such low esteem that birth-helping spirits were not developed, the birth-helping goddess Laima of the Latvians became the most vital and long lived of all divinities.

chapter
6

The Human Condition: Mesopotamia

I F we turn from the cultures of northern Europe, Asia, and America to those of the ancient Middle East, it is as if we left a somber half-lit place for a realm of dazzling riches and dizzying complexity. Even in their preliterate period the settlers of the land between the Tigris and Euphrates had achieved a state of civilization in which urban centers had emerged in the cultivated farmland, and where the towering places of devotion rose beside the palaces of kings. With the invention of writing (about 3000 B.C.E.), the continued construction of monuments, and the recording of literature and legal codes, Mesopotamia became, with Egypt, the leading intellectual force of the Mediterranean regions.[1]

The Sumerians organized their life around towns that controlled surrounding farms. Every town was complete with its administration, artisans, and priests; each was governed by a king and protected by its special god. At times a town or city was able to enforce its dominance on the others. Throughout its history the country lay open to incursions of fierce tribes from the desert and the mountain ranges.[2]

Though many nations succeeded one another in conquering the fertile region, the fabric of the ancient religion remained intact. The Akkadians gave the deities new designations in their own Semitic speech; the Amorites, Cassites, Assyrians, and even the Persians respected native tradition so that the ancient tablets were copied and recopied, translated, and provided with new comments.[3]

Thus we come upon a corpus of religious beliefs that are surprisingly homogeneous, the earlist lists of gods containing names which were still current in later sources. Our knowledge is derived through archaeology that excavated clay tablets, cylinder seals, reliefs, and ancient structures.

It is clear that so complex and rich a culture would also practice a complex and rich religion, yet like all religions it had grown from a beginning in the Paleolithic past and shared in the spiritual life of hunters. It will be of interest to see in what ways the ancient patterns might still be discerned and in what way they might have changed, and also how the new life had come to bear upon the image of a mother goddess.

THE ARCHAIC HERITAGE

Like the North Eurasian peoples, the inhabitants of Sumer and Akkad lived in a fully animated world; and the elements of their surroundings—the grain that feeds them, the flame that scorches, the stones and the trees—were thought to be living beings that might be approached in supplication.[4] The powerful elements of nature, the sky, the sea, the storms and winds, provided, as in the North Eurasian context, the overwhelming numinous experience from which the great gods of the pantheon developed. The universe is thus governed by the godheads of the sky, the mountains, or the water, and, as their relatives of hunting villages, these gods were seen both in the element that they represent and also in the form of humans. The reed goddess Nidaba, for instance, is the force of reed, present in every blade, enabling the scribe to record his accounts, or the shepherd to lure music from his pipe, but Nidaba is also a human woman.[5] Tiamat and Apsû embody the chaotic waters, but they are also man and wife, embracing, begetting, and bearing children.

It was earlier noted that every city or city-state lay under the protection of its special god, housed in a splendid dwelling, and feeling the anguish of the town in his own flesh.[6] We may recognize in this god the counterpart of the tutelary forces of a hunting or fishing community who guards its welfare and its strength. And also, as in the northern cultures, some godheads were devoted as midwives, nurses, or mothers to the special needs of women.

THE NEW VISION

Systematization of the Pantheon

At one time every settlement must have had its set of divinities, gods of the sea, the sky, or the mountain ranges. In historic times, however, one of these would be singled out to become the chief protector of a city (rather than an ancestral spirit). The town of Erech was beholden to Inanna, the goddess of love and war, and Enki, god of the sweet waters, was beloved in the town of Eridu. The various city gods were woven into one family so that Marduk became the son of Enki of Eridu and Ningirsu of Lagash was made into the son of Enlil of the town of Nippur.[7]

Besides the guardianship of a town, every god also held a function in the running of the cosmos. The god Ninurta/Ningirsu defended the other gods as a warrior, and Enki purified the water and supervised the growth of plants. The gods, combined into a governing body, would sit in council and decide the fate of gods and men. By such a council meeting, for instance, it was decided that the town of Ur should fall before the enemy.[8]

Ascendance of the Human Form

It is clear that the feeling of inferiority of mortals before the superhuman has given way to accepting, asserting, and defining in triumph or anguish the condition of being human. It is true that individuals appear as slaves and playthings of the gods, helpless creatures tossed about by forces without mercy, drowned by floods, or famished by an unyielding earth; but their fate is decided by beings in human form.

Animals have vanished from the myths of the creation, and the marriage between beast and human from the stories of descent. The emergence of the world is envisaged in the image of a family genealogy where a male and female being unite; in this way the male and female horizon gave birth to sky and earth, and these in turn to Lord and Lady Wind.[9]

In hunting cultures meteorological phenomena are frequently attributed to the action of a beast, such as a bird that creates storms and thunder. A bird of this kind was known to the settlers of Mesopotamia in the form of a lion-headed eagle. The bird was slowly transformed into the human-shaped Lord of Storms, Ningirsu/Ninurta. Seals of the Second Dynasty show a bird that possesses in its lower portion the body of a human. Gudea, the ruler of Lagash (about 2000 B.C.E.) saw in a dream the god Ninurta who was "winged and ending below in a flood." In a temple relief the god was pictured as a human with bird-wings growing from his shoulders, and throwing darts at a lion-headed eagle (i.e., against his own animal epiphany). We also have accounts in which the god Ninurta/Ningirsu fights and overcomes the thunderbird.[10]

We recognize in the tales of the stormbird two ways of dealing with a theriomorphic power: transforming him into human shape or subjugating him as an enemy. The myth of Ninurta's battle with the thunderbird represents the first recorded instance of the widespread narrative in which the monster is defeated by a creature in human form.

Triumph Over Nature

Incidents in which a primeval power is overcome by a creature in human shape occur also in the epic of creation. Here Marduk, begotten like a man in a union of the sexes, destroys the self-begotten Tiamat who represents the primeval ocean; and Ea, the anthropomorphic god of the sweet waters, overcame the more amorphous Apsû of the same element. Thus the defeat of the nonhuman form is endowed with ultimate importance in the creation of the world.[11]

The stories of Gilgamesh, king of Uruk, present incidents in which the powers of the nonhuman environment are vanquished. Fully equipped with splendid arms, he sets out to destroy the monster Huwawa, guardian of the cedar forest, and seeks the monster in his distant dwelling. When Gilgamesh and his companion reach the wooded mountain, they cut down the cedars in defiance of the ruler of the wilderness. In the ensuing battle the friends prevail, and Huwawa eloquently pleads for mercy. Though Gilgamesh is moved by pity he ultimately strikes the deadly blow, which deprives the mountain ranges forever of their guardian and protector.[12]

We may easily recognize the kinship between Huwawa, the master of the forest, and the master of the forest of the North Eurasian cultures, such as *vir-ava*, the Lady of the Forest of the Mordvins, or *vöris-mort*, the ruler of the forest of the Komi, who are rendered honor and respect by the human population.

The scholar Thorkild Jacobsen ascribes the ascendance of the human form to the end of the proto-literate period in the beginning of the third millennium. His dating would indicate that the triumphant rise of the anthropomorphic god coincides with a spectular growth in human achievement.[13]

Value of Human Activity: The Craft of Building

The importance of the builder's craft is greatly emphasized in Mesopotamian myth and ritual. In the Babylonian epic of creation the triumph of Ea over Apsû is crowned with the erection of a dwelling, and a temple is built after Marduk had vanquished the monstrous Tiamat. A Chaldaean myth of creation describes the chaos by stating that in "those days there existed no sacred places, no houses for the gods."[14]

The builder's work is imbued with such significance that the king himself must participate in raising the sacred structures; he was therefore entrusted with the portentous task of molding the first brick. Amidst much ceremony he would pour the clay into the form, and after it had dried, he would break the mold and show the sacred object to the population.[15] King Nabopolassar declares: "I bent my neck for Marduk, my Lord; and girding up the robes of my royalty, I carried bricks and clay upon my head."[16]

Sexual Activity

Whereas in hunting cultures the intercourse between man and beast holds a place in legend, sexual traffic between partners in human form acquired prominence in Mesopotamian myth and ritual. The wild half-human creature Enkidu, the friend of Gilgamesh, was taught the refinement of human ways through the seduction of a harlot. The powerful and widely adored divinity Inanna was the patron goddess of harlots and was herself a harlot.[17]

The union of a god and goddess, a "sacred marriage," is celebrated in many

songs and poems and constitutes possibly the most popular theme of Sumero-
Akkadian tradition. The goddess Inanna freely expresses her erotic longing:

> ... (my crescent-shaped) "Barge of Heaven", so (well) belayed,
> full of loveliness, like the new moon,
> my untilled plot,
> left so fallow in the desert,
> ... my parts piled up with levees,
> ... who will be their plowman?
> who will put plow oxen on them?[18]

In yet other texts the traffic of a chosen being with the goddess assures
his fitness for the royal office and the protection of the deity. Again it is the
goddess Inanna who declares:

> ... since by his fair hands my loins were pressed
> ... (Since) the hair (of) my lap he ruffled for me
> ... since on my pure vulva he laid his hands
> ... a good fate I will decree for him
> ... the shepherdship of the land I will decree as his fate.[19]

The Legitimacy of Suffering

The texts abound with dirges and lamentations: the wailing of the goddess
Ninhursag for her lost son, the weeping of the goddess Ningal for her sacked
city, and above all, the lamentations for the god Dumuzi, who was cut down
in the flower of his youth.[20]

It has been thought that the expression of such sadness points to a pes-
simistic view of life. It may also be assumed that it recognizes, explores, and
renders dignity to the experience of suffering and loss. If a godhead must die
and feel anguish like a human, the ultimate in his humanization is achieved.[21]

Let us summarize at this point that in Mesopotamian tradition inherited patterns of belief came to express new attitudes in which mortals, their fate,
achievements, and sorrows, stand in the center of concern. The goal is establishment on earth and not transcendence of the human condition, and the
sacred master of the forest becomes the monster to be destroyed. We shall
now consider what forms and functions were given to maternal divinities in
a culture so strongly oriented toward human accomplishments.

MATERNAL DIVINITIES

A maternal divinity is indeed encountered in the pantheon. Many names and
epithets are recorded, sometimes alternating in designating a single being,
sometimes employed for various deities. It is likely that mother goddesses
had been venerated in many communities, that they had fused in the course

of time, and that various names and epithets had remained alive. We may categorize the function of the deities under the following main headings: nurse or mother of kings; Lady of the mountain and mistress of wild and domesticated beasts; goddess of birth and medicine; and creatress of men. Her principal names are Ninhursaga (Lady of the Mountain), Nintur (Lady Birth Hut or Lady Womb), Ninmenna (Lady of the Tiara), Ninmah (August Lady), Aruru (Birth Water), Damgalnunna (Great Consort of the Prince)ıı Bēlit-ilī (Akkadian) (Mistress of the Gods), and Nagarnam-lúulu (Carpenter of Mankind).[22]

Nurse and Mother of Kings

In a poem in which Enki is in charge of organizing the universe, it is stated that Mother Nintur "has the power to give birth to kings and lords."[23] This function is also attributed to the goddess Ninmug (Lady Vulva).[24] In the tale of the creation of the hoe, Ninmenna is the "Mistress" of giving birth to priests and kings.[25]

On the victory stele of King Eannatum we find the inscription: "Ningirsu implanted the seed of Eannatum in the womb and Ninhursaga bore him."[26] King Hammurabi asserts that he had been born by Nintur, the Mistress of the land.[27] King Samsu-iluna claims Ninmah or Ninhursag as his mother.[28] King Nebukadnezzar was brought forth by the goddess Mah, and King Abonid was the son of Ninmenna.[29] The King Luggalzaggisi was suckled by the "milk of life" of Ninhursag.[30]

Lady of the Mountain and Mistress of Beasts

The Mesopotamian plain was flanked by the stony plateau of the Arabian desert in the West and the rocky foothills of Iran on the eastern border, both denoted as *hursag*. The mistress of this region would thus be the Lady of the stony wilderness. In a poem where Summer and Winter hold a dispute, the mountain itself, the *hursag,* was impregnated by the god Enlil in the form of a wild bull; thus the sons Summer and Winter were engendered.[31] The mountain as a ravished woman is also envisaged in a hymn to the god Ningirsu, in which the waters rushing down the cliffs are designated as the semen of the god Enlil, reddened in the deflowering of the hills:

> Oh my master Ningirsu, lord, seminal waters
> reddened in the deflowering;
> able lord, seminal waters emitted by the
> "great mountain" (Enlil) . . . [32]

In a more anthropomorphic aspect the goddess received the foothills as a present from her son. Ninurta was encouraged by his mother to go forth and fight a mountain demon; after the god had defeated the monster, he built a wall of stone, and through this construction the waters were made to flow into the proper channels. Thus the hillside became green with plants and vibrant with the creatures of the pasture and the forest. After she had received the gift, the name of the goddess was changed from Ninlil to Ninhursag.[33]

In yet another text, the god Ningirsu (Ninurta) is said to be born of the Hursag and suckled by the "milk of deer."[34] It is thus possible that the Mistress of the Mountain might assume an animal epiphany. In a lament the goddess mourns for her beloved son, a young donkey, to whom she had given birth and whom she lost to human hunters or to the treacherous cliffs:

> I gave birth to a choice donkey steed, a lord mounted it
> —what have I for it?
> I gave birth to a strong mule, a lord hitched it up . . .
> —what have I for it?[35]

In this poem the goddess appears as Mistress and Guardian of Wild Beasts, who might herself assume the features of a forest animal. And in some traditions she is wedded to Shulpae, a warrior and ruler of the desert creatures.[36]

In yet another aspect of the maternal goddess, she watches in tenderness over domesticated animals. According to a Babylonian hymn, the cow and her calf low to her in longing, and she in turn calls plaintively to them.[37] A sign, resembling the Greek letter omega, recurs on representations of the goddess, and it has been interpreted by scholars as the image of the uterus of a cow.[38] The sign *tur* of her name Nintur coincides, with slight orthographic variation, with the sign meaning "cowpen," so that her name would mean Lady of the Cowpen.[39] More specifically the sign *tur* of her name has been interpreted to mean the hut to which pregnant cattle are led for the delivery of their young.[40] Friezes on the walls of Ninhursag's temple at Al Ubaid show cattle being milked by priests; it is believed that these beasts belonged to the sacred herds of Ninhursag. Large numbers of bull sculptures were also discovered at the site of excavations.[41] And the Lady of the Mountainside and Guardian of its Beasts also appears to have offered her protective powers to the herds of men (Figure 30).

Medicinal Goddess

In one of the best-known myths, the tale of Enki and Ninhursag, the goddess causes the origin of healing gods. In the dawn of time Enki and Ninhursag dwelled on the island Dilmun, a kind of paradise, a pure, fresh region where the lion did not kill and the wolf did not devour the lamb, a place without sickness or old age. The two deities united and gained a daughter through this union, whom they named Nintur. When the maiden matured, the father took her in his arms and she consequently bore the goddess Ninkurra, Lady of the Mountain. Ninkurra also was embraced by the virile Enki and bore a

Figure 30. Cylinder seal of Uruk, around 3000 B.C.E.

daughter, the spider goddess Uttu, a weaver. Ninhursag tried to shield the child from Enki's attention, but he prevailed by offering fruit of the soil to Uttu as a wedding gift.

Ninhursag, however, removed Enki's seed from Uttu's womb to place it in the earth, and soon eight plants began to sprout. Enki ate these when he returned to the scene of his adventures, arousing the wrath of Ninhursag through this deed. She laid a curse upon him so that he sickened while the plants were growing in his body. He would have been destroyed if the goddess had not relented and hastened to his rescue. She placed the ailing deity in her vagina and thus was able to help in giving birth to eight gods, one for every part of Enki's body that had been stricken. These were then given places in the cosmic order.[42]

The myth appears grotesque today and is difficult to understand. It is a cosmogonic myth, for it explains the origin of healing plants. Since Enki is the god of the waters, his aggressive virility might symbolize the invincible and generative force of water. In this tale Ninhursag, Lady Mountain, has greater power than the mighty Enki. We must also realize that the line between myth and story is not always clearly drawn; we might have here a tale for the entertainment of travelers or sailors.

Goddess of Birth and Motherhood

We already encountered Ninhursag/Nintur as mother of kings and of wild and domesticated beasts. She is moreover named Mother of all Children and Mother of the Gods.[43] In the tale concerning the great flood sent by the gods to destroy all humankind, the mother goddess Nintur weeps bitterly for her children.

The divinity, moreover, actually shapes the child within the womb. A hymn to her temple E-hi-za states: "Mother Nintur, the lady of . . . Within your dark place she performs her task."[44] King Ur-Nammu asserts that he was fashioned by Nintur, and Sennacherib declares that "Bēlit-īlī Mistress of shaping," molded his form within his mother's womb.[45] The role of the goddess as creator of the child seems underlined in such epithets as Lady Fashioner, Fashioner of All Things in Which There Is Breath of Life, Lady Potter, Bronze Caster of the Nation, and Carpenter of the Inside.[46]

The act of parturition itself unfolds under the direction of the goddess. A hymn of her sanctuary in Kesh tells us:

> None but Ninhursağa, uniquely great, makes
> the innards (heart)/contract (var. pushes the innards),
> None but Nintur, the great mother, sets birthgiving going.[47]

The ability to set the birth process going is ascribed also to Ninmenna in the poem of the creation of the hoe,[48] while the temple of Nintur in Kesh is said to be a brick structure that promotes the act of birth.[49] In a tale of Enki's ordering of the world, the midwife goddess is envisaged with her water pail and the bowl of lapis lazuli that holds the afterbirth.[50] Therefore the birth goddess bears such names as Mother Spreading Her Legs, Bloodstancher, Midwife of the Gods, Midwife of the Nation.[51] The maternal divinity thus holds the triple role of mother, shaper of the embryo, and power of the process of parturition. Some references also indicate that she decides the fate of the newborn child.

Creatress of Man

In a Sumerian text we hear of the dissatisfaction of those gods who must toil to keep the universe in order. To appease the angry forces, the other deities decide to create beings who will relieve them of their tasks. Nammu, Enki's mother, is approached, and she agrees to undertake the effort if she is advised and guided by the wisdom of her son. Enki instructs her to pinch off clay that lies above the abyss and to give birth to it, assisted by the goddess Ninma and seven other deities. Humans are indeed brought into the world in this fashion.[52]

An Akkadian childbirth charm gives a very similar account of the birth of humankind. Here the goddess Nintur is advised to mix the blood of a slain god with clay. After the blood has been obtained, fourteen wombs are formed from the mixture and in nine months' time, with the assistance of the midwife Nintur, seven male and seven female creatures are seen as they emerge from the wombs. A brick has been placed between the two rows of matrices, and a brick must still be placed in the house of a woman in travail so that she too may be delivered of her child. The gods, in gratitude, bestowed the name "Bēlit-ilī, Mistress of the Gods" on Nintur.[53]

In the poem of Gilgamesh, the goddess Aruru fashions the man Enkidu from clay. She acts with the gods An, Enlil, and Enki in creating the animals, and she laments the destruction of humanity, in the tale of the flood, the children to whom she has given birth.[54]

Status of the Goddess

In some lists of the gods the mother goddess (Bēlit-ilī, Ninhursag) appears next to the most important of the gods.[55] She has a function in the construction and arrangement of the world. The effectiveness of the curse she placed on Enki, a mighty god, underlines her power. In another episode the mother goddess (Ninmah) engages in some rivalry with the same deity.

The creation of humankind, accomplished by Ninmah and Enki, is celebrated in a rousing feast. In the course of the revelry Ninmah boasts that she could produce not only handsome but also ill-shaped creatures. And, indeed, defective human beings—a barren woman, a man with neither male nor female organ—are brought forth by the goddess. As part of the contest, Enki provides places for them within human society. He then produces a being so impotent and so decrepit that Ninmah can find no niche for the unfortunate entity. Her wrath rises against the god; the defectiveness of the tablet hides from us the outcome of the episode.[56]

The utterly helpless creature is named Udmuul ("premature," literally "the day was far off") and would represent a fetus that was not allowed to grow to maturity, or more generally, the phenomenon of abortion. In this case the wrath of the mother goddess is understandable, for this phenomenon would nullify and defeat the powers of gestation wielded by the deity. The titles Ninmah (August Lady), Bēlit-ilī (Mistress of the Gods), and the epithet Mother of the Gods point to the high rank of the goddess, an equal among the most illustrious of the rulers of the world.

Cult

The lowest of the temples of Al Ubaid contains a foundation tablet stating that A-anni-padda, king of Ur, and son of Mesi-padda, king of Ur, had built the temple for Ninhursag. The raising of the structure is attributed to the time of the First Dynasty of Ur. We already noted that the temple friezes show images of cows milked by priests. A large relief of the building depicts the lion-headed stormbird resting on two stags.[57]

The excavators of the temple at Mari found a bronze plaque whose inscription says that the governor of Mari, Niwar-Mer, had built the sanctuary for Ninhursag.[58] The statue of a seated woman, her hands joined above her lap, was discovered in the structure attributed to her, the middle one of three, raised on top of one another, ascribed to post-Sargonic time (2350–1975 B.C.E.).

One of the most important places of the cult of the mother goddess of various names is Kesh, of which no remains have been discovered. It seems to have lain south of Nippur. At the time of Eannatum (ca. 2440 B.C.E.) Kesh seems to have been the center of Ninhursag worship; the town still existed at the time of Hammurabi. Afterward there is no sign of the city. The name of Kesh, where Ninhursag had lived with her husband

Figure 31. (*Left*) Terra-cotta relief of the mother goddess, old Babylonian.
Figure 32. (*Right*) Bronze figure with omega symbol, 14 to 13 B.C.E.

Shulpae, appears in litanies among towns that were devastated and destroyed.[59]

The worship of the goddess was continued in Adab, her temple named E-sa-
ra or Emah, after Kesh had been annihilated.[60] An inscription on a statue of
King Gudea states that he had built a temple for the goddess in the town of
Girsu.[61]

Iconography

Her most famous image is a relief in clay showing the goddess with a child
on her arm, two emaciated figures huddling in the corners (possibly the demons from whom she snatched the infant; they seem to be too big to represent
embryos), children's heads emerging from her shoulders, and the omega-like
symbol associated with the divinity (Figure 31).[62] We also possess the description of a terra-cotta relief on which a child drinks from a woman's breast; the
image is said to be of Nintur.[63] Several seal cylinders show a seated woman

with an infant on her lap.[64] The omega-like symbol of the goddess is incised on boundary stones and on reliefs (Figure 32).[65]

A woman nourishing an infant appears as sculpture or in relief from the Ubaid period into Hellenistic time. Three basic types were discerned by Helmut Kühne: a standing naked figure, a standing clothed figure, and a seated woman.[66] It is not clear, however, whether these were goddesses or mortals.

Relation to Archaic Forms

We may recognize a kinship between the Middle Eastern forces and the maternal divinities of the more archaic hunting and herding cultures of Eurasia. The nurse and mother of kings finds a parallel in the Animal Mother of the shaman, the numinous force whose fostering care imparts a measure of sacredness to a chosen being. In Sumero-Akkadian tradition the chosen being is obviously not a shaman but a king, and the goddess is in human form, though according to one text a king takes nourishment from the four breasts (teats?) of a divinity.[67] We deal here, possibly, with the cow form of the goddess, and Ninsuna, Lady of the Wild Cows, is named as mother of several kings.

Ninhursag, the Lady of the Mountain, has counterparts in many Masters and Guardians of Nature, and protectors of forests and its beasts. Like these, Ninhursag might have had an animal epiphany, and as a Guardian of wildlife may extend his care to domesticated beasts, so Ninhursag is brought into relation with the herds and flocks of pastoral society.

By giving birth to healing gods and by shaping the momentous danger-filled and exhilarating process of parturition, she shares the role of medicinal and birth-helping goddesses of more primitive cultures. These deities, we may recall, are always present in herding and hunting communities where they belong to the women's sphere and dwell in the women's portion of the house, as do the *Akkas* of the Saami. These female beings wield the power to impart a living soul to the body and to shape the child within the womb, as does the Old Woman of the Earth of the Nentsi, who dwells beneath the human habitation.

We also find new elements. Ninhursag, the Lady of the Mountain, has blended with Nintur, Lady Birth Hut, that is, a divinity of male pursuits with a goddess of women's needs. This phenomenon parallels the social reality in which women are no longer excluded from the ritual life of their community. The fears concerning women's functions are the stronger the more men are in terror of the elemental powers, as is shown by the example of Eskimo religion. Such fears receded in the Middle East where men learned to master their environment. The acts of begetting and bearing children were, like other human activities, imbued with a new significance.

By shaping the first human the birth goddess was given a role in the creation of the world. Through copulation and birth the very features of the landscape were brought into existence in the Babylonian epic of creation. The event of biological birth took part in originating healing gods. The life-giving powers of the human womb are needed in some, though not in all, accounts to engender the first human, while in other mythologies humankind is shaped through the craftsman's or magician's skills, the molding of clay (Hebrew), the endowment of trees with life (Germanic), or the forming of a figure from earth and snow (Mansi). Clay is still molded, incantations still sung, and blood still spilled, at times, to create mortals in Mesopotamian myth, with the event of biological birth as an added component.[68] In equality with the other gods the birth goddess was visualized as a master craftsman in a tradition in which craftsmanship was held in the highest of esteems.

The personality of the goddess, however, remained curiously narrow in spite of her importance. From being the fashioner of the child within the womb, a Lady Potter, one might expect her to become a divinity of crafts- manship, from her help in medicinal matters she might rule the realms of wisdom and of magic; her role in birth giving might relate her to agricultural fertility. From being the Lady of the Foothills she might have grown into the mistress of the irrigated land; from being the nurse of kings she might have become their champion in battle. None of these processes has taken place.

Images of agricultural and pastoral abundance crowd around the goddess Inanna and her lovers. The god Enki sends water to the plowed land and thus allows the grain to rise. The moon god Nanna, deity of the cowherders, grants increase of the herds and an abundance of milk and cream; the storm and warrior god Ningirsu may cause the plants to sprout and the beasts to mul- tiply. There is no avenue, however, between the birth of children and the birth of plants; the names and epithets of the birth goddess do not relate her to the harvest. The realm of wisdom, magic, and craftsmanship is ruled by Enki of the deep. The goddess Inanna protects the king in battle. It has been observed that the mighty mother goddess lost importance in the course of time and was eclipsed by other deities.[69]

We can only speculate why the birth goddess did not attain a fuller form. It is possible that the Mesopotamians were concerned about the rapid growth of their population. In the narrative of the great flood, sent to destroy hu- mankind, the reason given for the catastrophe is the god Enlil's anger at the noise produced by the multitude of men. After the tragedy has happened, a kind of program of birth control is instituted by the gods Enki and Nintur to prevent the recurrence of the event: There would be from now on barren as well as fertile women, a demon that would snatch a child from its mother's arms, and a class of priestesses that would not be allowed to attain mother- hood.[70]

It might be that a godhead of the stony mountains could, in sun-parched Mesopotamia, not attain the importance of a god of the fresh waters, such as Enki. Thorkild Jacobsen suggests that the patriarchal values of society pre- vented a woman and a midwife from gaining prominence in the pantheon. Though plausible, this reason cannot fully be accepted, for the gods did allow the rise of a woman and a harlot to prominence (i.e., the imperious, violent, and often destructive Ishtar).

The ancient Middle East, where growing and harvesting the fruit of a generous earth had supplanted a harsher way of life, is generally seen as the place where the Great Mother unfolds to the fullest flower of her creative sovereignty. This study has not found a substantiation of this claim. It is true that a birth and mother goddess is depicted as a craftsman and creator. This role is also held, however, by the other gods, arising in the climate of admiration for human craftsmanship. The action of birth-giving forms part of the process through which the first human is generated. This involvement, again, is a result of the value accorded to human activity rather than to a special respect for the fertile womb. Though the goddess enjoys a station of importance in her group, there is no evidence that she ever ruled the other gods.

It has been claimed that with the advent of agriculture the birth-giving powers of the earth were assimilated to a woman's powers of fertility,[71] a claim not supported by Mesopotamian tradition. Here birth goddesses are related to the cattle byre or the birth hut, to the site of parturition, like the North Eurasian birth helpers, but not to the agricultural earth. No great earth goddess has arisen in this society of farmers, and the field is not envisaged as a fertile woman.[72] Here, as well as in the other agricultural communities of this study, no sexual rites are directed to the plowed land, nor is it approached by women in their wish for children. Birth-helping goddesses, on the other hand, who show a strong relation to the earth, were encountered in this study; these belong to communities of herders and hunters. Here the earth is visualized in its ancestral form as the resting place of the departed, and not as the site of growing grain.[73]

Much attention has been directed by the devotees of the goddess religion to the ancient Middle East. This, it is held, was the site of warfare between matriarchal and patriarchal forces, and here the noble goddess was dethroned. Then the pastoral invaders established their own gods of the sky, of thunder and lighting, and of war. While it is true that tribal forces poured into the area throughout the millennia it is also true that these accepted the native deities. The case is clearest with the Indo-European Hittites who adopted the many local gods of "Hatti land" and who also adopted the pre-Hittite pantheon, headed by a weather god.[74] The armed god of thunder had arisen and evolved among the planters of the soil.

In farming cultures great significance is accorded to the sky, as we noted in northern Eurasia, because it sends the fertilizing rains. In pre-anthropocentric faith, thunder and lightning and the ensuing rains are created by an animal, frequently a bird, or also by a stone or stone tool dropped from heaven.[75] When gods were humanized, the tool or stone was wielded by a mighty god (the English noun "thunderbolt" indicates the archaic belief). The armed weather god became the champion of man and defeated the chaos monster; in some areas he also became a god of war. He was not imported by pastoral tribes to the farming centers of the Middle East.

The defeat of the Goddess is said to be recorded in the Babylonian creation myth. The primeval mother Tiamat, who gave birth to all, was slain by her descendant Marduk, and from her broken and dismembered body the world was fashioned by the warrior god.[76] We must observe, however, that Tiamat did not bring forth her children through her strength alone. She was embraced by her husband "Apsû, their primordial begetter" before she was able to give birth.[77] Only monsters to fight the enemy were generated without copulation. Hence we meet with a primal couple rather than a primal mother. Moreover, it is Apsû who was killed before his wife. Fettered by his son Ea, he was slain in his sleep. In the Greek account of the creation, which is of the same kind, the defeat of the *father* is of essence to the establishment of cosmic order.[78]

Hence the battle of Enûma Elish is not between male and female, it is between amorphous and manlike forces.[79] The poem gives voice to a humanistic view. The creation and maintenance of ordered society are achieved through actions that are in fact performed by humans: biological propagation and the killing of the enemy. The fight is won by aggression, not by submission to inscrutable and inexorable powers.

chapter

7

The Mountain Mother: Anatolia

I N the previous chapter we noted the rise of a new humanism, a belief that through the application of their skills and rationality people could order and arrange their environment. Yet the voices of an older faith were never completely silenced. Men still felt their helplessness in the face of overwhelming forces; mortals still longed to break the limitations of their physical existence by merging with the superhuman and to achieve in trance and ecstasy the experience of a fuller life. The voices of the earlier belief are clearly heard in the traditions of Cybele.

Cybele, also named the Great Mother, Mother of the Gods, Phrygian Goddess, and Mountain Mother, was adored throughout the world in the last millennium preceding the triumph of Christianity. Her cult extended from Asia Minor to Italy and Greece, to the Balkans, the Danube, and the Rhine, and the shrill music of her priests resounded through the towns and harbors of northern Africa. She was praised as the All-Mother and All-Creator who heals the sicknesses of beasts and men, and she became the last bastion of pagan faith in the rising tide of Christian religion.[1] The first recording of her name appears in an inscription on a Phrygian stone monument of possibly the seventh century B.C.E., and an oration to Cybele was composed by the emperor Justinian in 363 C.E. Surely we meet in her the most impressive of maternal divinities, and we shall examine the elements that went into the making of the goddess.

HER HOMELAND

The high plateau of Anatolia where the goddess has her home is formed of layers of rock, encircled by the two arms of the Armenian mountains along the coastlines of the Mediterranean and Black Seas. Lying between Asia and Europe, open to entrance through the Bosporus and Syria, Asia Minor accepted in the course of the millennia streams of populations and of cultural influences from the two continents that it unites.

Here a splendid civilization arose as early as 7000 B.C.E. The town of Çatal Hüyük served as a trading center and as the matrix of craftsmanship in the arts of stone, clay, and even metal working. The great number of shrines and cult objects points to a systematically organized religious life.[2]

In the Bronze Age the country is believed to have been divided into city-states, ruled by kings. Rich finds at Alaça Hüyük indicate that the inhabitants, known as Hatti, in their turn, had achieved luxury and splendor in their style of living.[3]

Waves of Indo-European peoples began to sweep into the land from about 2000 B.C.E. onward. Among these were the Hittites who rose to power, extended their empire at one point to northern Syria, and had the town of Hattusha (Bogazköy) as their capital. After 1200 B.C.E. aggressive tribes from the West brought disaster to the realm and destroyed the kingdom of the Hittites. The ruthless actions of the conquerors found literary expression in the story of the fall of Troy, which itself had been established earlier by a group of Greek invaders.[4]

Troy was never rebuilt in its ancient splendor and disappeared as a bulwark against the Balkan tribes, now streaming into Asia Minor and rolling onward toward the Syrian border.[5] The tribe of the Mushki had departed from its home in Macedonia; they were ancestral to the nation that 500 years later, gathered enough strength, under its King Midas, to form the empire of Phrygia.[6] The centuries between the fall of the Hittite and the rise of the Phrygian empires were barren (1200–800 B.C.E.). The land was thinly populated and no monuments or urban centers have been laid bare by archaeologists. And obviously, there is no continuation between the Hittite and the Phrygian styles of art.

King Midas met defeat at the hands of the Cimmerians, and after these the land was ruled successively by Lydians, Persians, Alexander the Great, the Diadochs, and the kings of Pergamon. The last of the kings of Pergamon, who died childless in 133 B.C.E., bequeathed the realm to Rome so that it became a Roman province.

It was during the reign of the kings of Pergamon that the cult image of the Phrygian goddess was transported to Rome from her sanctuary in Pessinus (204 B.C.E.), for an oracle had told the Romans that the cult of the goddess would give them succor in their battles against Hannibal.

The Hellenization of the region started after the decline of Hittite power. The Hittites had employed cuneiform writing, and the Phrygians used the letters of Greek script. Hellenization continued in the reigns of the successive rulers. While native traditions were able to survive, the province belonged, on the whole, to the western rather than to the eastern world at the time of its conversion to Christianity.[7]

ANATOLIAN RELIGION

In wishing to regard the goddess Cybele in the context of her religion we come upon the fact that little is known about the faith of the Phrygians. They left no written texts, and most of their inscriptions, though composed of Greek letters, have not been deciphered. I shall therefore present some elements of the myths and rites practiced in Asia Minor to discover if any of these find an echo in the makeup of the goddess.

Insight into Anatolian beliefs comes to us through archaeology, through documents from the city of Kültepe (a merchant colony), and above all, through the Hittite texts. We find additional information in Ugaritic documents and the writings of Hellenistic and Roman times.[8]

The Pantheon

A process of syncretization, undertaken by a priestly class, had already occurred in the Hattic era, and it continued under Hittite rule. In this process the many local deities and those imported from abroad were welded into one divine and majestic family headed by a king and queen.[9] The Hattic weather god thus blended with the Hurrite Teshup to become the ruler of the group, and he was wedded to the sun goddess Arinna, a Hattic divinity who fused with the Syrian Hebat. The Hurrite Saushka, designated by the ideogram of Akkadian Ishtar, became the sister of the Hattic Telipinu, and both turned into children of the royal pair.[10]

The Weather God

Throughout Anatolia primary importance was accorded to the weather god, the highest deity in almost every town, who brought not only sunshine and thunderstorms but also victory, justice, and succor.[11] When larger communities came into existence, one weather god would become the ruler of his family and he might receive some of the local deities as his sons.[12]

Other societies of the Middle East (such as the Canaanites or the Hurrites) shared the adoration of the weather god. In the course of war and conquest a group might adopt the weather god of the defeated enemy, fuse him with its own, or place him into a family relationship.[13]

Among pre-literate finds, the figure of a bull is prominent in cultic contexts. Bulls' images, bulls' heads, and bulls' horns are abundantly present in the shrines of Çatal Hüyük.[14] It cannot be doubted that these artifacts represent the weather god in his animal epiphany. As already noted, King Hattusilis I reported that he had seized the silver bull from the temple of the conquered town of Zelpa and had placed it in the temple of the weather god of Hatti.[15] The sacred "Song of the Bull" was sung in honor of the weather god of Nerik.[16]

In his human form, the god may be standing on a bull, stationed in a bull-

Figure 33. (*Right*) A weather god on a seal from Cappodocia. Figure 34. (*Far right*) Relief of Sendjirli.

drawn carriage, leading a bull by a nose ring, or be himself adorned with a bull's horns (Figure 33).[17] He holds the bolt of thunder in his hand, and this may be symbolized by a club or axe (Figure 34).[18]

The Significance of Rocks and Mountains

Belief in the sacredness of stones and mountains found many expressions in Asia Minor. Raw, unhewn stones were erected in sacred places, in forests, near a well, on the summit of a rock, or in temples, as the altar of sacrificial offerings or the epiphany of a godhead.[19] Hittite architecture gave voice to the numinous validity of stone. The images of gods were carved into the rock face of the most famous of sancturaries at Yazilikaya, a roofless shrine. It is believed that cultic ceremonies were enacted in front of these reliefs.[20]

The mountains themselves were visualized as gods. Festivals were conducted in adoration of some mountain ranges, and a procession of the noblest men and women of the realm, including the king and queen, would make its way to these ranges to offer worship at a solemn feast.[21]

Some myths attest to the procreative power of stone and rock. When Kumarbi, a god of Hurrite origin, wished to create a power to fight his rebellious son, he shed his seed "ten times" upon a rock, and he begot the stone demon Ullikummi through this act. At another time the god bit off the phallus of his father Anu. He spat the phallus, filled with sperm, upon a mountain and the mountain bore two sons.[22]

The Battle with the Monster

That a monster is defeated by a god in human shape is told throughout the Middle Eastern texts.[23] This battle is of deep significance because it establishes the order of the world. The Hittite monster is the dragon Illuyanka who had defeated the weather god in their first encounter. At a later time the god prevails with the help of the goddess Inara.[24]

The chaos monster is represented in yet another form in Hittite tradition: as a creature of stone who was begotten by Kumarbi's seed upon a rock. The monster grew alarmingly and through his size threatened to obliterate the world. He too was confronted by the weather god, and though the text is fragmentary, we may understand that he was destroyed.[25]

We must note that the tale of a giant stone adversary, which had to be defeated, arose in a tradition that also accorded great sacredness to stones. And thus the battle was directed to the older god. In archaic forms of society, people stand in awe and humility before the nonhuman environment, its forests, rivers, stones, and beasts. The Hittites still revered the sacredness of stones and mountains, while simultaneously pitting their intelligence and strength against the ancient power.

The Mistress of Wild Beasts

In the earliest finds of Anatolia we recurrently encounter the monumental form of a woman.[26] Usually seated, she is shown in close connection with wild beasts of feline kind; she may be enthroned between panthers, may fondle a leopard cub, or may hold a leopard or a lion cub on her lap (Figures 35 and 36). She is clearly a protectress and mistress of wild beasts. Her alliance with feral beasts was preserved iconographically through the ages. In the Hellenistic and Roman periods she was still pictured seated between lions, standing between lions, or in a carriage drawn by lions. In historic times she was equated with Cybele.

Significance of the Female Form

Reliefs on the temple walls of Çatal Hüyük repeatedly portray a woman with widely separated legs (Figure 37).[27] Neither child nor lover are at large in the vicinity, and we cannot assume that the pose belongs with either childbirth or sexual surrender. The cylinder seals of Kültepe of Cappodocia recurrently show a creature who lifts her garments to expose her sexual parts. She is not seen with a lover and is not a figure in an erotic scene (Figure 38).[28]

Stories of various traditions might offer an explanation for the unusual exposure; these tell of incidents in which such an action shattered the emotions of anger or of pain.[29] In the most famous of these tales the Greek Demeter was shaken from the grief for her lost child when the woman Baubo bared her vulva to the goddess. The exposure is thus shown as an agent of magical protection. This belief finds expression in the Anatolian myth of Ishtar and Hedammu. Hedammu was an oceanic monster of such voracity that he devoured all the produce and the creatures of the earth, and the world was threatened with annihilation. The goddess Ishtar proceeded in her beauty to the shore, where she bared her body before the astonished beast. Ishtar and

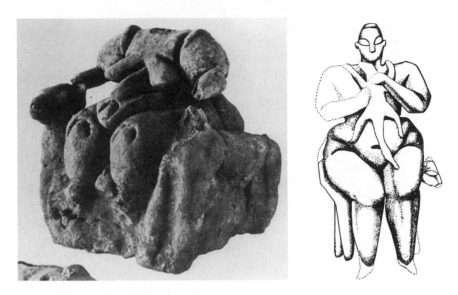

Figure 35. (*Left*) Clay sculpture of a woman enthroned between panthers from a shrine, A II, 1 of Çatal Hüyük. Figure 36. (*Right*) An artist's drawing of a clay sculpture of a female figure holding a cub, from a house, Q.VI.5 of Hacilar.

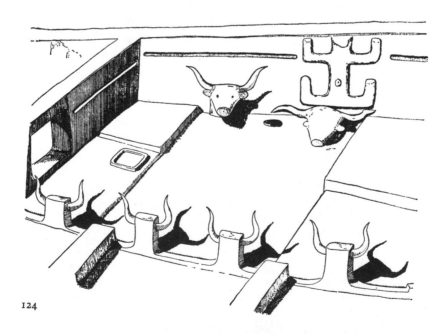

Figure 37. Relief in plaster on the west wall of shrine VI, B.8; bulls' heads of plaster and painted clay, Çatal Hüyük.

Figure 38. (*Left*) Old Syrian cylinder seals depicting a woman lifting her garments. Figure 39. (*Right*) Sculpture of Cybele of Büyükkale.

the monster engaged in conversation. The text is fragmentary, but apparently Hedammu was appeased.[30]

THE GODDESS CYBELE

Her Names

The names Kyvava in Lydian script and Kybebe in Ionian transcription are likely to have derived from the name Kubaba, the protective deity of Karkemish, adored already in the eighteenth century B.C.E. as the queen and mistress of the town.[31] The noun Kybabos denotes, in the writings of Semonides of Amorgos, a follower of Kybebe,[32] and in a tale recorded by Lucian, a youth named Kombabos lost his manhood through self-inflicted mutilation, an act practiced by the priests of the goddess.[33] The name, and probably also some aspects of the deity, wandered westward to Anatolia, and a dedication to *matar Kubileya* was inscribed on a Phrygian monument.[34]

In the cults and sanctuaries of the goddess the name Cybele is rarely used, for she carries the designation of her special domain, the specific locality that she protects and sanctifies—a mountain, a rock, a cave, a well, a village, or a town. She is Agdistis near the mountain Agdos next to Pessinus, and Idaia near the mountain range of Ida in the vicinity of Troy; she is adored in the Steunos cave of western Phrygia as Steunene, and as Silindene in the Lydian village Silindos.[35]

Her proper name is often prefixed by the title *meter, mater* (mother), as at Pontana near Meros where she is Meter Pontanene, or the title *meter* stands alone so that a town erected in her honor is a *metropolis* and her temple is a *metroon*. She is the *meter theon* (Mother of the Gods) or *meter oreia* (Mountain Mother). At times she would keep the name of her locality after her cult had spread to a new place; thus Dindymene, the Lady of the mountain Dindymon near Pessinus, retained her appellation when she was worshipped in the area of Kyzikos.[36]

We may thus consider her above all as a topical divinity, as the protective spirit of a specific place, a mountain, cave, or human settlement, who kept her separateness and did not fuse with others (except in her blending with Kubaba), though undoubtedly the various local numina showed great resemblance to one another.

The Monuments

Like the Hittites the Phrygians created their sacred monuments of rock and stone. Stones resembling seats with a backrest, planted in the forest and sometimes reached by steps of stone, have been interpreted as altars, as support for a cult statue, or as the throne of a divinity. Deep recesses cut into the vertical side of cliffs received the bones of the departed. The most striking of the sacred artifacts are the rock facades, reliefs hewn into the rock face in the image of a temple or a house to provide a place for the cult image of a godhead. Examination of the Phrygian monuments indicates the high position held by the Mountain Mother in Phrygian faith.

The greatest concentration of sacred sculptures and dedications incised into stone is found in Midas Kale in the Midas valley, a settlement built on a rock plateau that had been formerly surrounded by heavy walls.[37] Here was carved into a vertical surface the likeness of a temple adorned with a geometrical design and possessing a deep doorlike recess; within the recess stands a stone, now empty, that once served as a pedestal. Into the doorposts the word *mater* was repeatedly incised. This rock sculpture, known as the Midas Monument, is considered to be the most splendid of the sanctuaries, and we realize that it had been dedicated to the *mater,* the great Mountain Mother.[38]

In the valley of the Köhnus, a row of graves cut into the bordering cliffs is named "lion rock" by the peasants. Here, to form another striking rock

Figure 40. Cult relief of standing goddess from Gordion.

facade, doors were sculpted, opening into a cult niche in which the figure of the goddess was carved in relief and stationed between lions. A huge lion of stone, as if in protection, towers above the monument.[39] In close proximity, north of the road to Dögön, a plainer sanctuary contains the figure of a cruder goddess. Of a goddess, belonging to the monument of Büyük Kapi Kaya, only the headdress and the lower portion of a garment have remained; small pedestals at her sides might have served as bases for lions.[40]

In a niche of the wall of Büyükkale, the Acropolis of Hattusha, the statue of a goddess identified as Cybele wears a tall headdress and is flanked by two dwarf musicians playing a double flute and a kithara, respectively (Figure 39).[41] Recent excavations at Gordion in central Anatolia greatly add to our knowledge of Cybele worship. A well-preserved cult relief shows her standing within a frame; she is robed, veiled, crowned with a high headdress, and holds a bird of prey in one hand and a bowl in the other (Figure 40). Several other artifacts present her with the same attributes.[42] The finds belong to the most flourishing period of Phrygian culture (eighth to sixth century) and portray the goddess in a form that was yet free from Hellenistic influence. We realize that the lion was not always her attribute. A bird of prey, however, still marks her as a mistress of wild beasts. She is the only deity to be depicted, and the supremacy of her position is thus confirmed. The finds of the subsequent centuries are sparse; frequently, they are crudely made and lead us to assume that the goddess cult was carried on in the households.

The inscription of the "altar" or "throne" of a step monument, the Akkas Yuvasi rock of the Köhnus valley, actually names the goddess as *matar Kubileya*.[43] Yet more Phrygian inscriptions in villages and towns point to the worship of Cybele,[44] while many other dedications, not yet deciphered, allow us to assume the adoration of various other divinities. We may be safe, however, in understanding that the Great Mother was the most exalted, was honored in the most impressive of the monuments, and her image alone recurred in Phrygian iconology.

The Basic Myths

These were recorded in Hellenistic and Roman times and show some variations but also enough similarities to allow us to recognize the essential aspects of the goddess. Her experiences center on the loss of a young companion and her grief. Recurrently, we meet irruption of violence and madness, and references to a cult.

The fullest versions of her life are rendered, with minor variances, by Arnobius and Pausanius.[45] In this account she was conceived when Zeus struggled to embrace a goddess, whom he found in sleep on Mount Agdos, and spilled his seed upon the rock. The mountain became impregnated, in the way of Anatolian mountains, and gave birth to a wild, destructive, and monstrous being that was equipped with male and female genitals. The other gods wished to subdue the creature, and while it lay asleep, they fastened its male member to a tree. When Agdistis (as it was called after its place of birth) moved on awakening, the rope was pulled, the phallus torn from the body, and an almond (or an apple) tree sprouted where the organ touched the ground.

When a princess placed the fruit of this tree on her lap, she became pregnant and gave birth to a male child. When grown, the youth, named Attis, became the beloved companion of Agdistis until he set his mind on marrying the daughter of the king of Pessinus. Agdistis appeared in rage among the guests of the wedding feast and struck them with insanity, so that the king unmanned himself. Attis rushed in frenzy from the palace; beneath a pine tree he severed his male member and there he died. Agdistis, now grieving violently, begged Zeus to return the youth to life, but he only granted that Attis' body would not putrify, that his hair would grow, and that his little finger would be allowed to move. Attis was then buried at Pessinus, and a priesthood was installed in his honor.

In a tale transmitted by Ovid, Attis and Cybele were beholden to one another in chaste love. Attis vowed that he would keep his purity in order to serve his goddess, but he broke his promise when he became enamored of the nymph Sagaritis. In anger the goddess wrought the maiden's death and deranged the senses of her lover. The young god cursed the parts that had made him sin, as he cut them from his body. Flowers grew, according to one version, where his blood spilled on the earth, and his form changed to a pine tree, which is sacred to the Mountain Mother, according to another.[46]

A fully humanized account is presented by Diodorus. Here Cybele is the daughter of king Maion of Lydia. She was exposed at birth and raised by animals in the wilderness of the mountain Kybelon, and was named Mountain Mother by the villagers because of her loving kindness to men and beasts. Above all others she loved Attis and became impregnated by the comely youth. Her father wished to receive the girl again in her parental dwelling, but in anger at her condition, he slew the youth and cast away the unburied corpse. The girl raced in violent grief in frenzy through the countryside, wildly beating her tambourine and bewailing loudly the loss of her beloved. When a pestilence came upon the land, the inhabitants were told by an oracle that they must provide a burial for Attis and worship the girl Cybele as a goddess. They could not find, however, the lifeless body of the youth, and therefore they created a cult image and celebrated every year a festival of sorrow.[47]

Lucian reports that the Lydian Attes, the first priest of Cybele, had been emasculated by the deity and would travel in female clothing through many countries to exalt the glory of the goddess and to establish her cult.[48] Some Christian writers employed the legends to deride the worship of Cybele, depicting her as an old and ugly Mother of the Gods who unsuccessfully tried to seduce the handsome Attis and who emasculated him in anger and frustration.[49]

In some tales Attis finds his death through the teeth and claws of a boar, in resemblance to the fate of the Greek Adonis. Thus he was born, according to a Lydian tale, without the gift of male potency, and he wandered among the Lydians to instruct them in the rituals of the Mother of the Gods. He was so much loved and honored by Cybele that he aroused the jealousy of Zeus, who dispatched a ferocious boar to destroy him.[50] According to a *scholion* to Nicoander, Attis was a Phrygian shepherd, loved by the divinity, and he extolled and praised her in his hymns. He too perished when a boar attacked him on Zeus's command.[51]

The lions that draw the carriage of Cybele, so a Greek legend relates, are the human lovers Hippomenes and Atalante, changed in punishment into beasts because they had defiled the temple of the goddess through their sexual embraces.[52] Folk belief interprets the howling of the winds of spring as the lamentation of the deity who races through the forest in despair to search for her beloved, followed by her faithful and the piercing voices of their instruments, their cymbals, flutes, rattles, and drums; and she induces madness in those she meets.[53] It is also said that she roamed the forests in the company of Marsyas, and that he played the flute to console her in her grief.[54]

The central experiences of Cybele's life thus arise, according to the legends, out of her relation with her youthful companion; we may also note the consistently recurring themes of the youth's death, of emasculation, of self-inflicted wounds, of unnatural conception, of the sorrow of Cybele, and of the madness sent or suffered by the deity. There are references to her cult and to cult figures.

The Cult

In the loneliness of wooded mountains one may encounter the rude stones, erected as the throne, the altar, or the epiphany of the Mountain Mother.[55] She was adored in caves, as in the subterranean chambers of the mountain Lobrinos where her priests deposited their severed phalli, or in the grotto of Steunos, which held a greatly venerated image of the Lady.[56] She might also be associated with wells and springs, and she was the Mistress of the healing waters of Hierapolis.[57] Trees were sacred to the Mountain Mother, and her sanctuary might be surrounded by the pine trees of a grove.[58]

The goddess was adored, moreover, in architectural constructions. A community or town might grow around her temple or that of her companion, which might remain a simple center of religious life, inhabited mainly by her priests,[59] or it might develop into a bustling city, such as Attouda near the Carian border.[60] In Pessinus, at the foot of the mountain Dindymon, near the shores of the river Gallos, an entire temple city and theocratic state was created, served, and ruled by priests, and the highest, named Attis, received the honor and tributes of a king. Here the tomb of Attis was located, and here an unhewn stone was adored as the most sacred form of the Mother.[61]

In spring the great feast of the goddess was celebrated, its ritual based on the tragic events of Attis's life and on his triumph. The ritual was marked by its orgiastic nature, for the priests, named Galloi, Bakeloi, or Kybeboi, expressed the agony of grief through their frenzy. Through the sounding of flutes, cymbals, horns, and rattles, through rapid turning and dancing, through furiously shaking their heads, they induced in themselves a state of ecstasy in which they would become insensible to pain; they would wound and lacerate their bodies, and those who were about to enter the priesthood of Cybele would emasculate themselves with a sharp stone.[62] Afterward, the salvation of the god was announced with enthusiastic joy. The ceremonies began with felling a pine tree in the forest and ended with bathing the image of the goddess.

When the cult of Cybele was transplanted to Rome, her services were still conducted by her Phrygian priests, and we may assume that the practices were enacted much as they had been in their native land. Thus a pine was brought, as in the Phrygian ceremony, from Cybele's sacred grove and erected in her temple, initiating a period of intense mourning over Attis's death. On March 24, the third day of the festival, the "day of blood," anguish and frenzy reached their culmination, to be followed by the *hilaria,* the "day of joy." In Rome the image of the goddess, with the stone from Pessinus lodged in her head, her lions and her chariot, all of silver, were bathed in a river at the end of the celebrations.[63]

The cruel practice of self-mutilation has naturally aroused much interest and speculation. Some scholars believe that this act parallels a vow of chastity in the service of the goddess; others hold that through the severed organ the womb of the goddess is fertilized.[64] In their interpretations scholars have neglected to account for the feminine attire worn by the priests after their bloody deed.

The Galloi not only take to dressing in women's garments, but also to combing their hair in women's fashion, using perfume, adorning themselves with jewelry, and carrying mirrors in the way of women.[65] We are told by Lucian that the first priest of Cybele wandered in women's clothing through the provinces of Lydia.

Transvestism and the simulation of a sex change are not infrequently encountered in a cultic environment. The clearest examples of such practices are met in the context of the shamanistic traditions of Siberia, especially among the Chukchee and the Koryaks. While women may attempt to attain the role of men, the assumption by men of a woman's station is more frequent. In the first stage of "turning into a female," the shaman of the Chukchee plaits his hair like a woman; in the second, he wears women's clothes in the exercise of his craft; in the third, he withdraws from all pursuits of men, takes up sewing, becomes "soft and helpless" like a woman, chooses a "husband," and fulfills a woman's tasks.[66] A shaman of this kind is believed to have greatly enhanced his powers. In Koryak fairy tales such shamans are enabled to bear children; and among the Samoyeds the shaman wears a woman's hat.[67]

Herodotus reports that the soothsayers of the Scythians, named *enares,* traditionally wore women's clothes; it was believed that they had despoiled the sanctuary of Aphrodite at Ascalon and had been punished by the goddess with the "feminine disease"; in consolation she also bestowed on them the gift of divination. Hippocrates assumed that these prophets had contracted the "riding sickness" because they spent excessive time on horseback, and that this sickness had made them into eunuchs.[68]

The phenomenon of ritual perversion appears, even in our time, in a wide variety of regions, as in America, parts of India, northern Eurasia, or Borneo. The perversion may assume several forms—transvestism, homosexuality, or impotence due to castration. One can only speculate concerning the basis of the belief. It has been suggested that a creature in whom male and female elements are combined would be of greater spiritual effectiveness than a single-sex being, or also that the deviation from the norm would constitute a source of magic powers.[69]

We may note that the priests of Cybele were indeed credited with the gifts of healing and divination, the special talents of a shaman. The Galloi would utter prophecies in verse in the sacred fervor of their ecstasy; they received the truth of the goddess by entering a cave filled with noxious gases (in Hierapolis) from which no other living being could escape. They were trained in understanding dreams and interpreting the flight and song of birds. In some places the priests of Cybele healed diseases of both mind and body, such as hysteria, fevers, or the sicknesses of children.[70]

We may surely recognize many aspects of a shaman/sorcerer in these priests. Their actions and behavior, their castration, transvestism, and frenzy, and their curing of disease may be interpreted as activities and techniques of the sorcerer's craft. It is also likely that the rites of frenzy and castration had existed before the myth of the death of Attis was attached as explanation. The first description of the practices was given at the end of the fifth century, while the earliest Attis myth appeared in the Hellenistic Age.[71]

Iconography

The Phrygians portrayed the goddess with a bowl and a bird of prey; one sculpture also shows her flanked by lions. In an impressive representation she is seen with two dwarf musicians; sometimes she appears with a pomegranate or a pitcher. The goddess Kubaba of Karkemish, with whom she blended, may hold a mirror or a pomegranate; she may be seated on a lion or standing on a bull. It may be significant that there is nowhere evidence of a young male companion.[72]

Hellenistic and Roman imagery places her in close relationship with lions (Figure 41). Since both the Phrygian and the Hellenistic images ally her with feral beasts, it is possible to assume that she belongs in kind with the figures of the Neolithic sites, of pre-literate ages, who are linked with creatures of the wilderness. If this assumption is correct, then the Great Mother was already present in the earliest-known phase of Anatolian imagery. The Stone Age artifacts present her as a woman enthroned between panthers, fondling a leopard cub, or seated on a leopard, with an infant leopard on her lap, all indicating her nature as mistress and protectress of wild beasts.[73]

On the coins and terra-cottas of Hellenistic times Cybele may be stationed between lions or seated in a carriage drawn by these animals; frequently, she holds a tambourine.[74] As protectress of a city the Great Mother wears a mural crown, as on the coins of Pessinus; she may also share the space with other figures of belief; thus the images of Hermes and Men Ouranos (a celestial deity) are graven into a votive stele of Oukeh next to the form of Meter Kasamene. A coin of Pergamon shows her seated in her lion carriage and followed by a priestess with a tambourine, apparently in the presentation of a ceremonial procession.[75]

The Status of the Goddess

If we may interpret the sculptures of Hacilar and Çatal Hüyük as early forms of the Mountain Mother, then she was of great significance in Neolithic Anatolia, as seen by the recurrence of this figure. Also paramount in the shrines, however, were the bull's image, the bull's horns, and the bull's head of the weather god. Thus the Lady of the Wilderness shared her powers with at least one other divinity.

In Hittite art, female godheads are often stationed on lions; yet the texts

Figure 41. Statue of Cybele in Greek marble, Nettuno, Rome.

accord small importance to a Lady of Wild Beasts, while the Goddess of the Sun, Hebat, and the goddess of the crafts of war, Saushka, rose to prominent positions. And unmistakeably, the male weather god ruled the group.

In the empire of the Phrygians, on the other hand, Cybele held a place of supremacy. She was honored in the Midas monument, the most splendid of the sacred structures; her form was hewn into the great stele of Arslan Kaya and into the city wall of Büyükkale. She was the only deity to be depicted in the area of Gordion. Inscriptions to the *meter* recur throughout the Phrygian provinces, and her sacred animal, the lion, rose to sanctity throughout the realm. The image of a bull, who represents the Anatolian weather god, conversely, is not found among the Phrygian artifacts.

The Lydian rulers retained the high respect before the goddess. The name Attis was possibly incorporated into the name of kings, as in Aly-Attes and Sady-Attes.[76] In legend Attis (Atys) became a royal prince as the son of Kroisos;[77] the oldest Lydian coins bear the image of Cybele's sacred animal, the lion. We know, on the other hand, that the Greek gods had made their inroads into Lydian culture, and that the great sanctuary at Ephesus, built by Kroisos, was dedicated to the Greek goddess Artemis. During the time of Persian domination, elements of Persian faith were introduced, and the new Lords thus imported their goddess Anaitis.[78]

The kings of Pergamon, the Attalides, were named after the companion of Cybele; her sanctuary, the Mamurt Kale in the wilderness of Mount Aspordenon, was honored and supported by the kings[79] who also embellished and rebuilt the ancient temple structure of Pessinus. Inscriptions and cultic remains of the town of Pergamon indicate that a sanctuary of the deity had existed on the Acropolis in the proximity to Zeus's temple and that she bore the title Meter Basileia.[80]

While worship of the ancient deity thus persisted, the country had become so strongly Hellenized that in the fifth and fourth centuries the Greek Apollo was honored above all other gods,[81] and that the dynasty of the Attalides allied itself especially with the Greek Dionysus. When the region became a Roman province, a Dea Roma appeared on coins beside the other gods.

We thus realize that contrary to the opinion of most scholars, Cybele did not hold a position of sovereignty during all periods of the history of Asia Minor. She ruled supremely only in the reign of the Phrygian and, possibly, the Lydian kings. She shared her sovereignty with the bull-shaped weather god in the Neolithic and became eclipsed in Hittite religion. She stood alongside Zeus, Artemis, and Dionysus when Greek culture swept through the land. It is, however, very likely that in her many sanctuaries, on the level of folk religion, the devotion of her followers remained unbroken and unflawed through the ages.

The Functions of the Goddess

Iconography portrays her as the Mistress of Wild Beasts, but this role is not substantiated by the myths or the practices of her cult, for she is not concerned with caring for the creatures of the wilderness or the hunter's needs. She appears above all to be the protective spirit of a locality, mountain, village, or town. The Romans gave her credit for the defeat of Hannibal and for granting a splendid harvest. She was named Earth, All-Mother, and All-Creator, and was thus conceived as a universally beneficient divinity.[82]

If she had any special area of power, it was that of mantic inspiration. To a priest who spent the night sleeping in her temple she might reveal the future in a dream,[83] and the Gallos, descending into her sacred grotto and inhaling its noxious gases, returned raving, with the truth of the goddess on his lips,[84] and as healers and diviners her priests would travel through the countryside. She might indicate to her priests, both male and female, how the curse of a sickness could be lifted, especially a sickness that she herself had sent; and she was the Lady of the healing waters of Hierapolis. She is said to have devised an incantation for curing children.[85]

She was especially closely linked with the art of music. She consistently held the tambourine as her attribute, and the sounds of flutes, cymbals, drums, or horns were never absent from her ceremonies. When she was riven by her grief, the man Marsyas consoled her with his flute. The sculpture of Büyükkale portrays her as flanked by dwarf musicians, testifying that the sounds of music, thus probably ecstatic rites, belonged with the goddess in a fully Phrygian environment.

Relation to Anatolian Tradition

In several ways the deity partakes of the traditions of Anatolia. Neolithic artifacts allow us to infer that their creators adored a Lady of Wild Beasts, and the image of this Lady enthroned between her animals or holding and fondling an infant of the species was envisaged and produced through the millennia, persisting into the early era of Christianity. We may understand that a form of the goddess had existed in the earliest known layer of Anatolian religion. Though she did not retain in myth or cult her strong alliance with feral beasts, she did retain her attachment to the wild places, the wells, grottoes, forests, and mountaintops of untamed nature.

The rock altars, rock facades, and rock graves of the Phrygians indicate that they held, like the Hittites and the Hatti, a belief in the sacredness of stones, and the image of the goddess was carved into the living rock as were those of the Hittite, Hattic, and Hurrite divinities. The assumption that a stone might bring forth a living being, expressed in the Hurrite myths of Kumarbi and Washitta, is also evident in the tale of the impregnation of Mount Agdos and the birth of the androgynous Agdistis-Cybele.

Like other godheads of the Middle East, Cybele held a role in the drama of mourning for a slain divinity, and like Ishtar, Anat, or Inanna, she was devastated by the violence and fury of her grief. Magic powers were attributed to female sexuality in Asia Minor and northern Syria, as indicated by imagery and the story of Ishtar and Hedammu; belief in the powers of female sexuality also seems to underlie the simulated sex change of Cybele's priests.

In some important aspects, however, the goddess stayed aloof from the traditions of western Asia. She was never incorporated as a sister, daughter, spouse, or mother into a family of gods; thus she did not become a member of a pantheon such as that envisioned by the priests of Babylon or Hattusha. And she remained a local goddess, the tutelary spirit of a certain place, a mountain or a town, and her many names testify to this condition: She was the Lady of Mount Sipylos or Mount Dindymon, and as Agdistis, the potent mistress of Mount Agdos, she was brought to Rome. She transcended her nature as topical deity only in her blending with Kubaba, who herself had been a local goddess as the Queen of Karkemish.

Derivation of the Goddess

We do not know from where the Phrygians received their sovereign goddess. She was not part of the Hittite pantheon and thus was not taken over from Hittite faith. The Phrygians had driven the Hittites from their dwellings and had devastated the countryside, which lay bare for centuries, devoid of urban settlements and centers of higher culture. The conquerors met only with communities of simple farmers and the worship of their local gods. They found an archaic layer of belief rather than a theology that had been constructed and refined by the priesthood of a royal state. The Phrygians themselves retained their semi-nomadic ways for centuries until their statehood was consolidated under Midas.

It is likely that the Phrygians accepted the various local Ladies, in the form of the Neolithic Mistress of Animals, into their belief. It is only puzzling that they did not adopt the local weather gods, who also belonged to the archaic Neolithic heritage. Bull symbols are not present in Phrygian imagery, whereas the feline of the goddess is a sacred beast, and the legends of Cybele do not contain the figure of a weather god.

We may speculate concerning this phenomenon and possibly find an answer by considering the traditions of the Phrygians. They were a Thracian tribe that had marched to Asia Minor from the Balkans. In their home the Thracians were, according to Herodotus, a cattle-raising people, much given to plundering and warfare. They did not adore a weather god, but believed in Sabazios (equated with Dionysus), in a god of war (equated with Ares), and in a goddess (equated with Artemis by Herodotus) who was worshipped in an orgiastic fashion.[86]

The Thracian goddesses Kotys and Bendis were, like Artemis, deities of wild nature and were worshipped in ecstatic rites. In the feast of Kotys cultic dances were performed by men in women's clothes, called *hemigynoi* (half-women), to the sound of frenzied music. The *baptai,* immersion in water, formed part of the ceremonial. We find the following striking parallels between Cybele and the Thracian Kotys: the nature of a Mountain Mother, presence of transvestite priests, immersion in water, and orgiastic rites.[87]

Let us recall, moreover, that on entering Anatolia the Phrygians retained much of their ancient way of life for centuries, and thus, most probably, their ancient beliefs. Not having a weather god of their own (a deity important among farmers), they did not adopt the Anatolian god of storms, but they recognized in the local goddesses a kinship with their own Lady of the Wilderness. They would accept them in their belief and honor them in their own way.

They might also have grafted the Middle Eastern motif of a dying god and a lamenting goddess onto an already existing, orgiastic festival of their own deity.[88] This assumption receives support from the knowledge that the act of ritual castration has been attested for the fifth century B.C.E. whereas the attendant Attis myth was not recorded before Hellenistic times.[89] And a variant motivation for the mutilation is given by Lucian in the story of Kombabos: this youth cast off his manhood because he would then be unable to give in to debauchery and disloyalty.[90]

If we consider that Attis shares his name with the high priest of Cybele, and that, like a Gallos, he experiences loss of manhood and loss of rationality, that, in the myths, he wanders, sometimes in a woman's garments, through many lands to proclaim the glory of his goddess, we realize that he is modeled on her human followers; he is, in fact, a deified shaman-priest. Hence the basic unit of Cybele tradition is not a ruler and his wife, a mother and a father, or a mistress and her lover, but a goddess and her priest. It is likely that the festival of the Mountain Mother reenacts a man's entry into the priesthood of the deity and celebrates, as stated in some myths, the introduction of her cult. In other Mediterranean legends the world is restored through the returning of a god, but here a cult is established through his death.

We may observe several distinct strands in the matter of Cybele. We recognize the local Ladies of the Wilderness who were adored in Neolithic Anatolia; these were blended by the Phrygian invaders with their goddess Kotys, celebrated in orgiastic rites; she fused with the goddess of Karkemish; the Mediterranean theme of a dying and much lamented god also entered the tradition.[91]

The Titles of the Goddess

She is consistently named *meter, mater*—"mother", a town erected in her honor is a *metropolis,* and her temple is a *metroon.* Those whom she afflicts with madness are *metroleptoi;*[92] she is also the Mother of the Gods.

She is, however, not a mother. She does not give birth, and she is also not concerned with the parturition of others or with caring for young humans. Unnatural conception and gestation are exalted in her myths, for she, a healing and protective force, and also her beloved Attis, were begotten in unexpected ways. Erotic relations that would lead to biological conception and to birth seem to be abhorrent to Cybele. We do not know whether the love of Attis and Cybele was ever physically consummated (except in one humanized account). Her priests voluntarily sacrifice their ability of procreation.

She is named the Mother of the Gods, but she stands outside of any family relation with the ruling divinities.[93] She is designated as Mountain Mother, but we know that mountains did not originate in her womb or even, metaphorically, through her agency. We find an answer to this apparently puzzling phenomenon if we recall that recurrently in cultures of this study the noun "mother" does not denote a genetrix, in a literal or figurative sense, but rather a personage of noble status, a goddess or queen. Thus we encountered a Cloud Mother among the Mari, a Bee Mother, and even a Tobacco-pouch Mother among the Latvians. We may assume that Cybele as Mountain Mother is not the procreator but the ruler of the mountain, as Mother of the Gods she is the highest of all deities; as Magna Mater she would be the Great Queen.

The Nature of the Goddess: The Hunters' Heritage

The tales and cult practices of Cybele enshrine the concepts and beliefs of an archaic faith, such as had developed in communities of fishermen and hunters.

She represents the force of irrationality and frenzy through which, in this belief, salvation is attained, and she remained the Lady of the Wilderness who was worshipped as an unhewn stone.

Middle Eastern rituals and tales frequently convey an emotion of triumph over nature, a conviction mixed with guilt, that through human skills and human prowess the order of the cosmos was created in the midst of chaos. The widespread tale of slaying a monster, often recalled at the most important festival of the year, is expressive of this view, and the weapon of victory, the cudgel, club, axe, or mace, are always named, and often also the fabricator of the artifact. Humans had attained a measure of security and even luxury in the ancient Mediterranean towns. It is not surprising, if we consider the stout walls, the towering temples, the finely chiseled tools, the variety of the earth's produce, all wrought by humans, that they were proud of their achievements.

In the unsheltered villages of hunting nations, on the other hand, mortals bow in humility and in the knowledge of the insufficiency of their strength before the threatening, mysterious, all-surrounding, nonhuman world. Salvation of individuals and their community is attained not through human skills but through magic, not through the employment but through the loss of rationality. To achieve his goals of healing, gaining knowledge, and fighting starvation, the shaman sheds his human individuality to become transformed into a beast or possessed by a superhuman agent.

As in the vision of the hunting nations, the nonhuman is exalted in the traditions of Cybele. The monster-slaying myth is told from the monster's point of view. In this myth the monster almost always originated through magical conception, whereas his human adversary was begotten in the image of man through sexual embraces.[94] Cybele-Agdistis was brought forth, we may recall, in the same way as the monster Ullikummi, through seed spattered on a rock. In this way Cybele herself is the monstrous form; the god Attis, adored in many temples, was also begotten through magical impregnation. The priests of Cybele discard the organ by which biological conception may be worked.

The goddess does not fight her battles, like the divinities of human assertiveness, with a manmade tool, but by sending madness (i.e., her power over the mind of men that she may inspire or derange). She is not alone among divinities to use this weapon. When King Lykurgos wished to cut a vine of Dionysos with an axe, the god, he too a force of irrationality, so confused the senses of Lykurgos that he killed his own son with the instrument forged in a human smithy.[95] The tale is told by the Thracians and clearly emphasizes the impotence of human craftsmanship and ingenuity in the face of the divine.

Let us consider other ways the traditions of Cybele mirror the beliefs of hunting nations. These revere the spirit owners and guardians of wild beasts and also the supernatural owners of the local landscape, the many Lords and Ladies of the mountains or the streams. We cannot doubt that as a Mistress of Wild Beasts, as Mountain Mother, and as the Lady and protectress of a specific locality, Cybele belongs with these deities.

The shaman is the vital force in the religious life of hunting communities, and he is transported to his state of ecstasy through chanting, beating his drum, or through the frenzied movements of his body. These techniques of achieving ecstasy stayed very much alive with the priesthood of the goddess, for her devotees would induce in themselves a transcendental state through the piercing music of their instruments and the violent motions of their dances. A tambourine, reminiscent of the shaman's drum, belongs with the image of the goddess. Like a shaman, a Gallos possesses the gifts of healing and of mantic vision.

The agony, inflicted on the bodies of the priests, recalls the voluntary suffering of a shaman's initiation, born in the belief that true wisdom can only be attained by the experience of pain. The central importance of mutilation recalls the central importance accorded to mutilation in the tales of Sedna of the Eskimo. The emasculation described in the tales of Cybele is always self-inflicted and would thus present an act of dedication rather than the suffering of violation and defeat. Like some shamans, Cybele's priests simulate a change of sex. Attis appears in the form of a shaman-god, and Cybele herself partakes, in her frenzy, her emasculation, and in her powers of healing, of some shamanistic experiences and gifts.

The trees of the forest hold great sacredness among hunting nations and in the traditions of the shaman's craft. And pines figure prominently in the cultic matter of Cybele. Beneath a pine tree Attis lost his manhood, and in one account his lifeless and mutilated body changed into a pine. A pine tree was planted in Cybele's temple at the onset of her festival. We may also note that the eating of cereal fruit is forbidden to Cybele's priests.[96] In her myths trees and flowers grow from spilled blood rather than from planted seeds.

The goddess, who was venerated in lonely forests even after splendid temples were erected in her honor, who was worshipped in Pessinus in the form of an unhewn stone, who did not join a family shaped on a human model, stands for the exaltation of irrationality, for the triumph of the monstrous and nonhuman, for a trust in magic rather than the skills of men. Her rites and myths enshrine the heritage of very archaic times, even though they were recorded and enacted in urban societies and in centers of urban refinement and intellectual endeavor. She became the goddess of the extraordinary experiences of life, of the transports and the ecstasy by which mortals try to transcend their human limitations.

We may wonder why the elements of an archaic faith still found expression in a highly developed society. We find the answer if we realize that religious beliefs do not ever fully die. Even in their mastery of nature, men are still helpless in the face of certain forces. At the heart of mystery religions lies the concern with death, which cannot be defeated by human ingenuity and strength. And the desire for a merging with the infinite has stayed alive in human consciousness through the ages.

The powers of Cybele came to extend over many areas in the course of time: warfare, agriculture, protection of cities, and fertility. Yet in her persona she became less integrated in society than other godheads of this study. She did not enter a family relationship but stayed, like her priests, at the edge of the human community. She remained a Lady of the Wilderness, deeply allied with the craft and techniques of the magician. While in a place like Mesopotamia, human activity was admired and respected, Cybele stayed aloof and was repelled by the human way of giving birth and by the social custom of marriage. She was significant because she could assuage the need to rise above the human condition. She is frequently cited as an important form of the great sovereign Mother. While Cybele is sovereign in her realm, no creature could be further from the celebration of biological motherhood, and the title Magna Mater surely designates her as a great queen.

Demeter, the Ravished Earth: Greece

T HE earliest farming communities of Greece are dated to the seventh
millennium B.C.E. and were centered in the fertile regions. A truly splendid civilization originated in the third millennium on the island of
Crete, dazzling in its sophistication and accomplishments, and closely related
to a similar, somewhat later culture on the mainland. The two groups share
so many common elements that they are designated in conjunction with one
another as Minoan-Mycenaean civilization.

At about 1200 B.C.E. a catastrophe broke in upon the villages and towns
of Greece, caused possibly by invading forces. The inhabitants, driven from
their homes, lost their systems of government and their cultural achievements. By about 800 B.C.E. the turmoil abated. We do not know how much
of the Minoan-Mycenaean heritage was lost in the centuries of dispersion. We
do know that names of important deities had survived the wreckage (Zeus,
Hera, Poseidon).[1] In the succeeding era the Greeks received the craft of al-
phabetic writing from the Mediterranean states and henceforth were able to
transmit to posterity the glory of their intellectual endeavors.

GREEK RELIGION

Since Greek religious traditions do not reach us through a set of sacred writings, we meet them through the media of literature, sholarship, and art: the
poetry of Homer or Pindar, the works of Hesiod, the sculpture of Greek tem-

ples, or the paintings on Greek artifacts. The superhuman forms and figures therefore bear a double image, as expression of Greek piety and as products of artistic creativity. In learning about Greek religion we thus receive with the information the awe and impact of an aesthetic experience.

Religious forms and beliefs inevitably bear the imprint of the harsh reality of early life on earth, the fear and horror of creatures placed in a merciless environment, and the violence and bloodshed by which survival was achieved.[2] Greek mythology and rites clearly testify to the grimness of the human experience, for tales of rape and castration, of the demand for a victim's blood, of eating human flesh, or killing a child or a father are often told.[3] In other traditions a priestly class might have concealed or refined the raw facts of existence; in the culture of the Eskimo, conversely, human anguish surely left its mark upon the myths. Yet these did not reach us through Inuit artistic creativity, recorded as they were by Christian explorers.

The poignancy and haunting power of the expressions of Greek faith lie in their bipolarity, in the revelation of the gap between the luminous attainments and the wild roots from which these grew.[4] We are shocked and shaken both by the grim nature of the contents and by the beauty of the form.[5] I intend to show in the following examples how the ancient themes have stayed alive in their new frames.

The Sacrifice

The central rite of religious festivals, the essential act that establishes sacrality, is almost always the ceremonious killing of a beast. The Greek act of sacrifice was governed by many rules. Garlanded and with gilded horns the animal was taken by a festive crowd amidst the sound of music to its death. Men and women purified themselves before the blazing fire of the altar. The women shrieked loudly when the deadly blow was dealt, and then the blood was captured and sprinkled on the stone.

In a prescribed manner the carcass was divided and roasted in the fire to be consumed by the faithful in a sacrificial meal. The bones, skin, and sometimes the gallbladder, were placed into the flames so that the gods would also have their share.[6] There was indication in the ritual that the beast had willed its death.[7]

The scenario of the Greek sacrifice parallels the scenario and recalls the themes of the festivals of hunting societies after the slaying of a dangerous beast. In both events we encounter the joyous procession that leads the victim in its midst, the pretence of innocence, the honor rendered to the creature, the special treatment of the bones (hunters believe that from these the beast will be resurrected). In both events the preparations end in the rousing enjoyment of a festive meal. We may understand that the farmers and urban dwellers of Greece enshrined in their traditions the act of bloodshed and the attendant emotions of shock, fear, guilt, and exultation that had been central in primordial communal life.[8]

The themes of death and murder and ensuing guilt, of devouring one's victim, so frequent in Greek myth though motivated in various ways and often punished, may be traced to the central importance of inflicting death in archaic belief. The Greeks tell, for instance, of Zeus fettering his father Kronos, of Kronos devouring his children, of Semele perishing in Zeus's embrace, of Dionysus torn to pieces and eaten by the Titans, of Tantalos killing his own son and setting the flesh as a meal before the dwellers of Olympus.

The Sacred Places

In accordance with the central significance of the sacrifice, the altar and its sacrificial flame formed the most important portion of the temple. It might be represented by a rock, a structure built of brick and mortar, or a mound rising from the ashes of past offerings.[9]

The altar stood within the *temenos,* the sacred area marked off from its surroundings by a wall. In most sanctuaries a structure housed the cult image of the god, which might rest on a pedestal next to the table for votive gifts; often a lamp would burn before the godhead.[10] In time the image of the god, earlier carved in wood, became more splendid, cast in bronze or shaped in marble, or in its most luxurious form, in ivory and gold. It was known, however, that these latter were human creations and not the gods themselves, and devotion might still be directed to the older wooden form.[11]

While devotional gifts heaped up before the statues in their beauty, the sacred action, the shattering experience that welded humans into a community, still took place before the altar where blood was spattered on the stone and the fragrant vapor of roasting meat would rise to the sky.

Festivals

In Athens the Arrephoria, a feast performed by girls, marked the end of the service of Athena. The girls were to go at night to a place outside of the city and deposit in an underground chamber a basket holding an unknown and mysterious load. The rite commemorated the mythical event in which three girls were entrusted by Athena with a basket that they were forbidden to unseal. When they disobeyed the order they found the child Erichthonius, and a huge snake rolled toward them in threatening coils. They were overcome with horror and fell to their death from the steep cliff.

Erichthonius was the child of the virgin goddess. Athena had been pursued in lust by Hephaistos, and he had come close enough to shed his seed upon her thigh. The piece of wool that was used to wipe the seed from her body was thrown by the goddess to the ground, and from this grew the child.[12]

We thus find that Athena, a goddess of calm rationality, was subjected to the violence of sexual desire, acquired a son through monstrous birth, and unleashed a horror which brought death. And this tale was commemorated in a city of culture and political enlightenment.

The Peloponnese town of Olympia offered its site to the performance of contests and of games. Dedicated to the display of manly excellence and attracting participants from all areas of Greece, it became the symbol of Panhellenic unity.[13] In a sacred grove rose one of the finest of Greek temples, housing Phidias's statue of Olympic Zeus. Yet as many sacrifices as were rendered to Zeus where also rendered to a very different being.

The sanctuary of Pelops, the ancestor of the inhabitants, lay close to the temple.[14] In his myth Pelops was murdered by his father Tantalos, and the flesh of his body was cooked and set before the gods. The gods, however, reassembled his bones, so that Pelops returned to life. His bones are enshrined in a sanctuary of Artemis in the vicinity. And thus Olympia, the site of human striving and achievement, fully remembers the archaic tale of savage violence and crushing guilt.

Around the mystery religions systems of abstract thought developed that were concerned with spiritual matters, such as the fate of the soul after death, and the initiates might lead a life of ascetic austerity. The members of the Orphic sect,[15] dedicated to inner growth and searching thought, still retained as their foundation a tale of violence and deep sin: Demeter was raped by her son Zeus, and she bore the child Persephone, who, in turn, was violated by her father and gave birth to Dionysus. When still a child, Dionysus was killed, torn to pieces, cooked, and eaten by the Titans. In his wrath Zeus destroyed the Titans with his thunderbolt and restored the life of Dionysus.[16]

The Gods

We know that in complex societies the spiritual leaders shape a divine family out of a bewildering variety of local gods, the Lords of the forest and the household, the tutelary spirits, and the goddesses of women. In Greece it was above all through Homer and Hesiod that the gods, as we know, them received their forms.[17] And, as noted elsewhere in Greek tradition, archaic features might stay with a figure through the ages of its refinement.

Zeus, who had become the god of supplicants as Zeus Hikesios, and of the laws of hospitality as Zeus Xenios, might still be visualized as lightning and as rain.[18] Portrayed by sculptors in manliness and noble majesty, Zeus might change his form in the manner of a shaman to become a bull, a cuckoo, or a swan.[19] Apollo, the god of the measured chords and the harmony of music, would produce his truth through the incoherent words of a raving woman in his Delphic temple. The goddess Hera was the patroness of legal marriage, but she conceived without sexual encounter and brought forth a monster that threatened the social order.[20]

Some archaic deities might also merge with another and sometimes incongruous form. The function of the deities of childbirth was exercised by Artemis, the mistress of the wilderness, and by Hera who in myth is cruel in her persecution of birth-giving mothers and the newborn child.[21] Demeter, whose love and sorrow were commemorated in the poetic cadences of a Homeric Hymn and who offered a glimpse of eternity to the initiates of her mysteries, retained her form and function as the nourishing, fruit-bearing earth.

THE GODDESS DEMETER

Demeter was of such importance that her festival, the Thesmophoria, was the most honored of all Greek celebrations, and that her mysteries at Eleusis were attended by men and women from all areas of Greece and, later, of the Roman world. Her name has not been successfully interpreted: The second part clearly means "mother"; the first segment, *de-,* was related to the Cretan word for barley, or to a Greek word for earth; however, neither derivation is linguistically convincing.[22] Homer and Hesiod mention the goddess only fleetingly; her image is most clearly rendered through the vividness and poignancy of a Homeric Hymn dated to the seventh century.[23]

The Myths

Homer uses the image of the "sacred threshing floor" where "yellow Demeter sifts the corn from the chaff on the hurrying blasts."[24] Hesiod notes that her daughter was taken from her by Aides.[25] The Iliad also states that the fair-haired Demeter was among the women loved by Zeus.[26]

The Homeric Hymn allows us the fullest vision of the fair-haired goddess. It relates that Demeter's daughter, Persephone, also known as Kore, was gathering flowers on the Nysan Plain, that the earth gaped open as she was about to pluck an especially fragrant blossom, that she was seized by Hades, and that her mother heard the girl's despairing cry. With flaming torches Demeter sped in anguish "over the dry land and the sea" to search for her beloved child. After she was told the circumstances of her daughter's disappearance, she left in anger the assembly of the gods to go wandering among mortals. Arriving in "rocky Eleusis," she rested near the maiden's well and showed herself to the inhabitants in the form of an old woman. She then stayed in the royal palace to nurse the late-born child of the queen until she was disturbed in her attempt to bestow on him eternal life. Again she rose in fury, and revealing the full glory of her divinity, she demanded that a temple be erected for her.

Into this edifice she withdrew, and in her bitterness "she fashioned a savage year for mankind over all the nourishing earth," for she did not allow the planted seed to sprout, "and much white barley fell in vain to the ground," as she sat yearning for her daughter. She did not give way to the messengers of Zeus, come to soothe her, until the ruler of the gods commanded Hades to release his prize. Demeter's sorrow turned to overflowing joy when she beheld the maid and once again could hold her in embrace. Afterward the earth began to bloom and soon was laden with the ripening fruit. Demeter taught the rites of her mysteries to the princes of Eleusis and then ascended to join the assembled gods on Mount Olympus.[27]

A different kind of Demeter emerges in Arcadia. Pausanias tells us that an image of the goddess with a horse's head had once been worshipped in a cave near the town of Phigalia. Into this cave the goddess had withdrawn in wrath, for she had been ravished by Poseidon of the sea while she was searching for her child. As long as the goddess stayed away, the earth lay barren; seeds did not germinate, buds did not open into blossoms, and people were wasted by their hunger. The gods desperately tried to find the vanished deity; she was finally discovered by goat-footed Pan. She gave in to persuasion and returned to restore the fruitfulness of fields and meadows. In this form she was offered unbloody gifts—fruit, honeycombs, or uncarded wool—placed on votive tables before her cave, and she was designated as Demeter Melaina—Black Demeter.[28]

In Thelpusa of Arcadia, Demeter changed into a mare to escape the embrace of Poseidon, but transforming himself into a stallion, he raped her and begot on her the horse Areion as well as a daughter whose name was not to be revealed. Demeter became enraged, and she was honored in Thelpusa as Demeter Erinys (angry Demeter), though according to Pausanias, she was gentled after bathing in the river Ladon. A coin of the fourth century depicts the angry divinity wild-eyed and with hair coiling snakelike around her head; the other side of the coin shows the horse Areion.[29] In the tradition of Lykosura the fruit of the union of Demeter and Poseidon, a daughter, bore the name Despoina.[30]

Another of her lovers, however, Demeter met not in anger but in tenderness, and she lay with him in a thrice-ploughed furrow, and later bore the child Ploutos (wealth).[31] Yet another ravished and wrathful Demeter comes before us in an account by Clement of Alexandria in which she is raped by her son Zeus and gives birth to the child Persephone.[32]

The stories of Demeter contain the recurrent motifs of ravishment and anger and of the disappearance and return of the earth's fruit. The Lord of the Sky, Zeus, the Lord of the Ocean, Poseidon, the Lord of the Underworld, Hades, violated the goddess or her child. It is significant that the withering of the harvest is caused by Demeter's wrath, not by her sorrow.

Cultic Worship

Demeter's festival, the Thesmophoria, was widely observed. We know most about the Athenian form, and we may assume that there existed an essential similarity between the various celebrations. The ritual was performed by women only, and they fiercely guarded the secrecy of their communal gatherings. It was told that the women of Kyrene, their faces stained with blood, castrated a man who had come to spy.[33] During the three days of the Athenian festival the women would leave husbands and households, and bringing the sacred utensils of the ritual, they would gather in the sanctuary of the goddess.

Their most striking act was the casting of live piglets into the *megaron,* which was a cleft or chasm in the earth or a manmade excavation.[34] Other "ineffable" sacred objects, replicas of male organs and snakes shaped in dough and pine branches with their cones, were also thrown into the pit. Especially selected women would bring up the remnants of decayed flesh (of last year's festival?), for these, mixed with the seeds of the autumn planting, would bring rich harvests to the farmer.[35] The custom, so it is explained, was performed in memory of the herd of swine of Euboleus that sank into the earth when it split open to receive Persephone.[36]

The second day of the feast was filled with gloom and sadness, the women fasting and sitting on the ground in remembrance of Demeter's bereavement. And as Demeter's sorrow turned to joy, so the celebrations ended with a life-affirming festive meal and a sacrifice to Kalligeneia who "gives fair offspring" or who "gives good birth."[37] Lascivious and sexually charged speech was exchanged by the women in the ritual action, and this has been related by modern scholars to the jesting of a servant maid of the Homeric Hymn, whose jokes and jibes dispelled the sadness of the goddess, and to the promotion of fruitfulness of women.[38]

The concerns of the Thesmophoria are clearly with agricultural fertility and the functions of women's lives. We recognize a kinship of the Greek celebration with women's religious expressions of the North Eurasian cultures. The women worship their own special godheads devoted to their needs, and they exclude men from the ritual. In some villages, we may recall, a woman's feast is held for the Mistress of the Field to promote the harvest, and women are allowed to strike men with sticks and poles if they come to close to their activity. Demeter, in whose honor the Thesmophoria are enacted, is surely a woman's goddess.

The Mysteries

The town Eleusis, where according to some traditions the first stalks of grain had risen above the ground, lies at a distance of about thirty kilometers from Athens. Here the secret rites of Demeter were enacted from the time of the earliest documented evidence (the Homeric Hymn of the seventh century) to the time of destruction of the sanctuary by the Gothic hordes of Alaric in 396 C.E. The sanctity of the site, however, predates by far the time of the Homeric Hymn.[39] Archaeologists ascribe the first temple structure, a rectangular room with a portico, to early Helladic time (1600–1400 B.C.E.). The rocky and fortified settlement was ruled by the kings or priests of Eleusis, who later were defeated by the mightier Athenians.[40]

Revelation of the mysteries was punishable by death, and their secrecy was guarded loyally by the faithful; it is only through the indiscretion of disbelievers, such as the Christian Clement, that we gain some, possibly authentic, glimpses into the forbidden realm. The festival, held in the middle of September, was open to men, women, slaves, and foreigners, and its ritual entailed the sacrifice of an animal, which was in this case a pig. The ceremonies in the mystery hall led, as we know, beyond the bloody deed toward events and performances that would grant spiritual salvation through eternity to the ador-ant. The Hymn thus asserts: "Happy is he among earth-dwelling men who sees them; but whoever is not initiated in these secret rites and has no part in them never has a share in similar good things once he is dead and beneath the misty darkness."[41]

The *mystes* declared, according to Clement, that he had fasted, had drunk the *kykeon* (a drink made of barley, which had also been drunk by Demeter in her tiredness), had taken objects from a sacred basket, had worked them and returned them to their place.[42] We do not know what these "objects" were, possibly tools for preparing the *kykeon,* possibly, as it is hinted, entities of a sexual nature. The indiscretion of another Christian relates that at the high point of the ritual a single ear of grain was solemnly revealed and that the birth of a "holy" child was announced by the priest: "The Mistress has given birth to a sacred boy; Brimo to Brimos."[43]

Even the iconography does not tell us what shattering events took place in the light of torches and amidst the sounds of brazen gongs. Could it have been the performance of a play, actions evoking fear and horror, or simply the combined effect of darkness changing to the sudden light of blazing fire, of the previous dances and the previous fast, or the infectiousness of shared emotions?[44]

Obviously we know more of the public part of the celebrations: the bathing in the sea, the nine days' preparatory fast, the festive crowd that walked, danc-ing and uttering ecstatic cries, from Athens to Eleusis in remembrance of Demeter's wandering in search of her daughter.[45]

It is clear that a goddess of Demeter's stature was adored in mysteries and public festivals in many places and in many forms, such as Demeter Chthonia (Demeter of the earth) in Hermione, as Demeter Chloe (the verdant Demeter) in Athens, as Demeter Megalartos (Demeter of the big loaf) in Delphi. We may also assume that in the extension of her cult throughout the provinces of Greece she would merge with and absorb features of the local deity.[46]

ASPECTS OF DEMETER

Agricultural Goddess

Most conspicuous of her qualities is her relation to the produce of the soil. Hesiod admonishes the farmer to pray to 'Holy' Demeter and to Zeus Chthon-ius when he plants his seeds, "in order that Demeter's holy grain when ripe may yield a heavy crop."[47] Homer pictures the blonde goddess on the thresh-ing floor where she separates the fruit from the chaff. The reapers' harvest songs are called Demetro-ouloi, "and they call both the fruit and the reapers' songs in honour of the goddess."[48] In Cypros the labor of the harvest is called *damatrizein,* and the month of sowing is named Damatrios by the Boeotians. In agricultural festivals, such as the Thalysia, offerings are rendered to the goddess,[49] and the putrefied remnants of the sacrifical victims of the Thesmophoria are mixed with the autumnal seed.

The *kykeon,* made of barley, is sacred to the deity, and a stalk of grain is lifted at the high moment of her mysteries. Her cult image, an unhewn stone, stands in the Rarian Plain of Eleusis where the first grain was sown, and she sends Triptolemos with ears of grain to foreign lands. She herself holds, in her images, stalks of poppy and of grain. In the Homeric Hymn she has sovereign powers, not given to another divinity, of granting or withholding the produce of the earth. A number of her cult names testify to this power of the goddess; she is thus named Karpophoros (she who brings up fruit), Eualosia (she who fills the threshing barn), Himalia (she who surfeits with an abundance of food), and Megalartos (she of the big loaf) (Figure 42).[50]

The Lady of the Beasts

The cult image of Demeter Melaina at Phigalia was fitted with a horse's head and mane. Transformed into a mare, she mated with a stallion (Poseidon) and gave birth to a famous horse in the tradition of Thelpusa. Female terra-cotta figures of Roman times with the heads of cows and sheep were discovered in the sanctuary of Lykosura. And here a sacred hind is stationed behind the figure of Despoina.[51]

In the cited instances, Demeter appears as Mistress of Animals (especially horses), a role, usually held by Artemis in Greek religion. That Demeter had been worshipped in a cave points to her relationship with untamed nature, to a function of the Lady of the Wilderness. We may assume that in this form Demeter had fused with a divinity of local faith.

Demeter as a Women's Goddess

The Thesmophoria, as noted earlier, were women's feasts, and women predominated also in other Demeter celebrations, such as the Haloa.[52] The presence of men was accepted in the temple of Despoina at Megalopolis only once a year.[53] The roots of this exclusiveness may reach back to archaic forms of society when men and women worshipped separate gods. Women's goddesses were concerned with childbirth, with caring for the young, with women's crafts, and possibly with sexuality.

In the Thesmophoria a sacrifice was rendered to Kalligeneia, "she who gives fair offspring" or "who gives good birth." In the Homeric Hymn Demeter served as nurse to the queen's son, an episode that is not intrinsic to the story, and we may suspect that it was added to enshrine Demeter's aspect of divine nurse. A local legend of Lebadeia made her the nurse of Trophonius.[54] Certain epithets show her relationship to children: *paidophile* or *paidoteknos* (cherishing children).[55]

Figure 42. (*Above*) Sending out of Triptolemos; skyphos painted by Hieron, about 480 B.C.E. Figure 43. (*Below*) Terra-cotta Baubo figure from Priene, fifth century B.C.E.

Ribald jests and speeches were exchanged by the participants of the Thesmophoria in Athens; in Syracuse cakes made with sesame and honey in the form of a cunnus (female sex organ) were baked as offerings to Demeter;[56] a cunnus (of clay?) was dedicated to Demeter in Epidaurus.[57] When Demeter sat in silence and dejection, she was cheered by the jests of a serving maid, according to the Homeric Hymn. The poem does not state the nature of these jests, but we know a variant form of the same episode, transmitted by the Orphic tradition; in this the goddess, unable in her sadness to drink the *Kykeon* offered by her hostess Baubo, is delivered from her gloom when Baubo shows her private parts. These are in the likeness of an infant's face.[58] Statuettes depicting a woman's legs that end up in a woman's face were found in Demeter's sanctuary in Priene (Figure 43).[59]

Scholars link this concern with sexuality, especially female sexuality, with the wish to bear children. In archaic belief, however, sexual potency need not be restricted to procreation. The women of archaic hunting societies are banned from the site of the pursuit of game. Yet the hunting men are frequently pictured in their aggressive manhood, their organs huge and erect. It is as if their virility and strength were to be gathered to the noblest of all goals: the bagging of the reindeer and the bear.

Sexual restraints were placed on women before they undertook the sacred action of the Thesmophoria. Demeter, to whom a cunnus may be offered in piety, is often designated as *hagne* (chaste). The power of the female sexual organ was clearly demonstrated when Baubo bared her vulva to the goddess; it did not increase Demeter's childbearing ability, but it dealt a liberating blow to the evil force of her gloom. It thus performed a cleansing, apotropaic deed. Analogues to Baubo's action are found around the world.[60] Especially noteworthy are sculptures of hags fastened onto edifices of the Irish or English countryside, especially churches, hags who bare their vulva between widely separated legs to ward off the evil spirits from the house of god.[61]

It is natural that a woman's group would include among its rites those that would strengthen and affirm the magic power of female sexuality. It appears that the sexually directed action in Demeter's service belongs to the rites of female sexual magic though undoubtedly neither the faithful nor the commentators on the rites were still conscious of this function.

Relation to Death

In Hermione Demeter was adored as Chthonia. In her sanctuary a pathway led to the realm of death. The temple of Klymenos, the Lord of Death, lay opposite the temple of the goddess.[62] According to a decree ascribed to Lykurgos, the citizens of Sparta were urged to end their mourning on the twelfth day after death with a sacrifice to Demeter.[63] The Plutonium, sanctuary of the god of Death, was placed within the sacred precinct of Demeter in Eleusis, and here also an entrance opened into the underworld.[64] And the Athenians called the dead *demetreioi* (Demeter's folk) and sowed grain upon their graves.[65] Since Persephone, Demeter's daughter, is the Mistress of the Dead, the goddess retains through her a connection with the nether realms.

Anguish and fears concerning death and questions concerning human existence in the world of shadows are central to the mysteries of Eleusis. As mistress of the rites Demeter becomes the force through which a transcendental vision is achieved. "Blessed is he who, after beholding this, enters upon the way beneath the earth: he knows the end of life and its beginning, given by Zeus"; so Pindar stated.[66] And thus the goddess here obtained a new dimension as guide and helper in human quest, a divinity not only of death but also of the defeat of death.

In the Homeric Hymn she attempts to bestow immortality on the young prince. Even though she is thwarted in her effort, she is shown in the poem in her ability to grant eternal life. The goddess acquired her relation to death and afterlife when she was given a new dimension: Representing the earth of agriculture, she came to represent to some extent the earth that holds the dead.

The Culture Bringer

After Demeter's wrath had been assuaged, she revealed the secrets of her rites to the princes of Eleusis, to "Triptolemus and to Diocles the horse driver and to Eumoplus and to strong Celeus, the leader of the people." In pictorial representations Triptolemus is singled out as the one who receives the gift of grain from the goddess or the goddesses and who is ready in his winged chariot to spread the knowledge and the hope throughout the world.[67] "It is due to Demeter," Isocrates declares, "that men rose from a more primitive and beastlike state to enjoy the hope of a happy afterlife and the fruits of the field." Himerius speaks of Demeter's gift of corn and of the mysteries as the greatest benefit conferred on archaic peoples. And Diodorus Siculus asserts that grain was first brought by Demeter to Sicily, then to Athens, and from the Athenians others received it until the entire earth was brought under the plow (Figure 44).[68]

According to a local legend of the Argives, recorded by Pausanias, Demeter offered her gifts in gratitude because in Argos she had received hospitality from Pelasgos, who also told her of the circumstances of Kore's fate. According to an Orphic poem, the goddess had entered the dwelling of Baubo and Dysaules in Eleusis and showed them in thankfulness the ways of planting and reaping.[69]

In the instances of this section the role and function of Demeter have shifted from that of other versions of her adventures. Not restoring the order and the rhythmic flow of nature, she acts as innovator and creator, for grain had not existed for the ease and happiness of men before she came. Since tales of growing the first grain are later than the Homeric Hymn, Fritz Graf believes that in these the basic function had been altered.[70] But we don't know

Figure 44. Demeter with ears of corn; inside of cup; around 450 B.C.E.

Figure 45. Demeter and Kore; terra-cotta from Thebes; about 620–600 B.C.E.

the age of the tradition transmitted by the later tales. If, as one informant has it, an ear of corn rises in glorious epiphany before the *mystes* at Eleusis at the most important moment of the festival, then here also the appearance, the origin, and the creation of the fruit are celebrated. And then even in her mysteries two (contradictory) aspects of the goddess—one who restores and one who creates—would have been revealed.

MYTHICAL THEMES ATTACHED TO DEMETER

Withdrawal and Return

During the time of Kore's absence the earth lies bare and wasted, and the bloom of nature is restored only with the happiness of her return. The sequence will repeat itself, according to the Hymn; for every year, the girl will have to spend four months with her husband beneath the earth. Already in ancient time these events were thought to symbolize the yearly withering and growth of vegetation. A closer examination of the material shows a somewhat different web of relations.

The space of time of the loss of vegetation does not coincide in the Greek provinces with the time of absence of the girl.[71] We may also note that the barren season is not initiated by Kore's plunge. After the girl was seized, the goddess "sped like a wild bird" without tasting food or drink for nine days, until she heard the awful truth. She wandered yet more time among humans and then came to Eleusis where she stayed to nurse the prince. It was only after she withdrew to her temple that the earth began to waste. Thus it was not Kore's capture but Demeter's retreat that caused the blight; nor did Kore's ascension restore the bloom. This was brought back at a later moment by a soothed and gentled Demeter. When she was asked by her own mother Rhea to forgo her wrath, "Fair-crowned Demeter did not disobey, but sent the fruit up again on the rich lands." In the same manner life withered when Black Demeter stayed in anger in her cave in Phigalia, and life was restored with her return.

It is Demeter, rather than Persephone, who may be ranged with other "disappearing" gods. This "disappearance" always brings disaster to the world. When the Hittite god Telipinu hid in anger, the fields lay barren and the wells ran dry and women could not give birth to children until he reentered the community of gods.[72] When the goddess Ishtar turned her steps to the lower regions, all sexual desire ceased among men and beasts, so that the ass would no longer mount the jenny and men would no longer embrace their wives. She too was, with much toil and trouble, brought back to the living.[73] When Amaterasu of the Japanese closed the door of her retreat, the world lost its celestial light. The tale of the hidden or lost divinity thus voices a concern that goes beyond the worry about next year's crop: that of a catastrophic break in cosmic order.

The Mourning Goddess

The figure of the anguished Demeter finds analogues in other lands, usually envisaged in female form. When the Canaanite goddess Anat loses her brother she

> wanders in mourning o'er the upland,
> . . . cheeks and shin she gashes;

she scores the forepart of her arm;
... She lifts her voice and cries: Baal is dead![74]

This goddess is, surprisingly, as deeply hurt by the death of a youth whom she herself had caused to die. Inanna of Sumer weeps for her husband Dumuzi: "Gone is my husband,/ Gone is my love, my sweet love ... My beloved bridegroom has been taken."[75] She too had sent the same Dumuzi to his death, according to another poem. Dumuzi's mother wails for her beloved son, her "heart plays a reed pipe of dirges, for him in the desert ... where the lad dwelt ... he who is captive ... where Dumuzi dwelt."[76] The goddess Ninhursag laments the fate of her son, a wild donkey, who was taken from her by human hands. Maddened by her grief for Attis, Cybele rushes through the forests; and yet it was through her that he had died. The goddess Freyja of Germanic myth seeks her lost husband, wandering through many lands and shedding golden tears in her journey.[77]

It appears that sorrowing or wailing were thought to be a woman's business. It may be that the wailing of the goddess has a counterpart in ritual lamentations, as for instance in the "weeping for Adonis (or Tammuz)," performed by women of Greek and Semitic communities.[78] The lamenting goddesses are, as we have seen, by no means always gentle creatures.

The Ravished Goddess

The abduction of Persephone is central to Demeter's tale. But the goddess herself had suffered the invasion of her womanhood, for Zeus as well as Poseidon had, in varying accounts, worked their will upon the blonde divinity; and every time she had responded with her wrath. Incidents of rape are numerous in Greek myth, and they usually cause the birth of an important being, such as Arcas, the ancestor of the Arcadians, through the rape of Callisto; Perseus, the founder of Mycenae and the son of Danae; or Epaphos, the ancestor of the Danai, who was born because Io had been violated.[79] Since the union is so fruitful the action does not seem to be condemned.

The fate of the Sumerian maiden Ninlil shows some resemblance to Kore's experience. She was the daughter of Nunbarsegunn, and her maidenhood was taken by the tempestuous Enlil as she was bathing in a canal. For this misdemeanor the other gods banished the offender to the netherworld. The girl, being pregnant, followed her husband to the lower regions and was seduced in her journey several more times by the same divinity. Of the children begotten in these unions several stayed in the underworld and one of them, the moon god Nanna, rose to heaven. The tale serves to explain the creation of various gods and in no way points to expressions of anger or anguish by either mother or maid.[80]

The strong reaction of the Eleusinian divinities to the sexual aggression of a superior god is unusual in myth. It may be that the status of Demeter as Olympic goddess forbade the forcing of the woman (the goddess Ishtar, who was violated in her sleep, also reacted with great anger). It may also be that the act of rape served as a motivation for Demeter's aspect as an angry goddess.

Demeter's Wrath

The love and sorrow of Demeter are poignantly depicted in the Hymn: Demeter speeding like one demented through the land, sitting in speechless grief on a stool in the king's palace, wasting away with yearning in her temple, and clasping the returned Persephone in tenderness and joy. And Demeter has been called the Mater Dolorosa of Greek mythology. It is not, however, by sorrow but by anger that Demeter is moved to her decisive action. Her sorrow surely commences with the disappearance of her child and is terminated with her return. But it is Demeter's anger on hearing the truth that makes her leave the dwelling of the gods. In her anger she withdraws from the palace to her temple "on the rising hill"; not the ceasing of her sorrow but the soothing words of her mother cause her to restore the wasted earth. So that "she would put aside her anger," Zeus finally decides on sending back the girl. And Zeus's messenger orders Hades to release his bride so that "her mother when she sees her with her eyes, will desist from her terrible wrath against the gods."

The fury of the goddess, casting her royal nursling to the ground, induces a paralyzing terror in the queen and fear and trembling in the other members of the household. "All night, quaking with fear, they sought to appease the glorious goddess." The wrath of the goddess and its effects are also manifest in her Arcadian form. She must be soothed and persuaded in Phigalia to restore the flow of life. The Angry Demeter of Thelpusa grows mild after bathing in a river. Surely one of the basic themes of Demeter's tales is of the rising and the fading of her wrath.

It is in its effective action on nature and on men, its power to cause catastrophe or bring salvation, that a force is experienced as divinity. Since Demeter's actions are determined by the rise or ebb of her wrath, it is as a furious or a soothed goddess that she is a figure of belief. The beautiful and haunting vision of the sorrowful mother would be born in artistic and poetic creativity. It would be related to the earlier shape as the statue of Athena Parthenos by Phidias, in its splendor, is related to the older wooden *xoanon;* it was the older image for which every year a new garment would be woven by the pious.[81]

It is only natural that the figure of poetry would touch us more profoundly and impress itself more deeply in our memory than the earlier figure of belief. It is also true that the poetic elaboration added a new and lasting dimension to the goddess. The tradition of Demeter illustrates a characteristic of Greek religion that was earlier discussed: an older basic form is clearly visible in a sophisticated setting. The force that fills mortals' stomachs is still present in the noble and mournful divinity of the Hymn.

Demeter and Her Daughter

Some scholars believe that the story of the mother goddess and her daughter gives voice to an *Urerlebnis:* the mother-daughter pair suffering male intrusion into their sphere of tenderness and care.[82] If this pattern were primary and basic, it would consistently show two actors fixed in some measure in their roles: one experiencing aggression and the other loss, one violated and the other anguished. We have noted, however, that many events of Kore's life happen also to her mother. Like her daughter, Demeter suffers male aggressiveness; she herself has vanished and returned; she ascends Mount Olympus to join the assembled gods, paralleling Persephone's ascension from the underworld; and in one version Demeter herself descends to the regions of the dead.[83] The Roman Tertullian speaks of the rape of Ceres, and Servius of her marriage to the god Orcus in the realm of death.[84]

Cult practices show the two deities in great resemblance to one another. They were designates as the Great Goddesses in Megalopolis, as Thesmophoroi in Athens and in Syracuse, as the "two goddesses" in Eleusis, as Despoinas in Lykosura. The two may be worshipped side by side; thus there is reference to the "holy altars of Demeter and Kore" in the fields of Eleusis.[85] Pictural representations frequently draw them in great resemblance to one another (Figure 45).[86] In some places the daughter appears more important than the mother, as in Lykosura, and in others each may stand alone.[87]

The roles of the two deities clearly are not firmly fixed. It is true that boundary lines in mythology and cult are fluid, and that even the earliest references know Demeter as Kore's mother. It might therefore be argued that the members of the archetypal pair had, in the course of time, coalesced or grown away from one another (such a process surely did not take place with Inanna and Dumuzi, Attis and Cybele, Venus and Adonis). If, however, the union of mother and daughter, forged by the power of love, had existed as a widespread and primordial pattern, it would exist in various societies. The love of the Greek goddess for her daughter stands alone. The folklore figures of the Cornmother and Cornmaiden have been cited as analogues, but these beings, even if they could be called divinities, do not interact with one another. Moreover, if Demeter's function as a mother in her love and sorrow had been primary, it would have left its mark on Greek speech and would have given rise to epithets in the same way as did her power over agricultural fertility.[88] Demeter and Kore are, to some extent, parallel divinities.

SUGGESTED GENESIS

I suggest that Demeter, as we know her, developed in the following fashion: A powerful divinity of the growing grain acquired many new aspects as her faith spread through the provinces of Greece. She became not only the earth that holds the dead but also mistress of the human quest for salvation, a goddess of the life of women, a culture hero and creator. In some areas she fused with the local Lady of Wild Beasts. She was adored in several places as one of two, apparently, very similar divinities. She became the focal point of a number of traditional tales: of a disappearing and returning deity, of ravishment and birth, of mourning for a lost beloved.

In the last cited of the themes, Demeter was obviously in need of an object for her love. This appeared in Kore/Persephone, herself a complex being whose nature cannot be discussed fully in this study.[89] Let us merely note that she might have arisen in a fusion of the Queen of the Dead with one of the double forms of Demeter. We learn that Demeter changes age, turning in the Homeric Hymn from a crone into an epiphany of timeless beauty. We also know of an inscription that names Demeter "Maiden and Woman."[90] And we know of her epithet "verdant Demeter." The goddess seems to have presented various stages in the life of women (as did Hera). If the theme of the mourning deity called for a beloved being, the younger form of Demeter might easily become her daughter.

Many disparate bits and pieces, originated by cult and myth, were woven by the composer of the Homeric Hymn into a stirring and harmonious tale, and he created the poignant and time-transcending figure that combines the majesty and power of divinity with the deep emotions of a human woman.

RELATION TO ARCHAIC POWERS

Many instances of European folklore were adduced by Frazer and Mannhardt to prove that similar beings and a similar relation had existed in various lands. An examination of the many corn spirits, which still exist in modern times, shows them as threatening rather than kindly creatures. Appearing in many forms and with many names, such as Corn Mother, Corn Angel, Corn Wolf, Jew, and Devil, these demons are said to cower in the waving grain and to frighten and devour children. The *Kornweib* or *Zitzenweib* of East Prussia and central Germany, for instance, catches children to press and choke them against her iron bosom. Less harmful are the Corn Mother, the Old Woman, the Old Man, etc., when they represent the last sheaf of grain that was stacked at harvest time and became the object of many harvest customs, including singing, dancing, or the offering of gifts. It is still difficult to find resemblances between these fetishes and the goddess of many titles and many cults.[91] We may also observe that these spirits do not interact with one another.

It is in keeping with the method of this study to turn to the cultures of northern Eurasia in the attempt to trace a concept or a figure to its more basic form. In this reservoir of archaic traditions early types of godhead were and are still found in modern time in the context of a living faith. The area has been well explored and has been useful in previous chapters of this book in exposing the roots of later configurations. Here we find not only hunters, herders, and fishermen but also communities of early farmers. Whereas in hunting groups devotion would be rendered to the Lords and Guardians of Beasts, the planters turn in trust and hope to the fruit-giving earth, the rain-giving sky, and the waters of a river or lake. These elements are animated beings, visualized in their own form but also humanized and endowed with humanly structured families, human emotions and possessions.

Demeter corresponds in several ways to those spirits of northern Eurasia who represent the animated field of grain. There is the consistent and recurrent reference to her golden hair. In this she retained some of the physical appearance of her element, as did *linad-äma,* the Lady of the Flax, of the Erza, whose long yellow hair reaches to the ground as she wanders through her blossoming fields.[92] Like the northern spirits the Greek deity is honored with the title "mother." Sacrificial victims were cast in the Thesmophoria into a hollow in the earth. In a very similar fashion the bones of the animals sacrificed to *molanda-awa,* Mother Earth, are buried in the soil in the communities of the Mari; and the blood of the beast slain in honor of *muzjem-mumi,* the earth deity of the Udmurts, is poured into a pit dug especially for the event.[93] It is clear that in these instances the spirit is still visualized as the animated element, the earth itself, which receives within her bosom, as it were, the gifts of the devoted.

Demeter's wrath, as we know, causes disaster and despair. The northern farmer also dreads the anger of his deity. The Udmurts of the former district of Mamadysch do not like to dig in certain hills where the Mistress of the Earth is said to dwell, for they do not wish to disturb her rest. The Mordvins ask *pakś-ava* to forgive them because they might have dispersed her soil (herself) in the course of plowing. One must never hit the ground with a stick or any other object, for it is believed by the Erza that such an act would offend the Lady Earth.[94] Thus the Greek and the northern farmer are alike in their fear of the power and vengeance of the angry earth.

In her more anthropomorphic aspect the deity may dwell beneath the ground and be surrounded by her family.[95] Demeter embraced her lover Jasion in a furrow, and her daughter Persephone stays within the earth for a portion of the year.

The women of Mokshan villages gather in honor of *pakś-azorava,* the Mistress of the Fields, in her domain; a rich meal is spread upon the ground and consumed among many prayers for the bounty of the harvest. The feasting women possess the liberty to use a stick on any man who comes too close to their place of celebration. A similar ritual is enacted at sowing time for the Lady of the Grain by the women of the Mordvins.[96] We cannot fail to see the parallel to the Thesmophoria, a women's feast at the time of planting the new seed, and to the right of privacy of the ritual action.

Demeter is a complex being and shows parallels with yet other creatures of archaic faith. The goddess, helping to separate chaff from grain, her cult image standing on the threshing floor, belongs with the Threshing Barn Mothers of northern farmsteads. In her association with the underworld she shows kinship with the Mother of the Dead, such as *velu māte* or *zemes māte* of the Latvians. As Lady of the Horse and Mistress of the life of women, Demeter finds her analogues in even more archaic systems of belief. A Guardian and Master of Beasts prevails in communities of hunters, where there are also found deities that are dedicated exclusively to the biological and spiritual needs of women.

The observation of the North Eurasian farmers' fears, needs, and concerns might lead us to understand the occurrences of rape in the stories of Demeter. The work of agriculture was felt in some regions as an intrusion, as a violation of the life-sustaining Lady Earth. In the poetic and metaphoric language of Greek myth the guilt-producing labor would be transformed into the act of ravishment.

It need not be emphasized how far Demeter grew from her origins to become a helper in men's quest for spiritual growth and cultural development, nor how deeply she entered into the story matter of her Mediterranean environment. It is in keeping with what has been considered characteristic of Greek tradition, of archaic themes retained in works of high intellectual achievement, that a figure come to us in awesome beauty, created by the poet's and the sculptor's craft, should so clearly have retained aspects of her origin in the field of yellow grain (Figure 46).

We have seen that motherhood was not primordial with Demeter, the most poignant of maternal figures. She received it in her role of "mourning goddess," and it became integral to her being. Demeter, the earth that feeds living bodies, also became the earth that holds the dead, the ancestral force from which life is generated. Hence she also was a deity of women's lives and a cherisher of children. And through her closeness with the world of death she became a goddess of the mysteries. It was her experience of suffering and joy, of things lost and things reattained, and not her biological creativity that gave her power over human souls so that she could lead them from anguish to release and from fear of death to hope of eternal life.

THE GREEK GODDESSES OF WOMEN

In the hunters' world of fear and insecurity women's experiences and women's functions were enmeshed in a web of prohibitions. In this climate numina originated who are devoted exclusively to women's needs in their ritual isolation. In the more open society of the cities and communities of Greece, where women moved with greater freedom, divinities of women's needs, of childbirth and child nursing, were still highly visible and significant to allay the anxieties that surround parturition and the caring for the young. Sometimes the office was performed by specialized deities, and sometimes a great goddess would exercise this craft.

Figure 46. Demeter
Thesmophoros; Clay, Attic
period, about 450 B.C.E.

The Goddess Eileithyia

Eileithyia is the force most specifically related to the act of giving birth; thus she bears the title *mogostokos* (helper in travail) or *eukoline* (the one who softens pain).[97] Her presence is essential if a woman is to bring forth a child. The Homeric Hymn to Delian Apollo describes how Leto suffered the pangs of labor for nine days and nights because the jealous Hera kept Eileithyia with her on Mount Olympus. The goddesses who had gathered on Delos around Leto sent for the divinity of birth and promised her a golden necklace strung with amber for her help. As soon as Eileithyia set foot on the island, Leto clasped a palm tree as she knelt upon the ground. The earth smiled, Apollo was brought forth, and the goddesses emitted the "shout of birth." According to another account, the shrubs, earth, and rivers of the island turned to gold.[98]

Hera also kept the "helper in travail" from attending when Alkmene was to be delivered, thus delaying the birth of Heracles.[99] In these myths Eileithyia appears subordinated to the goddess Hera, and indeed she was, according to Hesiod and Homer, born to Zeus and Hera in the cave Amnisos on Crete.[100]

In the caves and grottoes of Crete she was worshipped through the ages; at such places as Amnisos, Patso, Krateros, and Inatos-Tsoutsouros many votive statues testify to the faith of Cretan women.[101] She was also greatly honored on Delos, where she had softened Leto's pain; here a temple was erected to her, crowded with gifts of vases, jewelry, and votive plaques of gold and silver; a yearly festival, the Eileithyeia, was celebrated, and a special hymn was sung in her worship.[102]

In images on coins and vases she raises in a characteristic gesture her hand with palms tuned upward to promote and hasten birth, and she also sometimes holds a torch.[103] Her by-name *eulinos* (the one with the good thread of life), indicates her power over the fate of the newborn child,[104] and her by-name *kourotrophos* marks her as nourisher or nurse of the young.[105] The name of the goddess occurs also in the plural so that we meet with several birth-helping spirits; thus vases frequently depict a deity in travail assisted by several Eileithyias.[106]

The divinity did not extend the narrow sphere of her activity, and she remained a minor goddess. Her function, however, was also performed by others. The goddess Hera sometimes bears the by-name Eileithyia, and the goddess Artemis and nymphs would be invoked by pregnant women.

Kourotrophos

It appears that the nurture of a child was thought to be as important as its birth, and often it was not reared by its true mother. Thus Apollo was taken by Themis from Leto, and his lips were smeared with nectar and ambrosia. The infant Zeus was snatched from Ge by Rhea, and he was nourished in a cave. Demeter nursed Damophon, the son of Keleos, king of Eleusis, and according to a Hellenistic source, she nursed Triptolemos. She nourished King Trophonius in Lebadeia.[107] According to a Theban legend, Hera gave her milk to Heracles.[108] Nymphs often took part in caring for children, as did the nymph Ino of Nysa who guarded Dionysus; nymphs are named as nurses of the infant Zeus, and three nymphs fostered Apollo.[109]

Animals may receive and raise a child. Zeus was suckled, in various accounts, by a goat, bees, a bear, or a bitch.[110] Even a monkey may hold and guard a swaddled baby, as in a votive offering of Corinth.[111] Sometimes men performed the task of caring for the young. The god Hermes was pictured with the infant Dionysus and also with the infant Heracles. Silenus was seen with Dionysus and Triton with Theseus.[112]

A Kourotrophos (nurturer of children) was in fact adored as a separate divinity and worshipped, especially in Attica. An inscription to this deity appears on an altar in Eleusis, and shrines were erected to her in the demes of Orchia, Piraeus, Sounion, and Marathon.[113] Pausanias states that her oldest cult was established on the Acropolis by Erichthonius, and a Milesian relief depicts a female divinity, inscribed as Kourotrophos, together with Leto, Apollo, and Artemis.[114] There is mention of a ritual, performed by women for

Kourotrophos, in Samos on the crossroads.[115] An inscription from Euboea in Eretria mentions a *hieron kourotrophon,* a sanctuary of the Kourotrophoi.[116]

The features of the spirit, however, remain shadowy; it is possible that she was not a separate being, but one of the goddesses cited by her epithet. The by-name Kourotrophos is held by Artemis, Ge, Hecate, Demeter, Hera, and Leto, by nymphs, and even by rivers. According to Hesiod's *Theogony,* Hecate was made by Zeus into a Kourotrophos.[117] The cult of Kourotrophos was established on the Acropolis, but only the goddess Ge Kourotrophos possesses a shrine in this site. Sacrifices to Kourotrophos took place in the sanctuaries of Artemis, Hecate, and Hera in Erchia. Votive statues of a kourotrophic nature were offered to the goddess Aphrodite in her sanctuaries in Cypros and to Artemis in Brauron.[118]

The number of incidents in which an infant is taken from its mother to be nurtured by another being does not indicate a high significance of the birth-giver. In the cases where the child is nourished by a beast, we may find an echo of the belief of hunting cultures: that a shaman (i.e., a chosen being) must be nursed by an animal.

The Moirai: Goddesses of Fate

The birth hour is also attended by the Moirai who determine the infant's fate. According to Hesiod, they were born to Zeus and Themis,[119] and they too may help or hinder parturition. We are told in a Theban narrative that the Moirai closed their hands on Hera's command and in this way delayed the birth of Heracles.[120] Hence they may bear the by-name Lochiai Moirai (the Moirai of the Childbed).[121]

The high stature accorded to these forces arises from their dreadful powers over the destiny of men. Three Moirai are named by Hesiod: Clotho, Lachesis, and Atropos, who "give mortal men evil and good to have."[122] The determination of fate is often, though not always, accomplished by the labor of spinning, so that one Moira may spin, the other wind, and the third cut the thread of life. The supremacy of the Moirai sometimes clashes with the sovereignty of the highest god, and in one instance Zeus is unable to save his son Sarpedon from his appointed death.[123]

Belief in the all-encompassing power of the Moirai remained vital through the centuries. An Orphic hymn addresses them as the "daughters of the night."[124] The dramatic poets probed man's relation with destiny, and in their plays they gave shape and expression to the agony. Folk belief retained the figures into modern time and visualized them as hags of great ugliness or as women dressed in white. As in ancient tradition they make their visit to the newly born and are received with hospitality. They may also, as in ancient time, be attendant at a wedding feast.[125]

The power of the Moirai was not meted out to other deities, and their name was not employed as epithet. Except when their ordinance conflicted with the will of Zeus, as it sometimes did, they remained the unquestioned source of good or evil destiny.

It may be argued that the Moirai should not be included among the goddesses of women's lives, that they were primarily personifications of an abstract notion and allied with childbirth only because at this time the fate of the human was decreed. We do not know which form preceded the other, but we do know that in most cultural contexts discussed here, the deity of birth is closely linked or even identified with the deity of fate. The birth-brick of the Egyptians, for instance, was personified, and the goddess, who had arisen in this way, fashioned the child's fate during gestation and announced it at its birth.[126]

Folklore retained the connection of the Moirai with marriage and birth-giving, two decisive moments in a woman's life. The spirits traditionally carry out their task through a craft that is symbolical of women's labor: the spinning of a thread. In the exercise of this craft they would clearly be classed as goddesses of women's lives.

THE GREAT GODDESSES

Artemis

Artemis is invoked by women in travail who beg her to be merciful and to visit them without her arrow.[127] And women offer her a lock of hair after their delivery.[128] As childbirth goddess she bears the by-names Lochia in Delos and Iphigeneia (of the good offspring) in Brauron. She is also named *mogostokos* and *despoina gynaikon* (ruler of women).[129]

As protector and educator of the young she is named Kourotrophos and Paidotrophos (nourisher of the young, nourisher of children).[130] In the festival of the Tithenidia in Sparta, nurses brought their charges to Artemis Kory-thalia;[131] small girls danced at her festival in Brauron;[132] and fierce fights were enacted by adolescent boys at the festival of Artemis Orthia in Sparta.[133] Homer relates her to a woman's craft by naming her *christelakatos* (the lady with the golden spindle).[134]

Hera

The goddess who "sleeps in the arms of the great Zeus" is closely allied with "the ancient ordinance of the wedding bed,"[135] with the union of marriage. The embrace of Zeus and Hera is poetically described in the *Iliad;* an erotic scene between a naked Hera and her husband is depicted on a terra-cotta relief of Hera's sanctuary on the island of Samos; and her marriage is ritually reen-acted in Knossos, according to Hereus.[136] The feast of the Daidala, held in her honor in a number of Euboean towns, contains elements of a wedding feast, such as a bridal procession and a wooden image decked out as a bride.[137]

Two statues of Hera in her temple in Plataea carry the epithets Nympheuo- mene (the one led as a bride) and Teleia (the one fulfilled [married]).[138] Three sanctuaries of Stymphalos in Arcadia honored three stages of her life: the virgin, Hera Pais; the married woman, Hera Teleia; and the separated, Hera Chera.[139]

Hera's life thus mirrors more closely than that of other goddesses the existence of mortal women, and she is the patroness of human marriages.[140] In the wedding month Gamelion, honor is rendered to her in Attica.[141] She protects the young bride and receives her veil after the ceremony is completed. As the one who "prepares the wedding," her by-name is Gamostolos.[142]

Hera is also the goddess of a woman's festival; every four years the girls and women of Olympia organized a celebration in her honor, where they engaged in footraces, resembling the athletic contests of men.[143] In various places Hera is worshipped as Eileithyia, the birth-helper, and she is able to delay or hasten birth, as in the case of Heracles and Eurystheus.[144] She gave, so it was stated earlier, the milk of her breast to Heracles, and she also nour- ished the baby Hermes (Figure 47).[145]

Hera is deeply entwined in the rhythm and the crises of a woman's life. She mirrors its various stages as virgin, woman, or "separated." She is in- volved in birth-giving, marriage, and nurture of the young; she also rules a woman's festival. It is possible to interpret her hostility and violence and her conflicts with her husband as the heritage of the mistrust and hostility be- tween men's and women's gods of primitive communities. The jealousy of Hera might be derived from the jealousy of the spirits who protect the young woman in an alien place.

Demeter

We have already noted the qualities that make Demeter a women's goddess. In many places she presided over women's festivals, above all over the secret rites of the Thesmophoria. And the bloody punishment inflicted in some tales on male intruders may recall the prohibitions of hunting cultures of male entrance into the ritual sphere of women. A sacrifice was offered in the Thes- mophoria to Kalligeneia (of the beautiful birth). Demeter, it was observed, acted as a nurse and foster mother to Damophon, Triptolemos, and Trophon- ius.[146] She bore the title Kourotrophos (nourisher of children).[147]

COMPOSITE IMAGE

Let us merely state that such goddesses as Hekate and Ge were actively en- gaged in caring for the young. The office of a woman's goddess is carried out in Greek tradition by a number of female divinities, by such specialized spirits as the Eileithyias, and by important goddesses. Of the latter, Hera is the one who is primarily allied with the stations and stages of a woman's life. The

Figure 47. *The Origin of the Milky Way* by Jacopo Tintoretto. Heracles is given suck by Hera.

office of nurturing the newly born was held by an even wider range of figures. It seems that some special virtue and benefit could be imparted to the child by a certain being that could not be offered by the woman who had given birth.

In the multifaceted society of Greece, in urban centers and in farming communities, goddesses were worshipped that have generic counterparts in the other cultures of this study. Artemis is, like Cybele of the Phrygians and the Mistress of the forest of the Moksha (*vir azerawa*), a goddess of the wild places of the world. Demeter found her origin, like the Mistress of the Earth of the Mari (*molanda awa*), in the animated field of grain. Like other earth deities, she became assimilated to the earth that holds the dead and, through this assimilation, to the creation of new life in birth. Demeter's maternal role unfolds in relation to the death and return of her daughter. In analogy to the birth-helping spirits of North Eurasian culture and the Latvian Laima, a number of birth-helping divinities attend to the Greek woman in travail.

It need not be emphasized how far the Greek deities developed beyond their basic form. Hera became the queen of Mount Olympus; she represented the essential forms of womanhood, the beauty of the maiden, the fullness of maturity, and the dignity of age. She presided over contests of female excellence that paralleled the Olympic games of the men. Demeter was cast in the haunting image of the grieving mother, and she led mortals on their initiatory journeys in her mysteries. None of these goddesses received her stature through the powers of her womb.

chapter
9

The Exaltation of Death: Mexico

T HE first inhabitants of the Americas probably arrived about 30,000 B.C.E. As they spread gradually through the vast territorial expanse they developed a great variety of cultures, as hunters and fishermen in some parts, and in others as builders of empires that could rival in sophistication the urban centers of the ancient Middle East.[1] They brought with them the hunters' heritage and developed the art of cultivating the wild seeds in the new land in probably more than one location. The techniques were improved and refined and brought forth in time a copious variety of plants, such as beans, squash, maize, cacao, tomatoes, and tobacco.

The fertile valley of Mexico, bounded by high mountain ranges and containing a lake in its center, offered its inhabitants cultivatable soil, the game of its forests, and the fowl and fish of its waters and reeded marshes. Here early peasant cultures (Zacatenco and Tícoman) expressed their religious faith through statuettes of clay shaped realistically into the forms of animals and humans.[2]

The first temple mounds were erected in La Venta, built of unbaked brick and terraced to hold a stone altar on the summit. In this tradition the animal form ascended over the human; jaguars and jaguar faces, creatures part man, part jaguar crowd the imagery, and an entire ritual scene could take place between an animal's gaping jaws.[3] Serpent forms are also apparent.

The succeeding culture of Teotihuacán continued earlier traditions, erecting its own temple mounds of even greater splendor and retaining the symbolism of jaguars and snakes.[4] The physical magnitude of the ceremonial buildings points to the power and importance of a priestly class, which tended to the needs of a farming population in an arid land. Pictures of flowing water and aquatic animals abound in religious imagery, as in the temple frescoes of Teotihuacán. The water god himself, rising from the sea, is drawn onto the walls of houses.[5] The period of Teotihuacán culture was peaceful; fortifications have not been unearthed and the images of priests were shown more frequently than those of warriors.

By about 900 C.E. the sites of this culture were abandoned and the entering Toltecs built their empire on the earlier foundations. They were a military nation, and the class of warriors rose above the class of priests. In their reign bloody sacrificial rites reached great dimensions; while the religious heritage of the earlier population was assimilated, new importance was accorded to the spheres of heaven and the stars.[6]

The rule of the Toltecs was shattered by the assaults of invading tribes from the North. Among these were the Aztecs who are said to have departed from their homes at Lake Aztlan or, according to another source, from the "Seven Caves."[7] They named themselves Mexica when they beheld the fruitful valley and asserted their sovereignty by subjugating the settled population.[8] They assimilated and adopted the Toltec heritage, while retaining some themes and godheads of their own nomadic past.

The religion of the Aztecs is well documented. Christian missionaries carefully recorded native habits; they added commentaries to the chronicles and almanacs of the Aztec priests. Mexicans themselves, acquiring the art of writing, would compose accounts, half-mythical and half-historical, of the early ages of their nation.[9]

MEXICAN RELIGION

It is likely that a class of priests had existed during the formative period of Mesoamerican civilization, and clearly it remained through the successive eras up to the time of the Spanish conquest. The raw materials of native faith were shaped, refined, and intellectualized through the centuries. The beliefs of various peoples were blended and invested with a new symbolism. Mexican mythology is also interwoven with history, with the wanderings of tribes and the conquest of the land. Possibly, some tribal leaders were turned into gods. The gods were roughly divided by some scholars into nature gods, tribal gods, and gods of creativity.[10]

The Divinity of Animals

The sculpture in the settlements of the most ancient period was mainly of humans, though animals might be found among the figurines. In the more advanced culture of the Olmecs (La Venta) the animal clearly rose above the man. Jaguars above all were invested with a new and terrible sanctity. The great altars of La Venta symbolize the heads of jaguars, the jaws represented by the niche. A ritual scene taking place within a jaguar's jaws is carved into a stela in Les Zapotes.[11] In the reliefs of Teotihuacán, which are devoted to the gods of moisture, streams of water issue from the mouths of jaguars.[12]

Later the jaguar was overshadowed by the serpent and by a special serpent bearing plumes. The temple priests of Teotihuacán wore the form of a plumed serpent on their heads.[13] The stone balustrades of the temple stairs of Chichén Itzá in Yucatán consisted of the bodies of feathered snakes.[14] Snake walls (*catepetl*) enclose the temple of Huitzilopochtli in Tenochtitlán, and the railing of the stairs was formed by snakes.[15] A glowing snake is wielded by the god of fire as his weapon.

A god's name may contain the word *coatl* (snake), as in Coatlicue (the snake skirted), a mother goddess, or in Mixcoatl (cloud serpent), a hunting god. The goddess Coatlicue stands, in a monumental sculpture, on legs strewn with feathers and ending in a jaguar's paws, and two snakes instead of a human head emerge from her shoulders.[16] The earth is imagined as a toad, a fish, a crocodile, and the fierce warrior Huitzilopochtli is visualized as a humming-bird.

We noted that a feathered snake could represent such diverse elements as the weapon of a god or the enclosure of a temple. A serpent (*coatl*) could be related to such diverse godheads as a mother goddess (Coatlicue) or a hunting god (Mixcoatl). The warrior god Huitzilopochtli is visualized as a humming-bird, a being without warlike qualities. The affiliation thus did not rest on any individual quality. The animal was the carrier of a sovereign and unspecified sanctity. The battle against the beast shape of an earlier god, which was fought in the Mediterranean, was not carried out in Mexico.

The Spheres of Male and Female Power

The elements of the cosmos do not bear a marked sexual aspect in Mexican thought. Two creative beings, one male and one female, brought forth the primeval gods.[17] The fruit of the soil is personified in Cinteotl, the god of maize, and in the goddess Chicomecoatl (by whom we live). The flower prince Xochipilli has a partner in the flower goddess Xochiquetzal.[18] The process of childbirth was equated with the encounter of the battlefield. When a woman brought forth a child she was hailed as a brave warrior, and when she lost her life she received the honors due to one who fell before the enemy; she then became a *mociuaquetzque* (warrior in the shape of a woman).[19]

It is true, however, that the creator god Quetzalcoatl had no female counterpart, and that female deities concerned with childbirth, the arts of healing, and female handicrafts are part of Mexican mythology.

Emphasis on the Celestial Spheres

The priests created an accurate and sophisticated way of counting time, in which a deity presided over every day and every week and over every hour of the night and day.[20] It must be because the minute observation of ritual was thought indispensable to the continuation of life, and because the timing of the rituals was calculated by the circuit of the stars, that such great importance was accorded to the spheres of heaven.[21]

The five intercalendary days of every year were fraught with the anxiety that time might not renew its passage. When after fifty-two years an era ended, anguish overwhelmed the population, so that in fasting and lamentations it mortified its flesh in countless tortures. At nightfall of the last day priests would climb to the top of a volcano in the hope of seeing the stars travel in their wonted paths. When certain stars had passed the meridian, messengers would race to every village and fires would be relit with jubilation.[22]

Countless sacrifices were enacted so that the sun would continue on its journey. Warriors who died in battle, victims who died on the sacrificial stone, and women who perished in childbirth were accorded the glory of escorting the sun in its orbit. Sahagún cites: "the brave warriors, the eagle-ozelot warriors, those who died in war, went there to the house of the sun . . . and when the sun was about to emerge . . . they arrayed themselves, they armed themselves, as for war, met the sun as it emerged . . . came skirmishing."[23]

Important gods might receive a stellar epiphany. When Quetzalcoatl, as a human leader, took his life, he stayed for four days in the underworld and after another four days his heart rose to heaven: "The old people tell that it was transformed into the star which rises at the time of growing light . . . and he was called the Lord of Dawn."[24]

The dwellers of the sky did not live in peace in Mexican religion. When the sun stayed immobile after he had been created, the morning star shot an arrow at him but failed to kill the deity. The sun, returning the assault, was more successful, and the morning star was slain.[25] In pictorial representations the two are shown as warriors who hold spears, clubs, and shields.[26] The *Anales de Quauhititlan* relate of the morning star that he "strikes various people with his rays, shoots them, sheds his light on them."[27] The Codices, depicting the phases of the planet Venus, show him in his various states of aggression.[28] Thus the alternation between day and night was envisioned as a bloody battle that must be continually repeated while the cosmic order is maintained; and the sky is peopled by a race of warriors.

The Exaltation of Death

The numbers of victims slain at every festival would indicate that the gods were unsatiable in their thirst for human blood. The victim might be hurled to death, as in the festival of the ancestral goddess Toci. He was tossed into the fire in honor of the fire god; then the body was taken half-roasted, from the flames, and the heart was cut from the flesh to be offered as a pious gift. Children were brought to the mountains to be handed to the deity of rain. And the fire of the New Year blazed from within the breast of a slaughtered being.[29]

The motivation for the cruel rites (i.e., their mythical antecedents) are revealed in several tales. In one creation story the earth, a female being, was torn to pieces, and from her severed parts the earth and sky were created. To console her the gods promised that all manner of fruit would grow from the parts of her broken body: trees and flowers from her eyes, mountains and valleys from her shoulders. But she cried and did not wish to bear fruit until she was drenched with human blood.[30]

In order to generate the sun and moon, two gods were chosen to give their bodies to the flames. Though they hesitated at first in fear and trembling, they finally took courage, and after four days of penitence they plunged into the blaze. Soon the luminaries were seen as rising in the East, but they did not continue in their course. Then the entire assembly of the gods decided "[let] this be that through us the sun may be revived. Let us all die."[31]

The wandering Aztecs beheld some gods as these fell from heaven and landed on the melon cactus. The tribesman killed them and through this act received the bows, arrows, and netbags, which made them into hunters, and also a new name: Mexica.[32] And wars were created to provide a sufficiency of blood for the thirsty sun.[33]

The Mexican belief in the creativity of death finds a parallel in a myth that is spread through parts of America, Indonesia, and Melanesia; in this myth the first food plants originated in the body of a slain divinity. This being may be buried, burned, or cut to pieces; it may be killed or voluntarily seek its death; but always the staff of life, rice, yams, or maize, henceforth feeds and sustains the human group.[34]

MATERNAL DEITIES

We encounter several mother goddesses who share some qualities but are also drawn as separate and distinct beings. They might have developed from god-heads of the same generic type of several tribes that were taken into the Mexican pantheon and accepted qualities from one another. I shall present these deities as separate creatures even though I realize that the separation may at times be artificial.

Chimalman: Shield in Hand

This goddess swallowed some precious stones and afterward bore a son, the god Quetzalcoatl. In a variant the hunting god Mixcoatl met the naked mistress of the land of the Huiznak; he shot several arrows at her, but she remained unharmed and withdrew into a cave. In his anger the god devastated the countryside, and Chimalman was persuaded by the women of the land to leave the shelter of her cave. When she emerged the god embraced her, and she conceived and bore a son, the god *ce actli* (Quetzalcoatl), but she died in giving birth.[35] In another tale she was married to Camaxtli and the mother of several children, one of them Quetzalcoatl.[36] I have not found any ritual observances in honor of this goddess.

Coatlicue: The Snake Skirted

A pious woman dwelled on the mountain Coatepec near Tollan, and one day as she swept the path, a feather ball descended on her, which she buried in her bosom. The ball later disappeared, and she realized that she was with child. She had earlier born a daughter and many sons—the 400 southerners—and they were overcome with shame when they learned about their mother's state. They proceeded against the woman with the intent of killing her for her offence, but she was soothed and calmed in her fears by the voice of the child within her womb. He burst forth at the moment of the greatest danger, in full armor with shield and spear, and defeated the overwhelming numbers of his enemies. And thus the god Huitzilopochtli slew hundreds in the first few hours of his life.[37]

The emperor Montezuma wished to know more about the birthplace of his nation; magicians told him of Lake Aztlan and the mountain Colhuacan where his ancestors had dwelled, and he sent his messengers to these parts. As they came to the "crooked mountain," Colhuacan, they encountered an old and dirty woman who shocked them with her ugliness. She was, so she told them, the goddess Coatlicue, who had grown old and dirty in her sorrow and longing for her son. And the fertile land around her had turned into a wilderness of thorns and thistles.[38]

Coatlicue is also the mother of Quetzalcoatl, according to the chronicler Camargo;[39] and she is married to Tlamatzincatl and Itzquitecatl, Chichimec gods of wine.[40] According to Sahagún, she is crowned with eagle feathers, and eagle feathers adorn her shield. Her skirt is plaited of writhing snakes, and she holds a snake staff in her hand (Figure 48).[41] The most striking image of the goddess appears in a stone statue of more than eight feet in height: She is clad in a skirt of writhing snakes, her legs end in a jaguar's paws and are covered with eagle feathers. Her head is formed of two snakes and her necklace strung of human hearts and hands with a human skull as its central ornament.[42] Those who plait flowers into wreaths honor her in the third festival of the year, which is devoted above all to the rain god Tlaloc, and she is given pancakes of amaranth in this celebration.[43]

Cihuacoatl: Female Snake

This deity is also known as Quilaztli, a name without known meaning or derivation (Figure 49). When Quetzalcoatl, Chimalman's son, was left without a mother after birth, he was nurtured and brought to manhood by Cihuacoatl/Quilaztli.[44] In order to create the human race, Quetzalcoatl wrenched the bones of dead men from the ruler of the underworld and brought them up to Tamoanchan, the House of Descent, and there he met Cihuacoatl, who ground the bones and placed the powder into a bowl filled with gems. Quetzalcoatl then let the blood of his male member run into the container, and from the paste men were shaped. The goddess thus was instrumental in an act of life creation.[45]

Sometimes she is seen as a mother, for she carries a cradle on her back as she mingles with the crowd in the marketplace. Yet when she disappears and leaves the cradle, it is empty except for the knife that is used in sacrifice.[46] At other times she is beheld with a child on her hip. In images she holds a shield inlaid with eagle feathers and also a weaving stick.[47] She has some relation to the work of agriculture, for she gave farmers the hoe and tumpline for their labor in the fields.[48] The goddess is named Deer of Colhuacan in her hymn, and in a picture manuscript her head emerges from a serpent's jaw.[49]

Her hymn exalts her as a warrior:

> Our mother warrior [woman], our mother warrior [woman], deer of Colhuacan, they have pasted feathers upon her. Day hath dawned; war is heralded. Let [captives] be dragged down and the land wasted. Deer of Colhuacan, feathers have been pasted on her. Eagle feathers are thy array; thy array is of one who fighteth boldly in war.[50]

When she walks weeping and wailing through the night, she announces to men that war is near.[51] The vice regent, a man, bears her name, Cihuacoatl, and he dresses in her female garments after battle.[52] A woman in the throes of childbirth is admonished by the midwife to be brave in the manner of the goddess: "be thou a brave woman . . . imitate the brave woman Cihuacoatl/Quilaztli." If the woman perishes she is praised: "Thou hast taken, raised up, used the shield, the little shield, which thy beloved mother Ciuapili, Cihuacoatl/Quilaztli placed in thy hand."[53]

The goddess received special honors in Xochimilko where her festival was held on the eighteenth of June. Durán declares: "In this temple and in honor of this goddess more men were slain than in any other." Here she received fire sacrifices in which victims were pushed into the fire, then taken out while still alive, and the heart cut from the body. Her priests scorched themselves in her service.[54]

Teteo Innan: Mother of the Gods

She also bears the name Tonan (Our Mother) and Toci (Our Grandmother) and is equated with Itzpapalotl in her hymn. Sahagún explains her title: "The ancients held that this one gave birth to the gods, whence men came on earth. Hence they named her Toci (grandmother)."[55] She is designated as Woman of Discord by the chronicler Durán, who explains that she brought discord between the Aztecs and the king of Colhuacan.[56] Images show her with a broom, with eagle feathers on her skirt, and with the healing plant *totoicxitl* in her hand. Often she carries spindles in her cotton headband (Figure 50).[57]

She alone of the figures discussed here is mistress of her own festival, *ochpaniztli* (the sweeping of the way), held in the eleventh month (August–September), and brooms play a part in the celebrations.[58] The scenes are enacted on the temple mound of Huitzilopochtli, for the goddess has no shrine within the town. A mature woman personifies the deity; she is closely attended by three midwives; and midwives, physicians, leeches, and diviners are prominent in the festival. For several days the woman-victim is entertained and cheered by her attendants, for she must be happy when she meets her death.

She is swiftly killed, and then her skin is drawn from the body. The skin of the thighs is severed from the rest and placed upon the face of a priest who represents her son, the maize god Cinteotl. The other portion clothes another priest who turns symbolically into the goddess through this act. He also wears the rest of her attire, including the garment she herself had woven before her death. Mock battles are enacted between the armed warriors of the town and the priests with their blood-stained brooms; the skirmishes continue as the festive crowd moves from the temple to the shrine of Toci at the border of the city, which also is the boundary of the province. Here the thigh mask is deposited, and sometimes real fights ensue between the faithful and a real enemy. The emperor then distributes in a solemn and ceremonial manner precious arms to leading warriors. Afterward the seeds of maize and squash are scattered, then snatched up by the pious throng.[59] The hymn to the goddess seems to contain a reference to the thigh mask of the priest: "The yellow flower hath opened—she . . . with the thigh skin of the goddess painted on her face departed from Tamoanchan."

In her departure from Tamoanchan she left a place of origin and birth that was envisaged as a flowering garden. In this hymn she is also seen as a deer, like Cihuacoatl: "I saw thee turn to deer in the land of the gods Xiuhnel and Mimich," and like Coatlicue, she appears in white: "Once again with chalk, with feathers she is pasted."[60] When Cortés made his entrance into Tenochtitlán, he was shown much respect and honor, given costly gifts, and taken to the shrine of Toci at the border of the town.[61]

Tlazolteotl: The Goddess of Dirt

She also bears the names Tlaelquani (eater of dirt [excrement]) and Ixcuina (four faces), because four sisters were represented by her name.[62] Ixcuina was among the deities who gave their lives so that the sun and moon would continue in their passage. When this goddess came from Huaxteca to Tollan she told some captives: "we wish to go now to Tollan with you . . . to fecundate the earth with you," and thus she instituted the battle sacrifice.[63]

By arousing carnal desire, this goddess leads men into sin, and her designation Tlaelquani coincides with the designation of a sinner, "he who eats his excrement." Sahagún declares that "her realm was that of evil and perverseness—that is to say, lustful and debauched living."[64] Conversely, she has the power to cleanse men from their moral blemishes if they confess their misdeeds to her priest and accept and endure the penance laid upon them. She is, above all, of calendrical significance, as the seventh of the nine regents of the night, the fifth of the thirteen daylight hours, the goddess of the fourteenth day and of the thirteenth week. She also rules a geographic region of the world and a phase of the planet Venus.[65]

Her images reveal a great resemblance to Teteo Innan (Toci), the Mother of the Gods, who was discussed earlier. Her lips are covered, like those of Teteo Innan, with a layer of liquid rubber; like her, she wears a cotton headband with spindles. Unlike her, she never holds a broom. And she is frequently adorned with a nose ornament in the form of a sickle (the Aztec symbol of the moon). The goddess may be shown in her nakedness, nursing a child, offering a captive for sacrifice, standing next to a serpent or an owl; she may also be in a coital position.[66] The most striking of her representations draws her in the act of giving birth, covered with the skin of another that ends in the middle of her thigh, as is the skin worn by the priest of Teteo Innan in her festival (Figure 51).[67] Considering the resemblance between Tlazolteotl and Teteo Innan, scholars have virtually equated the two deities. I present them here as separate entities because Fray Bernardino speaks of them consistently as two beings and draws two separate divinities in his illustrations. We may also note that the name Tlazolteotl is never held by the mistress of the *ochpaniztli* celebrations.

We may observe that the goddesses were honored and their memory preserved in diverse ways. Teteo Innan is mistress of an important cultic event, yet has hardly any myths. Myths are related of Coatlicue, Chimalman, and Cihuacoatl. Hymns are dedicated only to Cihuacoatl and Teteo Innan. Tlazolteotl belongs mainly to the calendar.

SPHERES OF FUNCTION AND ACTIVITY

Motherhood and Birth

Coatlicue gave birth to Huitzilopochtli and, in a variant, to Quetzalcoatl; more frequently this god is held to be the son of Chimalman. Tlazolteotl is portrayed as a child issues from her womb. An unmarked sculpture shows a woman in the act of giving birth, but we do not know if a goddess is depicted.

Teteo Innan (Toci) received the adoration of owners of sweat baths who would put her image at the entrance and name her Grandmother of the Baths. The use of sweat baths belonged with the customs surrounding parturition; the young mother would be bathed in a steam bath five or six days after her delivery, according to Durán, and Sahagún states of a woman in the throes of

Figure 48. (*Left*) The Goddess Coatlicue. Figure 49. (*Middle*) Cihuacoatl. Figure 50. (*Right*) Teteo Innan.

Figure 51. (*Left*) Tlazolteotl; Codex Borbonicus, 13. Figure 52. (*Right*) Sacrifice to the sun.

labor; "in order that she would quickly give birth, they quickly bathed her in a sweat bath."[68] The goddess was also held to be the ancestress of humankind.

Cihuacoatl was occasionally represented with a child upon her hip. She was invoked by the midwife who exhorted the woman in travail to emulate the brave action of the goddess. Since a woman's struggle to bring forth a child was equated with a warrior's struggle against his foe, it may be that the warrior aspect of the deity was of essence in this invocation. Cihuacoatl also had a share in the creation of the human race, and she nursed the orphaned infant Quetzalcoatl.

Warfare

Durán designates Teteo Innan as Madre de la Discordia, Woman of Discord.[69] Mock battles were enacted for several days in her festival in which priests wielded blood-spattered brooms against the weapons of the eagle and the jaguar knights. An arrow sacrifice was offered before Toci's shrine: "Remembering the wounds inflicted by arrows caused by that goddess, they now offered her men killed in an arrow sacrifice."[70] The emperor presented warriors with arms in a solemn ceremony at the conclusion of the feast.

It was believed that war was near when Cihuacoatl wandered howling through the night.[71] She was exalted in her hymn as a warrior who exhorts to battle:

> Our Mother warrior [woman], our mother warrior [woman] ... they have pasted feathers on her. Day hath dawned; war is heralded; let captives be dragged down and the land wasted. Deer of Colhuacan, feathers are thy array; thy array is of one who fights boldly in war.

The group of fighters known as eagle knights wore a costume of eagle feathers in representation of the noble bird. Thus eagle feathers marked and symbolized the warrior. Eagle feathers were everpresent in the apparel of the goddesses: Coatlicue and Cihuacoatl were crowned with eagle feathers, and eagle feathers adorned their shields. Toci's shirt was strewn with eagle feathers or embellished with the image of an eagle.[72] And Ixcuina (possibly the same as Toci) introduced the "battle sacrifice."

The Healer's Craft

As patroness of the sweat bath Toci partook of the craft of healing, and she carried the medicinal plant *totoicxitl*.[73] "Her devotees were," as told by Sahagún, "physicians, leeches ... those who purged people (and) eye doctors. Also women, midwives, those who brought about abortions, who read the future, who cast auguries ... who cured sickness by removing stones or obsidian knives from the body ... who removed worms from the eyes." Physicians and midwives figured prominently in her ritual. In a variant description of Toci's feast, dances were performed by nobles and princes who were disguised as medicine men, and the mock battles were carried out by midwives and physicians.[74]

It may be that Tlazolteotl's power to cleanse men of their sins is related to an ability to cure diseases; it was thought among some Mexican tribes that sicknesses were caused by evil deeds, and that by making confessions and enduring penitence, men would be relieved of their afflictions.[75]

The Crafts of Women

The goddesses were skilled in the craft of weaving. Cihuacoatl held a wooden weaving stick, and spindles were stuck into the headband of Tlazolteotl. Spindles and bundles of uncarded cotton also belonged with the headgear of Teteo Innan in the performance of her ritual, and the woman who impersonated her spun the cotton, wove a dress, and offered it for sale in the marketplace before her death. Later the dress was worn by the priest over the skin that had once covered her living flesh.

Origin and Ancestry

Teteo Innan, also known as Toci (grandmother), is an ancestral figure. Sahagún observes, and this was noted earlier, that in Mexican belief the race of gods and men had originated in this deity. Her shrine contained, in Durán's account, the image of an aged woman, and a woman of about forty to forty-five was chosen to represent her in her festival.[76]

The goddesses Cihuacoatl and Coatlicue were both related to the mountain of origin, Colhuacan. This name designates both a mythical and an actual location. The real town lies on the canal that connects Lake Texcoco with Lake Xochimilko.[77] The mythical place is deeply entwined with the experience of Aztec immigration. It was in Colhuacan that the wanderers found the idol of Huitzilopochtli to guide them in their future travels. It was here that the Mexica separated from the other tribes.[78] Colhuacan is drawn in the picture manuscripts as a mountain with its summit turned into a coil, and a cave or sanctuary with an idol may be seen within the mound.[79]

When Montezuma's men wandered in search of their nation's roots, they came upon the goddess Coatlicue at the foot of the "crooked mountain," Colhuacan. Cihuacoatl is named in her hymn the "deer" and "protectress" of Colhuacan. In their relation to this place where the Mexicans awakened to their national identity, the two goddesses were deeply part of the formative, archaic past. Teteo Innan came from Tamoanchan, according to her hymn. Tamoanchan, the House of Descent, where the bones of the dead grew into living men and women, represents the point of origin from above.[80] Thus Teteo Innan likewise possessed links with a site of primordial birth.

Tribal Affinity

Coatlicue, visited by Montezuma's men, had stayed near the cave of Aztec origin and had given birth to the Aztec god Huitzilopochtli and thus belongs to the heritage of the invading tribes.

Teteo Innan is equated in her hymn with Itzpapalotl, the "obsidian butterfly," a goddess of the nomadic Chichimecs. Several tales are told of this divinity: When the wanderers rested in their journey the two "cloud serpents," Xiuhnel and Mimich, beheld two double-headed deer descending from the sky; the two hunting men chased the deer all day through the steppes and forests and the deer turned into women when evening came. After some adventures of seduction, murder, and cannibalism, one of the two women fell upon a cactus plant; she was shot by Mimich and later burned. In the flames she turned into knives of various colors. She was Itzpapalotl, and the white knife was taken by the god Mixcoatl, the hunter, and henceforth carried in his sacred bundle.[81]

In another version it is merely stated that Itzpapalotl was slain by Mimich's arrow when the tribes came to Tepenenec. A version that does not mention the goddess Itzpapalotl by name says that deities landed on a melon cactus, and after they were shot, the Aztecs received the name Mexica and also the arms that made them into hunters.[82] Itzpapalotl thus is clearly related to a decisive, formative moment of the history of the invading tribes.

A resonance of these tales is discernible in the hymn of Teteo Innan, which declares: "She has become a goddess on the melon cactus, Our Mother Itzpapalotl," and also "I saw thee turn to deer in the land of the gods Xiuhnel and Mimich." And an arrow sacrifice recalling the death by arrow of Itzpapalotl is conducted in the feast of Toci, according to Durán.[83]

The goddess Cihuacoatl, the "deer of Colhuacan" and the mother of the hunting god Mixcoatl in her hymn, belongs in these aspects, likewise to the hunters of the northern steppes. The name Quilaztli, given to the goddess, also designates the deer of the hunting god Mixcoatl. Chimalman, the mother of Quetzalcoatl, was brought by the invading tribes from their home in Aztlan.[84]

Chimalman is conversely also the mother of the Toltec god Quetzalcoatl. Coatlicue received special honors in Coatlinchan, lying to the east of Lake Texcoco. Sahagún states that Tlazolteotl, often equated with Teteo Innan, was unknown among the Chichimecs (the hunting tribes) and adored by the Huaxtecs, Olmecs, and Mixtecs.[85] The feast of the goddess Cihuacoatl/Quilaztli was held in July in Xochimilco, where she was greatly treasured and adored.[86] She had also nurtured the Toltec Quetzalcoatl.

We must understand that a divinity may be claimed and revered by more than one tribal unit. We may assume that generically related deities of various nations were blended and assimilated in a process of syncretization that not only made the hunting god Mixcoatl into the father of the Toltec deity Quetzalcoatl, but also provided a common habitation for the rain god Tlaloc, rooted in an archaic layer of belief, and the late-arriving Huitzilopochtli on the temple mound of Tenochtitlán. The hunters' heritage, to be sure, is very much in evidence in the goddesses of this discussion.

Relation to Flora and to the Earth Itself

The hymn of Cihuacoatl visualizes her in a maize field where she is resting on her "rattle stick." This kind of stick, producing musical sounds when shaken, is of magical significance and is wielded by various gods. The interpreter of the passage explains that by means of this stick the earth is dug and the seed is planted.[87] This goddess also gave humans the hoe to work their fields.[88]

Agricultural rites were blended with the war games in the *ochpaniztli* festival, which was held at harvest time. Seeds of various kinds, "white maize grains, yellow, black, red, and squash seeds" were flung, sowed, and scattered among the onlookers. The maize god Cinteotl took an active part in Toci's festival; an illustration of the event shows a woman in the garments of Chicomecoatl, the female deity of maize.[89]

Teteo Innan is named Lord of the Earth and also Heart of the Earth in her hymn. The latter designation is hers, in the explanation of the interpreter, because she causes the earth to tremble. Durán reports that a strange tremor of the earth is felt at the moment of the celebration after the victim was hurled from a high scaffold to the ground.[90]

Coatlicue is the patroness of flower workers and is honored by them in a festival. Teteo Innan is likened to a flower in her hymn:

> The yellow flower hath opened—she, our mother with
> the thigh skin of the goddess painted on her face
> ... the white flower hath opened ...

Sexuality

In her feast Teteo Innan assumed a pose that suggests sexual surrender: "And when [Toci's impersonator] had come to the foot or the base of [the temple of] Uitzilopochtli, then she raised her arms, she spread arms and legs, at the foot of [the temple of Uitzilopochtli]. She put herself facing [the god] . . ."[91] Phallic men are among the figures drawn in illustrations of the rites. Tlazolteotl is the goddess of carnal lust, and she appears sometimes in a coital position in the calendars.

COMPOSITE IMAGE

The goddesses, designated by various names and undoubtedly of varied origin, and preserving some of their individuality, nevertheless have blended and taken over one another's function in many ways. Their reign extends over the realms of women's lives: childbirth and women's crafts. They also have ancestral aspects; as ancestral godheads they would be protective of a special tribe, and they retained qualities belonging with the spirits of a hunting nation. As strong as their relationship to the concerns of women is their relationship to the wars of men. In this and in their less prominent alliance with agriculture, they reflect the values of a militarily powerful and settled nation. They are also associated with the craft of healing.

The figures are commonly held to be various forms of the Earth Goddess and to embody the maternal fruit-giving aspect of the earth. My examination has not revealed a strong affinity with any portion of the natural environment; therefore, the complete identity between motherhood and earth cannot be substantiated.

It is true that in Aztec thought the earth may be a power of life-giving. After Tlalteutli, the unformed earth, was torn to pieces, fruit and flowers grew and ripened from her severed limbs. And when the arrow of the sun had cleft the earth, men and women emerged into the light. These tales are not brought into relation with the mother goddesses of this study and left no imprint on their forms. When the earth is visualized, it is a toad, fish or crocodile, or a creature of many jaws.[92] The goddesses of this essay show no resemblance with these shapes, for they are addressed as eagles, adorned with eagle feathers, visualized as deer, and Itzpapalotl is a butterfly.

Also, the goddesses are not stationed beneath or within the soil. When Quetzalcoatl left the underworld with dead men's bones in his hands, he rose to Tamoanchan, the House of Descent, and there he met Cihuacoatl. Teteo Innan has come from Tamoanchan according to her hymn (i.e., from above). Itzpapalotl, with whom she is identified, descended from the heights. Ixcuina (Tlazolteotl) was among the gods, presumably in heaven, who were intent on creating the sun and moon.

It may be argued that Coatlicue is envisioned in or near the mountain Colhuacan, which may contain the "Seven Caves." These represent, at least in some accounts, the birthplace of the invading tribes of hunters. In the culture of hunting peoples, caves and mountains are not experienced as manifestations of the fruitful earth, but as the awesome and sacred places of the wilderness. The role of the goddess here would resemble that of a Guardian of Nature or of a Lady or Mistress of the Mountain.

Scholars understand the relation between Teteo Innan and her son Cinteotl, the god of maize, to symbolize the birth of grain from the womb of the earth. The relation is, however, encountered only in the *ochpaniztli* where agricultural rites join the more prominent warrior celebrations. Elsewhere Cinteotl was born by the flower princess Xochiquetzal, and he saw life in Tamoanchan in his hymn. Teteo Innan, according to her song, bore the hunting god Mixcoatl, the "cloud serpent," and we cannot understand this event to recall the growth of fruit in the fertile earth.[93]

The goddess Tlazolteotl is drawn in the act of giving birth, and it is held that here she brings forth Cinteotl, but we see a female child emerging from her womb, wearing a cotton headband like her mother (Figure 51). Footsteps near the goddess indicate that the child has entered the woman's body from above, probably from Tamoanchan. The picture thus testifies to the life-giving powers of the upper spheres.

Teteo Innan is designated as Lord of the Earth in her hymn; since she is named with a masculine epithet "Lord," she is not visualized as a mother. The title Heart of the Earth, of the same poem, is accorded to her because the earth will tremble at her wish, and not because she is the earth.

Let us note that no title marks the goddesses as forces of nourishment and growth, while such titles are indeed bestowed on others, as on the god of rain "who makes things sprout" and on the goddess Chicomecoatl, "It was thought that she was our sustenance."[94] We may conclude by observing that in one thought pattern of the Mexicans life and fruitfulness emerge from the caverns of the earth. To the examples already cited we may add that of the flower princess, who was impregnated by the sun god in a cave and who brought forth the god of maize.[95] We must also observe that the mother goddesses have only a small share in this belief.

In attempting to trace the derivation of the mother goddesses, we may observe that in their role of birth-helpers and healers, in their relation to women's crafts, they perform the offices of the goddesses of women's lives of archaic forms of society. In their links with the tribal past, in their protective and ancestral aspect, they show a likeness to the ancestral tutelary spirits, specific to each tribe, which also form part of archaic faith. The warlike qualities of the godheads would have arisen in the function of a tutelary spirit at a time of conquest and of danger, for it is natural that such a power would be protective of its people and would exhort it to attack.

I suggest the following course of formation of the Mexican deities: goddesses of the lives of women and tutelary ancestral spirits belonging to various hunting tribes were blended. They acquired qualities and functions of the godheads of a farming population after the invaders had settled in the fertile lands. They were further shaped by the vision of the Mexicans: They shared in the sanctity of serpents, they demanded their toll of human suffering and human blood (Figure 52), and Tlazolteotl took her place amidst the rulers of the days and weeks and the hours of the night and day of the almanacs.

The composite image of the Mexican divinity shares aspects with deities of Asia and Europe. Like Nintur and Laima, she assists in childbirth; like Amaterasu, she is ancestral to her tribe. Like the Japanese deity, she is allied with the female craft of weaving. Like Laima, she is related to the bathhouse, a place of parturition and women's rituals. As in North Eurasian cultures, Toci, a healer and birth-helper, is also an ancestral spirit. It is in keeping with the Mexican reverence of death that the growing of new life should be linked with the world of the departed. The Mexican divinity alone possesses a warrior's spirit. She does not represent or rule a natural phenomenon, though she has some relation to agricultural activity. There is no evidence to show that she ever ruled supremely, or that she achieved her station through her biological fertility.

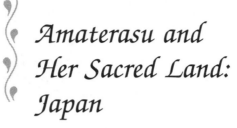

Amaterasu and Her Sacred Land: Japan

THE four main islands of the Japanese archipelago stretch in a slender arc east of the Asiatic mainland and are divided from their nearest neighbor by more than a hundred miles of ocean. Extending a considerable distance in the north–south direction, the land experiences a variety of climates, from heavy snowfall in the North to subtropical rains in the southern zone.[1] Close enough to the mainland to have received the impact of the brilliant Chinese civilization, the Japanese, surrounded by the ocean, were able to retain a separate identity and to develop the imported cultural achievements according to their own distinctive genius.

According to a Chinese document of the third century, the country was divided into many principalities and clans. Sometime around the fourth or fifth century one of these rose to consolidate the others and to establish its court in the Yamato plain. It elevated its members to chieftainship and its gods to superiority over the gods of other clans. From that time onward the Japanese saw themselves, in spite of inner struggles, as a national community led by a divinely instituted emperor.

In subsequent centuries the land continued to lie open to Chinese influences; the inhabitants adopted Chinese writing and the Buddhist faith, which came to be the official religion.[2] By the twelfth century a new power structure originated; it consisted of land-owning families, each with its group of loyal warriors, the Samurai, beholden to the shogun, a warrior aristocrat of absolute authority.[3] The figure of the emperor himself remained unviolated as focus and symbol of national identity.

The system was to stay until the second half of the nineteenth century; it was marked by turbulence and strife in its first period, and by tranquility in its later half (1600–1887), bought at the price of the full subordination of the individual within a rigid hierarchy, and the complete isolation of Japan from all traffic with other lands, so that no Japanese was allowed to leave and no foreigner could enter the terrain.[4] The isolation was shattered in 1853 by an American demand to have two ports opened to American ships. The archaic government of the shogun collapsed, and the Japanese set out to modernize their land with the same zeal with which they had accepted Chinese culture.[5]

During all times of Japanese history, through periods of violence and of tranquility, the arts were cherished. Paintings and sculptures adorned the earliest temples; prose writing flourished at the early courts. The shogun surrounded himself with men of letters; these developed the No drama, which expressed its message through the media of poetry and dance. Under the influence of Zen Buddhism the art of painting was refined, and landscape gardening developed to a degree unexcelled in other lands. The bustling towns of modern time saw the development of the Kabuki plays, Haiku poetry, and the invention of the wood block print.[6]

RELIGION

Syncretism

Throughout the ages there existed a great readiness among believers to accept the forms and concepts of a different faith. The Kami, gods of early belief, later named Shinto (the way of the Kami), were closely related to a local group and received worship from their local followers. When Buddhism became the preferred religion it overshadowed but did not eclipse the earlier divinities. At the pinnacle of triumphant Buddhism a chronicle of Japanese history was composed, and the emperor was seen as, and remained through the ages, the descendant of a Shinto goddess.

The ardent Buddhist, Prince Shōkotu, fostered the establishment of a Shinto priesthood in the same ways as he fostered the Buddhist orders, for its potential to support the central rule.[7] Buddhist priests realized that a Shinto shrine in their domain would enhance them in the eyes of the Shinto faithful, and, conversely, Shinto priests came to believe that a Buddhist statue in their temple would shelter and protect the native god.[8]

A deity of native tradition might be considered as a form of Buddha, as was Hachiman, renamed Daijizaiten-bosatsu.[9] Mountains, sacred to the ancient faith as dwelling places of divinity, became in Buddhist teaching the site for the realization of Buddhahood.[10] The founder of the Shingon school of Buddhism is said to have stated that the most potent way of achieving Buddhahood is the way of the Kami.[11]

It is clear that both processes took place: that Buddhism was wholeheartedly accepted and that it was greatly altered: shedding its negative view of earthly existence and serving the prevailing order.[12] Shintoism lost its clan-determined position and its exclusiveness and acquired a more intellectual and less pragmatic base. The combination of the beliefs of rice-growing farmers and their warrior chiefs with that of sages and philosophers from abroad received the name Ryōbu Shinto.[13]

Syncretism occurs not only between Buddhism and Shintoism but also between central and local religions, between the "great tradition" brought by wandering priests and the "little tradition" of local village life.[14] The countryside is dotted with countless monuments of worship, stone pagodas, statues of Shinto and Buddhist deities, and pilgrimage testimonials, indicating the intensity and vitality of religious faith.

THE RELIGIOUS AND THE SECULAR

Government and Religion

Queen Himiko of prehistoric time was of religious stature; she was a shamanic diviner and thus a mediator between gods and mortals. Throughout Japanese history the ruler retained his special status vis-à-vis the gods, as one to whom governance is given by divine decree. He himself is of divine descent, tracing his ancestry to the ancient goddess of the sun. He still meets this goddess yearly in his private chambers to partake with her of the new harvest of the crop.[15] His earthly court is modeled on the court in heaven, and her emblems, symbolic of her presence, may reside in his palace.[16]

There was always mutual support between government and religious institutions. Prince Shōkotu established during his reign a great number of Buddhist temples served by many priests and nuns.[17] He also aided the Shinto priesthood, and it became a group of privilege and wealth.[18] The religious institutions repaid the rulers with their loyalty. The monastery founded in the eighth century by Kōbō Daishi was named "Chief Seat of Religion for Ensuring the Safety of the Nation."[19] Rituals for the protection of the state would also develop around Shinto shrines.[20]

Religion and Aesthetic Experience

Even the earliest documents of native faith accord high value to men's physical surroundings, indicating that sacredness resides in the beauty of the natural environment. The attribution of numinous qualities to objects imbued certain activities, such as artistic performance, craftsmanship, or ceremonial, with spiritual value.[21]

The belief in the aesthetic base of numinous encounter received yet another dimension with the coming of Zen Buddhist teaching: that even in performing the acts of daily life, such as drinking tea with perfect grace or contemplating a bare branch rather than a branch of flowering blossoms, the sacred presence may be touched. The man Ryki, who brought the tea ceremony to its fullest form, was fond of quoting the following lines:

> To those who await
> Only the cherry blossom,
> How I wish to show
> The green patches of spring
> Through the Snow of the mountain village.[22]

We may consider the interaction between the humble acts of daily life and the aesthetic-religious ordering of existence to be a strong and striking feature of Japanese religion.

Religion and the Community

The smallest social unit of the rural community, the *dozoku,* consists of the main family with several branches. The members meet and visit one another on the festive days of the year, especially at the New Year's celebrations and the memorial feasts for the dead. At the latter occasion the *dozoku* assembles in the house of the main family where the tablets of the ancestors are kept. The communal cemetery is visited, and worship is rendered at the common shrine.[23] The village unit thus expresses and retains its cohesion through its acts of common rituals. It is clear from these brief glimpses that religious beliefs touch most areas of human activity, and that profane and spiritual existence are never truly separated from one another.

THE SUPERHUMAN POWERS

Divine Visitors

The Japanese dwell in a landscape made sacred by the presence of the gods. A Kami, residing in the Plain of Heaven, frequently chooses a place on earth as his permanent or temporary habitation. The deity may alight on a stone, a tree, or a mountain, and thereby sanctify the point of contact and its surroundings. A shrine is then erected and it may contain, as a sacred relic, the object first touched by the divinity.[24]

Divine visits are frequently experienced; in fishing villages it is believed that the godhead would arrive from the sea, seated in a boat or on the back of a tortoise.[25] In springtime gods travel from their mountain dwellings to the fields to foster and protect the growth of rice. Ancestral deities arrive in the *niiname* festival to share a bowl of the new rice with their descendants.[26] Male and female shamans receive the god within themselves and need not leave, like their North Eurasian counterparts, the world of men in a dangerous journey for their meeting with the superhuman.[27]

Tutelary Spirits

The country had been divided into clans, *uji*, in ancient time, each under the protection of its own god, the *uji-gami*. The *uji-gami* of modern time, also named *yashiki-gami*, may be enshrined on the land, the field, or in a grove of the main family, but he may sometimes belong to an even smaller unit.[28]

The spirit is revered at agricultural festivals in spring and autumn and may acquire the features of a harvest god.[29] He may also acquire the aspects of an ancestral being, and in some areas an ancestor is deified as a *yashiki-gami* in every generation.[30]

Ancestral Gods and the Powers of the Dead

Some believe that a deceased will turn into a Kami after thirty-three years have passed from the time of death and that the spirit will thereafter protect the family.[31] The ancestral tablets are kept in the house of the main family of the kinship group;[32] here the members gather to pay respect during the Bon festival of summertime. Dedicated to the dead, the Bon is one of the most important celebrations of the year.[33]

Some of the deceased may, however, turn into evil beings, such as *goryō-shin*, and at one time all catastrophes were ascribed to the action of such fetches. Through elaborate ceremonies and services these ghosts are sometimes turned into kindly spirits.[34]

We have observed that the divinities fuse and accept qualities from one another, tutelary gods mingling with ancestral beings, accepting aspects of harvest Kami or of regional divinities. Throughout all of Japanese religion there is a sense of blending and acceptance, of the boundaries between god and god and god and mortals, the dead and the living, art and nature, the sacred and the secular, abolished rather than affirmed.

THE ANCESTRAL GODDESS: AMATERASU ŌMIKAMI

The Basic Myth: Origin

Two great gods, the male god Izanagi and the maiden Izanami, united in precosmic time, and their embraces brought forth many children, some not viable, but others turning into the islands that compose the landscape of Japan and into gods to dwell upon the land: a god of mountains and a god of water, a god of trees and a god of fields.[35]

In giving birth to the god of fire the goddess was burned to death, and she was buried in a mountain. In anger and in sorrow Izanagi beheaded the son who had caused his grief, creating yet more gods through this deed and also through the tears shed in his pain. He then set out to retrieve his beloved mate from the region of the dead. In his great desire for the woman he looked at her, though she had admonished him against such action, and he noticed in horror that she was already decomposing. Shamed and angered at the discovery of her state, she sent monsters to pursue the god, and she vowed in wrath, when he escaped, that she would destroy a thousand humans every day, and he countered that he would create 1,500 others to populate the land.[36]

When he safely arrived on earth, he began to rid himself of the pollution of staying in the country of the dead; new gods arose as he washed his garments and his body in a river. Through washing his left eye, the goddess Amaterasu Ōho-mi-kami, "the great august shining one," the solar divinity, was engendered; through washing his right eye, the godhead of the moon was born; and when he cleaned his nose, he gave birth to Take-haya-Susanoo, a turbulent and noisy spirit. The god was pleased at the arrival of these splendid children, especially the girl, and he offered her a precious torque and also the queenship of the daylit sky. The moon received dominion over the nocturnal land, and the third the dominion of the sea.[37]

The Basic Incident in the Life of the Sun Goddess

The turbulent brother, Susanoo, did not fulfill his duty, so that his lands soon lay devastated and despoiled, and he was banned from earth in punishment. He came to heaven to take leave of his sister, and they entered a contest in which she brought forth female children by biting her brother's sword to pieces and he created males by chewing the jewels of his sister. His joy in what he took to be his victory knew no bounds, and in his boisterous excitement he destroyed the rice paddies of Amaterasu and fouled with his excrement the great hall in which the feast of tasting the new rice was to be held.

His sister accepted these pranks with understanding, but she lost composure when he threw a horse, flayed backward, into the hall where a maiden was entrusted with the task of weaving; she was so frightened by the incident that she wounded herself mortally with her shuttle. In anger or in sadness Amaterasu withdrew from heaven to a rock and, closing the door behind her, left the world to darkness and to gloom.[38]

Eight hundred myriad Kami gathered before Amaterasu's door and thought of ways of bringing back the sunshine to the sky. After several attempts had failed, a goddess of grotesque appearance performed a dance and bared her body in an obscene manner. At this the gods broke into laughter, and Amaterasu peeped curiously from her cave at the sounds of such merriment; she was gently made to join the throng. There was great rejoicing at the return of the glow of light.[39]

The Conquest of Japan

Amaterasu then decided that the land of "splendid reeds and of a thousand harvests" should be governed by her son Oshi-ho-mimi; but first the unruly spirits, settled in the country, had to be subdued by the celestial powers.

When the domain was finally secured, with the help and guidance of the goddess, her son ceded the kingship to his child. This child, Ninigi, receiving the emblems of the deity—her mirror, jewels, and a sword—to be the emblems of his royal office, descended to earth. With him went other gods who became the ancestors of various groups related to court structure and ceremonial, and Ninigi became the great-grandfather of the Emperor Jimmu.[40]

Amaterasu and the Craft of Weaving

Three types of endeavor, we have noted, were disturbed by Amaterasu's brother: the planting of her fields, the performance of ritual, and the act of weaving cloth. All three are labors carried out with patient toil and discipline, and they create and uphold the order of civilized society. Amaterasu's close association with these tasks shows her as a force of calm and order.[41]

In this episode weaving is presented as an activity of high importance, as significant as planting crops or religious ceremonial. Since weaving is seen throughout the world as a woman's task and occupation, this incident emphasizes the female aspect of the deity. The weaving maiden dies because in her fright she injures her female organ with her shuttle. Thus the sexual association is emphasized. It is as if the wild impetuous maleness of the god, whose name has been translated as "swift, impetuous, male augustness" or as "valid, intrepid, male Lord," was counterpoised destructively against a female creative ordering of the cosmos.

The importance of the products of the loom in Japanese society may be realized from the fact that cloth had served at one time as a medium of exchange. In the rituals of Shinto religion woven matter receives a prominent position. Thus a list of items presented to the gods includes meat (fish), rice, skin, and silk cloth. Twice yearly the festival *kammiso-sai,* the "ceremonial of the august garments of the gods," was enacted at Amaterasu's shrine in Ise and in these ceremonies precious garments woven by selected weavers were presented to the sanctuary.[42]

In another cloth-related celebration the emperor's garments are shaken by the priestess in a festival named "the shaking of the august soul"; apparently the emperor's soul is here equated with his robes, and the purpose of the ritual is to retrieve the ruler's soul.[43] The belief that garments may create or modify a being is also attested in other cultures. The Siberian shaman believes that by covering his body with the hide of a beast he will be turned into the animal whose strength or swiftness he desires. That in Japanese culture silk garments take the place of hides merely testifies to the high value attached to the products of craftsmanship. That Amaterasu's role as weaver has been retained in religious memory is shown by the presentation of a miniature loom, spindle, and reels which takes place every twenty years at her shrine.

Amaterasu and the Emperor

The emperor is consistently regarded as the descendant of the goddess of the sun. The deity, represented by her emblems, dwelled as member of the family in the imperial palace until one ruler, overwhelmed by the awesome nearness of her divinity, placed her emblems in a shrine.[44] In ancient time only the emperor was allowed to offer his worship at the sanctuary of the deity, but it gradually opened up to other portions of the population.[45]

In a custom that persisted through several centuries, an imperial princess would be chosen to devote her life to serving the goddess in the seclusion of Amaterasu's temple compound.[46] We already noted earlier that the emperor is visited yearly by the goddess for an intimate and private meal.

In some ways the emperor is shown as the earthly counterpart of the goddess, who experiences in his person the experiences of the deity. The court of Yamato was modeled on the court of heaven. It contained the presence of families of shamanic diviners, priests, and ablutioners, just as Amaterasu's court contained the prototype of each group.[47] Amaterasu sent grains of rice for the nourishment of mortals with her grandson when he descended to earth, and in similar fashion the seed of rice was sent yearly by a special envoy from the palace to the emperor's estates.[48] A certain ceremony named "calling back the lost soul of the emperor" is believed to reenact the recalling of Amaterasu from her hiding place.[49] The rice-eating feast in heaven, disturbed by Susanoo, according to the *Kojiki*, was conducted by the goddess, just as the rice-eating feast on earth is conducted by the emperor. We may understand that the emperor enjoys close contact with the deity and appears at times as her earthly counterpart.

Amaterasu and Agriculture

The *Kojiki* speaks of the rice fields owned and cultivated by Amaterasu; she presides over the feast of eating the new rice. She declares, when Ninigi descends to earth, "I will give over to my child the rice grain of my pure rice fields which I tasted in the plain of heaven."[50] Ceremonies to ensure the growth of the planted seeds are enacted at her shrine, such as the "grain petitioning festival" in the second month and the feast of the "requesting of mild weather" in the fourth month; in the ninth month the first fruit of the crop is offered to Amaterasu, and the great harvest festival of eating the new rice is celebrated in November.[51]

To obtain a fruitful harvest, celebrations are conducted throughout the countryside at crucial points of the year: at the times of sowing, transplanting, and reaping. A prayer for good crops in February and a harvest ceremony in November are enacted at the court, and at both festivals the emperor formerly presided.[52]

We may note that Amaterasu is not pictured in physical proximity to the fruitful earth; she is not a goddess of the rice field, just as the emperor is not pictured as a farmer. Her role parallels that of the emperor: in sending seeds to distant fields and in presiding over ceremonies, both ensure the growth of food through their sacred presence in the performance of the ritual.

Amaterasu and Her Sacred Objects

To lure Amaterasu from her hiding place the gods transplanted a sacred *sakaki* tree to set up before her door and decorated it richly with precious things: the Magatama jewels (jewels kept in the innermost, most sacred portion of a Shinto shrine) in the upper branches, a mirror in the middle branches, and "soft objects" (cloth) in the lower part of the crown.[53]

A mirror, jewels, and a sword were handed, as symbols of her presence, to her grandson when he rose to the lordship of Japan, and the goddess advised him to look into the mirror as if it were her soul. The objects were housed in the emperor's palace until they were removed to a new home. The princess Yamato, so legend tells us, enshrined the goddess in a temple compound, and a tree still stands in her sanctuary, as it had stood before the closed door of her hiding place.[54]

The emblems of Amaterasu are indeed endowed with a significance that might have preceded their contact with the goddess. It is believed that the simple sanctuaries of early times had consisted of a tree or stone or a combination of the two.[55] Both mirrors and jewels were found as grave gifts of prehistoric burial places and might have been endowed with ritual value. Jewels, swords, and mirrors made of clay or stone were discovered in the chieftains' tumuli; shaped of clay or stone, they were obviously of a symbolic nature. Jewels and mirrors belong with the equipment of the shaman of the Manchu-Tungus, an East Asian tribe, who is supposedly able to see the soul of a departed in the shining surface.[56]

Hanging mirrors and clothes offerings on trees appears to have been a widespread ritual practice. A tree so decorated becomes, so it has been assumed, the dwelling place of a deity.[57] We may notice once again that the objects sacred to Amaterasu were created by human labor and are the products of human skill, and not the raw elements of the natural environment. Even the tree had been transplanted from its natural position. The objects are also marked by a sacredness of their own.

Amaterasu's Shrine at Ise

Set at the foot of the mountains Konigi and Shinogi, the sanctuary of Amaterasu at Ise is naturally a focal point of Japanese spiritual life, functioning in many festivals and also on decisive historical occasions.[58]

I shall briefly describe some phenomena that are related to the shrine of Ise and illuminate some deep-seated beliefs, that is, the virtue of ceremonial but also the value of spontaneity at special times. The first is expressed by the institution of the *saigū* and its priestess. The *Nihon shoki* (or *Nihongi*), a chronicle, relates that Yamato Hime, the daughter of the emperor Suinin, was assigned to serve the goddess at her shrine. Undertaking a long, meandering journey, which seems in the nature of a pilgrimage, the woman built a "house of abstinence" on her arrival and a place to shelter the deity; she then stayed to serve in full devotion. On the model of this legend an imperial princess was selected through divination and sent to serve the goddess, fully isolated from worldly society, in a practice that continued until the fourteenth century.[59]

Even the selection of the maiden was regulated by extensive and minutely described ceremonies, as were the following years of her preparation in abstinence and seclusion. After the festival of her departure, which was conducted with the utmost pomp and splendor, she set out on a journey that recalls the circuitous wanderings of her legendary prototype. Removed from the circle of the court, but surrounded by a large retinue of priests, servants, and maidens-in-waiting, she performed essentially the same Shinto services that were performed at the palace (which differ from those performed at the shrine).

Three times a year, on important holidays, she would leave the privacy of her enclosure and conduct a ritual at the Grand Shrine. She was released from her position when a new emperor came to the throne; throughout her tenure the movements of her life were minutely ordered and prescribed. The institution of the priesthood of the princess testifies to the belief that the well-being and harmony of the world may be obtained through the discipline and structure of ceremonial, that, in the words of Ellwood, "the imposition of hierarchy and of an external and objective ritual pattern on society and each individual liberated the subjective life of the individual for the appreciation of beauty and pathos."[60]

Another diametrically opposed tendency asserts itself in Japanese religious life, that divine enlightenment and grace can be attained through ecstatic fervor and through a breakthrough in the order of the world. The belief found expression in the practices of the ancient healers and diviners and in the action of the semimystical mountain priests. Pilgrimages to the shrine of Ise testify to the rise of a joyous enthusiasm at certain specified occasions.

During the Tokugawa shogunate, when heavy restraints were placed on the individual and a hierarchical pattern was rigidly imposed on the population, the pilgrimages to Ise, the *okage mairi,* were instituted to take place every sixty years. In fact, the intervals were greatly shortened by spontaneous outbreaks of the phenomenon; moreover, this grew to enormous proportions.[61]

More than three million people marched in the first of these adventures, mainly the underprivileged, servants, women, children, and apprentices, leaving the wearisome burdens of their daily life and supported by the pious on their way. With the bonds of order already broken, lawlessness would erupt in many places, so that the pilgrims might fall prey to thieving, plundering, or sexual abuse. Sometimes dancing might break out among the travelers and infect the dwellers of the towns in the pilgrims' passage. Communities in the path of the procession might send jesters and entertainers to greet the wanderers and to participate in dancing to the music of bells, gongs, and shamisens. Towns seized by the seductiveness of the excitement might have the order of their life disturbed for a long period of time. The phenomenon also fostered a rich growth of legends, some telling of the punishment befalling those who hindered the progress of the pious, and some telling of miraculous cures and rewards.[62]

Though the upper classes and the authorities might frown upon the uproar, they could not help but support the pilgrimages because of their dynamic power, and also because it was probably realized that these provided a release for rebellious feelings, accumulated and stored through years of subjection to a rigid pattern, and thereby prevented the full rupturing of the social order.[63] We may note that the devotion was not as strongly directed to the inner shrine of Ise where Amaterasu has her residence, as to the outer shrine that houses the goddess of fertility. It appears that in these instances, that of the *saigū* princess of imperial blood and the spontaneous and ecstatic movement of the masses, both directed to the goddess, her figure retreated before her symbolic value as focal point of religious emotion.

Parallels to Amaterasu's Myth

The sun and moon as brother-sister pair are encountered in many regions of the world; we find them also in southeastern Asia where much of Japanese tradition originated. In Chinese myth the sun and moon were engendered, as in the *Kojiki,* through the eyes of a superhuman being, the giant Panku. This motif occurs also in an Indonesian tale.[64] A yet closer parallel to the story of the Japanese exists among the Mon Khmer nations. Here a third, a demon, is joined as brother to the sun and moon (who may both be male). The three fight about their share of rice and are in punishment fastened onto heaven. Whenever they resume their squabbles they cause the darkening of the world. In a Siamese version of the theme three brothers decided to give alms to monks. The first gave gold, the second silver, and the third rice in a dirty bowl. After death the first brother turned into the sun, the second into the moon, and the third became a demon who wished to devour the other two. Eclipses originate when these beings have their clashes, and the Siamese create much noise to prevent the extinction of the celestial light.[65]

There are yet more variants among the Siamese and among some Tai tribes. Obayashi believes that the tale of the sun-moon pair, with their evil, ill-tempered brother whose behavior may cause an eclipse, belongs to the Mon Khmer nations but had originated in a wider Austro-Asiatic context.[66]

Amaterasu and the Sun

The goddess is equated with the sun. It has therefore often been assumed that the sun itself had been worshipped at one time by the clan that attained domination of the others, that the sun became personified and then fused with tutelary and ancestral spirits. And it is therefore believed that the chief clan of the country had been devoted to a solar cult. The tale of Amaterasu's disappearance from the sky and the resultant darkening of the world pictures her in the image of the shining star. She has not, however, kept any other aspect of the natural phenomenon. She is not described as golden, as warming, or as riding through the clouds of heaven; she is not greeted at sunrise, and her festivals follow, above all, the rhythm of agricultural activity rather than the rhythm of the solar course.

Let us note that Shinto rituals do not concern themselves, in general, with celestial phenomena, concentrating as they do on honoring sacred places or the ancestral spirits, intent on securing the harvest or on other basic needs of human life. Among the folktales one does not find the resonance of a theme in which the glow of light has vanished from the sky and then is restored among rejoicing, though some, to be sure, relate to aspects of the moon, and there is evidence of his ritual importance.[67]

Celestial symbolism, on the other hand, is strongly emphasized in Chinese tradition, especially in relation to the office of the emperor.[68] In 601 C.E. the Chinese solar-lunar calendar was introduced in Japan to supplant the purely lunar reckoning of time. We know that many strands went into the weaving of the chronicles of Japan which were meant to legitimize the position of the imperial house, historical events, native myths, and learning acquired from abroad. I suggest that the solar aspect of Amaterasu was added as a foreign accretion to exalt the status of the native deity and of her descendants. She could not, after all, be so different from other *uji-gami,* among whom a solar deity does not seem to be presented. The tale of the eclipse was extant in some Austro-Asian countries and would have been imported by the chroniclers.[69]

Kukubyashi Fumio understands likewise that Amaterasu was not originally a solar deity. He points out that no solar rituals are performed at her shrine in Ise. Her earlier name was Amaterasu Ōhirume, according to the *Nihongi* (Chronicles of Japan). The noun *hi* of this name has two meanings, "spirit" and "sun." The noun *me* means "wife" and also "woman." He believes that her name was misunderstood and that it simply means "spirit woman." Because of the misunderstanding a solar aspect was added to the deity.[70]

Amaterasu's Guidance and Inspiration

Though not herself a fighter, Amaterasu guided and directed the conquest of Japan from her heavenly abode. She sent a messenger to the unruly land, and when he, unfaithfully, did not return to report of his accomplished mission, she sent another. He too did not fulfill his task. The next two gods, however, proclaimed Amaterasu's will to the native rulers, and these bowed before the greater power.[71] The going was not always smooth, and at one time the emperor Jimmu was forced to offer battle to the deities of Mount Kumano. A sword was sent from heaven to the descendant of the goddess, and it slew the rebellious warriors through its magic powers.[72]

At times the goddess reveals her wishes directly to her friends. When Yamato-Hime, the daughter of the emperor Suinin, wandered from province to province in search of a place to house the divinity, Amaterasu herself informed her of the location, on the upper reaches of the river Isuzu, where she henceforth wished to dwell.[73]

A chosen human was told by the goddess in a dream that certain rice fields should be offered to the god Taka-mi-musubi. The message was presented to the emperor who complied and also built a shrine for the god.[74] The location of the sword that magically killed the enemies of Jimmu was revealed in a dream to a certain man who found it and brought it to the battlefield.[75]

Many elements of native faith have contributed to shape the figure of the goddess. Like other ancestral beings she imparts divine charisma to her family; like other *uji-gami* she deeply concerns and sometimes identifies herself with her kinship group. She visits members of her family, as do other deities of her kind, on prescribed occasions, and she may descend on them in trance or dream to offer guidance and inspiration. Like others she partakes in agricultural rites, and she has chosen as her emblems objects of numinous significance in their own right. She transcended, as did her kin, the framework of local worship and became a symbol of the divinely ordained statehood of Japan and of the national community, thus a focal point of religious emotions.

The figure of Amaterasu is expressive, in yet other ways, of the spiritual values of her nation. Diverse peoples have diverse ways of facing the natural environment: the North Eurasians meet the world around them in humbleness and fear, the Eskimo in outright terror, and the Mesopotamians in guilty and triumphant aggression. Japanese tradition shows a gentle sense of trust, an expectancy of divine visitation, a belief that humans may to some extent share in the sacredness of nature, a faith that through patient reordering of the elements of the world, through craftsmanship and labor, and through the patterning of ritual, individual and cosmic harmony may be attained. Indeed, the evil powers of *goryō-shin* were turned, through ceremonies, into forces of benevolence. And the shrines and temples, resting against hillsides or sheltering beneath trees, indicate the desired union between the work of mortals and the sacred land.

Amaterasu is a gentle goddess and deeply allied with human accomplishments, brought into relation with the craft of weaving, with the toil of agriculture, and with the patterns of the ceremonial. Her very being originated in a ritual act, in the purification performed by her father; and her offspring arose through her dealings with an artifact. A tree was planted before her cave and decorated with the fruits of craftsmanship. The gifts offered to the goddess in later time consist of objects wrought through human effort, and not, as they often do in other cultures, of the victims of human violence.

Amaterasu partakes, to some degree, of another thrust of Japanese religion:

that through a state of irrationality, through fervor and excitement, mortals might achieve a meeting with divinity. Amaterasu enters this stream of spiritual life by giving inspiration to chosen beings and by accepting the homage of pilgrims to her shrine.

It is fitting that in a country where loyalty and dedication to one's family or clan were of overriding importance through the ages, the tutelary goddess of a clan should have risen to the highest station in the land. The survey of other cultures has shown that the tutelary spirits of a family or clan are the only fully beneficial forces. They do not hold the aspects of violence, capriciousness, or downright cruelty that is attributed, without resentment, to other divinities. And the Eskimo, as we have noted, who dwell in a merciless environment, did not develop the concept of protective and ancestral godheads. Amaterasu remained true to her basic nature of guardian and protector; thus the mightiest deity of Japan is a creature without violence or malice. She responds to insult and disturbance by withdrawal and not by the aggressiveness of attack.

I suggest the following genesis for Amaterasu: the tutelary deity of a family merged with, or became, an ancestral being. She rose in importance when her kin group ascended to the kingship of Japan, and she received her solar aspect through influences from abroad. The godhead never turned into a full-blooded woman, subject to passions or emotional entanglements, but grew into a symbol of the national community and of the indwelling sanctity of the land.[76]

Amaterasu shares some aspects with the western deities. Like Saule she personifies the sun, like Nintur she is an ancestress of kings, like Sedna she provides the food of men, like many western goddesses she applies herself to women's crafts. Analogous to the Mountain Mother of Phrygia, she is the highest godhead of the land. Both these sovereign creatures are far removed from the framework of normal life. In Cybele's case the restraints of civilized society are broken and salvation is sought in the frenzy of unleashed emotion. As shown by the example of the Saigū princess, the opposite path is followed by the devotees of the eastern goddess. These strive for harmony by subjugation of human passions, by the discipline of ceremonial, and by the patient application of craftsmanship; and a delicately wrought object would be rendered as a gift rather than a severed phallus. And the bonds of family and clan are exalted in her person. Neither of the two deities rose to supremacy because of the creative powers of her womb.

Mediterranean tradition did not travel to eastern Asia. And the Mediterranean tale that a monster must be slain in order to maintain or create the world of mortals is not part of Japanese mythology. Also the hunters' way of life has left few traces. The aggression unleashed in the hunt is turned inward toward mastering passions. If a human has been flawed by immorality or humiliation, the aggression may become complete. In this way the act of suicide has received ritual stature.

Conclusion

I N the previous chapters we considered important goddesses, figures that have often been classed as alternate forms of the Great Mother, said to be a timeless being of an infinite variety of functions and epiphanies. We have turned to various and often widely differing cultures: from those of nomadic hunters and herders, and of settled farmers, to inhabitants of the icy wasteland near the arctic waters, and to tillers of the sun-parched Mediterranean earth. We have noted, as was to be expected, that the individual godheads had received the imprint of their special spiritual environments. It was also found, however, that many of their characteristic qualities could be traced to very archaic configurations, such as had been preserved in the communities of northern Eurasia: to Lords and Guardians of Nature, to animated and deified elements of the surroundings, to tribal and ancestral spirits, and to the goddesses of women's lives. Sometimes the sophisticated goddesses of literate societies had accepted within themselves the qualities of more than one archaic group.

We noted the aspect of a Ruler and Guardian of wild nature in the Mesopotamian Ninhursag/Nintur, who is a Lady of the Mountain, in the Anatolian Cybele, the Mountain Mother, and in Sedna, the mistress of sea animals. Elements of the environment became personified in Amaterasu and Saule, the sun, and in Demeter, the plowed earth. Amaterasu and the Mexican divinities Tlazolteotl, Coatlicue, Cihuacoatl, and Teteo Innan show the aspects of ancestral tutelary forces. Sedna, likewise, is an ancestress. The offices of the goddesses of women's lives, relating to childbirth, health, and female occupations, are carried out by the Mexican deities and by Demeter and Nintur (see Appendix B).

The image and function of the goddesses grew and extended beyond the archaic frame. Demeter brought to men the arts of civilized society and the

consolation of her mysteries, and she aquired an affinity with the kingdom of
the dead. Cybele combined in herself the dynamics of many deities: she offered
victory to warriors, salvation to the devotees of her cult, fruitful harvests to
the farmer, and healing to the sick. Nintur was vital, as potter and master
artisan, in creating the first human. Sedna presides over the dead and Amaterasu symbolizes the sacred national community of Japan. The maternal divinities of Mexico showed an alliance with agriculture and the crafts of war
(see Appendix C).

On the basis of these observations we realize that the goddesses originated
in diverse forms and developed further in various ways. We may safely state
that the deities did not find their origin in one single archetypal creature and
did not derive significance through the power of the womb. Their importance
was attained in various ways: through the ability to provide the food of men
(Demeter and Sedna); to guard and protect a locality (Cybele); to aid in warfare
(Cihuacoatl and Teteo Innan); to illuminate the world (Saule and Amaterasu);
to establish and shield the nation (Amaterasu); to assist in the birth of children
(Nintur, Teteo Innan, and Cihuacoatl), and of cattle (Nintur). Tales of how a
child was conceived and brought forth by the goddess are related only of
Chimalman, Coatlicue, and Sedna. Only Chimalman and Coatlicue received
their significance from having borne a splendid son, i.e., from their motherhood.

That the possession of a fertile womb in itself is not a guarantor of strength
and power is well illustrated by the tale of Apollo's birth, which was previously
cited. Leto was prevented from release because Hera, in her jealousy, did not
allow Eileithya to aid the woman in travail. Compassionate goddesses gathered
around Leto and offered Eileithyia a precious jewel for her help. The offer was
accepted, and when Eileithyia reached the island, Leto, clasping a palm tree,
was able to bring forth her glorious son. Thus among the personages of the
episode, the jealous Hera, the friendly goddesses, and the competent Eileithyia,
the fertile woman was the weakest—helpless in the hands of benign or hostile
forces.

Even the Virgin Mary, one of the most celebrated of all mothers, had no
choice about her destiny. In shock and fear before the apparition of the arch-
angel Gabriel, she was informed: "Thou shalt conceive in thy womb, and bring
forth a son and shalt call him Jesus" (Luke 1:31–32). Truly, she had no greater
command of the events than a Victorian servant girl who gives birth behind
a shed. The mothers of great heroes may even be the subject of rape or de-
ception. Hercules was born to Alkmene because Zeus assumed her husband's
shape. Bödvild, the mother of the Germanic warrior Videge, was overcome by
Völund's wiles.

While we may realize that the ability to bear a child does not bestow
sovereign powers on a woman or sovereign powers on a divinity, we must also
realize the deep impact of the process of birth on human awareness and religious belief. The countless taboos concerning pregnancy, parturition, and
menstruation of hunting cultures underline the awe inspired by the *myster-*

ium tremendum of women's biological functions. By giving birth to a future hunter or to the mother of a future hunter the woman asserts her determination to continue existence in a hostile environment in the same way as the man who summons in courage and in unceasing aggression his god and master from a cave, to carry him in triumph to the human dwelling. In both instances life hangs in the balance; man and superhuman stand face to face, and the real dangers of the situation are overshadowed by the fears of insulting the mighty forces.

In the tales of more complex societies the bringing forth of a great man often is experienced in the midst of dangers. All male children of the Israelites were to be slain when Moses's mother was delivered; and her son was hidden in the reeds. Herod demanded the death of infants and Jesus's parents fled the town. Zeus would have been swallowed by his father had he not been sheltered in a cave. Romulus and Remus were born to a vestal virgin and left to die on a hill. Huitzilopochtli defended his young life, at the hour of his birth, against an overwhelming number of his enemies. In a Jewish legend Abraham was born amidst dangers while his mother took refuge in a cave.[1] It is likely that these tales give concrete shape to the fears and perils surrounding every human birth.

We thus encountered forces that attended especially to this time of crisis. Excluded from the worship and the protection of the gods of male pursuits and of the household of their marriage, the women of the hunting and herding societies of northern Eurasia would turn, in their spiritual and physical needs, and especially at the time of giving birth, to their own and special deities: Madder-akka and her daughters ease the labor pains of the Saami woman; and the 'earth carrying old woman' of the Nentsi, who lives beneath the tent, sends the child into the world and determines its length of life. In more highly developed pantheons the group of women goddesses is not so clearly marked off from the others, just as the women's realm has expanded in the human sphere. Important female deities might devote some of their attention to caring for the women's lot, such as Demeter, Hera, or Artemis of Greece, Nintur of Mesopotamia, Laima of the Latvians, and Teteo Innan and Cihuacoatl of the Mexicans. The Japanese Amaterasu is pictured in the woman's craft of weaving. Women's deities are not encountered, on the other hand, in the culture of the Inuit or in the entourage of Cybele.

It may be argued that there is no basic difference between the concept of the Great Mother, so widely accepted on many levels, and the goddesses of women which are here described, for both are concerned with motherhood and deeply involved in fashioning and maintaining human life. The two configurations, however, spring from very different sources. The Great Mother is shaped in the image of a fertile human woman. The Birth Goddesses have not necessarily given birth, i.e., Artemis and Laima. They may be beyond the age of bearing children, frequently addressed as 'old woman' or 'grandmother,' i.e., *akka*. They would not celebrate or represent the triumph of human biological fertility, for they are not forces from within but from without, emissaries of the overwhelming and enduring world in which the human is a stranger and shortlived guest.

These godheads may fashion the child or the child's soul, yet their creativity does not extend to other realms and they do not evolve into universally creative beings. They often hold the power over the future life of the newly born, however, because it is believed that destiny is determined at the time of birth. The godheads of fate are usually visualized in female form. In the myths of some more complex cultures we meet an unresolved power conflict between the highest god and deities of fate, between Odin and the Norns, Zeus and the Moirai, and Dievs and Laima. We might find the explanation of this phenomenon in the archaic separation between men's and women's deities, each group supreme and sovereign in its sphere. The fierceness displayed by women in guarding the privacy of their festivities against men might also find its derivation in this root. Considering the power of the Birth Goddesses over human fate we realize, once again, that the act of birth-giving does not evoke godheads of a joyful creativity but rather those somber powers of no recourse, who in the hour of the birth of mortals already know the hour of their death.

In the context of the early cultures women's goddesses are represented in concrete form, as puppets, and they are stationed in the human dwelling. In both aspects they parallel the tutelary ancestral deities of the man. Indeed, the woman's numina are inherited by her from her family and blend to some measure with her ancestral spirits. Thus we realize that the promotion of new life issues, to some extent, from the world of the departed, less from the transitory and perishable organ of a woman's body than from the enduring beneficial power of the dead.

Some of the birth goddesses show a relation to the earth. The noun *madder,* of the name Madder-akka, has cognates in related languages meaning "earth." The birth helper of the Nentsi lives within the earth, wears seven belts, a skirt and a hat of earth. A modern observer might assume that here the fruit-bearing earth is seen in analogy with the woman who brings forth a child. Yet neither the Saami nor the Nentsi have developed agricultural techniques. They do not view the earth as provider of the food of men but as the place that holds the dead. We may note, again, that life is thought to spring from the deceased. The earth as progenitor of humans, and as such she is sometimes viewed, achieves her creativity through her nature of ancestress and not through the nature of a fertile woman. In some cultures children are named after dead ancestors; the German noun *Enkel* (grandchild) was formed from the noun *Ahne* (ancestor), thus meaning "little ancestor." Both phenomena may be traced to the belief that life flows from the dead. A poem by Richard Beer-Hoffman entitled "Lullaby for Miriam" encapsulates this faith (in the final stanza):

> Miriam, my child, have you fallen asleep?
> We are only as banks to keep and to hold

The blood of our fathers, which runs ceaseless and deep
full of unrest and pride, to the young from the old.[2]

The images of godheads that emerge in this study differ greatly from those which inspire and console the followers of the new religion of the Goddess. These believe that the Goddess originated in one basic archetypal form, in one overwhelming experience that left its imprint on the human soul. I have argued that goddesses grew from a variety of contexts and desires, unfolding their nature in a variety of ways. Not the infants' longing for their mothers' breasts shaped the contours of the divine, but the needs of adult men and women faced with the cruel exigencies of archaic life, exultant in their triumphs and burdened with the everpresent knowledge and spectacle of death. To trace the power of goddesses to their biological functions is to diminish the stature and flatten the form in the images of divine and human women.

The devotees of the Goddess cult assert that the themes of violence in myth and the wars and bloodshed of human society were introduced by fierce and warlike invaders; these tribes and nations also brought a patriarchal order into the agricultural, matriarchal societies of the Middle East where the Goddess ruled supreme. In the course of this study, however, we have seen that the theme of the creative battle germinated in the farming communities themselves and was not derived from foreign powers. In the villages and towns of the Middle East mortals experienced the surge of pride that came with being able to force nature to their will. And they told the story of how the cosmos originated in the slaughter of a living creature.[3] Those who wish to study the themes of violence in myth and the nature of aggressiveness in human society are not helped by following a slanted and fictitious story.

How a goddess may lose in depth through the idealization of a Goddess worshipper, and through emphasis on her feminine experience, can be seen in the portrait of the goddess Inanna of Sumer, as it is rendered by Diane Wolkstein. The author traces the development of the divinity from unformed girlhood to the fulfillment of her destiny. In the poem of the *huluppu* tree the goddess is given her "throne and bed,"[4] the symbols of her rule and of her womanhood, she receives these after some beings were vanquished, creatures that are in fact her own unexpressed desires and fears.[5]

Afterward Inanna obtains the Tablets of Destiny and is ready to assume the rule over her land, but she has not yet gained full womanhood. The poems of Dumuzi's love and courtship of Inanna show her in the flowering of her passion; in the poems of her wedding with a king she bestows the lordship of the country on a chosen being.[6] In her longing for a deeper wisdom she descends to the underworld, "the great below" where she must suffer a temporary death to return to the living in the manner of a shaman.[7]

While Wolkstein has shaped the image of a vibrant and appealing creature, she has not done justice to her diversity. She has arranged the events in an invented sequence and thus pointed to a development of which there is no indication. Inanna (and she cannot be separated from the Akkadian Ishtar) is not shown in the violence of her anger and vindictiveness. Inanna sets the "wild bull of heaven" on Gilgamesh after he has spurned her love.[8] She invariably destroys those who have held her in their arms. These are enumerated by Gilgamesh: the varicolored bird whose wings were broken, the war horse for which she destined whip and spurs, the shepherd whom she turned into a wolf so that he was turn by his dogs, Dumuzi for whom she ordained lamentations every year.[9] Inanna also is a harlot and the patroness of the girls of pleasure; as such she is praised in a hymn:

> O harlot, you set out for the ale house
> O Inanna you are bent on going into your [usual] window
> [namely to solicit] for a lover.[10]

Moreover, Inanna is the power of the rainstorm, and she caused a deadly drought to defeat the ruler of Aratta. She is the force of war, as related in a song of self-praise:

> When I stand in the midst of the battle,
> I am the heart of the battle,
> the arm of the warriors,
> when I begin moving at the end of the battle,
> I am an evilly rising flood.[11]

We do not know why Inanna descended to "the great below," but it appears to have been ambition for a greater realm to rule, the same ambition that caused her to abduct the tablets of destiny from the god of the watery deep.

By leaving these and other aspects of Inanna out of her description, Wolkstein reduces the fullness of Inanna's image and the multiplicity of religious experiences that went into her making. A number of godheads must have fused in the course of time to create the figure. By further integrating the various epiphanies Wolkstein continues a process that was interrupted by the rise of Christianity. She has acted as a theologian, not as an explorer of the numinous.

In her book of feminist mythology, Carolyne Larrington enumerates the accusations leveled, in the course of a banquet, at the female godheads of Scandinavian tradition.[12] She does not present the accusations directed against the men. In her method she has given us half a myth and deprived the reader of the full flavor of the scene; she has served her theology but not the understanding of Norse beliefs. Many books on the theology of the Goddess have recently been written, and they have their place in modern society. My study is addressed to those who wish to gain a truer sense of the ways in which humans transformed the disparate and disturbing elements of their existence into the poetry of myth.

Since the "Goddess" appears to satisfy the needs of many modern women, it might be inferred that the concept was constructed for just this purpose in modern times. The idea of an archetypal Great Mother, however, was extant before the era of the modern women's liberation movement. In the nineteenth century J. J. Bachofen proposed the theory of a primordial matriarchal society in which a Mother Goddess ruled the other gods. Robert Briffault extended and supported Bachofen's ideas in his book: *The Mothers.* C. G. Jung and Erich Neumann saw the archetypal principle of the "feminine" as a structure of the human psyche. A. Dieterich vigorously expounded the idea of Mother Earth, the earth as primary maternal deity, whose worship preceded that of all the other gods. And his views are still widely accepted.[13]

E. O. James traced the outlines of the Great Mother Goddess; Mircea Eliade spoke of the sacrality accorded to women with the advent of agriculture.[14] Archaeologists, such as J. A. Evans and James Mellaart, eagerly embraced the belief in a primordial goddess of childbearing and fertility in their interpretation of prehistoric artifacts.[15]

In his *Faust,* Goethe avowed, "The eternally feminine draws us upwards to the stars." Friedrich Schiller named women as the purveyors of celestial light:

> Honor the women! It is woman who grows
> In terrestrial life the celestial rose.[16]

The "eternally feminine" (*das ewig Weibliche*) is surely an abstraction in line with "the brotherhood of man," the "sanctity of life," and the "sacredness of motherhood," all based on human qualities or relations. Such constructions and ideals came to the fore when people turned from the gods of their revealed religions. Intellectual concepts were substituted for the older forces who found their origin, as we have seen, in the elements of nature, in human surroundings, or in the world of the dead.

Abstractions, as guide to ethical action, came to special prominence in the eighteenth century through the intellectual movement of the "Enlightenment." People were exhorted to liberate themselves from the shackles of outmoded thought through the powers of their "reason." "Tolerance" was sought in religious matters; "equality" and "liberty" were the goals to be achieved by the French Revolution. And the statue of "Liberty" stands at the gateway to the United States, which was founded on the principles of the Enlightenment. A ruler was to govern because of personal qualities and virtues, not because the being had been chosen by a god.

Fully confident in the powers of human capability and human growth, modern thought interprets the relics of archaic religions in an anthropocentric fashion. Caves, for instance, are likened to the womb of Mother Earth and are said to symbolize an especially feminine sacrality, that of sheltering and feeding.[17] There is no evidence to show that the Paleolithic inhabitants saw the caves in the same light. Female figurines were not unearthed from caves but from sites of habitation. The picture of a woman engraved into the rock does not appear at the entrance but at some distance from the cave of Laussel. The cave walls exhibit pictures of phallic men and of animals of the chase; some of the beasts are slain or wounded by manmade tools.[18] The hunt is a specifically male pursuit, and thus no female imagery, pointing to a feminine sacrality is to be seen in the Paleolithic caves.

In a human-centered approach, a sovereign goddess was formed on the model of a human mother. She nurtures and she consoles, she chastises and she inspires, she is all-loving and all-giving, and she submits to the biological lot of a mortal woman. If we agree with Rudolf Otto that the primal religious experience arose in fear and trembling, in the awe before the *mysterium tremendum,* the utterly different, the unknown and unknowable, then we cannot assume that "Supermom" was the fountainhead of religious life, even if we had no other evidence. In the archaic thought pattern of the Ob-Ugrians, a bear, not a woman in human shape, is seen as the source of sustenance and strength.[19] And we must know that the belief in our own power and imagination, our potential and responsibility, the valor of our brain and of our body is a late flower in the growth of human thought.

Abbreviations

In citing works in the notes and appendices, short titles have generally been used. Works frequently cited have been identified by the following abbreviations:

ANET	*Ancient Near Eastern Texts Relating to the Old Testament.* Ed. J. B. Pritchard. Princeton, 1969.
AS	*Assyriological Studies.* The Oriental Institute of Chicago. Chicago, 1931–.
BE	*The Babylonian Expedition of the University of Pennsylvania.* Series A. Cuneiform Texts. Philadelphia, 1896–.
Boas I, II, III, IV	Boas 1888–1907. See bibliography entry: Boas (used in Appendix A)
Gudea Cylinder	F. Thureau-Dangin. *Les cylindres de Goudéa découverts par Ernest de Sarzec à Tello.* Paris, 1925.
HRET	*Historical, Religious and Economic Texts and Antiquities.* Niels and Keiser. New Haven, 1920.
ISA	*Les inscriptions de Sumer et d' Akkad.* Thureau-Dangin, F. Paris, 1905.
KB	*Keilinschriftliche Bibliothek,* I–IV. Schrader, E. Berlin, 1889.
KBo	*Keilschrifttexte aus Boghazköi.* Leipzig/Berlin, 1916–.
KUB	*Keilschrifturkunden aus Bogazköi.* Berlin, 1921–.
OECT	*Oxford Edition of Cuneiform Texts.*
Sculptures	*Assyrian Sculptures in the British Museum; Reign of Ashurnasir-pal 885–860 B.C.* W. A. Wallis Budge. London, 1914.
SEM	*Sumerian Epics and Myths.* E. Chiera. Chicago, 1934.

TRS	*Textes religieux sumériens du Louvre.* Henri de Genouillac. Paris, 1930.
UET	*Ur Excavation Texts* I-VIII. London, 1928.
VAB	*Vorderasiatische Bibliothek.* Leipzig, 1907–16.

Appendix A
The Sedna Tales

The following list cites variant forms of the tales concerning the Sedna figures. The list does not claim to be all inclusive.

1. The Ancestress

1.1 We meet with a recurrent tale of a girl's marriage to a dog, a marriage that originated various races.

    1.1.1 Sometimes no reason is given for the marriage (Boas I, 637, Central Eskimo, her name is Niviarsiang; Boas II, 207, Alaska; Boas IV, 492–93, Pond's Bay; Lantis, 132, Kodiak; Lantis, 133, Nunivak; Rink, 471, Greenland and Labrador).

    1.1.2 The girl refuses to get married; her father becomes angry and threatens to marry her to a dog; a dog soon appears and impregnates the girl (Kroeber, 168, Smith Sound; also known in Greenland).

    1.1.3 The father wants her to marry a dog; she flees to an island, but the dog follows her and marries her (Kroeber, 169, Smith Sound; Greenland).

    1.1.4 The girl marries her father's dog, who appears in the form of a man in dogskin trousers; the father's name is Aspasinasse (Boas III, 165–67, Cumberland Sound).

    1.1.5 When the girl does not want to get married, her father suggests that she marry a dog and she agrees; a dog soon appears who had transformed himself into a man for the occasion (Boas III, 327, western coast of Hudson Bay).

    1.1.6 A red-and-white stone was transformed into a dog and he marries the girl; her name is Uinigumissuitung or Aiviliayog (Boas III, 163–65, Cumberland Sound).

1.2 The girl finds herself on an island.

    1.2.1 She is sent there by her father because the puppies, her children, make too much noise (1.1.4; 1.1.6).

1.2.2 Her father places them on an island without any reason while her lover is away (1.1.5; 1.1.1 Lantis).

1.2.3 The pregnant girl was chased away, and her husband carried her to an island (1.1.2).

1.2.4 She fled to an island before her marriage (1.1.3).

1.2.5 Her father sends them to an island because the dog husband does not provide for her (1.1.1 Boas I).

1.3 There are several ways of providing for her.

1.3.1 The dog brings meat in a pair of boots tied around his neck (1.1.4; 1.1.6); later the father brings the food (1.1.4).

1.3.2 The dog swims back and forth with the food in a bag (1.1.5).

1.3.3 the dog brings meat from the father in a skin float (1.1.2).

1.3.4 The father brings food (1.1.3).

1.3.5 The father brings food after the dog has died (1.1.5; 1.1.4).

1.4 The dog drowns or almost drowns.

1.4.1 The father puts stones into the dog's bag; the dog almost drowns, but manages to reach the island; the next day the father puts sand into the pouch and the dog goes down (1.1.5).

1.4.2 The father puts stones into the boots that are hung around the dog's neck or in his pouch and the dog drowns (1.1.1 Boas I; 1.1.4).

1.4.3 In one instance the father does not succeed in killing the dog even though he puts stones into the float (1.1.2).

1.4.4 The dog grieves for a long time; when he learns about the location of his family he swims toward the island but he drowns (1.1.1 Lantis).

1.4.5 The father drowns the dog after he has drowned the daughter (1.1.6; this story presents a fusion of the dog marriage tale with that of the creation of sea animals).

1.5 The father is destroyed.

1.5.1 The girl tells the pups to kill or to devour her father (1.1.1 Rink; 1.1.4); she tells the pups to kill their own father (1.1.2).

1.5.2 The girl tells her children to kill her father; when he lies wounded on the beach, a tidal wave sweeps over him (1.1.5).

1.5.3 The young dogs gnaw off the hands and feet of their grandfather (1.1.1 Boas I, this is also a fusion tale).

1.5.4 In revenge, the young dogs tear their grandfather to pieces when he comes to visit them (1.1.1 Lantis).

1.6 The young dogs are sent away and become ancestral.

1.6.1 The mother makes a boat out of the sole of a boot and in this vessel some puppies sail across the ocean; others she sends inland to live on caribou meat. They become the ancestors of the Ijiqat, who are larger than men; others generate the Inuarudligat, the dwarfs; and yet others stay with her and become the ancestors of the Eskimo (1.1.4).

1.6.2 Some became the ancestors of the Europeans, others the ancestors of the Indians (1.1.5).

1.6.3 Some of the children were Adlet (half man, half dog), five were dogs; they became the ancestors of the Europeans (1.1.1 Boas I, fusion story).

1.6.4 Some puppies became the ancestors of the Kodiaks; some went farther North; there had been three male and two female children (1.1.1 Lantis, 132);

there were five male and one female child (1.1.1 Lantis, 133).

1.6.5 Five of the children became the ancestors of the Erkileks, a mythical race, the others of the Europeans (1.1.1 Rink).

1.6.6 Five of the children were dogs, the others humans; the humans became ancestors of the Indians (1.1.1 Boas II).

1.6.7 Five races developed from the girl's offspring: Europeans, Nakassungnaitut (unidentifiable), wolves, Tornit (giants), dwarfs; they had been sent away in pairs of male and female (1.1.2).

1.6.8 They became the ancestors of the Inuarudligat, the Ijiqat, Adlet, Eskimo, and white men (1.1.6).

1.6.9 Nuliayoq is identified with the mother of dogs and of white men (Boas IV, 497, Iglulik Eskimo).

1.6.10 A red dog married to Aiviliayoq (also known as Anavigak) is the father of white men, dwarfs, and Eskimo; she is also known as Kunna or Katuma or Uinigumissuitung (1.1.1 Boas IV).

1.7 The girl's fate

1.7.1 She becomes Nuliayoq and lives with her father and her dog under the sea (1.1.5); she becomes Sedna and lives with her father and her dog under the sea (1.1.6).

1.7.2 She goes back to live with her father (1.1.2); in her old home (1.1.1 Lantis).

1.7.3 She starves on the island (1.1.3).

1.8 In one tale the girl is in dog form and the man is human; from them the Kodiak people have descended (Lantis 131, Kodiak).

1.9 A girl appears as the ancestress of land and sea animals. She is the niece of two old men. When the girl is brought to bed with child, they act as her birth helpers; and they throw each animal, as it emerges, into the place where it is meant to dwell (Lantis 134, Kodiak).

2. The Mistress of the Sea and Creatress of Sea Animals

2.1 The tale often begins with a marriage.

2.1.1 The girl marries a bird, a petrel or fulmar (Rasmussen I, 113, Smith Sound, her name is Nerrivik; Boas I, 583–85, Davis Strait and South Baffinland, her name is Sedna; Boas III, 119, Cumberland Sound, Sedna; Boas IV, 496, Hudson Bay).

2.1.2 She marries a dog (fusion with origin story); she is called Aiviliayoq; a petrel, disguised as a man, later takes her from her husband (1.1.6).

2.2 Her marriage is unhappy; she must live in a tent of fish skins rather than of furs, she must eat fish instead of seals; she is taken from her husband in a boat.

2.2.1 She is taken by her father (1.1.6, fusion; 2.1.1 Boas I,583; 2.1.1 Boas III; 2.1.1 Boas IV).

2.2.2 Taken by brothers and father (2.1.1 Boas I, 585).

2.2.3 Taken by brothers and grandfather (2.1.1 Rasmussen I).

2.2.4 In one tale her father kills her husband (2.1.1 Boas I, 583).

2.3 The boat is followed by angry pursuers who create a sea storm by flapping their wings (they are storm birds); the boat fills with water and is about to sink.

2.3.1 The husband causes the storm (1.1.6; 2.1.1 Rasmussen I; 2.1.1 Boas III; 2.1.1 Boas IV; 2.1.1 Boas I, 585).

2.3.2 The relatives of the slain husband cause the storm (2.1.1 Boas I, 583).

2.4 To save the boat the girl is thrown overboard; she clings to the edge of the boat.

2.4.1 Her grandfather chops off her hands and she drowns; at the bottom of the sea she becomes Nerrivik, the ruler of the ocean and its creatures (2.1.1 Rasmussen I).

2.4.2 Her father chops off her fingers, but later lets her climb back into the boat when the sea is calmer. In revenge she tells her dogs to gnaw off his hands and feet (fusion with origin story). All of them, the dogs, the father, and the woman are swallowed by the earth; she becomes mistress of the underworld, Adlivum (2.1.1 Boas I, 583).

2.4.3 Her father cuts off her fingers and then pierces her left eye; afterward he drowns her dog (fusion); he himself lies down on the beach, covered by his tent, and a wave takes him. All three, the dog, the father, and the girl, live beneath the sea; she becomes Sedna (1.1.6, 2.1.1 Boas III); a similar account is given concerning Nuliayoq (2.1.1 Boas IV). Her fingers are cut off, her eye is pierced, and her body is carried ashore by her father; here she is covered by a wave (2.1.1 Boas I, 585). The same is told about Nuliayoq or Aiviliayoq by the Iglulirmiut of Baffinland (2.1.1 Boas I, 585; 2.1.1 Boas IV).

2.4.4 Her father chops off her fingers (Boas II, 205, Alaska).

2.5 Sea animals originate from the severed fingers.

2.5.1 Whalebones arise from her fingernails, the first joint turns into whales, the second into seals, the stumps of her fingers into ground seals (2.1.1 Boas I, 583).

2.5.2 The first joint turns into whales and whalebones, the second into ground seals, the third into seals (1.1.6; 2.1.1 Boas III).

2.5.3 The first joints turn into salmon, the second into seals, the third into walrus, the metacarpal bones into whales (2.4.4).

2.5.4 Unspecified sea mammals originate; her name is Nuliayoq (2.1.1 Boas IV).

2.6 The creation of sea animals is not connected with a marriage.

2.6.1 A poor orphan is thrown overboard out of sheer cruelty; her lamp and dog are tossed after her. Her fingers are cut off as she clings to the boat. Sea animals originate in the incident, and she becomes the mistress of the sea; her name is Nivikkaa, and it means "she who was pushed backward" (Thalbitzer I, 393–94, Greenland).

2.6.2 A woman tries to devour her parents while they lie asleep; they wake up in time and manage to escape. The father returns, takes the girl with him into the boat, and there he cuts off her fingers because she didn't want to marry (some sort of fusion). Various types of seals arise from this act (except *Phoca barbata*), also walruses and narwhal (Kroeber, 179, Smith Sound).

2.6.3 The father throws the girl overboard because her dogs had gnawed his hands and feet (fusion story); her fingers become whales and seals (1.1.1 Boas I).

2.6.4 The girl Nuliayoq was, as an orphan, mistreated and despised. While playing with other children on a raft, she was pushed into the water and her fingers were cut off as she clasped the boat. The fingers turned into seals and she herself, sinking to the bottom of the sea, became its ruler and the mistress of its beasts; she also extended her dominion over land animals (Balicki, 206, Netsilik Eskimo).

2.7 Aspects of the Lady of the Sea; her origin is not stressed in these tales.

2.7.1 A woman lives at the bottom of the ocean, and she is the source of all nourishment; from the vessel that receives the oil dripping from her lamp, sea animals come forth and swim through the waters. Her name is Arnarkuagsac, "the old woman" (Rink, 40, Greenland). The story is also told in Baffinland where her name is Nanokuagsac (Boas I, 587).

2.7.2 Sedna, the mother of sea animals, dwells in the lower world in a house of stone and whalebones with her father and her dog. Her father cannot walk and has only one eye (2.1.1 Boas III).

2.7.3 Nuliayoq, also called Aiviliayoq, is mistress of land and sea animals. When she is angry she places herself at the entrance of the Wager river and upsets the hunters' boats (Boas III, 145, western coast of Hudson Bay).

2.7.4 Aiviliayoq has a fine house, much food, a dog without a tail; her father is a dwarf, called Anautalik or Napayoq (Boas I, 585–86, among the Iglulirmiut of Baffinland).

2.7.5 Kannakapfaluk lives in a snow house at the bottom of the sea; two bears, one white, one brown, and a dwarf, named Unga, share her residence; she controls the supply of seals (Jenness, 188, among the Copper Eskimo); a slightly different version is known in Bathhurst Inlet: here a big woman lives with a small woman who may be her daughter.

2.8 When the Mistress of the Animals is angry she withholds these and must be appeased.

2.8.1 The violation of hunting taboos brings pain to the souls of the slain animals. When these souls return to Sedna she feels the pain in her hands (the animals are, after all, part of her) (2.1.1 Boas III, 120, Cumberland Sound).

2.8.2 When the shaman visited Arnarkuagsac he found her in a rage; seizing her hair, she flung down bloody clothes and a crying baby; the shaman was able to calm her down (Rink, 466, Greenland).

2.8.3 Nerrivik cannot comb her hair because she has only one hand; the shaman must go down to do it for her. In gratitude she sends seals and other sea creatures (2.1.1 Rasmussen I).

2.8.4 A man in possession of helping spirits reached the bottom of the sea; there he met the mother of Tôrnârssuk by her lamp; she wept and picked things from behind her ears. He tickled her to improve her spirits, and she became appeased; she then released the animals (Rasmussen I, 75, South Greenland).

2.8.5 The sins committed by mortals give pain to the blind eye of Nuliyaoq; the shaman has to remove the cause of pain (2.1.1 Boas IV).

2.8.6 The shaman must subdue Nanokuagsac or deprive her of the charms with which she holds the animals; then she will release them (2.7.1 Boas I).

2.8.7 The shaman repeats the action that originally caused the growth of living creatures. He cuts off parts of her hand. After cutting the nails, bears are released. The first joint brings forth the *pagomys;* cutting off the second joint liberates the seals; the knuckles bring forth walrus, and the metacarpal bones the whales (2.7.4).

2.8.8 The shaman must tear off the parasites that have fasted in the woman's hair, the *agdlerutit* (this term also means "abortion"), which tumble like snakes around her face, or take hold of her hair to wrestle with her until she is exhausted (Thalbitzer I, 393–95); he must relieve her of her *agdlerutit* (2.7.1 Rink).

2.9 The shaman's road is dangerous and difficult.

2.9.1 He must pass sharks; the entrance path to Sedna's house is as narrow as a woman's knife (2.8.4).

2.9.2 He first passes the place of the happy dead, then comes upon an abyss; he has to walk over a slippery, ever turning wheel, pass a kettle with boiling seals, brave the fierce dogs and seals that guard the house, and then walk over a bridge that is as thin as a knife (2.7.1 Rink); the tale is also told in Baffinland about Nanokuagsac (2.7.1 Boas I).

3. The Mistress of Land and Sea Animals

3.1 All game, caribou, foxes, fish, birds, come from her; she is Nuliayoq, mother of the beasts (Rasmussen II, 195, Caribou Eskimo).

3.2 Nuliayoq, also called Aiviliayoq, is mistress of land and sea animals on the western coast of the Hudson Bay (2.7.3); Nuliayoq is mistress of land and sea animals also among the Netsilik Eskimo (2.6.4).

3.3 A woman, probably Sedna, created the reindeer from some fat taken from her belly and created the walrus, also from fat, in the water. The reindeer frightened her because it would not run away. She knocked out its teeth and kicked it so that its tail came off. And that is why reindeer have missing teeth and hardly any tail (Boas I, 587–88, Hudson Strait). She still hates reindeer.

3.4 A woman created reindeer from her boots in the hills, and walrus in the sea from her breeches. At first the walrus bore antlers and the reindeer possessed tusks. This arrangement was too dangerous for the hunters and it was reversed by an old man (Boas I, 588, Davis Strait). In other places also a woman transformed her garments into caribou and walrus; here she herself exchanged the antlers and the tusks (Boas III, 122, Hudson Bay; Boas III, 167, Cumberland Sound).

3.5 Pinga is the "Mother of the Caribou," and she lives in heaven (Hultkrantz, 389, Caribou Eskimo).

4. The Mistress of the Dead

4.1 After the dogs had gnawed off the hands and feet of the girl's father, all sank into the earth; the woman became mistress of the underworld (2.1.1 Boas I).

4.2 Idliragijenget, "she who sleeps in the house of the wind," is the mother of the underworld; her father Savirqong lies on a ledge; the dead are brought to him and must stay with him for a year snd suffer his pinchings. Across the threshhold lies Sedna's dog (Boas I, 588, Central Eskimo).

4.3 Those who die of sickness or were transgressors go to Sedna where they stay for a year; after being healed and purified they go up to second heaven. Here they hunt, but are plagued by ice and cold; murderers never leave. Those who are really good go to another heaven where they are truly happy (Boas I, 590, Davis Strait). This is also said about Nuliayoq or Aiviliayoq of the Hudson Bay (2.7.3).

4.4 Those who die of disease go to Sedna for a year; those who die by violence go to the lowest heaven. Those who had a premature birth go to Sedna and stay in the lowest world (Boas III, 130, Cumberland Sound).

4.5 The mother of sea animals lives in a house of stone and whalebones in the lower world. She cannot walk; her dog and her father stay within her dwelling (1.1.6; 2.1.1 Boas III).

4.6 Transgressors go to Nuliayoq; the good go to heaven where they play football with the head of a walrus; their playing manifests itself to men in the form of the northern lights (Boas III, 146, Cumberland Sound).

4.7 After three days the human soul goes to Sedna (Boas I, 591, Davis Strait).

4.8 Sedna's father sits beside the entrance of the house, covered with a blanket, always ready to snatch an entering soul and to draw it under his cover (Boas IV, 483, Cumberland Sound).

5. A story of the Labrador Eskimo blends the elements of the Sedna cycle in such a way that it must be told by itself.

A man married a woman and from this union came all the Eskimo. He, Tôrnârs-suk, set some puppies out into the sea in an old boot. One dog came back with the Indians, the other with white people. The man turned himself into a dog and married a young woman. Her father took her to an island, threw her overboard, and then cut off her fingers as she clung to the boat. Her thumb turned into a walrus, her first fingers into a seal, and the middle finger into a white bear. She now lives under the sea (Hawkes, 152).

6. The Names of the Deity

To indicate the role of the figure, each name will be followed by one or more of the following letters: A, ancestress; D, Mistress of the Dead; M, Mistress of Animals. Aiviliaoq (A,D,M); Akuilarmiut (M); Anavigak (A); Arnakuagsac (M), "the old woman"; Idliragijetinget (D), "she who sleeps in the house of the wind"; Kannak-apfuluk (M); Katunna (A); Kuma (A); Nanokuagsac (M); Nerrivik (M), "food vessel"; Niviarsiang (A); Nivikkaa (M), "the girl who was pushed backward"; Nuliayoq (A,D,M); Pinga (M); Sedna (D,M); Uinigmissuitung (A), "she who didn't want to marry"; Unisavagis (A).

The father is named Anautalik (he who has something to cut) or Angutas (her father), Savirqong (he with knife), Aspasinasse, or Napayoq.

We may note that some figures exercise more than one function. It is also true, though this is not shown by observing the names, that one persona may be designated by several names. In a tale of Cumberland Sound, Aiviliayoq was also named Uinigmissuitung because she didn't want to have a husband and became Sedna after she had drowned (1.1.6). Both instances point to the fusion of the various themes.

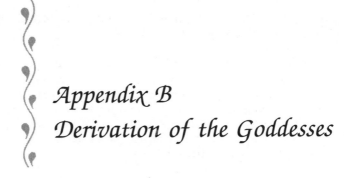

Appendix B
Derivation of the Goddesses

Goddess	Guardian of Nature	Animated Element	Ancestral tribal spirit	Women's Goddess
Nintur/ Ninhursag	Mountain Mother			Childbirth, Cattle goddess
Saule		Sun		
Sedna	Mistress of seals		Ancestress of tribes	Prototype of the ritually impure woman
Amaterasu		Sun	Ancestress of emperor	Women's crafts
Demeter		Plowed earth		Women's festivals Childbirth Nursing
Cybele	Mountains, forests, wells			
Mexican Goddesses			Tribal goddesses	Childbirth, women's crafts

Appendix C
Development and Growth
of the Goddesses

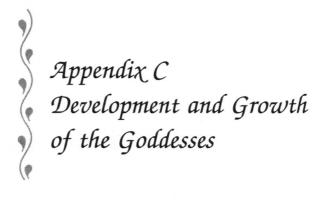

	Nintur/ Ninhursag	Saule	Sedna	Amaterasu	Demeter	Cybele	Mexican Goddesses
Agriculture		×		×			×
Actual mother		×			Sorrowing mother		×
Mysteries					×	×	
Universal force						×	
Craftsmanship				×			
National goddess				×			
Creation of men	×						
Death			×		×		
War							×
Culture bringer					×		
Disappearing god					×		

Not all ramifications and developments could here be taken into account.

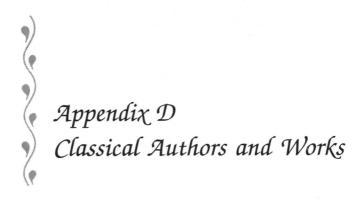

Appendix D
Classical Authors and Works

The following list cites the classical authors and works, and their abbreviations, used in this book.

Aeschylus
Antimachus of Colophon
Apollodorus Apoll.
Apollonius of Rhodes
Apuleius
Aristophanes
Arnobius
Athenaeus
Callimachus
Clement of Alexandria
Cleomedes
Cratinus
Diodorus Siculus
Eratosthenes
Eunapius
Euripides
Gregorius (Gregory of Nazianz)
Heracleides (Heracleides Ponticus)
Herodotus
Hesiod
Hesychius
Himerius
Hippocrates
Hippolytus

Aesc. *suppl.* Aeschylus, *Supplices*
Aesc. frg. *Aeschylus,* fragment
Ant. Lib. Antonius Liberalis
Ant. Pal. *Anthologia Palatina*
Apoll. *bibl.* Apollodorus, *bibliotheca*
Apul. *Met.* Apuleius, *Metamorphoses*
Arch. frg. Archias, fragment
Arist. *Lysist.*—Aristophanes *Lysistrate*
Clem. *Protr.* Clement of Alexandria, *Protreptikos*
CAF—*Conicorum Atticorum Fragmenta,* Th. Kock, ed. Leipzig, 1880–88.
Call. *hymn* Callimachus, *hymni*
Cleomedes *cycle theor* Cleomedes, *cyklike theoria mataron*
Cratinus fr. Cratinus, fragments
Crinagoras of Lesbos, *Anthologia Palatinum*
Danais fr. *Danais,* fragment
Diod. *bibl.* Diodorus *bibliotheca*
Diod. Sic. Diodorus Siculus
Eratosthenes *katasterisma*
Eunapius *Vitae Sophisticarum*
Eur. *Iph.* Euripides, *Iphigenia in Aulis*

Homer	Eur. *Phoen.* Euripides, *Phoenissae*
Horatius	Eur. *Sup.* Euripides, *Supplices*
Isocrates	Gregor of Nazanz *Orat.* Gregory of Nazanz,
Julianus (Julian the Apostate)	*Orationes*
Juvenal	Hes. *Theo.* Hesiod, *Theogony*
Lucian	Hesiod, *Works*
Lucretius	Hesych. *Anesidora,* Hesychius, *Anesidora*
Lycurgus	Himerius, *Orationes*
Minucius Felix	Hippocrates, *de Aere, Aqua et Locis*
Nicander	Hom. *Od.,* Homer, *Odyssey*
Olen	Hom. *Hymn, Hymni Homerici,* Hom. *vitae*
Ovid	Horatius *od.* Horatius *carmina*
Pausanias Paus.	*hymn. Apoll. Hymnus ad Apollinem*
Pindar	*Il, Iliad*
Pisander	Jul, *or,* Julianus, *Orationes*
Plato	Juvenal *sat,* Juvenalis *satiri*
Plutarch	Minucius Felix, *Octav, Octavius*
Prudentius	Lucian, *de dea Syria*
Pythagoras	Lucian, *de theon dialogoi*
Sallust	Luc. *schol, scholion* on Lucian
Semonides	Nicander, *Alexipharmaca*
Servius	*Orphic Hymn*
Sophocles	Ovid, *Fasti*
Strabo	Ovid, *met. Metamorphoses*
Suidas (Suda)	Pindar *Ol.* Pindar, *Olympians*
Tacitus	Plut. *Dio,* Plutarch, *Dio*
Tertullian	Plut. *Lyc.* Plutarch, *Lycurgus*
Theocritus	Prud. *Persisteph.* Prudentius, *Peristephanon*
Theophrastus	*liber*
Tibullus	Sallust, *de diis*
Virgil	*Serv. Verg. Georg. Servius commentary* on
	Virgil's *Georgica*
	Tert. *ad. nat.* Tertullianus, *ad nationes libri*
	Theocrit. *Id.* Theocritus *Idyls (bucolici*
	graeci)
	Theog. Theogony.
	Theophrastus, *On Pity*
	Vita Herodotea
	Vitae Homerici

Appendix E
Mexican Sources

The Mexican sources cited and their abbreviations are as follows:

Anales de Quauhtitlan; Noticias historicas de Mexico y sus contornos (Codex Chimal-popoco), 1882. Edited by José Ferdinand Ramirez. Also edited and translated by Walter Lehmann, 1906, 1938. *anal. quauht.*

Codex Bologna (Codex Cospi). *A Pre-Columbian Codex in the Library of the University of Bologna.* Published by the Duc du Loubat. Rome, 1898. *Cod. Bol.*

Codex Borbonicus: *A Pre-Columbian Codex preserved in the Library of the Chamber of Deputies in Paris.* Published by the Duc du Loubat, 1899.

Codex Borgia: *A Pre-Columbian Codex preserved in the Ethnographical Museum of the Vatican.* Edited by George E. Seler 1904–09.

Codex Boturini. García Cubas, *Atlas Geográfico y Estadístico de los Estados Unidos de Mexico.* Mexico City, 1858.

Codex Telleriano-Remensis; *A Post-Columbian Codex published by the Duc du Loubat.* Paris, 1899.

Codex Féjerváry-Mayer; *An old Mexican picture manuscript in the Liverpool Free Public Museum.* Published by the Duc du Loubat. Paris, 1901. Seler 1901.

Codex Vaticanus A (3778); *A Post-Columbian Codex preserved in the Library of the Vatican.* Published by the Duc du Loubat, Rome, 1900. *Cod. Vat.*

Codex Vaticanus B (3773); *A Pre-Columbian Codex preserved in the Library of the Vatican,* Rome. Published by the Duc du Loubat, Rome, 1896. *Cod. Vat. B.*

Florentine Codex; Codex Florentino. Illustrations for Sahagún's *Historia de las Cosas de Nueva España.* Edited by Arthur J. C. Anderson and Charles E. Dibble. Santa Fé, 1950–82. FL.

Historia de Colhuaca. Edited and translated by Walter Lehmann. Berlin, 1938. (*Anales de Quauhtitlan*).

Historia Ecclesiástica Indiana (Sixteenth century) by Fray Gerónimo Mendieta. Edited by Icazbalceta J. García. Mexico City, 1870.

Historia General de las Cosas de Nueva España by Bernardino di Sahagún. *Florentine*

Codex. Edited and translated by Arthur C. Anderson and Charles E. Dibbles. Santa Fé, 1950–82. FL

Historia de las Indias de Nueva-España by Fray Diego Durán (Sixteenth century). Translated by Doris Heyden, Fray Diego Durán. *The Aztecs: the History of the Indies of New Spain.* New York, 1964.

Histoire du Méchique. "Histoire du Méchique; Manuscrit Français inédit du XVI Siècle." E. D. Jonghe. *Journal de la société des Américanistes* de Paris, 1905.

Historia de los Mexicanos por sus pinturas (Codex Ramirez); Icazbalceta García: *Nueva Colección de documentos para la Historia* de Mexico. Vol. 3. Mexico City, 1891. *hist. mex. pint.*

Histoire Mexicaine, Documents pour servir á l'Histoire du Mexique. Catalogue Raisonné de la Collection de M.E. Goupil. Edited by Eugene Boban Paris, 1891. *hist. mex.*

Histoire de la nation Mexicaine (Reproduction du Codex 1576) in the Goupil Collection, Paris. J.M.A. Aubin ed. 1893. *hist. mex.* 1576.

Historia de los Reynos (Anales de Quauhtitlan).

Historia de Tlazcala. Camargo D. Muñoz (Sixteenth century). Edited by Alfred Chavero. Mexico City, 1892.

Historia Tolteca-Chichimeca. Edited by K. T. Preuss and E. Mengin. Die mexikanische Bilderhandschrift Historia Tolteca-Chichimeca. Berlin, 1937–38. *hist. tolt. chich.*

Notes

Chapter 1

1. Levy, *Gate of Horn,* 62; she is called by James the "life-producing Mother as the personification of fecundity" behind whom lies "the mystery of birth and generation in the abstract, at first in the human and animal world with which Paleololithic Man was mainly concerned" (*Cult of the Mother Goddess,* 228).

2. Neumann, *Great Mother,* 96.

3. Mallowan and Cruikshank, "Excavation," 87.

4. James, *Cult of the Mother Goddess,* 41.

5. Guthrie, *Early Greek Religion,* 39, quoted by Petterson, *Mother Earth,* 77.

6. Eliade, *History of Religious Ideas,* vol. 1, 40.

7. Pettazzoni, *Allknowing God,* 435; Eliade asserts "since women played a decisive part in the domestication of plants, they become the owners of cultivated fields, which raises their social position and creates characteristic institutions, such as, for example, matrilocation" (*History of Religious Ideas,* vol. 1, 40).

8. Gimbutas, *Gods and Goddesses,* 195–96.

9. Piggott, *Prehistoric India,* 127.

10. Campbell, *Masks of God,* vol. 3, 70–75, assumes that the best-known mythological expression of this happening is contained in the Babylonian creation myth where the female all-mother is destroyed by her descendant Marduk.

11. Apuleius, *Metamorphoses* XI.

12. James states that "the function of the male in the process of generation became more apparent . . . as the physiological facts concerning paternity were more clearly understood and recognized. Then the Mother-Goddess was assigned a male partner" (*Cult of the Mother Goddess,* 228); ibid., 22.

13. Hančar examined ninety-five hunting stations in Siberia, the place from which the figurines might have found their diffusion ("Problem der Venusstatuetten"). Alexander Marshack, *Roots of Civilization,* 281–340, describes not only the statuettes of

women but also the engravings of female forms found throughout Europe and Asia on many objects.

14. Ränk, *Die heilige Hinterecke,* 10, 11; in the Finno-Karelian regions the men's part is called *misten-puoli* and the women's part *naisten-puoli;* the Votiaks (Udmurts) name the area in which the bed stands *kisno-pal*—"women's part"; the Russians have the name *ženskaja polovina*—"women's part"—for the screened-off portion of the house. Ränk published his study in 1949. He had based himself frequently on older sources; many of the customs described were no longer practiced at the time of publication, and more may have disappeared since then.

15. Ibid., 99, 100.

16. Ibid., the Siimsi pillar belongs to the Yurak (Nentsi) settlements, 107; the *akka-kerre* to the Saami, 185; the Samoyed tent is divided by a pole, 187. It is believed that if the sanctions are violated, a wolf might break into the reindeer herd or the men would lose their luck in hunting.

17. Ibid., 194–200. The door is called *påssjo-raike, påssjo* being the sacred portion of the house; among the Kola Saami the door is named *varr-lips* (bloody door) because the meat of the animal killed in hunting is brought into the house through this door.

18. Ibid., 203–7, the Ainu husband is not allowed to use the front entrance for six days following the birth of a child; if no second door exists, he makes his way through a window in the hind wall.

19. Ibid., 192–93; Hastings, *Encyclopedia of Religion and Ethics,* entry: Birth I, b.

20. Kühn, *Felsbilder Europas,* 91; Narr, "Bärenzeremoniell"; Jettmar, "*Aussage der Archäologie,*" 309.

21. Hastings, *Encyclopedia of Religion and Ethics,* entry: Birth 2.

22. Bächtold-Stäubli, *Handwörterbuch,* entry: Wöchnerin. The modern English term "confinement," the German *Wöchnerin,* referring to the weeks of the woman's seclusion, still indicate the earlier customs.

23. Lévy-Strauss, "La vie familiale," 108.

24. Neumann, *Great Mother,* 159.

25. Bächtold-Stäubli, *Handwörterbuch,* entry: Wilde, Wilde Weiber, 2; Harva, *Wassergottheiten, 64.*

26. The random sampling of twenty-one pictures of the Virgin Mary in the Founders' Room of the Ashmolean Museum in Oxford shows sixteen pictures of Mary holding, fondling, or playing with her child; in two she is seen in lamentation over her dead son. Only three portray her without a child: the *Annunciation* (Florentine School, anonymous), the *Allegory of the Immaculate Conception* (Vasari), and the image of Mary herself as a newborn child (Andrea di Ciene).

27. Hančar, "Problem der Venusstatuetten," 149–52. Marshack points to the wide variety of female forms, which might be pregnant or slim, naturalistic or so stylized as to show only breasts, buttocks, or a vulva, sometimes brought into relation with animals or male figures, and he believes that they had served many functions connected with women's experiences—maturation, menstruation, childbirth—but also with the cycles of the progress of time, the cycles of the seasons (*Roots of Civilization,* 281–340). Preston also thinks that the images of women in Paleolithic times related to a wide variety of stages and conditions of a woman's life Preston, "Goddess Worship"; See also Narr, "Bärenzeremoniell und Schamanismus in der älteren Steinzeit Europas."

28. Paulson, *Religionen der finnischen Völker,* 228; Udmurt women gather in one of the houses after the spring sowing has been completed; they then walk together

through the village, one of them dressed as Corn Mother; they visit other houses and finally celebrate a feast. Among the Moksha, the Mistress of the Fields is impersonated by one woman who leads the others through the settlement; all of the women are permitted to strike anyone they meet with their sticks; then they feast in a field, imploring the Mistress of the Fields to send a good harvest.

The raising of a woman's status in a farming community has been attributed, among others, to the assimilation of a woman's fertility to that of the soil. It could, however, also be that agriculturalists had moved away from the sphere of anxiety and fear that clouded the hunters' life and from the magic practices that had been created by these fears. Nor need the presence of a Corn Mother be based on an analogy between a woman's and agricultural creativity. Hunting people also have female rulers, such as, Mistresses of Wild Beasts; it is the participation of women in religious ritual that is new.

29. Helck, *Betrachtungen,* 62, points to the figurine of a woman with an infant that was found in an Egyptian grave. The figurine carried an inscription expressing the wish for a child. It seems that the object was deposited in the grave of an ancestor to intercede for the living person.

30. Ucko, *Anthropomorphic Figurines.* Three of the figures holding a child are from the assemblage of Hacilar in Anatolia, 356; two from the Ubaid culture of southern Mesopotamia, 361; and one or two from Greece, 369. We encounter seven mothers at the most.

31. Ibid., 443.

32. Gimbutas, *Gods and Goddesses,* 184–90; for the world view of hunting peoples, see Findeisen, *Dämon und Ahne.*

33. Narr, "Bärenzeremoniell," points to the bear representations in the caves of Trois Frères in Ariège and Les Eyzies in the Dordogne, 238, and to the deposition of bear skulls in caves of Central Europe, as in Reyersdorf of Silesia or in the Salzofen-höhle of Austria, 240–42. He then notes the bear ceremonies of modern hunters.

34. Martin Nilsson is one of the few who believes that a plurality of divinities is presented in Minoan art. He observes: "There is a tendency to explain the figures along one particular line. Evans finds everywhere the great Nature goddess with her paramour, Dusseaud the chthonic goddess, Earth the Mother. It is tempting to reduce the explanation of the figures to a single formula, but in this simplification there is a risk of doing violence to the evidence. For it is very possible that the Minoans had a multitude of gods." Nilsson 1925, *A History,* 18–19.

35. Wolfgang Helck, who disputes the maternal aspect of the Great Goddesses (Cybele, Anat, Ishtar, Astarte), points to their strong sexual appetites, their aggressiveness and cruelty, and the violence they frequently inflict on their lovers. He postulates the original form of a sexually oriented goddess in whose ritual a young man would become her lover and then be slain. In later times she merged with more benevolent divinities and was also associated with the fertility of the earth (*Betrachtungen*).

36. James, *Cult of the Mother Goddess,* 129 ff.

37. The Homeric Hymn to Apollo, among other sources, tells her story; it is the island Delos that, in most accounts, takes pity on the young woman. Rhea's concealment of the infant Zeus is related by Hesiod. Post-Homeric literature describes Thetis's loud wailing on her son's death.

38. Demeter's story is most fully related in the Homeric Hymn to Demeter of about 650 B.C.E. As told by Clement of Alexandria, Zeus attacked Demeter (Dio) in the form

of a bull; in her anger she called herself Brimo. Later she was appeased. Zeus also embraced his own daughter Kore, or Pherephatta, in the form of a snake.

39. James, *Cult of the Mother Goddess,* 169; in gratitude a temple was built to her on the Palatine.

40. Apuleius, *Metamorphoses* XI.

41. When the seed of Zeus spilled on a rock, a hermaphroditic creature, Agdistis, was begotten; later the gods tied its genitals to a tree and it emasculated itself, becoming the female Cybele. The blood flowed into the earth, and a tree began to grow. When a young woman gathered apples from the tree, she was impregnated and in time gave birth to Attis (Pausanias 7, 17). In an extended version the enraged Agdistis appeared at Attis's wedding feast and struck the wedding guests with madness. The young bride died from self-inflicted wounds, while Attis unmanned himself and died beneath a tree, much mourned by Agdistis. In another version Attis had fallen in love with a nymph; here also Agdistis's anger caused the woman's death and Attis's self-mutilation. Cybele was served in her cult by castrated priests. Considering that no normal birth takes place in the myths surrounding the goddess, that men mutilate themselves so that they could not even beget a child, one would have to consider Cybele an antibirth goddess.

42. Hastings, *Encyclopedia of Religion and Ethics,* entry: Pregnancy. The many myths in which a woman was fecundated by an external agent, a spark of fire, or a gust of wind indicate that an external agent was needed to stimulate conception and that the woman was not creative through her own inner force.

43. *Die Schöpfungsmythen,* 59; also 233–34, fn 48.

44. If the earth is assimilated to the womb in early belief, then one might think that the advent of agriculture would underline and exalt the male contribution to productivity, for now it is clear that nothing happens until the "seed" is placed into the ground.

45. Harrison, *Prolegomena,* 285; Harrison understands that in matriarchal times the relations of goddesses to men were of high dignity, as exemplified by that of Hera to Jason or of Athena to Perseus. However, "with the coming of patriarchal conditions this high companionship ends. The women goddesses are sequestered to a servile domesticity, they become abject and amorous," 273. Harrison does not observe that the relationships she cites are between divine women and mortal men. Such a tutelary bond persists in the masculine environment of heroic literature; such is the bond between Odysseus and Athena and between Germanic Helgi and his Valkyrie bride.

46. In her study, "Female Status in the Public Domain," Sanday concludes that the ratio between the percentage of female divinities and the female contribution to subsistence is high; there is no correlation between the number of female divinities and female status. James Preston points out that there is no correlation between the status of divine and human women; Preston, "Conclusion," 327.

We may also point to the notion of Courtly Love, the subservience to a high-born lady, and the practices of daily life; even Kriemhild of the *Nibelungenlied* was beaten, as a matter of course, by her husband Sigfried.

47. Delcourt finds in the goddess Hera the traces of an older type of divinity associated with a husband-son (*Hephaistos,* 39). James 228, states "that the function of the male in the process of generation became more apparent ... the Mother-goddess ... was assigned a male spouse ... even though, as in Mesopotamia, he remained the servant son of the goddess" (*Cult of the Mother Goddess,* 47).

48. James, *Cult of the Mother Goddess*, 237.

49. Bächtold-Stäubli, *Handwörterbuch*, entry: Fruchtbarkeit. Hastings, *Encyclopedia of Religion and Ethics*, entries: Harvest, Birth. It is true that in the Old Testament great value is placed on producing offspring and thus on the fertility of women. The Old Testament, however, is not typical in this concern.

50. The Finno-Ugric Cheremiss (Mari) turn to the Wather Mother on their wedding day and ask her to bestow fruitfulness on the young woman (Harva, *Wassergottheiten*, 122). Among the Udmurts the bride is led to a well and sprinkled with its water (ibid., 148–49). Barren women walk around a stone monument in Bombay; in St. Renan in France young women rub their stomach against a certain stone (Bächtold-Stäubli, *Handwörterbuch*, entry: Fruchtbarkeit, 5).

51. Lévy-Strauss, "La vie familiale," 66.

52. A tale in which the emphasis lies on conception and birth might relate how a barren woman achieved pregnancy. Such a story occurs in *Völsunga saga:* A queen who had not conceived for seven years of marriage was sent an apple by a god; after she had eaten the fruit she became pregnant. Similar themes are encountered in fairy tales; they are not, to my knowledge, widespread in mythology.

53. Petterson names A. Dieterich (*Mutter Erde*, 1905), as an apostle of the "Earth Mother Theology." Bachofen's *Das Mutterrecht* (1861) and Harrison's *Prolegomena to the Study of Greek Religion* point in the same direction and also had much influence in developing this theology.

54. Gimbutas, *Gods and Goddesses*, 176–77.

55. The Hacilar sculpture is reproduced by Mellaart, *Excavations at Hacilar*, vol. 2, plate CXXIX, statuette 525. The figures of Çatal Hüyük are shown in relief and may appear above the heads of bulls (Mellaart, *Çatal Hüyük*, figs. 23, 27, 28, 40).

56. See note 54.

57. Egyptian "birth-stools" are also mentioned in Exodus 1:16; Dhorme, "Terre-mère chez les Assyriens," 550–51.

58. Klein, *Three Šulgi Hymns*.

59. Jacobsen, *Harp That Once*, 86–89; the king is Shu-Suen, and the poems might have had a place in the cult of Inanna.

60. Mellaart *Excavations at Hacilar*, vol. 2; the proportion of the thighs is 75 mm to 50 mm in the drawing (1.5), and 53 mm to 43 mm in the photograph (1.2); the width of the hips is 60 to 27 mm in the drawing (2.2) and 43 to 25 mm in the photograph (1.7). The artist also extended the torso's right leg to break off below the knee so that it seems to rest against that of the woman rather than to enter between. The artist also completes some questionable fragments as children in two of the figures (202–203 for the photographs and 496–97 for the drawings). It is clear only in one of the many sculptures that the "mother goddess" has a child on her lap.

61. Mellaart, *Earliest Civilizations*, 108.

62. Fleming, 259.

63. Friedrich, *Meaning of Aphrodite*, 151.

64. Campbell, *Masks of God*, vol. 3, 54.

Chapter 2

1. Gimbutas, *Civilization of the Goddess*, 222.

2. Sjöö and Moor, *Great Cosmic Mother*, 84.

3. Gadon, *Once and Future Goddess,* 12.

4. Ibid., 22.

5. Baring and Cashford, *Myth of the Goddess,* 86.

6. Gimbutas, *Civilization of the Goddess,* 344–49.

7. Eisler, *Chalice and the Blade,* 24.

8. Ibid., 17–18.

9. Ibid., 27.

10. Sjöö and Moor, *Great Cosmic Mother,* 130.

11. Eisler, *Chalice and the Blade,* 19.

12. Gimbutas, *Civilization of the Goddess,* 399.

13. Ibid.

14. Eisler, *Chalice and the Blade,* 56–57.

15. Baring and Cashford, *Myth of the Goddess,* 405.

16. Stone, *When God Was a Woman,* 67.

17. Baring and Cashford, *Myth of the Goddess,* 167.

18. Campbell, *Masks of God,* vol. 3, 86.

19. Baring and Cashford, *Myth of the Goddess,* 158.

20. Campbell, *Masks of God,* vol. 3, 21, 22.

21. Baring and Cashford, *Myth of the Goddess,* 159.

22. Ibid., 281.

23. For climatic reasons, agriculture did not take hold in northern Scandinavia, whereas in the South a settled farming population erected megalithic structures. An archaic culture persisted also in the other arctic regions of Europe and extended also into Asia. Some of the pre-agricultural forms of life, of hunting and herding, were continued into historic times and some persisted even into the modern age; Shetelig and Falk, *Scandinavian Archaeology,* 85–121. The cave lies near the town of Leka; the paint consists of a mixture of iron oxide and pulverized stone; Gjessing, *Nordenfjelske ristningar,* 10–14.

24. The image of Zalavrouga belongs to a group that is dated from 1000 to 500 B.C.E. In this time span a Neolithic culture still prevailed in northern Russia; Kühn, *Felsbilder Europas,* 195.

25. These rock drawings appear on the eastern coast of Sweden and the southernmost portion of Norway. They are dated to the Bronze Age, 1500–500 B.C.E. The most frequently presented image is that of a boat, but we also find many animals. See Gelling and Davidson, *Chariot of the Sun.*

26. Helck, *Betrachtungen,* 95; the Hattic name Taru is also related to Hebrew, Arabic, Akkadian, Greek, and Latin nouns. We find here a common cultic word extending throughout the East Mediterranean region.

27. Haas, *Hethitische,* 73; the vase is from Inandik. In a relief of Alaça Hüyük a king offers a sacrifice to a bull, Helck, *Betrachtungen,* 98, citing Akurgal and Hirmer, *Hethitische Kunst,* pl. 92. Haas, *Kult von Nerik,* 63; Haas, *Hethitische,* 73, *KUB* XX, 10; IV 11 ff; Haas 1982, 73, *KBo* X, 2, I, 9–12. Bulls are drawn on standards found in Hattic graves near Alaça, Haas, *Hethitische,* 73, citing Bittel, *Hethiter,* 36.

28. Helck, *Betrachtungen,* 95, 170.

29. Ibid., 190–91, for the reproduction of the seals; they belong mainly to a colony of Assyrian merchants in Cappodocia in Asia Minor of about 1800 B.C.E. On a Ugaritic relief the weather god is shown with horns on his helmet and with club and spear, 189, fig. 174.

30. Pope and Röllig, *Syrien;* entry: Baal-Hadad 3.

31. Gaster, *Thespis,* 162, fn. Bull figurines were also found in Tell Halaf of Meso-potamia, Helck, *Betrachtungen,* 91; the Hurrite weather god Teshup, whose home is on the upper Tigris, is accompanied by two bulls, 98. Even a Hebrew text praises the splendors of the ox—*behemoth*—Job 40. The noun *abîr* of Genesis 49:24 is believed by some scholars to be an alteration from *abbîr*—"steer," so that the appellation for god would read "bull of Jacob," Gaster, *Thespis,* 162, fn.

32. Baring and Cashford, *Myth of the Goddess,* 86; these authors also state that the bulls of Çatal Hüyük represent the "visible image of her regenerative powers," 129.

33. Cameron, *Symbols of Birth and Death,* 4–6. This symbolism is accepted by Gimbutas, *Civilization of the Goddess.*

34. The connection between Anatolian and Cretan bull images is also recognized by Helck, *Betrachtungen,* 143.

35. Baring and Cashford, *Myth of the Goddess,* 155.

36. Jacobsen, *Treasures of Darkness,* 94, reproduces the seal of Adda.

37. Ibid., 129. This image is shown on Old Babylonian cylinder seals; Frankfort, *Cylinder Seals,* pl. XXII a.

38. Falkenstein and von Soden, *Sumerische,* 60–61, "Hymn to Ninurta."

39. The Akkadian myth "Ninurta and the Anzu Bird" parallels the Sumerian tale in which the storm bird is defeated; Jacobsen, *Treasures of Darkness,* 132, citing UET VI, nr. 2. The god of storm and rain himself seems to have evolved from the form of a lion-headed bird (as the Anatolian weather god was at one time in the form of a bull). The hymn, cited earlier, describes him as having the front paws of a lion and the hind parts of an eagle. He appeared to King Gudea in a dream in which he possessed the wings of an eagle, while his lower portion ended in a flood, Jacobsen, *Treasures of Darkness,* 128.

40. Helck, *Betrachtungen,* 98.

41. Ibid., 189–91, for representations of the armed human god. Some of these date from pre-Hittite time, such as a rock relief of Alaça Hüyük (ibid., fig. 169), a relief of Tell Halaf (ibid., fig. 183), or a seal from Cappodocia (ibid., fig. 176).

42. Ibid., 170–71; the chariot is drawn by bulls, and it storms across the mountains, obviously creating the thunder; citing Bossert, *Altanatolien,* fig. 778. In this form the god is designated on a stele as "Lord of the Wain."

43. See note 41; the most famous Hittite representation of the armed god of the storm is that of Teshup on a relief of Yazilikaya.

44. Haas, *Hethitische,* 38; the gods of Nerik and Zippalanda thus became the children of Hebat and Teshup. The Hurrite god Teshup had replaced the Hattic god Taru.
The high station of the storm god is shown by the fact that he received the title "king" in Hattic texts; Helck, *Betrachtungen,* 96 KUB XXVIII 7 Vs 1 a/2, and the title "lord" (*baal*) in Semitic texts.

45. The Sumerian account of Inanna's descent is found in ANET 52–57, translated by S. N. Kramer, and the Akkadian account, 106–9, translated by E. A. Speiser. The hymn is cited by Jacobsen, *Treasures of Darkness,* 137, from Reissner, no. 56, obverse 16–36. See also Edzard, *Mesopotamien,* entry: Inanna 2.

46. Gilgamesh appears to have been king of Uruk at around 2000 B.C.E. Several Sumerian poems were composed about him and were recorded from 1600 B.C.E. on-ward. A composition resembling an entire epic was composed in Akkadian at about 1600 B.C.E.; Jacobsen, *Treasures of Darkness,* 195.

47. Haas, *Hethitische,* 22; the Hittites accepted the gods of the Hatti, of Cappo-

docia, of the Syrians, the Canaanites, the Hurrites. The only remaining Indo-European god was Šius, deity of the sun, for whom a temple was erected in Kaniš. He lost importance in later times, 24–25. See also Laroche, *Recherches.*

48. Haas, *Hethitische,* 38–41. In the relief of Yazilikaya, two groups of figures face one another; figures 1–42 are male, figures 43–63 are female. Some of these gods are named, and we know that they are the family of King Teshup and Queen Hebat.

Concerning the Semitic invaders, von Schuler observes that the nomadic tribes of the Guttaeans, Elamites, Hurrites and Kassites, which entered the Middle Eastern regions as invaders and conquerors, lost their own language and civilization, and accepted native culture (*Kleinasien,* 20).

49. At about 1200 B.C.E. the Hittite empire was destroyed by violence. The Mushki, a Balkan tribe, were ancestral to the Phrygians. Some centuries after their arrival, the Phrygian empire was created by King Midas, and monumental buildings were erected; the *meter* was their highest goddess; Akurgal, *Die Kunst Anatoliens,* 3.

50. Hrungnir was a stone giant defeated by the Germanic god of storm, Thor; *Skáldskaparmál* in *Snorri Sturluson. Edda,* 77–80. Ullikummi, also a stone giant, grew so rapidly that his size threatened to obliterate the world; he was defeated by Teshup; Haas, *Hethitische,* 149–60. Typhoeus was the son of Earth and Tartaros, and he was defeated by the god of thunder, Zeus; Hesiod, *Theogony,* 820–68.

51. Fontenrose, *Python,* 465–66.

52. 1 Kings. 18.

53. Mellaart, *Earliest Civilizations,* 33.

54. For the validity of the belief in matriarchal and patriarchal systems of society, see Preston, "Conclusion," 325–30.

55. One of the founders of the movement was Z. Budapest; Stein, *Goddess Celebrates,* 12–13. A similar organization is the Fellowship of Isis, founded by Olivia Robertson in 1976; Matthews, *Voices of the Goddess,* 30.

56. Ardinger lists, among others, new moon rituals, Earth Day at the end of March, Candlemas rituals in February, midsummer celebrations, harvest and Hallowmas celebrations and midwinter feasts; *Woman's Book of Rituals,* 125–88.

57. Amini, "Path of Change," 218–30, describes a ritual for one who has suffered sexual abuse in childhood. Joyce, "Ritual Creating," 58–59, describes a ritual to celebrate a girl's first menstruation.

58. Gadon, *Once and Future Goddess,* 300.

59. Stein, *Goddess Celebrates,* 6, lists the following as basic elements of ritual: (1) purification; (2) casting the circle; (3) invoking the directions; (4) drawing down the moon (on full moons); (5) the charge of the Goddess (on Sabbaths and full moon); (6) invocations; (7) body of the ritual; (8) self-blessing; (9) raising the cone of power; (10) grounding; (11) opening the circle/thanking the elements; (12) endings/group hugs/sharing food.

60. Gadon, *Once and Future Goddess,* 309.

61. Ibid., 328.

62. Ibid., 376.

63. Lefkowitz, *Women in Greek Myth,* 268.

64. James Preston, "The Goddess Chandi," has pointed out that the appeal of the goddess Chandi increased and that her cult grew in popularity during a period of social change and modernization (nineteenth century) in the Indian city of Cuttack of Orissa. He understands the goddess to be an agent of social change.

Chapter 3

1. The peoples are of Mongoloid and European stock, speaking languages of the Finno-Ugric or Ural Altaic group or fully isolated idioms, such as that of the Chukchee or the Koryaks. Concerning the development of a homogeneous culture, Ivar Paulson declares: "Although we encounter in the vast region of northern Eurasia peoples of very different origin and level of civilization, we also find the substratum of an archaic cultural unity" (*Seelenvorstellungen,* 14). Hultkrantz, "Arctic Religions," observes: "The whole arctic zone constitutes a marginal area and an archaic residue of the old hunting cultures and hunting religions."

Careful and detailed ethnographic studies were composed chiefly in the first six decades of the twentieth century; they describe the state of culture of the time of their composition, frequently relying also on older reports. Some peoples had been converted to Christianity and some to Islam. They had certainly come into contact with influences from abroad. In some regions, such as that of the Finno-Balts, much erosion of tradition took place in the later decades. In this study the conditions presented are those described by scholars such as Harva, Paulson, Karjalainen, and Hultkrantz.

2. Hultkrantz has shown that the introduction of reindeer breeding into Saami (Lapp) economy did not disturb the patterns of the earlier religion ("Reindeer nomadism").

3. Many books were written on the subject of shamanism; for example: Findeisen, *Schamanentun;* Eliade, *Le chamanism;* Michael, ed., *Siberian Shamanism;* Diószegi and Hoppál, eds., *Shamanism in Siberia.*

4. To win his battles, the shaman must have the ferocity of a bear or a bird's ability to fly to heaven, as described for example by Prokofyeva, "Costume of the Enets Shaman."

5. Paulson, *Religionen der nordasiatischen,* 35; it was a robin in the mythical tradition of the Khets. The theme of mud brought by a bird for the creation of the world is widely diffused, ranging in area from Finland to South America, Harva, *Die religiösen Vorstellungen,* 103–07. In the lore of the Koryaks, the first living being was a raven with shamanistic powers, Bogoras "Folklore of North-Eastern Asia," 637–56. Thunderstorms arise through the flight of iron ducks in the belief of the Forest Nentsi (Yuraks), Lehtisalo, *Entwurf einer Mythologie,* 18; the Yakuts also believe that the cold is sent by a bull living in the North, ibid., 25. According to the Yakuts, the first shaman descended from an eagle, Sternberg, "Der Adlerkult," 133.

6. Lehtisalo, *Entwurf einer Mythologie,* 50.

7. Ibid., 51–53; the bear is called either son-in-law or daughter-in-law by the Forest Nentsi. The ceremonies are also described by Findeisen, *Schamanentun,* 23–26. The bear feast of the Mansi is described in great detail by Kannisto, *Materialien zur Mythologie,* 349–83. See also Tscherneijtzow, "Bärenfest." The celebration always lasts for several days.

8. Harva, *Religion der Tscheremissen,* 80; men never go silently through the forest; they sing, greet the trees, ask them for the way; this is recorded for the Mari (Cheremiss).

9. Lehtisalo, *Entwurf einer Mythologie,* 57 ff; Kannisto, *Materialien zur Mythologie,* 247, relates that among the Mansi (Voguls) near the river Loswa, women traveling in a boat must leave it when they come to a certain portion of the river and walk on land on the "woman's path," because the river contains a water sanctuary. One girl who did not leave the boat died during the journey.

10. Paulson, *Seelenvorstellungen,* 245 ff; the soul associated with the man's physical being has been designated as "life soul" or "breath soul"; the soul that may detach itself is known as the "free soul" or "wandering soul"; the two may somewhat interchange in function. An "ego soul," related to man's conscious intelligence, has also been discerned. Åke Hultkrantz introduced the term "guardian soul" for the soul that may turn into a tutelary spirit.

11. In some cultures the god of heaven may have a definite function; Num of the Nentsi grants luck in hunting reindeer, and reindeer are sacrificed to him; Lehtisalo, *Entwurf einer Mythologie,* 29.

12. These Lords are sometimes arranged in a kind of hierarchy so that the guardian of a certain beast would be subject to the Master of the species, and he in turn would be beholden to the Lord of the domain. The spirits of freshwater fish are thus governed by the Master of the Rivers—Ó'jin-pogil—among the Yukaghir, the spirits of the creatures of the sea by the Ruler of the Ocean—Čobuń-pogil, and the game of the forest by Lebie-pogil, the Owner of the Earth; Paulson, *Religionen der nordasiatischen,* 68.

13. Paulson, *Schutzgeister,* 64, 70; when he is in human form, fish are his domestivated animals. Vir-ava, the Queen of the Forest of the Mordvins, is tall as a tree and her legs are "thick like logs," Harva, *Finno-Ugric,* 184; she is described as having long sagging breasts and may also appear in the form of a wolf or dog, a whirlwind, or fire.

14. The Lord of the Mountain is named Pal'-ys, Sternberg, "Religion der Giljaken," 205. The name of the Lady of the Sea of the Livonians is Mjer-äma and she receives much honor; Paulson, *Die Religionen der finnischen Völker,* 201; she is given brandy and white bread every Easter, and also when men set out on their fishing expeditions. Some of the caught fish are thrown back into the sea. She is said to be the greatest benfactor of mankind.

15. Paulson, *Religionen der finnischen,* 251; he is called *maja haldjas,* Protector of the House. The Mari know *wit'śa kuwa,* the Old Woman of the Barnyard; the Estonians *sauna-vaim,* the Bath-house spirit. We also encounter *gid-kuzo,* Stable Man, of the Udmurts; *pertin-izand,* Lord of the Room, of the Veps; *riihen-haltija,* Protector of the drying barn, of the Finns.

16. Lehtisalo, *Entwurf einer Mythologie,* 111; she is called Earth Carrying Old Woman, Earth Grandmother, and Determiner of Fate. The Tundra Nentsi call her Earth Mother. The rulers of beasts and of localities are separate from the phenomenon that they rule, though they may share some qualities. It is believed that these beings originated in the "wandering soul" of the phenomenon. Ivar Paulson used the term "animistic" to define them (*anima,* "soul").

17. For the beings who arose out of a phenomenon itself, the term "animatistic" (*animare,* "to come to life") has been employed. We thus find that the cornfield itself (*noru-pak'śa*), and not its master, is listed among the Mokshan gods; Paulson, *Religionen der finnischen,* 227. The supporting pillars of the tent themselves are charged with holiness among the Chukchee, Ränk, *Die heilige Hinterecke,* 109.

18. Paulson, *Religionen der finnischen,* 224.

19. Harva, *Wassergottheiten,* 135; sometimes it is not possible to ascertain whether the spirit master of an element or the element itself is adored in cult or prayer; in some cultures the two exist side by side, as do *büt-ia* (the indwelling demon of the water) and *büt-awa* (the river or the lake itself) among the Mari, ibid., 115. Some cultures make a clear distinction between the two through their designations: the Udmurts consistently employ the noun *murt* (person) for the soul creature and *mumi*

(mother) for the element itself, ibid., 64ff, 74ff. Rivers are called by their names, prefixed with the word for mother, so that we find *sur-mumi,* Mother Sur, or *tsuptsi-mumi,* Mother Tsuptsi.

20. Ibid., 145; the Lord of the Water of the Mordvins is named *vetsa eräj,* "the one who lives in the water." Concerning this being, Harva states: "While he was pushed into the background and is hardly found nowadays as recipient of a cult, the "Water Mother" *ved-ava* (the water itself) became one of the most important deities."

21. Ibid., 162; thus the Owner of lakes and rivers of the Estonians (*näck*) draws humans to the water and drowns them in his element. Sometimes he appears as a precious ring. People reaching for it are invariably drowned.

22. Butter and milk are brought to tree stumps, heaps of stones, or empty fields for *maa-ema* (Lady Earth) by the Estonians; Paulson, *Religionen der finnischen,* 233; there is also a *maa-iza* (Earth Father) and a *maa-vaim* (Earth Spirit). Dark animals are slaughtered for *muzjem-mumi* (the earth) by the Udmurts, while their Lord Heaven receives white animals rendered to him from the height of a hill, 211, 213–14. Lady Earth is said to live in mounds of earth; the offerings are black sheep and oxen. The bones and some of their organs are buried in the earth and the blood poured into the ground.

23. Harva, *Wassergottheiten,* the Udmurts bring sheep and oxen to the well and implore it to send the needed rains; the Mari toss a lamb into the river when a drought has parched the land, 121. Fifteen Udmurt villages would gather at a well near the village Parvu: here they slaughtered a red-and-white ox and two sheep, 75. In later times people directed their supplication for rain to the god of heaven. When the Mari pray for rain to *büt-awa,* the bones of the sacrificial animals are lowered into the well, 121; the Mordvins also performed a rain sacrifice when they suffered from a drought, 147.

24. Ibid., 76–77, "Once man has noticed the mysterious power of water to create the growth of vegetation, he easily conceives the belief that water would exert the same magic power over men and beasts." (transl. mine)

25. Ibid., 149.

26. Lehtisalo, *Entwurf einer Mythologie,* the Tundra Nentsi have a story that relates that men could not slay a single forest creature until they obtained possession of their *haehe* and set them in their proper places, 103. Sometimes the household gods are taken on hunting expeditions and then returned to their station, 102–4.

27. Ibid., 79–80; one of the holiest places of the Nentsi is the island Waigatš; here live the Old Man and the Old Woman of the Earth who gave birth to mountains, such as the Minissei or the Urals.

28. The Saami turn to these *seide* in all their needs; the large stone formations are clearly related to the pursuits of hunting and fishing and may represent the Guardians of the game; Hultkrantz, *Religion der Lappen,* 291. Some of the *seide* are manmade (i.e., deposited by men); Harva, *Finno-Ugric,* 100. See also Hultkrantz, "Reindeer Nomadism."

29. Paulson, *Religionen der nordasiatischen,* 98, among the Chanti. Karjalainen, *Religion der Jugravölker* II, 209.

30. Sternberg, "Religion der Giljaken," 257–58; he is not represented as an idol. We cannot be sure whether the protective spirits that were adored in sacred sites had found their origin in the owner of the locality, who became the guardian of a special group, or whether household spirits had been moved into the wilderness. The worship of tutelary forces at sacred sites is very difficult to classify, for it is exceedingly complex.

Sometimes spirits are worshipped in their natural dwelling places, sometimes in special sacrificial sites that may be near a village or behind a house. Some of the nature sanctuaries contain idols; in others, the godhead is not represented. Some of the sacrificial huts and storage places are abandoned dwellings, whereas others were erected for the purpose.

31. These deities also have a place in myth; the Madder-akka of the Saami receives the child from the highest god and plants it into the woman's womb (Ränk, *Lapp Female Deities,* 10–14). The Yakuts believe that the childbirth goddess Ajysyt must be present at every delivery or else the mother and child will die.

32. Findeisen, *Schamanentum,* 29.

33. Campbell, *Masks of God,* vol. 1, 266; the informant is G. V. Ksentofontov.

34. Bogoras, "Folklore of North-Eastern Asia," 618.

35. Ibid., 643; Kannisto, *Materialien zur Mythologie,* 79–80; Sokolova, "Representation of a Female Spirit," 499.

36. Other "mothers" are, for example, *maa-äma* (Earth Mother) and *linand-äma* (Flax Mother) of the Livonians; *šundi-mumi* (Sun Mother) and *muzjem mumi* (Earth Mother) of the Udmurts; *veden-äma* (Water Mother) of the Karelians; *vir-ava* (Forest Mother) of the Erza; *tolozi-awa* (Moon Mother), *büt-awa* (Water Mother), *pol-awa* (Cloud Mother), and *molanda-awa* (Earth Mother) of the Mari; *sou-änäse* (Water Mother) of the Tatars; *Tomam* (Mother of Tom [a river]) of the Khets; *loddiš-aedne* (Bird Mother) of the eastern and western Saami; *meantas-ajik* (Reindeer Mother) of the Kola Saami; *jurt-ava* (House Mother), *varma-ava* (Wind Mother), *vel-ava* (Village Mother), *tol-ava* (Fire Mother), *mastor ava* (Earth Mother), and *vir-ava* (Forest Mother) of the Mordvins; *pakš-ava* (Field Mother) and *neške-ava* (Beehive Mother) of the Mokshans; *veden-emä* (Water Mother), *mesten-emuu* (Forest Mother), and *karhun-emuu* (Bear Mother) of the Finns; *mjer-äma* (Ocean Mother) of the Estonians; *faxa-mama* (Fire Mother) of the Nanai (Goldes); *vagreg-imi* (Mother of the Sons of God) of the Mansi; and *dunde-enim* (Earth Mother) of the Yenisei Tungus.

Every "mother" of North Eurasian tradition has not been recorded, and I did not read all works on the religions of this area nor did I record all the "mothers" that I did encounter; thus one may appreciate how much larger the number is in actuality.

37. Paulson *Religionen der nordasiatischen,* 87. *Meantas-ajik,* the Reindeer Mother of the Saami, appears as a wild reindeer and is sometimes transformed into a woman; *tavia-ava* of the Kola Saami is of great benefit to hunters, Paulson, *Schutzgeister,* 165, 172. *Metsän-emuu,* the Forest Mother of the Finns, is asked to share the bounty of her forest, Paulson, *Religionen der finnischen,* 190; *ved-ava,* the Water Mother of the Mordvins, is sometimes seen as a fish, followed by a swarm of water creatures, ibid., 200. The female Owner of the Forest is designated as *emei* (mother) by the Nentsi.

38. Lehtisalo, *Entwurf einer Mythologie,* 111; *witš-ku-awa,* the Barnyard Mother of the Mari, might also be placed in this category.

39. Harva, *Religion der Tscheremissen,* 69; her name is *ket-še-awa.*

40. Paulson, *Die Religionen der finnischen Völker,* 228; some cases show with great clarity that we deal with the element and not with the indwelling spirit; a Mokshan prayer to the House Mother asks her to forgive him who erected her and heats her, Harva, *Finno-Ugric,* 168. A Mordvin prayer to the Earth Mother declares: "We have thrown seed upon you, let a thick root grow, give us full straw and heavy grain" (Paulson, *Religionen der nordasiatischen,* 225). The Udmurts ask the Earth Mother to forgive them for digging within her, Harva, *Wassergottheiten,* 13. The Estonians be-

lieve that her breast is wounded when a knife is thrust into the soil, Paulson, *Religionen der nordasiatischen,* 232; "You nourish us," the Mordvins state in prayer, "you fill our stomachs, on you we stand, on you we walk, on you we fall" (ibid., 225). They beseech the Water Mother to grant health to those who drink her: "Water Mother give good health to all Christians. To him who drinks of you give good health . . . give good health also to the flocks which drink you" (Harva, *Wassergottheiten,* 135); the Udmurts ask their River Mothers in prayer: "You mothers, who never run dry! . . . you who move swiftly, you mother streams, give to the grass and to the seeds of your moisture" (ibid., 85).

41. Paulson, *Religionen der nordasiatischen,* 217; such a title is given when the god in question has been humanized and embellished with many qualities; besides a wife, Jumo, the sky god, also has many servants and courtiers, such as Jumo's Treasurer and Jumo's Prophet; it has been suggested that the elaboration of Jumo's household shows the influence of a foreign religion, probably that of the Turco-Tatars, ibid., 217.

42. Harva, *Religion der Tscheremissen,* 90; the noun *šotšem* is related to the verb *šotšam* (to beget, to bear, to be born). There is also a *jumo šotšem;* Jumo is the god of the sky, but his name has come to denote divinity in general. The noun *perke* means "blessing," and there is also a *perke-awa,* Mother Blessing or Lady Blessing.

43. Ibid., 72. To honor the Earth Mother and to gain a promise of good crops, Mokshan women celebrate a feast in springtime when the seeds are sown, Paulson, *Religionen der nordasiatischen,* 227.

44. Harva, *Wassergottheiten,* 110.

45. Ibid., 121–30.

46. Ibid., 141; the people pray: "Silver-bearded Lord of Water, silken-haired Water Lady, bleach my flax."

47. Ibid., 150.

48. Ibid., 152.

49. Ibid., 152. Trust in the fertilizing powers of water is also met outside of the northern regions, and in German villages girls and boys are said to have their origin in "children's wells," or *Kleinkinderbrunnen,* Bächtold-Stäubli, *Handwörterbuch,* entry: Kindersteine.

50. Harva, *Die religiösen Vorstellungen,* 177–78. The Ocean Mother of the Livonians receives a husband and some daughters; the husband is named *mjer-iza* (Ocean Father) and the girl(s) *mjer-tidard* (Ocean Maiden), Paulson, *Religionen der finnischen,* 201.

51. Findeisen, *Schamanentum,* 20.

52. Harva, *Wassergottheiten,* 133. In the same magic formula in which Water Mother of the Udmurts flows as a silver ribbon through the lands, she sits with her children at the table. The Mokshan *ved-ava* washes and bleaches flax and is also a lady with hair of silk. The Corn Mother, who is "sown in the morning and reaped at dusk," sings with the voice of a human woman; *paksä-noru-ava* is scattered through men's labors, but she also wanders through the fields when the rye is in bloom.

53. Paulson, *Old Estonian Folk Religion,* 87; after a successful fishing expedition, the fishermen declare "Thank God, the Ocean Mother once again has given birth."

54. Harva, *Wassergottheiten,* 120; we cannot determine the derivation of the Drying Barn Mothers of the Livonians who are given bread and beer to clean the grain stored in their habitation; the woman's name is *ri-jema;* there is also a *ri-iza,* her

husband, and *ri-lapstöke*, their children. They are essential in preventing fire; if they are angry, they might burn the building; Paulson, *Religionen der finnischen*, 251.

Some Soviet scholars take the title "mother" very literally and assume that a "mother cult" had existed in Siberia. Nahodil and Simčenko relate this mother cult to a matriarchal stage of social organization. They point to the great significance of the Fire Mother, who was worshipped by several Siberian tribes and whose cult was also well preserved. They therefore believe that the stage of matriarchy was already present in preagricultural societies and represents the oldest system of descent. These scholars fail to realize, however, that Mother Fire was worshipped in her form of fire, and not in her capacity of mother. They also fail to realize that the presence of an important goddess does not necessarily reflect a matriarchal social system (Nahodil, "Mother Cult in Siberia"; Simčenko, "Mother Cult among the North Eurasian People").

55. Harva, *Die religiösen Vorstellungen*, 217–19. It is widely assumed that agricultural societies believe that a marriage between sky and earth, a "sacred marriage," is necessary for the growth of vegetation. This belief does not hold true for the agricultural communities of northern Eurasia. If the sky god receives a wife, she dwells with him in heaven. If the Corn Mother has a mate, he is the Old Man of the Corn (*norow-ava* and *norow-ata* of the Erza); the husband of the Ocean Mother is the Ocean Father by the same process. It is true that both sky and earth are worshipped as powers of the harvest; however, they are worshipped independently from one another.

56. Harva, *Wassergottheiten*, 121: "Dies erklärt sich daraus, dass *büt-aba*—ursprünglich ebensowenig wie die flussmutter der permischen völker etwas anderes ist als ein kultisches epithet des beseelten wassers. Den namen 'mutter' geben die tscheremissen auch anderen naturerscheinungen. . . . Dagegen werden die menschenähnlichen geister meines wissens nirgends *aba* genannt."

57. Karjalainen, *Religion der Jugravölker II*, 286: "Wir können zu keinem anderen Schluss gelangen, als dass die so gebrauchten Vaterbenennung nichts weiter ist als ein ehrendes und schmeichelndes Epithet."

58. Leach, *Lévi-Strauss*, 97. The Hungarian terms for uncle and aunt are *bácsi* and *néni*. In Thomas Mann's *Magic Mountain*, Hans Castorp muses about the strange custom of calling the waitress in a Swiss sanatorium a "daughter of the dining hall" (*Saaltochter*), not realizing that "daughter" merely means "young woman." The name Grandma Moses does not define the painter as a possessor of grandchildren or of grandmotherly actions, such as baking or knitting, but merely as an old woman.

59. Petterson, *Jabmek*.

60. Ränk, *Lapp Female Deities*; Bäckman, "The Akkas."

61. Hultkrantz, *Religion der Lappen*, 286–87.

62. Ibid., 286; Hultkrantz describes the minor changes in religious thought and practice after the adaptation of reindeer herding in the late Middle Ages, such as the introduction of a protective spirit of herds where there had formerly been a protector of the untamed beasts, or a change in the position of the sacred stones ("Reindeer Nomadism").

63. Hultkrantz, *Religion der Amerikanischen Arktis*, 291–93; Hultkrantz, "Reindeer Nomadism."

64. Ränk, *Lapp Female Deities*, 10–14.

65. Ibid., 21, citing Solander in Reuterskiöld, *Källeskrifter*.

66. Ränk, *Lapp Female Deities*, 21.

67. Ibid., 20.

68. Ibid., 22–23, citing Qvigstad, *Kildeskrifter,* vol. 1, 24 ff; she is also supposed to help in the parturition of reindeer.

69. Ränk, *Lapp Female Deities,* 24.

70. Ibid., 26; in some places Ux-akka is only the guardian of the door, protecting the entrance against evil spirits. In Christian time the Virgin Mary sometimes takes her place and is known as Marian-ugse.

71. Ibid., 28–30.

72. Ibid., 32; Ränk points out that the terrestrial function of the *akkas* is carried out everywhere, whereas the celestial function is limited to the Scandinavian Saami who also possess a highly structured image of the universe; this is divided into four or five layers and is believed to be a late-comer to Saami cosmology, ibid., 17; Hultkrantz, *Die Religionen Nordeurasiens,* 295 ff. Ränk, *Lapp Female Deities,* 17–21; among the Finnish Skolt Saamis the noun *māddâr ahkku* signifies ancestress, as does *māddâr akko* among the Swedish Lapps; the Finnish Lapps hold *madderakko* to be merely a maternal or paternal grandmother.

73. Ibid., 20; the Estonian noun *ämm* (grandmother) also developed the meaning of midwife.

74. Ibid., 21–23; Ränk cites Reuterskiöld, *Källeskrifter,* 98, for *skile-quinde.*

75. Ränk, *Lapp Female Deities,* 28–30. Ränk points out that the symbolism of the bow is widely diffused in northern and central Eurasia; it appears in rites of birth for male children and is obviously meant to ensure the luck and skill of the future hunter ("Symbolic Bow").

76. Ränk, *Lapp Female Deities,* 34–35.

77. Ibid., 38; in a Christian manuscript the rear door of the Saami dwelling, *passio,* is said to belong to the Christian god Immel, and the front door *ux* is said to belong to the devil *muben-aimo.* Sar-akka escapes the classification into good and evil spirits and libations are poured for her into the hearth, ibid., 41–42.

78. Ibid., 37–39.

79. Ibid., 40, citing Högström, *Beskriftning,* 50.

80. Ränk, *Lapp Female Deities,* 46–47; such an inheritance would be called *arb-saiva.* The departing bride's custom of taking idols from her parental dwelling finds a parallel in the biblical episode in which Rachel "steals" her father's household gods when she follows her husband Jacob; Genesis 31:19.

81. Lehtisalo, *Entwurf einer Mythologie,* 111 ff.

82. Ibid., 112.

83. Karjalainen, 1920–21 (*Folklore Fellows Communications* 41) 51–52. In the mythology of the Vasugian Chanti the soul is fashioned by Pūges, the daughter of the celestial god, who sends this soul from heaven; Ränk, *Lapp Female Deities,* 53, citing Karjalainen, *Religion der Jugravölker II,* 1922, 307 ff.

84. Ränk, *Lapp Female Deities,* 53.

85. Ibid., 53–54; Kaltaš-agke thus appears among several Chanti tribes; the goddess Pūges was invoked in difficult deliveries, and small images, spirits of obstetrics, received her name.

86. Ibid., 56–59, citing Yonov, and Seroshevski, *Yakuty.*

87. Ränk, *Lapp Female Deities,* 57, citing Seroshevski, *Yakuty,* 675.

88. Ränk, *Lapp Female Deities,* 57–59, citing Seroshevski, *Yakuty.*

89. Ränk, *Lapp Female Deities,* 59–61, citing Shirokogoroff (*Versuch,* 57 ff; *Social Organization,* 194, 261; *Psychomental Complex,* 153 ff).

90. Ränk, *Lapp Female Deities,* 62–65; thus *eme* (woman, wife), *emge* (old woman,

ancestress, paternal grandmother) of the Kalmyks; *ene* (mother), *eneke* (little mother), *ämägän* (little mother, old woman, wife) of the Teleuts; and *öröken-öreken* of the Shors and the Kumandines. Solomutina reports that she observed the making of such dolls among the Tuvas as late as 1982; the puppets are called *uruglar érens* ("Role of the Altaic Shaman," 193).

91. Ränk, *Lapp Female Deities,* 65–68; women who were barren or whose children had died would procure such dolls among the Soyots; among the Teleuts the spirits were thought to be especially effective in the case of eye disease.

92. Ibid., 70, citing Potanin, *Ocherki,* 28, 103 ff.

93. Ränk, *Lapp Female Deities,* 71–72 citing Batchelor, *The Ainu,* 236. The translations from the German of Harva, Findeisen, Paulson, and Karjalainen are mine.

Chapter 4

1. The distances between the three extreme points of Eskimo settlement—the Bering Strait, the southeast corner of Labrador, and Cape Farewell—are 6,000 miles each; Birket-Smith, *Eskimos,* 26. The Eskimo are generally divided, according to their station, into the Aleuts of Alaska and the eastern and western islands; the Pacific Eskimo in Alaska and on Kodiak Island; the Asiatic Eskimo on the Chuckchee Peninsula; the Bering Strait Eskimo at the mouth of the Yukon River; the Copper Eskimo on Victoria Island and Coronation Gulf; the North Alaska Eskimo; the Mackenzie Eskimo at the mouth of the Mackenzie River; the Caribou Eskimo on the Adelaide Peninsula, Repulse Bay, the Melville Peninsula, and in Baffinland; the Polar Eskimo in north Greenland; and the East Greenland Eskimo. Hultkrantz, *Religion der Amerikanischen Arktis,* 359–60.

2. Rasmussen believes that inland Eskimo had moved from the interior to the coast and that these tribes are the present-day Central Eskimo (*Across Arctic America,* 117).

3. The first reports concerning the Eskimo came from the Norsemen who set foot in Greenland and America in the ninth and tenth centuries. The Norse settlements disappeared in the later Middle Ages while new contacts were established through the expeditions undertaken by Danish, English, and Norwegian explorers with the aim of finding a northwest passage to the East. By the seventeenth century knowledge of the distribution of Eskimo tribes had been gained concerning not only those of Greenland but also those living on the arctic coast of America. In 1670 the Hudson Trading Company was established by the English as a permanent base for further journeys. In the eighteenth century the Russians set out on exploratory voyages and reached the St. Lawrence Island in 1741; somewhat later they reached the Aleutian Islands. James Cook and John Mackenzie met the Eskimo population in their passages through the Bering Strait. John Ross spent the winters of 1829–33 near the North Pole and discovered the Polar Eskimo. The last area to be entered by Europeans was eastern Greenland, where masses of packed ice cause great difficulties of approach.

While some accounts of Eskimo life have come to us from the early missionaries, the first scientific treatises were written by Franz Boas (concerning Baffinland) and Gustav Holm (concerning Agnmasalik). Others, such as E. W. Nelson, H. Rink, V. Stefansson, L. M. Turner, D. Jenness, W. Thalbitzer, and K. Rasmussen, described in a scientific manner the customs of the Eskimo before these gave way to the influences of modern times.

4. The lands inhabited by the Eskimo are in no way uniform in landscape. Greenland has inland ice and mountainous shores with fjords running into the ocean; in Labrador there are coniferous forests, tundras, and low plains. The flatlands of Alaska lead into a shallow sea, and an Alpine chain rises in southern Alaska and continues to the Aleutian Islands. Kodiak Island possesses a more abundant flora than other Eskimo regions; here the timberline crosses an area whose climate fosters a luxurious growth of vegetation—grasses, ferns, flowers, and mosses where there are no trees. Lantis, "Mythology of Kodiak Island," 126. See also Fitzhugh and Crowell, *Crossroads of Continents*.

5. This was declared by one of the Netsilik Eskimo: "Many people have eaten human flesh . . . after so much suffering that they were not fully sensible of what they did" (Rasmussen, *Across Arctic America*, 224).

6. Ibid., 225.

7. Hultkrantz, *Religion der Amerikanischen Arktis*, 365.

8. Rasmussen, *Across Arctic America*, 130–31.

9. Birket-Smith, *Eskimos*, 166.

10. Balicki, *Netsilik Eskimo*, 218–19.

11. Rasmussen, *Across Arctic America*, 134–35.

12. Ibid., 81.

13. Thalbitzer, *Légendes et chants*, 161–64; the tale comes from west and central Greenland.

14. Rasmussen, *Across Arctic America*, 83.

15. Thalbitzer "Gottheiten der Eskimos," 390–92; considering the shaman's experience we may understand why words relating to the weather and to human thought may come from the same root. In Alaska *sla* means "weather," "my senses"; the verb *slaugohaqtos* means "I am thinking." The wilderness experience of the shaman finds a parallel in the Old Testament Book of Job: After much suffering Job hears the voice of God in the whirlwind and experiences the fullness of God's majesty and power.

16. Hultkrantz, *Religion der Amerikanischen Arktis*, 396; this is conducted by the Central Eskimo.

17. Ibid., 386.

18. Thalbitzer, "Gottheiten der Eskimos," 388, quoting Glahn *Tagebücher* (1771), 347:

> . . . dass die Grönländer glauben, alle Dinge seien beseelt und dass auch die kleinsten Geräte eine Seele besitzen. So hat ein Pfeil, ein Boot, eine Schuhsohle, ein Löffel, ein Drillbohrer, jedes für sich eine Seele. Diese Seele ist von dem groben Stoff getrennt . . . doch von gleicher Gestalt.

Glahn gives the following meanings for the noun *inua:* 1. Man, 2. Owner, 3. Inhabitant, 4. Lord of an Entity, 5. Greenlander; as quoted by Thalbitzer, "Gottheiten der Eskimos," 388.

19. Merkur divides the spirits of the Eskimo into two kinds: The *inua*, genitive of *inuk* (man), is the indwelling force that imparts individual character to a phenomenon; it may become the object of cultic devotion (i.e., *sila*, the indwelling force of the wind). The other kind is the *tornaq*, the ghost of an animal or human; he never receives cultic reverence, but he may become the helping spirit of the shaman; Merkur, *Becoming Half-hidden*, 225. See also Fitzhugh and Kaplan, *Inua*.

20. Rasmussen, *Across Arctic America*, 385.

21. Thalbitzer, "Gottheiten der Eskimos," 407, 409–11.

22. Ibid., 407.

23. Ibid., 409.

24. Boas, *Eskimo of Baffinland,* 121–22; Cumberland Sound; for an interpretation of Sedna, see also Kleivan, "Sedna."

25. Hultkrantz, *Religion der Amerikanischen Arktis,* 395, among the Central Eskimo.

26. Jenness, *Copper Eskimo,* 188.

27. Boas, *Central Eskimo,* 603–5, Cumberland Sound.

28. Boas, *Eskimo of Baffinland,* 139–40.

29. Ibid., 141, Probisher Bay.

30. Paulson, *Schutzgeister,* 268.

31. These tales are systematically presented by Hatt.

32. See note 12.

33. Hultkrantz, *Religion der Amerikanischen Arktis,* 396.

34. Ibid., 397; see also Holtved, "Eskimo Myth."

35. Róheim ("Sedna Sage") declares that the Sedna cycle crystallizes the fears surrounding birth, death, and sexuality. The severed fingers of Sedna's hands represent children who "kill" their mother at the time of birth. The dangerous journey of the shaman symbolizes the descent into the vagina and its attendant fears. The fear of castration then appears in the rendering of this "coitus" as a cutting off (the shaman cutting off the parasites in Sedna's hair). The father with his knife symbolizes a castrating force, while the ocean, receiving Sedna as well as the *angakoq,* becomes the great mother into whose body one wishes to return.

36. Wardle, "Sedna Cycle."

37. Fischer citing Carpenter ("Changes in the Sedna Myth") for Sedna's continued power and validity ("Central Eskimo Sedna Myth," 27). He also presents a survey of 45 Sedna tales.

38. Sonne, "Mythology of the Eskimos." See also Sonne and Kleivan, *Eskimos.*

Chapter 5

1. Gimbutas, *Balts,* 14; in prehistoric times the country had contained more bodies of water that turned into swamps in later ages. These swamps figure greatly in folk belief and superstition. The large rivers are the Daugava, the Venta, the Lielupe, and the Gauja. The large number of fortifications on the banks of the Lielupe indicates the amount of fighting and guarding that must have taken place; Spekke, *History of Latvia,* 21–23.

2. According to Gimbutas, Indo-European tribes went in the direction of Central Europe. One branch settled along the eastern coast of the Baltic; another group pushed from the middle Dnjeper to the upper Volga and the Oka River in Russia (*Balts,* 39–43).

3. Ibid., 143; by 600 C.E. large trading centers had been established.

4. The Lithuanians, however, were not defeated by the Teutonic Knights. It took sixty years to defeat the Prussians. The Couronians, a Latvian tribe, achieved some autonomy through a separate treaty. The Letgallians, Semigallians, and Selonians were incorporated with the Prussians and the Finno-Ugric Livonians and Estonians into the Livonian Confederation, which was ruled by the Teutonic Knights. After losing their independence the Livonians fused with the Latvian nation. When Latvia emerged as

an independent state, it contained the territory of the medieval Livonians (Vidzeme), Semigallians (Zemgale), and Letgallians (Letgale).

5. After dispossessing the native nobility of their land, the Germans introduced the feudal system; thereafter the fiefs were converted into hereditary estates. Serfdom was fully developed at the end of the sixteenth century. The peasants sank to their lowest status under Russian rule; Spekke, *History of Latvia,* 195–6.

6. Sources of religious information are, among others, the *Cronica Terre Prussie* of Peter von Dusburg (1326) who was a Knight of the Teutonic Order, or the *Livländische Reimchronik* (1290) by an unknown author. Of the writings of the time of the Reformation, those of Stephan Bülow, Salomon Henning, and Paul Einhorn (seventeenth century) are important. When Latvia came under the rule of Polish Lithuania, the Jesuits established a Seminary in Riga where they stayed until the arrival of the Swedes in 1621. They published the *Annalen des Rigaischen Jesuiten Kollegiums von 1604–1618.* The Jesuit Johann Stribinš, especially, recorded many valuable observations gained in his missionary journeys. Of importance is the scholar Matthäus Praetorius who completed the *Preussische Schaubühne* in 1703.

7. The *dainas* are short lyrical poems, often consisting of no more than four lines; they are more often trochaic than dactyllic. They deal with various themes of human experience—love, war, sickness, death, motifs of folk belief. They often present the situation from a woman's point of view. The first printing of *dainas* took place in 1632, and the same poems recurred unchanged in collections published almost 300 years later. We thus notice the great conservatism of those who sang the songs. About 800,000 variants are held by the Folklore Archives in Riga. Many of them were published by K. Barons and H. Wissendorf. Some of these were translated into French by Michael Jonval. K. Brastinš published collections in 1928 and 1929. The numbers placed by me after a *daina* are the numbers in the collection of Barons and Wissendorf, as quoted by Zicāns and Biezais. A number preceded by a J refers to a *daina* translated by Jonval into French. A number preceded by an M refers to a *daina* cited by Mannhardt, "Die lettischen Sonnenmythen." The translation from the German of Mannhardt, Zicāns, and Biezais and from the French of Jonval is mine.

8. As reported by the Jesuit Stribinš, quoted by Mannhardt, *Letto-preussische Götterlehre,* 442.

9. Ibid., 107, quoting Nikolaus von Jeroschin (fourteenth century), *Die Kronike von Pruzinlant.*

10. Spekke, *History of Latvia,* 59.

11. Johansons, *Schirmherr des Hofes,* 76–150.

12. See note 7.

13. Biezais, *Baltische Religion,* 322; he is the Lithuanian Dieva and the Old Prussian Deivas.

14. *Historia Lettica,* ch. 11; von jhrer Ehe und Hochzeiten, quoted by Mannhardt, *Letto-preussische Götterlehre,* 485.

15. Biezais 1975, 329.

16. Saule may also play ball with the ocean water, tossing her silken handkerchief against the white foam of the waves (J161).

17. We also hear that she beds down beneath a tree and wakes up with apple blossoms in her eyes (J225, 1).

18. Saule also joins the dance at human feasts. She also participates in the singing of the so-called *ligho*-songs; these were sung by women at the solstice festival. A song always ends with the word *ligho,* which is a shout of joy and jubilation.

19. At another time Saule struck the moon with a stump of silver because his light was not sufficient (J303). Sometimes Saule descends to earth and walks across the fields; she is careful to raise her hem, for when it drops the grain sinks to the ground (32542, 8).

20. The goddess is frequently envisioned in relation to a tree. She may rest in slumber under an apple tree (J255, 1), be seated in a linden tree at the edge of the ocean (J227), throw mists over an oak tree with icy leaves which rise in the water of the Daugava (J228). On a birch growing near the path of her journey she hangs her belt every night (J235, 2).

21. Biezais, *Die himmlische Götterfamilie,* 505 ff.

22. Ibid., 512–13.

23. Many aspects of the goddess may be traced to more than one conceptual base. Her dancing in golden slippers on a silver mountain may have arisen in the visual experience of sunlight flickering on a hill; it may also retain the memory of a dancing divinity, such as is encountered in the Vedic texts; Indra, for instance, is a dancing divinity; Ogibenin. The labor of weaving undertaken by Saule belongs with her form as efficient countrywoman; it may also symbolize a cosmological concept, for in Baltic tradition the sky was thought to be a piece of cloth; Biezais, *Hauptgöttinnen,* 144–46.

24. Biezais, *Baltische Religion,* 335–36; Dievs is another god honored at this time; the consumption of food is important in the festival. It is believed that the richer the food the more prosperous will be the coming year. Sexual features are included in the celebrations, and the male organ may be designated as St. John's Herb.

25. Biezais, *Hauptgöttinnen,* 165, finds a slight intrusion of Saule's figure into the sphere of the goddess of fate; he also sees some merging of Saule with the Virgin Mary. In both cases the merging is slight. The goddess Laima is much more frequently identified with Mary. Biezais assumes some relation between Saule and the fertility of the fields. His assumption is based on the *dainas* in which Saule walks through the cornfield, lifting her garment so as not to crush the grain. There is, however, no reason to assume that lifting one's garment would have an effect on the crops.

26. *Wiederlegung der Abgötterey,* ch.1,642, quoted by Mannhardt, *Letto-preussische Götterlehre,* 464.

27. Biezais, *Baltische Religion,* 368–69 lists seventy "mothers": *abras māte* (Mother Baking Oven), *āru māte* (Mother of the Fields), *bangu māte* (Wave Mother), *bišu māte* (Bee Mother), *bišu māmulina* (Bee Mummy), *cela māte* (Road Mother), *cela māmulina* (Road Mummy), *dabas māte* (Mother Nature), *Daugava māte* (Mother Daugava), *debess māte* (Mother Heaven), *Dievs māte* (Mother of Dievs), *Diev' māmina* (God's Mummy), *dzīparina māmulina* (Yarn Mummy), *gausa māte* (Mother Blessing), *Gaujas māte* (Mother Gauja), *sāta māte* (Mother Moderation), *Jānu māte* (Mother of [the feast of] St. John), *Jumja māte* (Mother of Jumis), *joda māte* (Mother of the Devil), *juras māte* (Mother Ocean), *kapu māte* (Mother Churchyard), *kara māte* (Mother War), *krūma māte* (Bush Mother), *Laimas māte* (Mother Fortune), *mūža māte* (Mother Life), *lapu māte* (Leaf Mother), *lauka māte* (Field Mother), *Laumas māte* (Fairy Mother), *lazdu māte* (Mother Hazelbush), *lietus māte* (Mother Rain), *linu māte* (Mother Flax), *Māras māte* (Mother Māra), *mēra māte* (Measure Mother), *mēslu māte* (Dung Mother), *mēslu baba* (Dung *baba*), *meža māte* (Mother Forest), *miga māte* (Mother Sleep), *rauga māte* (Mother Yeast), *mieža māte* (Mother Barley), *miglas māte* (Mother Fog), *nakts māte* (Mother Night), *naudas māte* (Mother Money), *nāves māte* (Mother Death), *ogu māte* (Berry Mother), *Pērkona māte* (Mother of Pērkons), *piena māte* (Milk Mother), *pirts māte* (Mother Bathhouse), *rigas māte* (Mother Threshing Barn), *rozu*

māte (Rose Mother), *rūšu māte* (Pit Mother), *Saules māte* (Mother Sun), *senu māte* (Mushroom Mother), *senu māmina* (Mushroom Mummy), *skauga māte* (Mother Envy), *smilšu māte* (Sand Mother), *sniego māte* (Mother Snow), *sviesta māte* (Butter Mother), *tabacina ragu māte* (Tobacco Pouch Mother), *tirgus māte* (Market Mother), *udens māte* (Water Mother), *uguns māte* (Fire Mother), *upes māte* (Mother River), *vēja māte* (Mother Wind), *velu māte* (Mother Death), *velna māte* (Mother Devil), *zemes māte* (Mother Earth), *ziedu māte* (Mother Blossom), *ziemela māte* (Mother North), *žagaru māte* (Kindling Wood Mother), *laika māte* (Mother Weather), *briežu māte* (Mother Stag), *piegulas māte* (Night Guarding Mother), *dārzu māte* (Garden Mother), *lōpu māte* (Livestock Mother), *rīsu māte* (Spinning Mother), *zirgu māmulina* (Horse Mummy).

28. Dictionary arranged by Gotthard Friedrich Stender, quoted by Manhardt, *Letto-preussische Gotterlehre,* 622–23. Johansons observes that *māte* is the general name of a female Latvian divinity (*Schirmherr des Hofes,* 16).

29. Johansons, *Der Wasserherr,* 26.

30. Johansons, *Schirmherr des Hofes,* 14–20; the *mājas kungs* has been described as dwelling behind the stove or beneath the floor; he never wears shoes and also appears in other buildings of the farmstead. He was still honored in some places in 1935, ibid., 39.

31. Ibid., 159–62.

32. Biezais, *Hauptgöttinnen,* 119. Laima has to some extent blended with the spirit, named Māra, and it is difficult to draw a line of clear demarcation between the two. The names thus interchange in the variants of one poem; they are, however, also shown side by side as separate creatures. No systematic study comparing the resemblances and differences has been undertaken. I attempt to cite mainly the poems which contain the name Laima, but occasionally a poem with the name Māra is included. Most scholars believe that Māra arose in a mutilation of Maria, the Virgin Mary. Indeed, Māra is invoked, more often than Laima, in a Christian context, as in baptismal poems.

33. Ibid., 185.

34. Ibid., 185 ff. A nineteenth-century account gives a full description of a bath-house celebration. The logs to heat the stove had to be selected from special trees; the switch, with which the woman cleansed herself and also touched the child, was to consist of the twigs of one birch only, with one additional twig of oak, linden, or rowan. It was put together on the feast day of St. John. A chicken was slaughtered in the course of the ritual. In the place where the woman had belabored herself with the switch she left a gift—a garter or some coins. Religious significance is also attributed by other nations of the region to the bathhouse (i.e., Slavs, Lithuanians, Estonians, and other Finno-Ugric peoples).

35. Some poems indicate Laima's special significance to a woman in her fertile years. A girl declares that she did not need Laima while she wore her maiden's wreath, but she came in tears to the goddess after it was taken. Another poem admonishes girls to pray to Laima, while old women "have come to an arrangement."

36. *Daina* 1138 names Māra as the recipient of the woolen garter. According to the poems the beasts offered are chickens, piglets, and sheep; Biezais, *Hauptgöttinnen,* 184. The letter T before the number of a *daina* relates it to the collection of magic charms by Smitš.

37. *Historia Lettica* of 1649, as quoted by Biezais, *Hauptgöttinnen,* 73. Laima may also have a role in the procreation of domesticated animals; so-called Laima trees are seen on all roads; from such trees lambs and kids are born.

38. Much is known about the wedding customs of the Latvians; marriage seems to have been a celebration of great significance. Most of the *dainas* pertain to weddings; Biezais, ibid., 213 ff. Archaic customs, such as bride abductions, left their residue in the traditions. We also know that marriage ceremonies were performed in open fields without the presence of church officials (*daina* 15375, 6). The authorities, much concerned with the fact that a marriage was considered binding after the public celebration had taken place, demanded that another ceremony be performed in church.

39. Ibid., 122, notes that "fortune" appeared in two forms among the Latvians, both designated by the same word, an abstract notion *laime* and an anthropomorphic goddess Laima. The two may both appear in the same song (9208, 1).

40. Some *dainas* present a strange contradiction in Laima's character; she sorrows over the fate that she herself has determined. She is asked in one *daina* why she is crying over a misfortune that she herself has ordained (9259).

41. Biezais, *Hauptgöttinnen,* 155 ff, believes that besides sharing the office of setting fate, Laima and Dievs are united in marriage and have produced offspring—the Sons of God. He bases his assumption on a group of *dainas,* all variations on one theme: that an orphan girl is not really an orphan, for her father is God, her mother Laima, and the sons of God are her brothers as in *daina* 5045. I cannot agree with Biezais. Surely the poem is metaphorical. If the girl had God as father and Laima as mother she would not be an orphan. Is it to be assumed that the deities keep their male children and send their female children to earth to be orphans?

42. There is some relation of Laima with farming; according to one *daina* (58413) she sows winter wheat from a silver basket, and she is called Cow-Laima in a magic charm quoted by Biezais, ibid., 251.

43. Ibid., 71.

Chapter 6

Documentation of this chapter was difficult because I am not an expert in the field. Translations of the texts, and sometimes even factual information, vary widely; sometimes passages, even in translation, were not available to me. I therefore had to rely on the interpretation of experts. I relied primarily on Thorkild Jacobsen's interpretations because I find his analysis more penetrating and sensitive than that of other scholars. I will, however, sometimes note when his interpretation differs from that of others.

1. For a general survey of the ancient Near Eastern cultures, see Mellaart, *Earliest Civilizations.*

2. The Sumerians are thought to have entered the area during the course of the fourth millennium B.C.E. During the third and second millennium the country was invaded by the Guteans, Elamites, Hurrites, and Cassites. The period called Early Dynastic ended when Sargon founded the Akkadian empire at about 2340 B.C.E. Sumerian rule was restored during the Third Dynasty of Ur (2050–1960 B.C.E). After the Elamites defeated Dynastic Ur, the Akkadian language was adopted. The name Old Babylonian is applied to a period from the end of the Ur Dynasty to the reign of Hammurabi (1728–1689 B.C.E.). The Assyrians were predominant for about 300 years and collapsed at the end of the seventh century. The neo-Babylonian empire was founded in the middle of the sixth century by Nabopolassar and was conquered by the Persians in 539 B.C.E. The dates, however, vary somewhat in the various accounts.

3. Dhorme, *Les religions,* 5–8.

4. Jacobsen, *Mesopotamia,* 130, quotes from *Maqlû* Tablet VI a magic charm addressed to salt:

> O, Salt, created in a clean place,
> . . . I am . . .
> Held captive by enchantment,
> Held in fever by bewitchment.
> O Salt, break my enchantment;
> Loose my spell!

Part of the charm directed to fire is as follows:

> Burn, O Fire the man and woman who bewitched me;
> . . . Scorch them, O Fire;
> Take hold of them, O Fire;
> Consume them, O Fire
>
> > (*Maqlû* Tablet II, quoted by
> > Jacobsen, *Mesopotamia,* 134).

5. Ibid., 132, relating to a hymn to Nidaba, *OECT,* I, 36–39 (not available to me).

6. In a deeply moving lament the goddess Ningal speaks of the fated destruction of her city Ur, which she vainly tried to prevent:

> When I was grieving for that day of storm,
> that day of storm, destined for me
> laid upon me, heavy with tears,
> that day of storm, destined for me,
> laid upon me heavy with tears, on me, the queen.
>
> > (S. Kramer, *Lamentation,* quoted by
> > Jacobsen, *Treasures of Darkness,* 87)

7. Dhorme, *Les religions,* 5.

8. By such a council Marduk was chosen to be king over the other gods; this is related in the Babylonian epic of creation, named usually after its first line, *Enûma elish;* Marduk makes the establishment of kingship a condition for his fighting the monstrous Tiamat. The poem celebrated the superiority of the city god of Babylon; ANET 60–72. The destruction of Ur occasioned the lament of the goddess Ningal, cited in Note 6; it was carried out by invading tribes. The myth, however, interprets it as a storm sent by the god Enlil.

9. The best-known account of the genealogy is given in *Enûma elish,* but other lists also exist. The oldest account of about 2600 B.C.E. stems from Fāra; in a list of gods (called An:Anum) the name of a Sumerian god is juxtaposed with its Akkadian counterpart; in this list fifteen pairs of gods precede the god An, a deity of the sky. And the sky, married to earth, Ki, engendered Enlil, the god of storm. In the *Enûma elish,* on the other hand, Tiamat and Apsû, the salt and the sweet water mingled to bring forth Lahum and Lahamu, probably the silt deposited by the water; these in turn had Anshar and Kishar, the earthly and the heavenly horizons, and they engendered Anu, the god of heaven.

10. I follow in my account the interpretation given by Jacobsen, *Treasures of Darkness,* 128–29; see also Jacobsen and Kramer, fn 27.

The myth of Lugal-e mentions Ninurta's killing of Kur; Kramer, *Sumerian Mythology,* 117, fn 76. In an Akkadian myth Ninurta goes to fight the bird Anzu who had stolen the tablets of destiny, and he defeats him in his mountain; ANET 514–17. See also van Dijk, *Lugalud-me Lámbi Nirgal,* for the Lugal-e myth.

Other scholars do not think Ninurta/Ningirsu's relation with the thunderbird to be quite so clear-cut. The lion-headed eagle, however, is Ninurta's emblem; the battle with the monster is uncontestably ascribed to him. He does appear half bird, half flood in Gudea's dream. The temple relief is reproduced in Sculptures, pl. XXXVI–XXXVII.

A hymn addresses the god as a "dragon with the front paws of a lion and the hind paws of an eagle," Falkenstein and von Soden, *Sumerische,* 60.

11. In the Babylonian epic of creation Marduk shaped the world from the body of the defeated Tiamat by cutting her in half, making the sky from her upper parts and the earth from her lower parts. The god Ea who had destroyed Apsû built a house over the body of his defeated enemy. This house was also called Apsû. It is true that Marduk himself is not wholly in the form of man, for he possesses four eyes and four ears, but these features make him superhuman rather than monstrous. The *Enûma elish* is supposed to have been composed in the second millennium B.C.E., though the texts date from the first millennium.

12. Gilgamesh was a historical ruler of the city Uruk of about the third millennium. Stories about him remained alive long after his death. Several poems about him are recorded in Sumerian; a fuller version from about the middle of the second millennium is composed in Akkadian. Copies of this version were found in the library of Ashurbanipal in Niniveh and date from about the sixth century B.C.E. I follow the translation of Schott and Soden.

13. Jacobsen, *Treasures of Darkness,* 9.

14. Gressman, *Altorientalische,* 130 ff, quoted by Dhorme, *Les religions,* 301: "A sacred dwelling, a house of the gods, a sanctified place had not yet been created . . . the tree had not been made; the brick had not yet been placed, the brickmold had not been created." (translation from the French mine)

15. Frankfort, *Kingship,* 273; the process is well described in a text concerning Gudea who felt himself called upon to rebuild the temple of Ningirsu at Lagash. Gudea received instructions in a dream on how to design the sanctuary; *Gudea Cylinder* A I, of about 2100 B.C.E. (in cuneiform).

16. Langdon, *Die neubabylonischen,* 63, quoted by Frankfort, *Kingship,* 273.

17. She is addressed in a hymn:

> [Y]ou, my lady, dress as one of no repute
> in a single garment,
> the beads (the sign) of a harlot
> you put around your neck . . .
>
> *BE* 31, no. 12, 10–20,
> quoted by Jacobsen, *Treasures of Darkness,* 140.

18. Kramer, "Herder Wedding Text," cited by Jacobsen, *Treasures of Darkness,* 46. See also Wolkstein and Kramer.

19. Klein, *Three Šulgi Hymns,* 138–9.

20. Lamentations for the god Dumuzi were carried out in a yearly ritual. Witzel collected seventy laments that represent, as he declares, only a portion of the corpus. Dumuzi represents, in the view of Goddess devotees, the son-lover of the deity who is part of the archetypal pattern. The fact is, however, that Dumuzi is not Inanna's son;

Osiris is the husband of Isis; Attis was born to a princess and not to Cybele. Thus the combination son-lover does not exist. Baring and Cashford, *Myth of the Goddess,* 145–58.

21. Briefly note that the world of the Mesopotamians is clearly regulated and compartmentalized. The universe is run like a well-ordered estate with each compartment under the care of a special god. The arrangement of the universe forms the final part of the Babylonian epic of creation. We find three steps that lead to cosmic order: birth of aspects of the landscape, defeat of a monstrous form, and rational arrangement of the world. The ordering of the cosmos is also described in the poem "Enki und die Weltordnung," Bernhard and Kramer.

22. For the interpretation of Nintur as Lady Birth Hut or Lady Womb, see Jacobsen, "Notes on Nintur," 279–80.

23. Sjöberg and Bergmann, 142, 502–03.

24. Bernhard and Kramer, "Enki und die Weltordnung." 246.

25. Quoted by Jacobsen, "Notes on Nintur," 294.

26. Jacobsen, "Concept of Divine Parentage."

27. The Code of Hammurabi XXVIII, 43, quoted by Labat, 55.

28. KB III, 132, quoted by Labat, *Le caractère religieux,* 55.

29. VAB IV, 164, VAB IV 230, 3 (in cuneiform), quoted by Labat, *Le caractère religieux,* 55–56. Mesilim is the beloved son of Ninhursag, Sjöberg and Bergmann, *Collection of Sumerian Temple Hymns,* 143.

30. ISA, 58, 218, quoted by Labat, *Le caractère religieux,* 58.

31. Jacobsen, "Notes on Nintur," fn 28, quoting from the manuscript edition of the poem. I did not find this rendition in the translation by van Dijk, *La sagesse;* here Enlil poses his leg on the earth "like a great bull," 43.

32. Gudea *Cylinder* A VIII 15–16, quoted by Jacobsen, *Treasures of Darkness* 131–32.

33. Jacobsen, *Treasures of Darkness,* 131, citing the Lugal-e myth (of about the time of Gudea), tablet VIII, 13–25 SEM, no. 35 (in cuneiform); Kramer, *Sumerian Mythology,* 117. The demon is Azag and his shape is indeterminate. In an Akkadian myth of the same kind the goddess is Mami and the enemy is a bird named Anzu who had stolen the tablets of fate; ANET 514–17.

34. Jacobsen, "Notes on Nintur," 282, citing Gudea *Cylinder* BXXII.

35. Jacobsen, "Notes on Nintur," 283.

36. Jacobsen, *Treasures of Darkness,* 105; according to the poem of the Creation of the Hoe, Ninhursag is wedded to "the raging storm" Shulpae in her temple in Kesh, Sjöberg and Bergmann (Gragg), *Collection of Sumerian Temple Hymns,* 161.

37. Sjöberg and Bergmann (Gragg), *Collection of Sumerian Temple Hymns* 163; a hymn of the Old Babylonian period states:

> Nintu, lofty lady of Keš
> who with the great mountain Enlil is perfect;
> Nintu; to whom cows and their calves cry aloud.

A liturgy bewailing the destruction of Kesh speaks of the devastation of the "cattle pen of the Lady of Keš," ibid.

38. Frankfort, "Lady of Birth."

39. Jacobsen, "Notes on Nintur," 279.

40. Delougaz, "Animals Emerging"; the word *tur* denotes metaphorically the

womb, "the birth hut of the inside," so that the name Nintur would also mean Lady Womb, Jacobsen, "Notes on Nintur," 279.

41. Hall and Woolley, *Ur Excavations,* 93, pl. XXXI and XXXIII.

42. "Enki and Ninhursag," ANET 37–41.

43. The epithets *ama-dumu-dumu-ne, ama-diğir-re-ne-ke* appear on the statue of Gudea A, quoted by Jacobsen, "Notes on Nintur," 286.

44. Sjöberg and Bergmann, *Collection of Sumerian Temple Hymns,* hymn 39, p. 46, 500–503.

45. Jacobsen, "Notes on Nintur," 287.

46. In order of citation: *Nin-dim, Níg-zi-ğal-dím-dím-me, Nin-bahar, Tibira-kalam-ma, Nagar-šā-ga;* Jacobsen, "Notes on Nintur," 77–78.

47. Sjöberg and Bergmann (Gragg), *Collection of Sumerian Temple Hymns,* 77–78.

48. "Ninmenna sets birthgiving going," Jacobsen, "Notes on Nintur," 288, quoting from the poem of the creation of the hoe.

49. Biggs, "Archaic Sumerian Version," 195–96, quoted by Jacobsen, "Notes on Nintur," 288.

50. Jacobsen, "Notes on Nintur," 289–90, quoting Bernhard and Kramer, "Enki und die Weltordnung," lines 393–99,

> Aruru, the sister of Enlil,
> Nintur, the mistress of the foothills,
> verily holds in (her) hand the sacred brick causing
> birthgiving . . . verily holds in (her) hand her lapislazuli
> (vessel) in which the afterbirth is placed.

51. In order of citation: *ama-dug-bad, mud-keš-da, šag-zu-diğir-e-ne, šag-zu-kalam-ma;* Jacobsen, "Notes on Nintur," 289.

52. Kramer, *Sumerian Mythology,* 69–71, from a Sumerian tablet of the third millennium.

53. ANET, 99–100; this account agrees with the one given in the poem of the flood.

54. Jacobsen, "Notes on Nintur," 296.

55. Several lists of gods have been discovered. An Old Babylonian list (B) contains the name of the mother goddess together with An, Enlil, Enki, Ishkur, Utu, Ninurta, Inanna; another (C) cites fifteen divine couples and then An, Enki, Enlil, Ninhursag, Suen, Inanna; an Akkadian list (D) also cites primeval gods and after them An, Enlil, Bēlit-ilī (mother goddess), Ea, Sin, Ishtar, Ninurta, Nergal; Edzard, *Mesopotamien* entry: Götterlisten.

56. Jacobsen, *Harp that Once,* 151–53; "Enki and Ninmah", "Enki and the World Order"; unpublished mss by C. A. Benito; Microfilm, Ann Arbor, 1960.

57. Hall and Woolley, *Ur Excavations,* pl. VI.

58. Parrot, "Les fouilles de Mari," 6.

59. Sjöberg and Bergmann (Gragg), *Collection of Sumerian Temple Hymns,* 161–62; a lament states "Keš, built at the top of the plain has been delivered to the hand of the storm," ibid., 162.

60. Ibid., 164.

61. Quoted by Jacobsen, "Notes on Nintur," 277–78.

62. van Buren, "Clay Relief"; the relief is in the Iraq Museum and a copy in the Louvre.

63. Labat, *Le caractère religieux,* 67. "The belt is tied; her breast is bare; she carries

on her left a small child. It drinks from her breast and she offers her right (breast)" (translation from the French mine).

64. Porada, *Corpus*, pl. XXXVIII; Frankfort, *Cylinder Seals*, pl. XXII C.

65. van Buren lists the artifacts that show the symbol; she interprets it as a swaddling band ("Clay Relief").

66. Kühne, "Das Motiv."

67. Falkenstein and von Soden, *Sumerische*, 294; it is King Assurbanipal who sits on the lap of Sharrat-Ninua, suckling from two breasts and sheltering beneath the others; see Labat for divine cow-mothers, (*Le caractère religieux*, 67–68).

68. We do not know whether the birth process entered the account of the creation of the world because the act of parturition was seen as an expression and release of creative energy, or whether in the process of humanizing the universe all actions were visualized in terms of human endeavor and activity. I am inclined to the latter view.

69. Jacobsen, "Notes on Nintur," 293–94; she lost all importance during the latter part of the Isin-Larsa period (2000–1800 B.C.E.).

70. Lambert and Millard, *Atra-hasīs*, 103; Kilmer, "Mesopotamian Concept."

71. Eliade, *History of Religious Ideas*, vol. 1, 40–41; Gadon, *Once and Future Goddess*, 22.

72. Great Goddesses, such as Asherah and Ishtar, are "Queens of Heaven"; Stone, "Goddess Worship."

73. For instance, the "earth grandmother" of the Nentsi who sends the child into the world; Lehtisalo, *Entwurf einer Mythologie*, 111 ff.

74. As pointed out by Edzard, *Mesopotamien*, 20; he states that the Semitic, nomadic invaders gave up their dialects and accepted native speech and civilization.

75. Blinkenberg, *Thunderweapon*, shows that the belief in a stone flung from heaven is found throughout the world; this "thunderstone" is recognized in archaic stone implements that are discovered in the ground.

76. Baring and Cashford, *Myth of the Goddess*, 275–85.

77. *Enûmah Elish*, ANET 60–72.

78. Thus Ouranos, the primordial father, was destroyed by his son Kronos, and Kronos was overcome by his son Zeus, as told in Hesiod's *Theogony*, 453–506, 617–720.

Chapter 7

1. Graillot, *Le culte de Cybèle*, 421–533, traces the spread of Cybele cults from Asia Minor to Italy, Gaul, the Germanic regions, Spain, and the Roman provinces of Africa. Vermaseren, *Cybele and Attis*, 86.

2. Mellaart, *Çatal Hüyük*, 22–23. Twelve layers of settlement were discovered; animal bones show that the wild bull was about to become domesticated.

3. Bahadir, *Anatolie*, vol. 1, 127–28. Akurgal, *Art of the Hittites*, 15–29; metal working shows an especially high level of achievement.

4. Akurgal, *Die Kunst Anatoliens von Homer bis Alexander*, 2; this relates to level VI.

5. Akurgal, *Die Kunst Anatoliens*, 3.

6. Ibid.

7. Ibid., 120–21, distinguishes four stages of Phrygian culture: (1) 775–725 B.C.E., the founding of the small Phrygian states; (2) 725–675 B.C.E., the founding of the

Phrygian empire; (3) 675–585 B.C.E., the Cimmerian dissolution of the empire; (4) 585–500 B.C.E., Lydian predominance. He attributes the impressive stone monuments of the region, its rock facades, to the last stage.

Haspels, on the other hand, assigns the earlier facades, including the most famous, the Midas Monument of Midas City, to the last third of the eighth century (*Highlands of Phrygia,* vol. 1, 146).

8. The Hittite texts were written in a kind of Babylonian cuneiform and date from the fourteenth and thirteenth centuries, but are often copies of older texts. The Cappadocian documents (from a merchant's colony at Kültepe) include both visual presentations and clay tablets. The Ugaritic texts were probably recorded at about 1400 B.C.E. but are probably based on older traditions. They center on a cycle of myths, pertaining above all to the god Baal.

9. Laroche, *Recherches,* 129–33. Since the gods kept their names after they were incorporated into Hittite myth, it is easy to know their derivation. Basing himself on linguistic evidence alone, Laroche found among the divinities one god of Indo-European origin, Shiuna; gods of Hattic origin, such as Wurushemu of the town of Arinna, Taru, god of the Hattusha, Telipinu of Nerik; gods of Hurrite origin, such as Teshup and Hebat; and gods of Mesopotamian origin, such as Ningal, Enlil, Kubaba. Laroche considers the Hurrites as the agents of transmission of the Mesopotamian heritage, and he believes the Hattic divinities to be related above all to certain localities and the Akkadian gods to be expressive of abstract ideas.

10. Helck, *Betrachtungen,* 96–97. The title *kattah* (queen) was applied to several Hattic deities, appearing in conjunction with the weather god who bore the title *ka-a-te* (king). Thus we meet a royal couple already in the Hattic pantheon. The Indo-European god Shiuna was still revered in early Hittite time under King Anitta, but gave way to Anatolian deities. Hurrite influence became important at about 1500 B.C.E.; the most significant Hurrite divinities are Teshup, the weather god, and Saushka, a war goddess, the sun god Shumige, the moon god Kushu, the bull god Tilla (closely related to Teshup), the god Kumarbi. Their cult center was Niniveh. The Hurrites had absorbed much Syrian culture before they made contact with the Hittites. Haas, *Hethitische,* 35–36.

11. Thus he bears such epithets as *henwas, tethesnas, kunahuwas, handan-dannas* (KUB VI 45, II 60; KUB VI 45, I 49; KUB XX 60, 5). A full list is given by Helck, *Betrachtungen,* 130–36.

12. Thus the god of Zippalanda and the mountain god Sharumma became the children of the mighty Teshup; Haas, *Hethitische,* 38.

13. That the name Baal (Lord) appears in Ugaritic as the name of the weather god indicates the ruling position of the deity.

14. Mellaart, *Çatal Hüyük,* 77–130; other animals presented are stags, rams, and leopards.

15. Helck, *Betrachtungen,* 99; KBo X 1.

16. Helck, *Betrachtungen,* 95; Haas, *Der Kult von Nerik,* 24–42.

17. Helck, *Betrachtungen,* 170–71; the bull-drawn chariot of the weather god developed after the fall of the Hittite empire when the Hittites had regrouped themselves into smaller principalities. The station on the bull occurs in the final stage of iconographic development. In this form the god appears in Gebel Beda; Bossert, *Altsyrien,* figs. 446 and 447.

18. Helck, *Betrachtungen,* 99, citing Bossert, *Altanatolien,* figs. 412, 416.

19. Haas, *Hethitische,* 18–19.

20. Akurgal, *Art of the Hittites,* 118–22.

21. Such ceremonies with intricate and firmly established rituals were conducted in several places. Near Zippalanda the feast was in honor of the mountain gods Arnuwanda, Pushkurunuwa, Tuthalyia, Sharisha, and Telipinu, KBo XVII, 88t Rs II 9 ff, Haas, *Hethitische,* 56. In the festival of the mountain Pushkurunuwa sacrifices were offered to the deer sacred to the mountain god. There were also rites in honor of a tree, a well, and the god of the mountain, Haas, *Hethitische,* 58. The festivities always lasted for several days and included dancing, music, ritual performances, and sacrifices; Haas, *Hethitische,* 54–63.

22. Haas, *Hethitische,* 132, 144; KUB XXXIII 120 II.

23. The tale of the battle with the monster may therefore form part of the creation story; the event may be reenacted in certain festivals, such as the New Year's celebrations of Babylon and the *purulli* festival of the Hittites.

24. von Schuler, *Kleinasien,* 177–78; Goetze, "Myth of Illuyankas."

25. von Schuler, *Kleinasien,* 204–205; Güterbock, "Song of Ullikummi," 135 ff. Kumarbi is a Hurrite divinity from the North Mesopotamian town of Kurmish. He too had dethroned his father Anu (by biting off his phallus); Haas, *Hethitische,* 143–44; KUB XXXIII 120 II. The birth of a creature from a rock is not paralleled in western Syria and Mesopotamia, but the theme occurs in eastern Anatolia and in the Caucasus; Haas, *Hethitische,* 148.

26. Mellaart, *Excavations at Hacilar.*

27. Mellaart, *Çatal Hüyük,* 115–16; Mellaart, *Excavations at Hacilar,* vol. 2, 184, table CXXIX. Mellaart, the excavator, believes that the goddess is depicted in the process of giving birth. He points to the fact that beneath one of the reliefs (Figure 37) in the temple of Çatal Hüyük a bull's head is placed on the ground so that, in his view, the goddess has just given birth to a bull. His view is widely accepted. We must note, however, that the bull's head and the goddess are not part of the same artifact. The goddess is represented by a relief made of plaster on the temple wall. The bull's head is a sculpture in the round, planted on the floor, shaped of plaster and painted clay. The form of the goddess is stylized, and the bull's head is naturalistic; the scale of the two is incompatible. If the bull had indeed issued from the woman's womb, the head would be inverted, with eyes beneath the mouth and not in an upright position. We may find in Mellaart's interpretation one of the indications of the great desire to find a "mother."

28. Winter, *Frau und Göttin,* figs. 268–95.

29. See note 61 of chapter 8.

30. von Schuler, *Kleinasien,* 173; Güterbock, *Kumarbi,* 116–17.

31. Helck, *Betrachtungen,* 245–46; the name Kybele, however, could have derived from another root.

32. Burkert, *Structure and History,* 102; Cratinus *fr. 82.* CAF I, 38.

33. Hepding, *Attis,* 218; Lucian, *de dea Syria* 27, CAF I, 31.

34. It is carved into the rocks of the Köhnus valley, in the south of the Phrygian highlands; Haspels, *Highlands of Phrygia,* vol. 1, 97.

35. Helck, *Betrachtungen,* 250–51; Pausanias 7,17,9—Agdistis; Strabo X,3,12 (469) —Idaia.

36. Graillot, *Le culte de Cybèle,* 361, for Meter Pontanene; for Dindymene, Helck, *Betrachtungen,* 251; Apoll. of Rhodos I, 1123 ff.

37. This settlement was the religious and military stronghold of several unfortified

villages. Its important features are the strong cyclopean walls with gates and subterranean staircases cut into the rock.

38. The Midas site lies in the southeastern highlands (Haspels, *Highlands of Phrygia,* vol. 1, 29, and vol. 2, figs., 1–57, 494).

39. Ibid., vol. 1, 88–89, and vol. 2, figs. 186–91 and 523; "lion rock"—Turkish Arslan Kaya.

40. Ibid., vol. 1, 89, and vol. 2, figs. 185, 524; the monument lies behind the Arslan Kaya and is called Küçuk Kapi Kaya—"little gate rock." Ibid., vol. 1, 87, fig. 184; this is found east of the Köhnus valley.

41. The upper part of the figure was damaged and had to be restored. We do not know how the upper part actually looked.

42. Other figures found at Gordion were a red stone statuette and a limestone relief, both showing the same attributes; Roller, "Great Mother at Gordion," 129, fn 4; stone reliefs from Ankara again contain these attributes, ibid., fn 7. The only image of Cybele with a lion is from western Anatolia in Arslan Kaya; in Hellenistic times the lion became standard.

43. Haspels, *Highlands of Phrygia,* vol. 1, 97; vol. 2, figs. 138, 526.

44. Brixhe and Lejeune, *Corpus,* vol. 1, Inscriptions were discovered in the following places: the lines *materan areyastin* appear on the so-called Arezastis monument 1,700 meters north of Midas City (p. 38); a front rock of the same place has *materey* (p. 40); the village Findik of Bithynia has *matar* (p. 50); the village Germanos, also of Bithynia, shows a nine-line inscription containing the words *matar kubel* (line 3) and *mataroteko* (line 7), (pp. 66–68). See also Brixhe, "Le Nome de Cybèle."

45. Hepding, *Attis,* 103–10; Arnobius V, 5; Pausanias VII, 17.

46. Hepding, *Attis,* 113, 114; Ovid, *Fasti* IV, 22 ff; in this version flowers originate in Attis's blood; in *Metamorph.* X 10, 104; a pine tree is originated.

47. Hepding, *Attis,* 111–13; Diod. *bibl.* III, 58, 59.

48. Hepding, *Attis,* 103; Lucian, *de dea Syria,* ch. 15.

49. Hepding, *Attis,* 116, Minucius Felix, *Octav.* 22,4, p. 30; Arnobius IV, 35, p. 37.

50. Hepding, *Attis,* 100, Pausanias VII,17,9.

51. Hepding, *Attis,* 100; scholion to Nicander's *Alexipharmacos,* v.8, p. 9.

52. Ovid, *Metamorph.* X, 560–704.

53. Hepding, *Attis,* 123–24; Lucian, *de theon dialogoi* 12; those whom she meets are called *metroleptoi* (possessed by the goddess).

54. Roscher, *Ausführliches,* entry: Marsyas; Diodor.iii, 58; Marsyas is also said to be the composer of the "Phrygian tunes" played on the flute, Pausanias X,30,9–*metroon aulema.*

55. Graillot, *Le culte de Cybèle,* 394, as on the Dindymon of Kyzikos, Apoll. of Rhod. I,1123 or in Ibriz and Efflatum Bunar in Lycaonia (9, fn 4), and in Bogazköy, where the stone is near a well, ibid.

56. Graillot, *Le cult de Cybèle,* 394, 395; Lobrinos is in the area of Kyzikos.

57. Ibid., 395.

58. Hepding, *Attis,* 124; Pausanias VIII,44,3.

59. Graillot, *Le culte de Cybèle,* 355; Atou Kôme near the source of the Tembrogios.

60. Ibid., 356.

61. Ibid., 348–49; Strabo XII,5,3.

62. Hepding, *Attis,* 125–29; the earliest reference to the festival was made by Herodotu-s IV,76 concerning the celebrations at Kyzikos.

63. Hepding, *Attis*, 142; many Roman writers described the feast of the Magna Mater, as for instance, Lucretius, Vergil, Tibull, Ovid. Only Phrygian priests were active in the orgiastic celebrations when the cult first came to Rome, but beginning with the reign of Claudius, Romans were allowed to participate, 146–47. One must not forget that a Romanized form of Cybele was also in existence. Her cult appealed to the nobility and her festival, the Megalesia, was performed in April. It became part of the official Roman festival calendar and was a vital part of Roman life. No rites concerning Attis were enacted; Garth, "Magna Mater and Attis." See Gerard, "Légende," for her importance to Roman politics.

64. Hook, "Eunuchen im Orient," 25; Pauly-Wissowa, entry: Kybele, A par. 4, 1 speaks of the fertilization through the severed phallus.

65. The Galloi also used perfume and makeup; Juv. II, 93; Apul. VIII, 27; Graillot, *Le culte de Cybèle*, 300; Hepding, *Attis*, 103; Lucian, *de dea Syria*, ch. 15.

66. Baumann, *Das doppelte Geschlecht*, 16–19, citing Bogoras, *The Chukchee*, 107, 448 f.

67. Jochelson *The Koryak*, I, 19 ff, 49 ff, cited by Baumann, *Das doppelte Geschlecht*, 19.

68. Herodotus IV, 67. Hippocrates, *de Aere, Aqua et Locis* 22.

69. Baumann, *Das doppelte Geschlecht*, 39, ". . . cultic sex change is primarily a means of seeing a specific deviation from the norm, here heterosexuality, as an expression of increased magical and religious effectiveness." (translation mine)

70. Graillot, *Le culte de Cybèle*, 307–11; Hor. *Od.* I,16,5 compares the oracles of Dindymene to those of Pythia, Graillot, 306.

71. Burkert, *Greek Religion*, 179.

72. The goddess Kubaba appears on a relief from Karkemish of the eighteenth century B.C.E. with a mirror; an inscription on this relief states "Kubaba, Queen of Karkemish"; on an orthostat of Karkemish she holds a pomegranate and a mirror and is seated on a lion, whose head serve as her footrest. In an image from Birecik she has horns and holds a pomegranate and a mirror. A relief from Malatya shows her facing the weather god who is seated on a lion while she is seated on a bull (the emblematic animals are thus reversed), she also holds a mirror and the inscription names her Kubaba. Bittel, "Phrygisches Kultbild aus Bogazköy," 18–19. See also: Head, *Historia Numinonum*.

73. Mellaart, *Çatal Hüyük*, reproduces and describes the following: clay sculpture seated between felines A II, i, figs. 67, 68; brown limestone sculpture standing behind a leopard VI A, 10, figs. 73–76; and clay sculpture holding two lion cubs A III, i, fig. 49. Mellaart, *Excavations at Hacilar*, reproduces: a standing figure holding a leopard cub under her arm, vol. 2, plate CXXVII; figure seated on a leopard, holding long-tailed animal, vol. 2 plates CLV, CLVII, fig. 228, my Fig. 36; woman seated on two animals: this is very fragmentary, only the tail of one animal is left, as it curls up her back, vol. 2, plates CLVII, CLVIII, fig. 229.

The sculptures excavated by Mellaart and described by him (*Excavations at Hacilar*) from the village Hacilar are of clay. This village has not achieved the extension or urbanization of Çatal Hüyük; its founding has been dated to 7000 B.C.E.; it was inhabited by agriculturalists who practiced some craftsmanship in clay and stone. In the second half of the sixth millennium it was fortified with a wall; the sculptures were excavated from the houses of the settlement rather than from shrines.

74. Helck, *Betrachtungen*, 252–53. She appears seated and with lions on coins of Magnesia, Nakrasa, and Sardes; standing between lions in Attouda and Brinla; riding

on a lion in Hadrianeia and Akrasos; in a lion-drawn carriage in Serdica and Kyzikos; with a lion on her lap in Metropolis and Ion; before a temple with lions in Attouda and Magnesia. My examples are taken from a much richer store. A fuller list is provided by Helck.

75. Meter Kasamene is reproduced by Graillot, *Le culte de Cybèle,* table IX; Ohlemütz, *Die Kulte,* 189–91.

76. Pauly-Wissowa, entry: Sadyattes; they belonged to the dynasty of the Heraclides.

77. Hepding, *Attis,* 101; Herodotus I, 34–45. Atys, the son of Kroisos, was killed by the Phrygian Adrestos while hunting boars. The killing was an accident and in remorse Adrestos took his life on Atys's grave.

78. Akurgal *Die Kunst Anatoliens,* 167–74.

79. Ohlemütz, *Die Kulte,* 174 ff; Strabo 13, 2, 6: the sanctuary lay 30 kilometers southeast of Pergamon at a height of about 1,000 meters.

80. Ohlemütz, *Die Kulte,* 182.

81. Ibid., 4–16.

82. Roscher, *Ausführliches,* entry: Kybele; II, 2, *meter panthon, hymn homer.* 14; I, 1, *zoogonous thea,* Sallust *de diis* 4; Apollonius celebrated her as All-Mother who had created the air, earth, and the ocean.

83. Graillot, *Le culte de Cybèle,* 308; for instance at the Plutonium of Acharacea, Strabo XIV 1,44.

84. Graillot, *Le culte de Cybèle,* 307; Strabo XIII 4,14.

85. Graillot, *Le culte de Cybèle,* 310, fn 6; Diod. III, 58. She was associated in Greece with the god of medicine Asklepios in Tanagra and Athens; Pauly-Wissowa entry: Kybele A par. 3, 5; Diodor. III, 58.

86. Hastings, *Ency. of Religion and Ethics,* entry: Thrace; Roscher, *Ausführliches,* entry: Kotys.

87. Pauly-Wissowa entry: Kotys; Aesch. frg. 56 N; Juvenal, *sat.* II, 91; this description relates to the festival after it was brought to Greece; here worshippers were called *hemigynoi* (half-women); the *baptai* (cultic immersions) was the name of a comedy by Eupolis in which he used the Kotyia to satirize Alkibiades.

It appears that among warlike semi-nomadic, cattle-raising nations, orgiastic rites reminiscent of the techniques of shamanism, as well as other pre-agricultural elements of religion, persisted while these had retreated in agricultural and urban groups. See: Lincoln, *Priests;* Meuli, "Ein altpersischer"; Motz, "Ódinn."

We find the orgiastic phenomenon of the "battle fury" among the Germanic Berserks and the Indian Maryuts. The Scythians, also a warrior nation, possessed soothsayers of feminine bearing and also practiced orgiastic rites; the *Naharvali,* one of the Germanic tribes was, likewise, served by effeminate priests (Tacitus, *Germania,* ch.43). We may assume that the Thracian-Phrygians, one-time neighbors of the Scythians, had belonged to the same culture complex. If this is true, we may wonder why the Thracian-Phrygians kept their archaic heritage while a similar heritage had been given up by the Indo-European Hittites. We may recall that the Hittites did not destroy the culture of the Hatti. The Phrygians, on the other hand, appear to have been of more warlike and ruthless nature, as they devastated the countryside and forced the native settlers to escape. From the absence of urban remains following the invasion of the Phrygians, we may assume that these continued their nomadic or semi-nomadic existence for several centuries until King Midas formed the Phrygian state.

88. It has also been assumed that the Phrygians received the goddess Cybele from

the Middle East, as by Monigliano, and also by Burkert, *Structure and History,* 103; she was traced from the Euphrates to Anatolia.

89. Burkert, *Greek Religion,* 179.

90. See note 33.

91. One must distinguish between the "dying" and the "disappearing" god; the tales of the former (Adonis, Dumuzi, Osiris) give voice to anguish at the death of a beloved and the dead does not return (contrary to Frazer's claim); in the latter the concern is with cosmic order and the divinity returns (Demeter, Telipinu, Ishtar).

92. See note 53.

93. That an oracle of Apollo speaks of the birth of Zeus from Cybele (Ohlemütz, *Die Kulte,* 61, citing Kaibel, *Epigrammata,* 1035) cannot be considered a true description of the Anatolian goddess. In another Hellenized version of her life, she is the child of Zeus.

A clay figure excavated at Çatal Hüyük is generally held to depict the goddess in the process of giving birth. This assumption is based on the observation of what might be a child's head beneath her thighs. She is seated between two panthers. Those who hold this generally accepted view fail to consider the following: The woman is not in a position of childbirth, for her knees are closed and her thighs are parallel. She is seated solidly on a rock (Figure 35); she is never, in subsequent images, shown in the process of giving birth, whereas her pose of sitting between felines is especially characteristic. Myths don't make her a biological mother (though she becomes pregnant in one humanized account). The mass between her legs is not clearly recognizable (at least not in reproduction); it might represent an extension of the rock, or a river gushing from it; if a head may indeed be recognized, it could be that of a young animal sheltering beneath her knees; other sculptures show her with the young of animals (Figure 36). It is true, however, that in one account she bore the river nymph Nikeia to the river Sagarios; Roscher, *Ausführliches,* entry: Kybele I, 1a.

94. Teshup, however, represents an exception; he was born from the semen that Kumarbi swallowed when he bit off his father's genitals.

95. Roscher, *Ausführliches,* entry: Lykurgos 2, Diod. 1,20. 3,65.

96. Walter Burkert finds elements of the hunters' tradition in the following aspects of Cybele worship: the rule that her priests are forbidden to eat any form of grain; the fact that the *taurobolion,* the killing of the bull, was to be carried out with a "sacred hunting spear" (*Structure and History,* 119); Jul. *or.* 173 c, 174 ab, 175 b-177 d; Prud. *Peristeph.* 10, 1006–50.

Burkert also notes the treatment of the phalli, which he compares to the treatment of those of slain animals. See Meuli, "Griechische," 247 ff.

Chapter 8

In this, as in other chapters, I had to rely on work of scholars in the field. Experts such as Martin P. Nilsson or Lewis R. Farnell allowed me to gain some insight into Greek religious traditions. I was especially influenced and guided by the works of Walter Burkert.

In my notes, whenever possible, I give the references to both the secondary work and the primary source cited by the author.

Quotations without notes in this chapter are taken from Paul Friedrich's translation of the Homeric Hymn to Demeter.

1. Martin Nilsson traces many elements of Greek religion to the Minoan and Mycenaean heritage (*Mycenaean Origin* and *Minoan-Mycenaean Religion*).

2. Walter Burkert traces aspects of the ritual to an even earlier stage than the Paleolithic, to the time of men's evolving from the primates when they learned to kill for the sake of survival. The change from a hunted to a hunting creature was the essential factor in the creation of our species (*Homo Necans,* 12–22).

3. Living creatures were driven into the flames in the rites of Artemis Laphria in Patrai; Burkert, *Griechische,* 110, Paus. 7, 18, 11–13. Limbs were cut from living victims and thrown onto the altar of Despoina at Lykosura, Burkert, *Griechische,* 59, Paus, 8, 37, 8.

4. The anguish of noting the gap between painful reality and artistic achievement is expressed in modern poetry by W. H. Auden, and aptly he chooses a Greek image. I cite here parts of the poem "The Shield of Achilles" from *Collected Poems:*

> She looked over his shoulder
> For vines and olive trees,
> Marble well-governed cities
> And ships upon untamed seas,
> But on the shining metal
> His hand had put instead
> An artificial wilderness
> And a sky like lead.
>
> She looked over his shoulder
> For ritual pieties,
> White flower-garlanded heifers
> Libations and sacrifice,
> But there on the shining metal
> Where the altar should have been
> She saw by the shining forge-light
> Quite another scene.
>
> A ragged urchin, aimless and alone
> Loitered about that vacancy; a bird
> flew up to safety
> From his well-aimed stone;
> That girls are raped, that two boys knife a third,
> Were axioms to him, who'd never heard
> Of any world where promises were kept
> Or one would weep because another wept.
>
> The thin-lipped armorer
> Hephaistos, hobbled away
> Thetis of the shining breasts
> Cried out in dismay
> At what the god had wrought.

5. Walter Burkert points to the retention of archaic themes within a highly cultured environment (*Homo Necans,* xxiii).

6. Karl Meuli points not only to similarities between Greek sacrificial rites and the customs of modern hunting nations, but also to those of prehistoric peoples, as

interpreted by archaeological remains. In some Swiss caves, the bones and skulls of bears, ascribed to the Paleolithic, were arranged in a manner indicating a ceremonial burial that resembles that of modern hunters. Certain modern hunters of Africa place the skin and head of a slain leopard on a headless clay replica of the beast. The clay figure of a headless bear was found in the cave of Montespan, and between the paws lay the skull of a bear; Meuli, *Gesammelte Schriften,* vol. 2, 964–74.

7. Milk or wine might be poured over the victim's head; when the animal shook his head, it was taken as a sign of acquiescence. Meuli *Gesammelte Schriften,* vol. 2, 995. When the bull was given water to drink, he lowered his head; this too was seen as a sign of agreement; Burkert, *Griechische,* 102.

8. The customs and traditions made little sense to people in an urban context and the presence of an anthropomorphic pantheon. The philosopher Empedokles, the Orphic and Pythagorean sects deplored the atavistic fashion. In his book *On Piety,* Theophrastus condemned the customs of the sacrifice as replacement of an earlier cannibalism; Burkert, *Homo Necans,* 7–8. Yet the sacrifice remained, for it was apparently considered indispensable to creating a deep sense of human oneness through the primeval shock and horror of the spilled blood and through the shared exultation of the life-affirming communal meal.

9. Burkert, *Griechische,* 146–47.

10. Ibid., 152.

11. The wooden figures have not been preserved; the Greek word *xoanon* denotes a carved form, and the word is used to designate the divine statuettes. A god might at one time also have been represented by a single plank. Some temples remained without an image; ibid., 151–53.

12. Burkert, *Homo Necans,* 151; the name of the child Erichthonius is related to Erechtheus, the first king of Athens, Burkert, *Homo Necans,* 152, *Danais* fr. 2.

13. Burkert, *Homo Necans,* 96.

14. As stated by Pindar, "he is drenched in glorious blood offerings, lying at the ford of the Alpheios, with his busy tomb right next to the altar." Pindar *Ol.* 1.90–93; cited in Burkert, *Homo Necans,* 96.

15. Orpheus was a mythical poet; he was also said to be a historical personage of the fifth or sixth century B.C.E. Poems supposedly written by him became the sacred writings of the Orphic sect. The poems are extant in fragments only and were collected with other fragmentary poems of the same school. The thoughts and beliefs of the sect concerning the judgment of the dead and the migration of the soul are said to have influenced Plato. Pythagoras lived at the end of the sixth century and founded a religious sect. Some of his works are scientific, dealing with mathematics and the laws of harmony. He believed that only an austerely pure life allowed people to reach an intellectual understanding of the world.

16. Burkert, *Griechische,* 442.

17. Ibid., 191–99.

18. Zeus Xenios, Farnell, *Cults of the Greek States,* vol. 1, 71, citing Pindar; Zeus Hikesios, Farnell, *Cults,* vol. 1, 72, Aesc. *Suppl.* 385.

He is also known as Zeus Kataibates, "the one who comes down (as lightning)," Farnell, *Cults,* vol. 1, 46, Paus. 5, 14, 10; and as Keraunis "the thunderer," Farnell, *Cults,* vol. 1, 44, Paus. 5, 14, 7.

19. He turns into a cuckoo to win Hera; Burkert, *Griechische,* 211, Paus. 2, 36, 1, f. He turns into a bull to win Europa, Pauly, entry: Europa, Ovid *met* 2, 846 ff.

20. She brought forth Typhoeus who was going to destroy the order of Zeus, Burkert, *Griechische,* 212, *Hymn. Apoll.* 305–54.

21. She allowed no place on earth to offer asylum to the pregnant Leto; finally the small island Delos gave her shelter so that she could bear her children, Burkert, *Griechische,* 229, *Hymn. Apoll.* 25–126.

She tried to destroy Dionysus even before his birth; Burkert, *Griechische,* 212, Aisch. *Fr.* 355–8.

22. Farnell, *Cults of the Greek States,* vol. 3, 29; the Cretan word for barley is *deai;* the syllable *de-* has been posited as a variant form for "earth."

23. My quotations from the Homeric Hymn to Demeter are taken from the translation of Paul Friedrich, *Meaning of Aphrodite,* 163–80. There are also other accounts of Demeter's life; the poets Orpheus, Eumolpus and Musais are named in various reports as having composed poems about the goddess; Graf, *Eleusis,* 151. Of these only fragments have been preserved; especially important is a papyrus of the first pre-Christian century, ibid., 153. Modern scholars, such as Malten, tried to reconstruct the tales. Already in antiquity the stories had been retold, as by Pausanias 1,14,2 and by Clement of Alexandria, *Protr.* 2,21,1, Graf, *Eleusis,* 158–60.

24. *Iliad V* 499–504.

25. Hesiod, *Theog.* 912 f Farnell, *Cults of the Greek States,* vol. 3, 118.

26. *Iliad* XIV 326; Dionysus is said to be the son of Demeter and Zeus, according to Diodorus Siculus iii 62,6; Frazer, *Golden Bough,* vol. 7, 66.

27. There are some variations in the accounts concerning Demeter, as stated in note 23. In an account, transmitted by Pausanias, Demeter enters into the household of Baubo and Dysaules, inhabitants of Eleusis. Dysaules's sons tell the goddess of her daughter's fate, and in gratitude she bestows on them the gift of grain. According to an Argive legend she was received by Pelasgos and Chrysanthis in her journey, and she rewarded them for their hospitality, Graf, *Eleusis,* 158–59, Paus. 1,14,2.

28. Burkert, *Structure and History,* 125–27, Paus. 8, 42; a Delphic oracle had told the inhabitants of the region, on the occasion of a famine, to revive the cult in Demeter's sacred cave.

29. Burkert, *Structure and History,* 127, Paus. 8,25, 4–10; in the town Tilphossa of Boeotia the ravished goddess was named Erinys; in yet another variant the god Poseidon begat the horse Pegasus when he mated with Medusa; Burkert, *Structure and History,* 127, Apoll. 2 (32), 3, 2, 1.

30. Despoina, rather than Demeter, is the main goddess of the mysteries of Lykosura where unbloody gifts are offered. Artemis, Demeter, and Adytis are named in the cult. These divinities are also designated as Despoinas, Nilsson, *Griechische,* 346.

31. Hesiod, *Theog.* 969; the land is, in fact, plowed in Greece three times a year; Frazer, *Golden Bough,* vol. 7, 73.

32. Burkert, *Griechische,* 442; Kern, *Orphicorum fragmenta,* 60–235; Clement, *Protr.* II, 22 ff.

33. Nilsson, *Griechische,* 324, Suidas; in Aigila the celebrating women attacked and killed intruding men; ibid., 327, Paus. 4,17,1.

34. In the sanctuary of Agrigent an opening led to a natural chasm; in Priene a square underground chamber had been dug, plastered, and covered with planks; Burkert, *Griechische,* 366–67.

35. The time span between the casting of the piglets and their recovery is not

known; it must have been long enough for the meat to decay. The women who brought up the remnants were placed under special sexual sanctions; ibid., 366.

36. The tale of Euboleus is not contained in the Homeric Hymn; it is reported by Clement, *Protr.* 14.P and by a scholion to Lucian, Nilsson, *Griechische,* 320.

37. Kalligeneia is not otherwise known in myth and seems to appear only in the ritual. The customs described are those of the Athenian festival.

38. This action is named *aischrologia;* the women form two groups that mock one another with ribaldries; Nilsson, *Griechische,* 322, Cleomedes *cycle theor.* 2,1 p. 112.

39. The first plowed field was represented by the Rarian plain, Farnell, *Cults of the Greek states,* vol. 3, 44, Eur. *Supplices* though a Delphic oracle names Athens; Farnell, *Cults,* vol. 3, 34. Kerényi, *Eleusis,* 17, Eunapius, *Vitae sophistarum* VII, 3.

40. The sanctuary rises on the site of a Mycenaean fortification, Mylonas, *Hymn to Demeter,* 33. The settlement of Eleusis might have been ruled by a family of kings or priests. In later times the highest offices of the rites could only be carried out by members of certain native families: the Eumolpides and the Kerykes; Kerényi, *Eleusis,* 22–23. It has also been assumed that before the incorporation of Eleusis into the Attic state the mysteries had represented a tribal institution, and they were later opened to other Hellenic peoples; Farnell, *Cults of the Greek States,* vol. 3, 153–60.

41. *Homeric Hymn,* Friedrich, *Meaning of Aphrodite,* 179–80.

42. Burkert, *Griechische,* 427, Clement *Protr.* 2, 21, 2; Clement, who was a Christian, tried to belittle the ceremonies and hinted that objects of a sexual nature were hidden in the basket.

43. Burkert, *Homo Necans,* 289,

44. The *mystes* had fasted for nine days before he proceeded on his journey; a scholion to Theokritus II, 35–36 speaks of the sound of brazen instruments "like that which is beaten at the rites of Ceres," Kerényi, *Eleusis,* 84. Dances were performed around the well named Kallichoron, which lay still outside of the sacred precinct; and a great fire burned within the mystery hall; ibid., 70, 92.

45. The march began on the nineteenth of the Boedromenon in the middle of September after the pilgrims had taken their purifying bath in the sea. They proceeded shouting the name Iakchos and swinging branches of twigs; ibid., 60–66.

46. The feast of Demeter Chthonia in Hermione is described by Pausanias 2, 35, 5, Nilsson, *Griechische,* 329; an account of the Thalysia performed on the threshing floor, in Kos is given by Theocritus, *Id.* 7, 3, Nilsson, *Griechische,* 331; the altar and the image of Demeter are situated on the threshing floor. The *proerosia* were a feast of plowing, celebrated in Eleusis in the sacred plain; Farnell, *Cults of the Greek States,* vol. 3, 42–45. Demeter's mysteries merged in some places with the local mysteries, as, for instance, in Samothrake; here she participated in the mysteries of the Kabiri and received the name Demeter Kabeira; in Pheneos in Arcadia she received the name Demeter Kidaria, Nilsson, *Griechische,* 343, Paus. 8, 15, 1. She was especially popular in agriculturally fertile Sicily; here several places claim to be the spot where Persephone was swallowed by the earth (e.g., Kyane near Syracuse); the goddesses were worshipped as Thesmophoroi in Syracuse: Pauly-Wissowa, *Paulys Realenzyklopädie,* Diod. Sic. XI, 26, and as Theai hagnai in Akraia; Ovid, *fast* IV, 421, called Sicily the favorite land of the goddesses.

For Demeter Chloe: Farnell, *Cults of the Greek States,* vol. 3, 33, and for Demeter Megalartos: Farnell, *Cults,* vol. 3, 37.

47. Farnell, *Cults of the Greek States,* vol. 3, 35, Hesiod, *Works* 465.

48. Farnell, *Cults of the Greek States,* vol. 3, 36, citing Athenaeus.

49. Nilsson, *Geschichte,* 63, Hesych. Hesiod, *Works* 31–33, speaks of the "food which the earth sends up: Demeter's corn."

50. She is called Karpophoros in various places, such as Tegea, Farnell, *Cults of the Greek States,* vol. 3, 318, Paus. 8, 53, 7; Eualosia: Farnell, *Cults,* vol. 3, 318, Hesych. *Anesidora,* Farnell, *Cults,* vol. 3, 317; Paus. 1, 31, 4; Himalis: Farnell, *Cults,* vol. 3, 37, Athenae. 416, B. She is also Azesia, "the goddess of spelt," Farnell, *Cults,* vol. 3, 37, Hesych; or Haloas, "the goddess of the threshing floor," Farnell, *Cults,* vol. 3, 37, Theocr. *Id.* 7,155.

51. Nilsson, *Griechische,* 344; Burkert, *Griechische,* 418, Paus. 8, 37, 6; beings with animal features appear also on a peplos that had belonged either to Demeter or Despoina, Nilsson, *Griechische,* 347. Also ibid., 348, Paus. 8, 10, 10; Farnell, *Cults,* vol. 3, 56. Demeter Melaina of Phigalia was said to have had beast images in her sanctuary, a dolphin, doves, and snakes, Nilsson, *Griechische,* 348, Paus. 8, 42, 4.

52. Farnell, *Cults,* vol. 3. 45; the priestly office in the Haloa was held by a woman, and women were initiated into a secret group at this feast, according to a scholion to Lucian, ibid., 46.

53. Ibid., 112; Pausanias 8, 31, 8. Men were also excluded from Demeter's festival in Aigila, Nilsson, *Griechische,* 327; they were not allowed to enter Demeter's temple in Enna in Sicily or her temple near Etna; Pauly-Wissowa, *Paulys Realenzyklopädie.*

54. Here she is called Europe and her sanctuary stands in the grove of Trophonios, Farnell, *Cults,* vol. 3, 30, Pausanias 9, 39, 4.

55. The title Kourotrophos, "cherisher of children," is applied to her in Athens, Farnell, *Cults,* vol. 3, 81i C.I.A. 3.372, 373 (seat inscriptions in the Erechtheum).

56. Burkert, *Griechische,* 368.

57. Graf, *Eleusis,* 168; Wehrli, "Die Mysterien," 79, cites an account where the goddess herself bares her sex; Gregory of Nazianz, *Orat.*

58. Graf, *Eleusis,* 166; Clement *Protr.* 2, 21, 1.

59. Graf, *Eleusis,* 168; Winter, *Die Typen der figürlichen Terrakotten,* 223.

60. We may note that the Japanese Amaterasu was lured from her hiding place by the laughter of the gods aroused through the obscene dance of a goddess. Graf cites an Egyptian example in which Hathor shatters the anger of Re Harachta, the god of the sun, by baring herself (*Eleusis,* 169–70). Irish women of the royal court stripped naked and dispelled the murderous rage of Cuchulain.

61. Scott, *Phallic Worship,* 205–10; for a full discussion of the Irish and English Sheela-na-gig, see Andersen, *Witch on the Wall,* see also Motz, *Beauty and the Hag,* 14–30.

62. Nilsson, *Griechische,* 330; Paus. 2, 35, 9.

63. Farnell, *Cults,* vol. 3, 49; Paus. 3, 14, 5.

64. Kerényi, *Eleusis,* ill. 27.

65. Burkert, *Griechische,* 251.

66. Kerényi, *Eleusis,* 15; and Crinagoras of Lesbos stated in the last pre-Christian century: "yet set thy foot on the Attic soil, that thou mayest see those long nights of Demeter's holy rites, whereby while thou art among the living thy mind shall be free from care, and when thou goest to join the greater number it shall be lighter," ibid., 193, *Anthologia Palatina* XI, 42 3–6, transl. Paton IV, 91.

67. The first vase paintings, both black and red figured, are dated to the sixth century, and their number increases rapidly. Twice Triptolemus is shown with a plow. Especially famous is a relief found at Eleusis that depicts the youth between the two

goddesses; Farnell, *Cults,* vol. 3, plate XXV, now in the Central Museum in Athens. Triptolemus probably was a local god of agriculture in Eleusis; his altar stood on the Rarian Plain where the plowing feast was celebrated; ibid., 45; He became in time a Panhellenic hero. On presentations he changed in the course of time from a bearded man to a youth, Nilsson, "Die eleusinischen," 85. A play concerning Triptolemus had been written by Sophocles (486 B.C.E.) of which only fragments exist. Here too he is said to have spread agriculture throughout the world.

68. Graf, *Eleusis,* 182, Isocrates 4, 28; Frazer, *Golden Bough,* vol. 7, 58, Himerius *Oratio* ii, 5; Wehrli, "Die Mysterien," 87, Diod Sic. 4.4. Isocrates and Himerius name Athens as the source of dispersal of grain, and Diodorus names Sicily; we may consider the statements of these authors as patriotic efforts to glorify their homeland.

69. Graf, *Eleusis,* 158–59, Paus 1, 14, 3.

70. Graf, *Eleusis,* 174–76.

71. The seeds begin to sprout in Greece several weeks after the autumn sowing, and the grain continues to grow through the winter. Nilsson assumes that the girl's absence coincided with the storage of grain in underground containers during the four months of the summer; Nilsson, "Die eleusinischen," 105–14. The time of sowing wheat and barley extends from October to December; they are harvested in May or June; a less important crop is sown in April. Brumfield, *The Attic Festivals of Demeter* 11–53.

While it is frequently believed that Persephone represents vegetation that dies and returns, it has been pointed out by Johansen ("Thesmophoria") that in many places Persephone is not recovered from death and is considered in Greek faith to be a goddess of the underworld. Johansen understands the Thesmophoria to represent the initiation of a girl into womanhood; the feast thus would be of an initiatory nature. Barbara Smith also believes that the Thesmophoria celebrate a girl's *menarche,* symbolized by the red juice of the pomegranate that she eats in the underworld ("Greece," 89). For girls' initiation, see also Dowden, *Death and the Maiden.*

72. Gaster, *Thespis,* 353–77.

73. "The Descent of Ishtar to the Netherworld"; ANET 106–09.

74. Gaster, *Thespis,* 194.

75. Wolkstein and Kramer, *Inanna,* 86.

76. Jacobsen, *Treasures of Darkness,* 54, BE XXX nr.1, ii 3 to iii 4.

77. *Snorri Sturluson. Edda,* 35. Lamentations seem to be widespread in Middle Eastern tradition, and they may include weeping for a ravished city. The goddess Ningal mourns the fated destruction of her city Ur. The lament is cited in Chapter 6 of this study. The wailings for the sacked Jerusalem of Hebrew tradition might belong to this class.

78. The rite of "weeping for Adonis" took place in the late summer, Nilsson, *Griechische,* 386.

79. Burkert, *Structure and History,* 6–7.

80. Jacobsen, *Treasures of Darkness,* 103–4, "Enlil and Ninlil"; SEM 76–77.

81. Burkert, *Griechische,* 225.

82. This is the belief of Helck, *Betrachtungen,* 92–93, and of Kerényi, *Eleusis,* 145. Paul Friedrich (*Meaning of Aphrodite*) assumes that the tale and cult of Demeter spread so widely because there was a great need for a maternal, caring goddess, since none of the other important Greek goddesses showed strong maternal tendencies.

83. Wehrli, "Die Mysterien," 84; in the Orphic Hymn 41, Antatai (Demeter) is led into the underworld by Euboleus. If the disappearing divinity would represent the

vanishing of vegetation, then it would make more sense to have Demeter disapear, because she is much more closely identified with vegetation than Kore.

84. Farnell, *Cults*, vol. 3, 121. Tert. *Ad. Nat.* ii, 30; Serv. Verg. *Georg.* I, 344.

85. Farnell, *Cults*, vol. 3, 43; in a play by Euripides a queen speaks of having come for the sake of sacrificing, to the plowing field in Eleusis, "I abide here by the holy altars of the two goddesses Kore and Demeter."

Demeter and Kore are the chief deities of the Haloa festival of Eleusis; Farnell, *Cults*, vol. 3, 45,

Theai Megalai: Farnell, *Cults*, vol. 3, 125, Paus. 8, 31, 8; Thesmophoroi in Syracuse: Farnell, *Cults*, vol. 3, 74, Plut. *Dio.* 56; Despoina: Farnell, *Cults*, vol. 3, 334, Paus. 8, 37, 1. They are also known as Demeteres, Burkert, *Griechische*, 248.

A Roman arch in Eleusis bears the inscription "To the Two Goddesses," Kerényi, *Eleusis*, 67.

86. "On the more ancient vases and terra-cottas they appear rather as twin sisters, almost as if the inarticulate artist were aware of their original identity of substance." Farnell, *Cults*, vol. 3, 259.

87. Kore is not named in the reapers' harvest prayer of Theocritus, *Id.* 7, 42, Farnell, *Cults*, vol. 3, 115, and in dedications to the harvest, *Anth. Pal.* 6, 98; Farnell, *Cults*, vol. 3, 115. The worship of Demeter Melaina and Demeter Erinys seem to indicate that there was only one goddess, Farnell, *Cults*, vol. 3, 117. In places in Sicily there are festivals for Kore only, Nilsson, *Griechische*, 355.

88. Raindrops might thus be designated as Demeter's tears, in the same way that grain is designated as Demeter's fruit; *damatrizein* means "to reap"; if the sorrowful mother was primary, it might mean "to weep." If it was the need for a maternal deity that caused the Demeter cult to spread through the Greek provinces, as assumed by Friedrich (*Meaning of Aphrodite*), then we may wonder why she was exported in various forms: as goddess of the underworld or as Lady of the beasts.

The folklore parallels are brought forward by Frazer, *Golden Bough*, vol. 7, 131–213, and by Mannhardt, *Mythologische*, 296–350.

89. Many patterns may be discerned in Kore-Persephone; even the doubling of her name suggests a complex being; she appears frequently as a double of Demeter in cultic practices, but she is strongly differentiated from her in the Homeric Hymn. Homer cites her only as Queen of the underworld. The theme of a maiden ravished in the flower of her youth by death appears also outside of the Demeter tales, Malten, "Der Raub der Kore," 309–11; she has a relation to marriage in Sicily and lower Italy. (Clay reliefs of a sanctuary of Persephone in Locri indicate her role as a goddess and protector of marriage, Sourvinu-Inwood 1978, 105; the abduction of a girl is found also outside of Demeter's tale as a theme related to human marriage, Sourvinou-Inwood, "Erotic Pursuit." Kore may also be shown with stalks of corn, like her mother, Farnell, *Cults*, vol. 3, plate V. This very brief survey indicates that Kore overlaps in some ways with her mother, but appears more closely related to marriage and to the queenship of the underworld.

90. The inscription appears in a temple in Delos, Kerényi, *Eleusis*, 33.

91. Bächtold-Stäubli, *Handwörterbuch*, entry: Korndämonen, divides the spirits of the grain into three classes: the wind in the corn, the frighteners of children, and the puppets created in the course of the harvest, usually from the last sheaf of wheat. All may appear in male, female, and animal form. All three may carry the designation Corn Mother. The first two forms are truly threatening; drinking from the iron breasts of the *Zitzenweib* is as deadly as being crushed in her grip. Only the last of the groups

could have any relation to a beneficial force; the customs are quite varied. Whoever cuts the last stalk or shapes the last sheaf is called bride or bridegroom, according to sex, in Austria. The one who cuts the last stalks will marry an old woman or a widower in Silesia, Hesse, or Bavaria. In lower Austria the last sheaf is adorned with flowers and placed in a special location in the barn. In Saxony the last worker is covered with straw and field flowers, while the other harvesters perform dances around him. In Hesse it is a stick that is embedded in straw and flowers and becomes the focal point of dancing. Sometimes gifts are left in the field for certain spirits. In Zürich the first three stalks cut in harvesting are left for the Old Woman. Near Leipzig the replica of a barn, made of corn stalks, is given to the *Kornengel*. In upper Franconia stalks are left for the *Waldfräulein*.

92. Paulson, *Religionen der finnischen Völker*, 231; brandy is poured into the earth for her at the time of planting.

93. Ibid., 220, 214.

94. Ibid., 214, 227, 225.

95. Ibid., the Mordvins believe in the earth mother *mastor-ava* and in a male god *mastor-at 'ä*, 225; and as they have a field mother *pakś-azorava*, they also have a "field old man," *pakś-at 'ä*, ibid., 227.

96. Ibid., one of the women would be dressed up to represent the goddess, 227, 228.

97. Hom. *hym.* I, 97; *Il.* XI, 270; a shrine to Eileithyia Eukoline has been identified in Agrai in Attica; Price, *Kourotrophos*, 124.

98. Hom. *hym*, I, 97 ff: Hoenn, *Artemis*, 67, quoting a hymn by Kallimachos.

99. *Il.* IXX, 119; Ovid, *met.* IX, 285.

100. *Theog.* 922; *Il.* 11, 270. Pauly-Wissowa, entry: Eileithyia.

101. Price, *Kourotrophos*, 81 ff. In the cave of Eileithyia in Krateros a stone formation resembling a woman stands next to a smaller formation resembling a child; the two are surrounded by a stone enclosure, Faure, *Fonctions*, 13.

102. Delos was, with Crete, one of the most ancient centers of the Eileithyia cult from where it spread to other parts of Greece, Price, *Kourotrophos*, 150, citing Pausanias 1, 18, 5; the remnants of her sanctuary were not found, but its existence and the kind of offerings it received are attested by inscriptions and inventories; Price, *Kourotrophos*, 151, citing Bruneau, *Recherches*, 214 ff. Eileithyia had cults throughout Greece, as in Sparta, Arcadia, Paros; Price, *Kourotrophos*, 191.

103. Farnell, Cults, vol. 2, 612, 613.

104. This name is given to her in a hymn composed by Olen; Paus. VIII, 21, 3.

105. This name is mentioned by Antimachos of Colophon; Price, *Kourotrophos*, 89.

106. Pauly-Wissowa, *Paulys Realenzyklopädie*, entry: Eileithyia.

107. Demeter nursing Damophon, Price *Kourotrophos*, 119; Demeter nursing Triptolemos, Price, 61; Demeter nursing Trophonius, Pauly-Wissowa entry: Trophonius, G.

108. Pauly-Wissowa *Paulys Realenzyklopädie*: Hera VIII, 5; Diod. IV, 9.6; *Anth. Pal.* IX, 589.

109. Nurses of Apollo and Dionysos, Price, *Kourotrophos*, 126.

110. Call. *Hymn.* I, 46 ff; a bitch with a child appears on coins of Crete and on Minoan seals, Price, *Kourotrophos*, 73; the bee and bear nurses of Zeus are also cited by Price, 73.

111. Price, *Kourotrophos*, 77.

112. Price, *Kourotrophos,* 70, citing Zanker, *Corinth,* 77 ff; Price, *Kourotrophos,* 71, citing Robertson, *History of Greek Art,* 467; Price, *Kourotrophos,* 71.

113. Ibid., 107.

114. Price, *Kourotrophos,* 112; Farnell, vol. 3, 17.

115. Price, *Kourotrophos,* 152, citing *Vita Herodotea, Hom. Vitae* 399.

116. Price, *Kourotrophos,* 137.

117. *Theogony* 450–52.

118. As in Idalion, a sanctuary of Aphrodite, Price, *Kourotrophos,* 93–94, citing Ohnefalsch-Richter, *Ancient Places;* the shrine in Brauron is dedicated to Artemis Iphigeneia "who gives good offspring"; Price, *Kourotrophos,* 121.

119. *Theog.* 904 ff.

120. Pauly-Wissowa, *Paulys Realenzyklopädie:* Moira IX.

121. Pauly-Wissowa, *Paulys Realenzyklopädie:* Moira IX; Eur. *Iph.* T206.

122. Hes. *theog.* 904.

123. *Il.* XVI, 431 ff; he also cannot save Heracles, *Il.* XVIII, 117 ff.

124. Pauly-Wissowa, *Paulys Realenzyklopädie:* Moira V.

125. Pauly-Wissowa, *Paulys Realenzyklopädie:* Moira XII.

126. Lurker, *Gods and Symbols,* entry: Birth brick.

127. Pauly-Wissowa, *Paulys Realenzyklopädie:* Artemis III, 10; *Ant. Pal.* VI, 273.

128. Pauly-Wissowa, *Paulys Realenzyklopädie:* Artemis III, 10; *Ant. Pal.* VI, 201, 271.

129. Price, *Kourotrophos,* 151, citing Bruneau, *Recherches,* 191; Price, *Kourotrophos,* 121; Pauly-Wissowa, *Paulys Realenzyklopädie:* Artemis III, 10; Theokr. XXVII, 29; Artemis III, 11; *Ant. Pal.* VI, 269.

130. Diod. Sic. V.73.5; Paus. IV, 34, 6. Price, *Kourotrophos,* 189.

131. Pauly-Wissowa, *Paulys Realenzyklopädie:* Artemis III, 8; Athen. IV, 139 AB.

132. Farnell, *Cults,* vol. 2, 436; Arist. *Lysist.* 645 and Scholion.

133. Pauly-Wissowa, *Paulys Realenzyklopädie:* Artemis III, 8.

134. *Il.* XX, 70.

135. *Od.* XXIII, 296; cited by Burkert, *Greek Religion,* 132.

136. *Il.* XIV, 153–353; Diod. Sic. V, 72, 4; all cited by Burkert, *Greek Religion,* 132.

137. Paus. IX, 3, 3–8; cited by Burkert, *Greek Religion,* 135.

138. Paus. IX, 2, 7; Burkert, *Greek Religion,* 135.

139. Pauly-Wissowa, *Paulys Realenzyklopädie:* Hera II, A 15; Paus. VIII, 22, 2.

140. The "sacred marriage" is in Greek tradition the marriage between Zeus and Hera; several places lay claim to have been the site of its enactment, such as Samos, near Knossos, Euboea.

141. Deubner, *Attische Feste,* 176, citing Hesych.

142. Pauly-Wissowa, *Paulys Realenzyklopädie:* Hera VIII, 2; Diod. V, 73; Arch frg. 18, B; P-W: Hera III, Pisander in Schol. Eur. *Phoen.* 1748.

143. Paus. V, 16; cited by Burkert, *Greek Religion,* 133.

144. *Ill.* XVIII, 118; Price, *Kourotrophos,* 192.

145. Pauly-Wissowa, *Paulys Realenzyklopädie:* Hera VIII, 5; Erathost. *Katast.* 44.

146. Hom. *hym.* II, 226, ff. Paus. IX, 39, 5.

147. Farnell, *Cults,* vol. 3, 81; C.I.A. 3, 372, 373 (seats in the Erechtheum in Athens).

Chapter 9

As in other chapters I had to rely on translations and the works of specialists in the field for my information. I have been greatly helped by the works of such scholars as Eduard Seler, Walter Krickeberg, and Åke Hultkrantz. The information supplied by diverse sources is often overlapping, and I have not cited every variant of a myth or an illustration.

1. Krickeberg et al., *Die Religionen,* V–X.

2. Hultkrantz, *The Religions,* 168.

3. This scene is carved into a stele at Les Zapotec, Krickeberg et al., *Die Religionen,* 10. The La Venta culture is attributed to the Olmecs (a nation by this name was later living in the area); Hultkrantz, *The Religions,* 169–71.

4. The name of the creators of the Teotihuacán culture, which flourished from the third to the seventh century of our era, is not known; Hultkrantz, *The Religions,* 17.

5. Krickeberg et al., *Die Religionen,* 15–16; this culture is known as the classical period. Other important sites of this civilization are at Monte Albán in Oaxaca and El Tajín in Vera Cruz; ibid., 17–23.

6. Concerning the Toltecs, we may already consult written records, and according to one source, the Toltec kings ruled from 856–1168 C.E. Hultkrantz, *The Religions,* 243; Krickeberg et al., *Die Religionen,* 29, according to the *Historia de los Reynos (Anales de Quauhtitlan),* the capital city was Tollan-Tula, eighty miles north of Mexico City. Systematic excavations, begun in 1941, reveal a center of civilization; it has even been claimed that Tula was the great artistic center after Teotihuacán had been destroyed, Léon-Portilla, *Aztec Image,* 22–24.

The dating of the various cultures is still controversial. The following chronology has been drawn up by Doris Heiden in Durán, *The Aztecs,* 331: preclassical, 2000–200 B.C.E.; classical, 200 B.C.E. to 750 C.E.; Toltec, 750–1250; Chichimec invasions, 1200–1248; Aztec rule, 1428–1521. Michael Coe (*Mexico*) has a somewhat different chronology: early formative period, 1500–900 B.C.E.; middle formative, 900–300 B.C.E.; formative, 300 B.C.E. to 150 C.E.; early classical, 150–650; classical, 650–900; early postclassical, 900–1200; late postclassical, 1200–1521.

7. Durán, *The Aztecs,* ch. 2, p. 9; several tribes emerged from the caves, according to this chronicler, in 820 C.E.: the Xochimilca, Tecpanec, Colhua, Tlalhuica, Tlaxcalanchakas, Chalca. The Aztecs left 300 years later. It need not be emphasized that the chronicles vary in their accounts of the past.

8. Hultkrantz, *The Religions,* 242–44.

9. The most important of the Spanish informants is the Franciscan monk Bernardino de Sahagún, who arrived in Mexico in 1529 when native religion was still very much alive. He described the physical features of the country and the customs of society in minute detail and named his monumental work *Historia general de las cosas de Nueva España.* Diego Durán, another sixteenth-century friar, wrote a two volume history, *Historia de las Indias de Nueva España.* Gerónimo de Mendieta (1525?–1624) composed the *Historia ecclesiástica Indiana.* There also are a number of anonymous accounts.

The pictorial documents of the Mexicans are of great importance; some of these relate to the past, some to secular and religious customs, some to the counting of time and to astrological concerns. In some of these codices (*Telleriano-Remensis, Vaticanus A*) interpreters had written comments in Spanish. On the basis of these comments other unmarked codices could be interpreted. The great task of deciphering the pictorial documents was carried out by Eduard Seler.

10. Krickeberg et al., *Die Religionen,* 41; Theodor Preuss talks about tribal and nature deities *(Die mexikanische).*

11. Krickeberg et al., *Die Religionen,* 10.

12. Hultkrantz, *The Religions,* 171; Krickeberg et al., *Die Religionen,* 15–16.

13. Krickeberg et al., *Die Religionen,* 16.

14. Ibid., 30; Hultkrantz, *The Religions,* 171. The god Quetzalcoatl, followed by his alter ego, a feathered serpent, appears in a rock relief near Tula and in a picture of the chapel in Chichén Itzá in Yucatán, Krickeberg et al., *Die Religionen,* 33.

15. Ibid., 46; Durán, *Book of the Gods,* 76.

16. The statue had once stood in a temple of Tenochtitlán, the site of present-day Mexico City; Krickeberg et al., *Die Religionen,* 44.

17. Krickeberg, *Märchen der Azteken,* 3, citing *Historia de los Mexicanos,* 228–31.

18. Six pairs of gods are pictured as the rulers of the six regions of the world (Seler, *Codex Féjerváry-Mayer,* 35, 36, 37). The East is ruled by the Flower Prince and the Flower Princess, the North by the Pulque (wine) god and goddess, the West by the god and goddess of maize, the South by the rain god and the lady of the water, the sky by the Flower Prince and the Flower Princess, and the underworld by their rulers Mictlantecutli and Mictlanciuatl; reproduced by Seler, *Codex Borgia,* vol. 2, 172–76.

19. Sahagún, *Florentine Codex,* bk VI, ch. 29; her dead body would be carried through the streets, followed by the midwives who "bore their shields and gave war cries."

20. The priests employed a calendar of 20 weeks, each week composed of 13 days, covering a period of 260 days, and another system of 18 months where every month was composed of 20 days with 5 days added to complete the circuit of the sun. Each of the 20 days was marked by a specific symbol; the week, however, ended after 13 days, so that the first day of the new week would carry the sign of the fourteenth day; the first day of the third week would carry the sign of the seventh day. After 20 weeks the first day of the week would again carry the sign of the first day. Thus a unit of 260 days was established. This unit was used in *tonalamatl,* the Book of Days, which served astrological functions. A solar calendar was also used; the solar year consisted of 18 months, each containing 20 days, with 5 days added to complete the period. The days would still be known by their *tonalamatl* name, and the year would be designated by the name of its first day, (e.g., "one rabbit," "two reed"). After 52 years the circle was completed.

21. Eighteen great feasts were held, one for every month; among the honored gods were Tlaloc, the god of rain, Xipe, the god of vegetation, Chichomecoatl, the goddess of maize. After eight years a great feast of renewal was celebrated. Every eight years the end of the solar cycle coincides with the end of the cycle of the planet Venus (584 days). This coincidence may be the reason for the time of the feast.

22. Sahagún, *Florentine Codex,* bk VII, chs. 9–12.

23. Ibid., bk VI, ch. 29.

24. Quotation translated by me from German; Seler, *Codex Borgia,* vol. 2, 7. Krickeberg, *Märchen der Azteken,* 68–69, citing *anal. quauht.* 17–29.

25. Lehmann, "Traditions," 263.

26. Krickeberg et al., *Die Religionen,* 32.

27. Seler, *Codex Vaticanus B,* 287.

28. The aggressive morning star is named Tlauizcalpantecútli; in "one crocodile" he shoots old men and women, in "one rain" he shoots rain, in "one reed" he shoots kings. Calendar illustrations testify to his aggressive action: the god of the planet Venus shoots Cinteotl in his first phase (*Codex Vaticanus* B, 80; *Codex Bologna,* 9); he shoots the goddess of the water in his second phase (*Cod. Vat.* B, 81; *Cod. Bol.* 9); he shoots warriors in his third phase (*Cod. Vat.* B, 82; *Cod. Bol.* 10); kings in his fourth phase (*Cod. Vat.* B, 83; *Cod. Bol.* 10); and he shoots Ozelotl, the god of the North, in his fifth phase (*Cod. Vat.* B, 84; *Cod. Bol.* 11), reproduced by Seler, *Codex Borgia,* vol. 2, 141–48.

29. Durán, *Book of the Gods,* 234; Sahagún, *Florentine Codex,* bk II, chs. 9, 14, 20.

30. de Jonghe, "Histoire du Méchique," 27–29.

31. Both gods brought gifts before they died; those of Tecuciztecatl were precious, those of Nanauatzin were poor; he was syphilitic, but they testified to his piety. Sahagún, *Florentine Codex,* bk VII, ch. 2.

32. Krickeberg, *Märchen der Azteken,* 97, citing *Histoire de la nation Mexicaine,* sheet 4–27; *Lehmann et al., Geschichte,* 4–5.

33. Krickeberg, *Märchen der Azteken,* 22–23, citing *hist.mex.pint.* 236.

34. Hatt, "The Corn Mother"; the theme may be found in North and Central America but is absent from South America with the exception of Peru. The creature is often of a very kindly nature and may take care of orphan children. Often she (the spirit is usually female) is discovered in the act of producing food from her body, as, for instance, by rubbing herself. Those who see her are enraged and repelled, and she is killed, or she herself may offer to sacrifice her life. Sometimes she is buried, sometimes burned; soon afterward food begins to grow in the earth. In a variant the spirit is lost rather than destroyed, and then found. While the plant that arises in America is maize, it is rice in Indonesia; in Celebes rice and sago are produced. In these parts it is also held that the cocoa plant and the buffalo grew from the body of a boy. Yams came from the limbs of an old man.

35. Krickeberg, *Märchen der Azteken,* 37, citing *anal. quauht.* 13–15. Lehmann, "Traditions," 277–79.

36. de Jonghe, "Histoire du Méchique," 34. Lehmann et al., *Geschichte,* 112, *Histoire Mexicaine,* 40, Chimalman is here the older sister of the two spirits (Mimixcoa) who came from heaven and were killed. She is the wife of Mixcoatl in Lehmann "Traditions," 265.

37. Spence, *Gods of Mexico,* 185–87; his weapon is the fiery serpent *xiuhcoatl.* She is also called Coatlantonau, "our serpent mother"; her sons are the Centzonuitznaua and the daughter is Coyolxauhqui; Sahagún, *Florentine Codex,* bk III, ch. 1.

38. Durán, *The Aztecs,* ch. XXVII, 135–39.

39. Krickeberg, *Märchen der Azteken,* 330, citing Muñoz, *Historia de Tuzcala,* 40.

40. Seler, *Gesammelte,* vol. 2, 481, citing Sahagún, bk II, ch. 33.

41. In his description Sahagún also gives her name as Iztaccihuatl (white woman) and relates that she wears a white garment and white sandals and has her face painted with white earth; Seler, *Gesammelte,* vol. 2, 480.

42. A human skull, instead of a head, rises from the shoulders of another snake-skirted sculpture. The larger sculpture was found in Mexico City, the smaller one in Tehuacan in Pueblo.

43. Sahagún, *Florentine Codex,* bk. II, ch. 22; she is especially honored in Coatlan.

44. Lehmann, "Traditions," 279.

45. Ibid., 253. That new life springs from bones is a widely held belief among hunters; the grinding of a substance into paste seems to be an image created by an agricultural culture in which grain is ground into flour.

46. Lafaye, *Quetzalcoatl*, 212; Caso, *The Aztecs*, 54; Sahagún, *Florentine Codex*, bk I., ch. 6.

47. Sahagún describes her as wearing a crown of eagle feathers, a red-and-white skirt, sandals, bells, her face painted red and black, adorned with golden ear ornaments. She is also beheld in the garments of a noblewoman, her hair arranged in hornlike coils (*Florentine Codex*, bk. I, ch. 6); some of the elements of her appearance are given by Seler in his translation of a Sahagún ms in Madrid. (*Gesammelte*, vol. 2, 477).

48. Sahagún, *Florentine Codex*, bk. I, ch. 6.

49. Seler, *Gesammelte*, vol. 2, 1051, reproducing *Histoire Mexicaine*. She is also named "the Deer of Mixcoatl"; Seler, *Gesammelte*, vol. 2, 1052.

50. Sahagún, *Florentine Codex*, bk. II, appendix; The first part of the hymn is as follows:

> *Song of Ciuacoatl*
> The eagle Quilaztli, with serpent blood painted, with
> eagle plumes crowned, is protectress of the Chalmeca
> and (goddess) of Colhuacan.
> The maize is our hands and our feet in the field of the
> god, who resteth upon her rattle board.
> Maguey thorns, rest in my hand. In the field of the god,
> she resteth upon her rattle board.
> The grass bunch resteth in my hand. In the field . . .
> Aumei quauhtli, our mother, goddess of the Chalmeca,
> deliver me with the dread dart of thorns. It is my son
> Mixcoatl.

51. Ibid., bk. I, ch. 6.

52. The clothes are called "eagle garments"; Durán, *The Aztecs*, ch. LVI, 230.

53. Sahagún, *Florentine Codex*, bk. VI, chs. 28, 29.

54. Durán, *Book of the Gods*, ch. XIII, 217; he also states that she is dressed in woman's garb, all white.

55. Sahagún, *Florentine Codex*, bk. I, p. 40; she is also called "Heart of the Earth," Tlallilyiollo, ibid., bk. I, p. 40.

56. Durán, *The Aztecs*, ch. IV, 26.

57. Sahagún describes her as having a thick layer of rubber around her lips, a black mark on her cheek, a cotton headband, a shield with a golden disk, ear ornaments of blue feathers, white skirt and sandals, eagle feathers on her skirt, and a broom in her hand; she also carries a healing plant; Seler, *Gesammelte*, vol. 2, 468–69, in his translation of Sahagún's ms in the Biblioteca del Palacio in Madrid. Sahagún notes the medicinal plant, also a circle of rubber on her cheeks, a ball with palm strips, cotton flowers, a shell-covered skirt (*Florentine Codex*, bk. I, ch. 8). The spindles are seen in illustrations of the *ochpaniztli* festival in *Codex Borbonicus* 30, Seler, *Codex Borgia*, vol. 1, 159, or in an illustration of Durán, *Book of the Gods*, plate 24.

58. Sahagún, *Florentine Codex*, bk. II, ch. 30. The three medicine women are called Aua, Tlauitecqui, Xoquauhtli; illustrations of the festival are found in *Codex Borbonicus* and *Codex Tellerianus-Remensis*. The festival is also described in Durán, *Book of the Gods*, ch. XV.

59. Sahagún, *Florentine Codex,* bk. II, ch. 30.
60. Ibid., bk. II, appendix; the hymn continues:

> The white flower hath opened, she our mother with the thigh skin of
> the goddess painted on her face, departed from Tamoanchan.
> She hath become a goddess upon the melon cactus, our mother
> Itzpapalotl, she . . .
> Thou hast seen, in the nine dry plains, the deer's heart
> on which was fed our mother Tlaltecutli.
> Once again with chalk, with feathers she is pasted. In
> four directions hath the arrow shattered.
> They saw thee turn to deer in the land of the gods Xiuhnel
> and Mimich.

61. Durán, *The Aztecs,* ch. LXXIV, 290.
62. Sahagún, *Florentine Codex,* bk. I, ch. 12: "it was said that there were four women—the first named Tiacapan (the older sister), the second Teicu (the younger sister), the third named Tlaco (the middle sister), the fourth named Xocutzin (the youngest sister). These four women, it is said, were god(desses). These each separately were called god(desses) of luxury (Tlaçolteteu)." The name Tlazolteotl for the goddess of the calendars was given by the commentators of the *Codex Telleriano-Remensis.*
63. The name Ixcuina is not actually mentioned in the passage, but we are given four names that correspond to the names of the four sisters: Tiacapan, Teicu, Tlacoyehua, Xocoyotl; Sahagún, *Florentine Codex,* bk. VII, ch. 2. Lehmann, "Tradition," 294, fn. 3; also: Spence, *The Gods of Mexico,* 159.
64. Sahagún, *Florentine Codex,* bk. I, ch. 12.
65. She is the regent of the seventh night hour in *Codex Vaticanus* B, 22 and *Codex Borgia* 14, reproduced by Seler, *Codex Vaticanus B.* She is the regent of the fourteenth day sign in *Cod. Vat.* B, 41 reproduced by Seler, *Codex Vaticanus* B, table 91; regent of one of the phases of Venus, *Cod. Vat.* B, 41, *Cod. Borgia* 16, reproduced by Seler, *Codex Vaticanus* B, table 41, p. 199. She is the regent of the North, *Cod. Féjerváry-Mayer* 23, reproduced by Seler, *Codex Vaticanus* B, 67; regent of the fifth day hour in the *tonamalatl* of the Aubin collection and in *Cod. Borbonicus,* reproduced by Seler, *Das Tonalamatl,* 27; regent of the thirteenth week, *Codex Borbonicus* 13, reproduced by Seler, *Gesammelte,* vol. 3, 316, my Figure 51.
66. The coital position is found in *Cod. Vat.* B, Seler, *Codex Vaticanus* B, table 74; in *Cod. Borgia* 14 she is naked and offers a captive for sacrifice; her abdomen is marked by a wavy line indicating that she has given birth; she displays the usual attributes of black lips, spindles in her headband, and a nose ornament, Seler *Codex Vaticanus B,* 99; in *Cod. Féjerváry-Mayer* she throttles a child with a snake, Seler, table 28; she nurses a child in *Cod. Borgia* 16, Seler, *Codex Vaticanus* B, 199; she is shown with a snake between her legs in *Cod. Vat.* B, Seler, *Codex Vaticanus* B, table 22.

I must repeat that not all illustrations available to me are cited and that I did not consult all of the codices.
67. *Codex Borbonicus* 13, as sign of the thirteenth *tonalamatl* section; this image, in which she is painted yellow and white, has presented a strong argument for her identification with Teteo Innan.
68. Sahagún, *Florentine Codex,* bk. I, ch. 8; ibid., bk. VI, ch. 28; Durán, *The Aztecs,* ch. IV, 29.
69. Durán, *The Aztecs,* ch. IV, 26.

70. Ibid., ch. LXII, 245.

71. Sahagún, *Florentine Codex,* bk. I, ch. 6.

72. Ibid., bk. II, ch. 30. ". . . another offered her her shirt with the eagle design." It was put on the priest who impersonated her.

73. Ibid., bk. I, ch. 8.

74. Ibid., bk. I, ch. 8; the variant is cited by Seler, *Codex Borgia,* vol. 1, 154, from the Sahagún manuscript in Madrid. The war games, performed by midwives and physicians, lasted for four days; the warriors wore their hair in the manner of women.

75. Seler, *Codex Borgia,* vol. 1, 162; Sahagún, *Florentine Codex,,* bk. I, ch. 12. The belief is also reported from among the Indians of Yucatán and Guatemala.

76. Durán, *Book of Gods,* 231.

77. Lehmann et al., *Geschichte,* 2–3; the wanderers had started their journey in Aztlán; in Colhuacan they received the idol of the "devil" Huitzilopochtli; with them was the woman Chimalman. According to Durán, *The Aztecs,* ch. I, 6, the caves of origin were in Teocolhuacán, which was also called Aztlán. The Indians claimed that their ancestors were born in these caves; ibid., ch. II, 9. The name Chichimecs is usually given to nations dwelling to the north of Mesoamerica. The Aztecs sometimes are and sometimes are not included in this group. Durán states "they were called Chichimec because they were hunters" (ibid., ch. II, 11).

78. After leaving Colhuacan the Aztecs told the other tribes that they would have to go on without them; the tribes were sad; Krickeberg 1928, 96, citing Aubin, *Histoire 1576,* sheets 4–47. An illustration in *Codex Boturini* (1, 2) shows how the tribes set out from the water, reached the "crooked mountain", and the separation afterward, reproduced by Vaillant, *The Aztecs,* plate 25.

79. Durán, *The Aztecs,* ch. I, 7. 133–35; here Colhuacan lies in the middle of a lake. In *Historia Tolteca,* Colhuacan is brought into relation with Tollan, as cited by Seler, *Gesammelte,* vol. 4, 99.

80. It is said of Cinteotl that he was born at Tamoanchan, the place of rain and mist "where the children of men are made" (Sahagún, *Florentine Codex,* bk. II, 212). From Tamoanchan the goddess Xochiquetzal fell to earth; Brundage, *The Phoenix of the Western World,* 40.

In de Jonghe, "Histoire du Méchique," 27, however, Tamoanchan is a cave.

81. Lehmann, "Traditions," 1906, 271–76; Lehmann relates this form of the goddess to the women who become warriors after death, 274, fn 10.

82. The Chichimecs left their leaders Itztolli and Xiuhnel in Macatepec and went to Tepenenec; here Mimich shot Itzpapalotl with his arrow, Seler, *Gesammelte,* vol. 4, 87; it is also said that Itzpapalotl ate 400 Mimixcoa; one escaped revived the dead and they killed her. Seler, *Gesammelte,* vol. 4, 87, citing *anal. quauht.* She is considered a symbol of fire, ibid., vol. 3, 226. Her picture is shown in *Cod. Borgia* 11 with obsidian knives on her butterfly wings, and in *Cod. Telleriano-Remensis* vol. 18, with eagle claws on hands and feet and wearing a butterfly disguise, ibid., vol. 4, 75, 76. She is the regent of the sixteenth day in *Cod. Borgia* 11, Seler, *Gesammelte,* vol. 5, 138.

83. Durán, *The Aztecs,* ch. LXII, 245.

84. Lehmann et al., *Geschichte,* 2–3.

85. Seler, *Gesammelte,* vol. 3, 248, 249, citing Sahagún.

86. See note 54.

87. On the role of the rattle stick, see also F. Neumann, "The Flayed God."

88. Sahagún, *Florentine Codex,* bk. I, ch. 6.

89. Ibid., bk. II, ch. 30, "And when they had climbed up [the pyramid], then they

flung, sowed, and scattered the seed among the onlookers—white maize grains, yellow, black, red; and squash seeds. All scrambled for them . . . And the maidens who belonged among (the priests of) Chicomecoatl . . . They bore upon their backs the ears of dried maize, seven ears each." The image of a woman in the garments of the maize goddess is shown in *Cod. Borbonicus* 30.

90. Durán, *Book of The Gods,* 235.

91. Sahagún, *Florentine Codex,* bk. II, ch. 30.

92. Cipactli is the fish from which the earth was made, Krickeberg, *Märchen der Azteken,* 5, citing *hist. mex. pint.* 228–31.

"Two gods . . . brought the Goddess of the Earth, Tlalteutli, (Atlalteutli) down from heaven . . . she had mouths at every joint . . . with which she bit like a savage beast." (de Jonghe, "Histoire du Méchnique," 28, translation from the French mine).

93. The belief that Cinteotl descended from Tlazolteotl is also based on the fact that in the song of the feast of eating water tamales, which is held every eight years, Tlalzeotl is cited in the first stanza and in the following stanza Cinteotl is praised. Nothing, however, is said about the relationship between the two.

94. Sahagún, *Florentine Codex,* bk. I, 40; "she was the maker and giver of all those things which are the necessaries of life, that the people may live," ibid., bk. II, ch. 4.

95. de Jonghe, "Histoire du Méchique," 31.

Chapter 10

1. The four largest islands, from north to south, are Hokkaido, Honshu, Shikoku, Kyushu, and they extend from the 45th to the 29th parallel.

2. There is no agreement concerning the ethnic origin of the settlers of Japan. It has been suggested that Southeast Asian people entered in the so-called Jomon period (ending in 250 B.C.E.); South Pacific influence is also assumed for middle Jomon, and paddy rice field culture has been traced to Southeast Asia or Indonesia. The influence of Northeast Asian Tungusic tribes has also been discerned, and there is an assumption that an altaic pastoral tribe of mounted warriors had invaded the islands and had subjugated the native population. Kitagawa, "Prehistoric Background," 302–11.

3. Reischauer, *Japan,* 45–49. The fight for power had raged between two noble families of the land: the Taira and the Minamoto. At first the Taira were victorious, but later they were completely defeated by the Minamoto. Yorituro Minamoto was the first shogun.

4. Ibid., 77–95. The first centuries of the shogunate are known as the Kamakura and Ashikaga periods respectively. Three strong rulers accomplished the unification of Japan: Nobunaga (1534–82), Hideyoshi (1537–98), Iyeysau (1542–1616). The period of overpowering central control is known as the Tokugawa period; during this time were enacted the ruthless and cruel persecutions of the Christians, who were virtually stamped out after their great rebellion in 1637–38.

5. Ibid., 110. It was Commodore Matthew Perry who arrived in 1853 with a letter from the President of the United States demanding the establishment of trade relations. The Japanese realized that they were helpless before the technical achievements and the fighting powers of the West.

6. Ibid., 35, 98–101. The most famous of the literary works of the court at Nara was written by Lady Murasaki, *The Tale of Genji,* and deals with the adventures of an imaginary prince.

7. Kitagawa, *Religion in Japanese History,* 30–32; Prince Shōkotu lived from 573–627.

8. Ibid., 38.

9. Ibid., 38; in the middle of the Heian period (794–1185) the idea developed that the Kami's original nature was Buddhahood, 68.

10. Grapard, "Flying Mountains," 204.

11. Kitagawa, *Religion in Japanese History,* 64, fn 38; his name is Kūkai or Kōbō Daishi.

12. Kitagawa, "Buddhist Transformation," 325; the trend of presenting Buddhism as a gospel of salvation is represented by Gyogi, a shamanist Buddhist saint and archbishop (670–749). The Buddhists also fostered the establishment of philanthropic institutions. Several were promoted by Kūkai (773–835) of the Shingon school, 327.

13. Kitagawa, *Religion in Japanese History,* 58.

14. The village Satoyamabe-mura in the Nagano prefecture exemplifies the blending of the various traditions. The central Shinto shrine had been erected for a god that was said to have arrived on a pampas leaf; the villagers now worship Take-mina-katanokami, the ancestor of a well-known Samurai family, and Gozu-tenno, who had changed from an earlier god of epidemics to a spirit of benevolence. The inner shrine contains a miniature statue of Buddha and an image of Prince Shōkotu, the promoter of Buddhist faith. Near the central shrine stand a Buddhist temple (originally erected to serve the main Shinto shrine, and now belonging to the Shingon sect) and shrines for the tutelary spirits of the extended family. Hori, "Japanese Folk Beliefs," 412–15.

15. Hori, "Visitors," 78; this festival is now held on November 23, but may have been held more closely to the solstice in the past.

16. Kitagawa, *Religion in Japanese History,* 19.

17. Ibid., 26. At the time of his death in 627 C.E., forty-six Buddhist temples had been constructed, served by 816 priests and 569 nuns.

18. Ibid., 32–33, fn 72; Shinto priests became government officials.

19. Kitagawa, "Buddhist Transformation," 327; Kōbō Daishi lived from 773 to 835.

20. Grapard, "Flying Mountains," 215; by the middle of the Heian period (794–1185) twenty-two great Shinto shrines were supported by the emperor.

21. Ludwig, "Way of Tea," 33–34, quoting Warner: "Shinto has always been the artist's way of life" (*Enduring Art of Japan*).

22. Rikyū lived from 1521 to 1591; the poem is cited by Ludwig, "Way of Tea," 46–48.

23. Hori, "Japanese Folk Beliefs," 406–9; the New Year's festival is held on January 1 according to the lunar, and on February 18 according to the solar calendar.

24. Grapard, "Flying Mountains," 197, believes that a sacred site originated because a god chose it as his dwelling place and a shrine was then established on the spot; this site developed into a sacred area under the influence of Buddhism, spatially more extensive, and the locus for the realization of Buddhahood; in the Kamakura period the sacred area grew to include all of Japan, the land of a sacred nation.

Kitagawa assumes, on the other hand, that the entire area of Japan had originally constituted a place of unbroken sanctity, which in later time received some structure ("A Past of Things Present"). In relation with the Kami who has been considered to be, among other things, the sacredness dwelling in an element, we must also consider the concept of the *tamashii;* this dwells in people or objects as a kind of "soul" or animating principle and is not usually sacred. It may also possess, in contrast to the

Kami, a visible appearance. A *tamashii* may achieve sacredness and become a Kami. Matsudaira, "Concept of Tamashii."

25. Ogura, "Drifted Deities," 134, collected sixty-eight instances of stories in which a god had drifted in from the sea in the peninsula Noto, which is especially conservative in the preservation of religion, 138. The landing place usually receives as much reverence as the deity itself. Ebisu is said to have arrived in the form of a stone, and sometimes he is revered in this shape; Sakurada, "Ebisu-gami," 124.

26. Hori, "Visitors," 79; these visits of ancestral beings may take place several times during the winter months and vary with the locality. On the level of folk tradition, supernatural visitors are symbolized by visiting groups of actors, minstrels, or magicians, often at New Year's time, 86–91.

27. It has been pointed out that there are two basic kinds of shamanism, one in which the magician must leave the earth, as it has been described in a previous chapter, and another prevalent in Southeast Asia where the godhead takes possession of the human. The second kind does not involve animal transformation. Schröder, "Zur Struktur."

28. Harada, "Village Tutelary Deity," 215–217; members of the family group are selected to perform the devotions for this spirit; also Naoe, "Study of Yashiki-gami," 204.

29. Naoe, "Study of Yashiki-gami," 210; the god Inari, worshipped as *yashiki-gami,* is held to be an agricultural deity in some places.

30. Ibid., 207; from the Kumano region to Shikoku the word used for *yashiki-gami* is that of the deified ancestor. Naoe assumes the previous existence of a belief in which the deified ancestor became a *yashiki-gami,* 208.

31. Kitagawa, "Buddhist Transformation," 323, states that the native Shinto cult eagerly accepted the Chinese notion of ancestor worship. He points out that in the oldest anthology of poetry the Kami of the mountains and of the sea are mentioned much more frequently than ancestral beings; Kitagawa, *Religion in Japanese History,* 16, fn 29.

32. Hori, "Japanese Folk Beliefs," 409.

33. Ibid., 415–16; also at this time the dead may descend from the mountains where the paths have been made smooth for them to ease their journey and where fires have been lit in their honor.

34. Ibid., 419 ff; these spirits received special services; they took place in Kyoto in 863 C.E. under the auspices of the emperor and became widespread.

35. The myth is recorded in the Chronicles of Japan; *Kojiki* and *Nihon shoki* were written at the request of the emperor Temmu in 712 and 720 C.E., respectively; Florenz, *Die historischen,* 13. The feebleness of some children was the result of the goddess having made the first move in the sexual encounter. Such action is not proper to a woman. Altogether fourteen islands and thirty-five deities were produced. Philippi, *Kojiki,* bk. I, chs. 4–7.

36. Florenz, *Die historischen,* 25; Philippi, *Kojiki,* bk. I, ch. 10.

37. Florenz, *Die historischen,* 28–30; Philippi, *Kojiki,* bk. I, ch. 17. According to a version cited in *Nihon Shoki,* Amaterasu was engendered in the union of Izagami and Izanani, Florenz, *Die historischen,* 131.

38. Florenz, *Die historischen,* 37–38; Philippi, *Kojiki,* bk. I, ch. 11.

39. See note 53.

40. Philippi, *Kojiki,* bk. I, chs. 32–37. Florenz, *Die historischen,* 60–71; these were

families of priests, families of religious dancers, producers of holy mirrors and holy jewels, ibid., 71, fn 14.

41. Miller, "Ame-No," 35 points to the following contrasting qualities between the two:

Susanoo	*Amaterasu*
male	female
undisciplined	disciplined
chaos	cosmos
disorder	order
impure	pure
associated with earth	associated with heaven
warrior	weaver
carries a sword	wears jewels
founds rival clan in Izumo	founds rightful clan in Yamato

42. Miller, 1984–85, 38; the festival is celebrated in Ise only.

43. Miller, "Ame-No," 41–42; the name is *furi-mi-tama*.

44. Florenz, *Die historischen*, 243–44; the mirror of Amaterasu and the jewels of another deity were adored in the palace. The tenth emperor, Sujin, asked his daughter to build a shrine for the goddess in the village Kasanui in Yamato. In a variant, the mirror was meant to be in the sleeping place of the emperor, ibid., 196.

45. Davis, "Pilgrimage," 203, fn 22; in the early periods of Japanese history, even the members of the imperial family had to ask the emperor's permission to worship at the shrine. By the eleventh century, warrior aristocrats became patrons and worshippers. In the beginning of the fifteenth century, commoners formed fraternities to visit the shrine.

46. Ellwood, "The Saigū."

47. Kitagawa, *Religion in Japanese History*, 19.

48. Waida, "Sacred Kingship," 321, he probably granted the seeds at the spring festival called *toshigoi*.

49. Ibid., the festival of "calling back the emperor's lost soul," *chinkon-sai*, is performed before the *niiname*, 337; Waida understands that in this scene the emperor is mystically united with his ancestress, 341.

50. Ibid., 338; the name Ninigi means "grain spirit." Quotation from *Nihon shoki*, Florenz, *Die historischen*, 196 (my translation from the German).

51. Miller, "Ame-No," 37, fn 29; the names are *toshi-goi-no-matsuri, kazahi-no-mi-sai* (held in the fifth month of modern time), *kanname-sai* (held in the tenth month of our time), and the *niiname-sai* in the eleventh month.

52. Hirayama, "Seasonal Rituals," 59–61.

53. Florenz, *Die historischen*, 37–39; Philippi, *Kojiki*, bk. I, ch. 17.

54. The daughter of the eleventh emperor Suinin wandered through several provinces with the emblems, until she was informed by Amaterasu about the location of the sanctuary. It was to be in the district Ise near the river Isuzu; Florenz, *Die historischen*, 258–59. The tree in Ise's shrine has its branches cut so that it resembles a pillar; Grapard, "Flying Mountains," 198.

55. Grapard "Flying Mountains," 198. A branch of the *sakaki* tree or a bamboo skewer are important throughout Japan in rituals conducted for the *uji-gami*, the village tutelary deity. In such rituals, often a "holy rod", named *o-hake*, is also erected; Harada, "Village Tutelary Deity," 217–18.

56. Kitagawa, "Prehistoric Background," 322. Eliade, "Recent Works," 163, quoting Diószegi.

57. Philippi, *Kojiki*, 83, fn 13. It has been suggested that the sacredness of trees in Japan became reinforced through Siberian influences where shamans' trees are of high significance. The symbolism of the two entities is, however, completely different. The Siberian sacred tree unites the realms of the universe and is a means of reaching heaven, and therefore very important to the shaman in his celestial journey. The Japanese tree is important as the place on which the godhead has alighted in his descent to earth; this tree is wholly of this world.

58. The shrine is mentioned in records of 673–674 C.E. Kitagawa, *Religion in Japanese History*, 33.

59. Ellwood, "The Saigū," 36; the place of her stay is called *saigū*, "palace of abstinence"; the various groups of her retinue as well as the services performed by her parallel those at the court. A full account of the ceremonial surrounding the institution is given in the *Engi-shiki*, a book of court ceremonial composed in 927 C.E.

60. Ibid., 60.

61. Davis, "Pilgrimage," 100; pilgrimages took place in 1638–39, 1650, 1661, 1701, 1718, 1723, 1730, 1748, 1755, 1803, 1855. Without the support of alms the pilgrimages would not have been possible; the pilgrims might receive rice, dried seaweed, beans, tobacco, noodles, tea, lanterns, also services such as, haircuts, hot baths, rides on horses. Sometimes the luck would run out and the pilgrims might starve.

62. Ibid., 201–8.

63. Ibid., 213–21.

64. Obayashi, "Die Amaterasu-Myth," 23.

65. Ibid., 31–32.

66. Ibid., 39–40.

67. Waida, "Symbolism," 408–12; several folktales deal with the figure in the moon, which is said to represent a man with buckets; these may have contained the waters of life. In some areas of rural Japan a women's organization meets once a lunar month to worship the moon that appears at the next dawn; the moon is also believed to be a god who gives easy childbirth; Hori, "Japanese Folk Beliefs," 414.

The folktales considered by me appear in the extensive survey and collection of Hiroko Ikeda, "A Type and Motif," and also in the survey of Joanne Algarin, *Japanese Folkliterature*.

68. Miller, "Ritsuryō Japan," 104; the Chinese emperor was called the "Son of Heaven." The emperor Temmo, enthroned in 673 C.E., placed much emphasis on the Sutra of the Golden Light in his claim to the royal office. Some scholars believe that celestial orientation was brought to Japan through an invading Altaic tribe. They do not, however, cite the celestial or solar deity to whom Amaterasu is supposed to owe her solar qualities.

69. It has been assumed by some that the actions performed before Amaterasu's cave represented rituals for the strengthening of the sun: setting up a tree, making roosters crow, performing a dance, performing divination, chanting a liturgy. The claim is not substantiated. Philippi, *Kojiki*, ch. 17, fn 3.

70. Kukubyashi, "Amaterasu Ōmikami."

71. Florenz, *Die historischen*, 60–68; Philippi, *Kojiki*, chs. 35–37.

72. Florenz, *Die historischen*, 87; Philippi, *Kojiki*, bk. II, ch. 49.

73. Florenz, *Die historischen*, 259.

74. Ibid., 301–02.

75. See note 72.

76. We also find the view that the sun god had originally been male and was probably Takaki or Takamimusubi who appears next to Amaterasu in the texts. She had been his priestess-wife and turned later into a goddess; Waida, "Sacred Kingship," 338. Her role of supervising the weaving of sacred garments, and in some accounts, her own weaving is also said to point to her priestly function; Philippi, *Kojiki,* ch. 16, fn 9.

Conclusion

1. As related by Ginzberg, *Legends of the Jews.*
2. The German original reads:

>Schläfst du Mirjam, Mirjam mein Kind?
>Ufer nur sind wir und tief in uns rinnt,
>Blut von Gewesenen, zu Kommenden rollt's,
>Blut unsrer Väter, voll Unruh und Stolz.

3. The tales of the monster-combat were collected by Fontenrose, *Python.*
4. Wolkstein and Kramer, *Inanna,* 144.
5. Ibid., 141.
6. Ibid., 151–55.
7. Ibid., 160–63.
8. Jacobsen, *Treasures of Darkness,* 201.
9. Ibid.
10. Ibid., 140, citing BE XXXI, no. 12, 10–20.
11. Jacobsen, *Treasures of Darkness,* 137, citing Reissner, no. 56, obv. 16–30.
12. Larrington, *Feminist Companion,* 150–51; the banquet is described in the Eddic poem *Locasenna* in Neckel and Kuhn, *Edda.*
13. Preston, "Goddess Chandi," 325–30.
14. Eliade, *History of Religious Ideas,* vol. 1, 40; "religious relations with the animal world are supplanted by what may be called the *mystery of solidarity between man and vegetation* . . . in addition woman and feminine sacrality are raised to the first rank. . . . The fertility of the earth is bound up with female fecundity."
15. Mellaart, *Earliest Civilizations,* 129–32.
16. The German original reads: Das ewig Weibliche zieht uns hinan. (Goethe).

>Ehret die Frauen! Sie flechten und weben
>Himmlische Rosen ins irdische Leben.

17. As stated, for instance, by Auer-Falk, "Feminine Sacrality."
18. As seen in my illustrations: Figures 14, 15, 17: a wounded bear is shown by Baring and Cashford, *Myth of the Goddess,* fig. 25, p. 28.
19. Norlander-Unsgaard, "On Gesture," 199.

Bibliography

Akurgal, Ekrem. *The Art of the Hittites.* London, 1962.
———. *Die Kunst Anatoliens von Homer bis Alexander.* Berlin, 1961.
Akurgal, Ekrem, and M. Hirmer. *Hethitische Kunst.* Berlin, 1961.
Algarin, Joanne P. *Japanese Folkliterature: A Core Collection and Reference Guide.* New York, 1982.
Amini, Azuri. "A Path of Change: Healing from Childhood Sexual Abuse." In *The Goddess Celebrates,* ed. Diane Stein, pp. 217–31. Freedom, California, 1991.
Anales de Quauhtitlan: Noticias historicas de México y sus contornos. 1882. José Ferdinand Ramírez, ed. In Lehmann 1906.
Andersen, Jørgen. *The Witch on the Wall.* Copenhagen, 1977.
Ardinger, Barbara. *A Woman's Book of Rituals and Celebrations.* San Rafael, California, 1992.
Aubin, J.M.A., ed. *Histoire de la nation Mexicaine.* Paris, 1893.
Auden, W. H. *Collected Poems.* London, 1976.
Auer-Falk, Nancy. "Feminine Sacrality." In *The Encyclopedia of Religion,* eds. Eliade et al. New York, 1987.
Bachofen, J. J. *Myth, Religion and Mother Right,* trs. Ralph Mannheim. Princeton, 1967.
Bächtold-Stäubli, H. *Handwörterbuch des deutschen Aberglaubens.* 10 vols. Berlin, 1927–42.
Bäckman, Louise. "The Akkas: A Study of Four Goddesses in the Religion of the Saami (Lapps)." In *Current Progress in the Methodology and Science of Religion,* ed. W. Tyloch, pp. 31–39. Warsaw, 1984.
Bäckman, Louise, and Åke Hultkrantz. *Saami pre-Christian Religion: Studies of the Oldest Traces of Religion of the Saami.* Stockholm, 1985.
Bahadir, Alkim U. *Anatolie.* Vol. 1. Geneva, Paris, and Munich, 1968.
Balicki, Asen. *The Netsilik Eskimo.* New York, 1970.
Balys, Jonas, and Haralds Biezais. 1973. *Baltische Mythologie.* In *Wörterbuch der Mythologie II,* ed. H. Haussig, pp. 373–554. Stuttgart, 1973.

Baring, Anne, and Jules Cashford. *The Myth of the Goddess: Evolution of an Image.* London, 1991.

Barons, K., and H. Wissendorf. *Latvju Dainas.* 6 vols. Jelgava and Petersburg, 1894–1915.

Barrelet, Marie-Therèse. "Les déesses armées et ailées, Inanna-Ishtar." *Syria* 32 (1955): 222–60.

Barton, George A. *Miscellaneous Babylonian Inscriptions.* New Haven, 1918.

Batchelor, J. *The Ainu and Their Folklore.* London, 1901.

Baumann, Hermann. *Das doppelte Geschlecht.* Berlin, 1955.

Beitl, Erich, and Richard Beitl. *Wörterbuch der deutschen Volkskunde.* Stuttgart, 1955.

Benedict, Ruth. *The Chrysanthemum and the Sword.* London, 1947.

Benito, C. A. "Enki and the World Order." Unpublished manuscript on microfilm. Ann Arbor, 1960.

Bernhard, I., and S. Kramer. 1959–60. "Enki und die Weltordnung." *Wissenschaftliche Zeitschrift der Friedrich Schiller Universitat Jena.* (Gesellschafts-und sprachwissenschaftliche Reihe 9): 231–55.

Biezais, Haralds. "Baltic Religion." In *The Encyclopedia of Religion,* eds. Eliade et al. New York, 1987.

———. *Baltische Religion.* In Åke Ström and Heralds Biezais *Germanische und baltische Religion.* Stuttgart, 1975.

———. *Der Lichtgott der alten Letten.* Stockholm and Uppsala, 1976.

———. *Die Göttergestalt der lettischen Volksreligion.* Uppsala, 1961.

———. *Die Hauptgöttinnen der alten Letten.* Uppsala, 1955.

———. *Die himmlische Götterfamilie der alten Letten.* (Historia Religionum, 5). Uppsala (1972).

———. "D. Ward. The Divine Twins" (review). *Indogermanische Forschungen* 77 (1972):275–79.

Biggs, Robert. "An Archaic Sumerian Version of the Kesh Temple Hymn from Tell Abū Salābīkh." *Zeitschrift für Assyriologie* 61 (1971):193–207.

Birket-Smith, Kaj. *The Eskimos.* London, 1936.

Bittel, Kurt. *Die Hethiter: die Kunst Anatoliens vom Ende des 3. bis zum Anfang des 1. Jahrtausends vor Christus.* Munich, 1976.

———. "Phrygisches Kultbild aus Bogazköy." *Antike Plastik* 2 (1963):7–29.

Bleibtreu-Ehrenburg, Gisela. "Homosexualität und Transvestitismus im Schamanismus." *Anthropos* 65 (1970):189–228.

Blinkenberg, Christian. *The Thunderweapon in Religion and Folklore.* Cambridge, 1911.

Boas, F. *The Central Eskimo.* Annual Reports of the Bureau of American Ethnology, 6 (1888). Washington. Boas I.

———. *The Eskimo of Baffinland and Hudson Bay.* [Bulletin of the American Museum of Natural History 15, no. 1] (1901). New York, Boas III.

———. *The Eskimo of Baffinland and Hudson Bay.* [Bulletin of the American Museum of Natural History 15, no. 2] (1907). Boas IV.

———. "Notes on the Eskimo of Port Clarence, Alaska." *Journal of American Folklore* 7 (1894):205–8. Boas II.

Bogoras, Wladimir. *The Chukchee. Pub. of the North Pacific Expedition.* Memoirs of the American Museum of Natural History, 7. New York, 1907.

———. "The Folklore of North-Eastern Asia, as compared with that of North-Western America." *American Anthropologist,* n.s. 4 (1902):577–683.

258 BIBLIOGRAPHY

Bossert, Helmut T. *Altanatolien. Kunst und Handwerk in Kleinasien.* Berlin, 1942.
———. *Altsyrien.* Tübingen, 1951.
Brastinš, E. *Latvju Dieva dziesmas.* Riga, 1928.
Briffault, Robert. *The Mothers: A Study in the Origins of Sentiments and Institutions.* London, 1959.
Brixhe, Claude. "Le Nome de Cybèle." *Die Sprache* 25 (1979):40–45.
Brixhe, Claude, and Michael Lejeune. *Corpus des inscriptions paléo-phrygiennes.* 2 vols. Paris, 1984.
Brommer, Frank. *Satyroi.* Würzburg, 1937.
Brumfield, A. C. *The Attic Festivals of Demeter and Their Relation to the Agricultural Year.* Salem, 1981.
Brundage, Burr C. *The Fifth Sun.* Austin, 1979.
———. *The Phoenix of the Western World: Quetzalcoatl and the Sky Religion.* Norman, Oklahoma, 1982.
Bruneau, P. *Recherches sur les cultes de Délos à l'Epoque hellénistique et á l'Epoque impériale.* Paris, 1970.
Budapest, Z. 1991. "Teaching Women's Spirituality Rituals." In *The Goddess Celebrates,* ed. Diane Stein, pp. 14–21. Freedom, California, 1991.
Budge, W. A. Wallis. *Assyrian Sculptures in the British Museum: Reign of Ashur-nasir-pal 885–860 B.C.* London, 1914.
van Buren, E. D. "A Clay Relief in the Iraq Museum." *Archiv für Orientforschung* 9 (1933):166–71.
Burkert, Walter. *Greek Religion: Archaic and Classical,* trs. John Raffan. Oxford, 1985.
———. *Griechische Religion der archaischen und klassischen Periode.* Stuttgart and Berlin, 1977.
———. *Homo Necans: An Anthropology of Ancient Greek Sacrificial Ritual and Myth,* trs. P. Bing. Berkeley, 1983.
———. *Structure and History in Greek Mythology and Ritual.* Berkeley, Los Angeles, and London, 1979.
———. *Wilder Ursprung. Opferritual und Mythus bei den Griechen.* Berlin, 1991.
Cameron, D. O. *Symbols of Birth and Death in the Neolithic Era.* London, 1981.
Campbell, Joseph. *The Masks of God.* 4 vols. New York, 1959–68.
Carpenter, Edmund S. "Changes in the Sedna Myth among the Aivilik." *Anthropological Papers of the University of Alaska* 3,2 (1955):69–73.
Caso, Alfred. *The Aztecs: People of the Sun,* trs. Lowell Dunham. Norman, Oklahoma, 1958.
Chiera, E. *Sumerian Epics and Myths.* Chicago, 1934.
Clinton, Kevin. *Myth and Cult: The Iconography of the Eleusinian Mysteries.* Stockholm, 1992.
Codex Florentino. Illustrations for Shagún's *Historia de las Cosas de Nueva España.* Francisco del Paso y Troncoso, ed. Vol. 5, Madrid, 1905.
Coe, Michael. *Mexico.* London, 1984.
Crawford, E.O.G. *The Eye Goddess.* London, 1958.
Davis, Winston. 1983–84. "Pilgrimage and World Renewal." *History of Religions* 23 (1983–84):97–116, 197–221.
Delcourt, Marie. *Hephaistos, ou la légende du magicien.* Paris, 1957.
Delougaz, P. P. "Animals Emerging from a Hut." *Journal of Near Eastern Studies* 27 (1968):184–97.
Deubner, Ludwig. *Attische Feste.* Berlin, 1932.

Dhorme, Édouard. *Les religions de Babylone et d'Assyrie.* Les Anciennes Religions Orientales 2. Paris, 1945.

———. "La Terre-mère chez les Assyriens." *Archiv für Religionswissenschaft* 8 (1905): 550–52.

Dieterich, Albert. *Mutter Erde. Ein Versuch über die Volksreligion.* Leipzig, 1925.

van Dijk, J. A. *La sagesse suméro-accadienne.* Brill, 1953.

———. *Lugalud me-Lámbi Nirgal. Le récit epique de Travaux de Ninurta, de Deluge et de la nouvelle Création.* Leiden, 1983.

Diószegi, Vilmos, ed. *Popular Beliefs and Folklore Tradition in Siberia,* trs. Stephen B. Dunn. Budapest, 1968.

Diószegi, Vilmos, and M. Hoppál, eds. *Shamanism in Siberia.* Budapest, 1978.

Dorson, M. Richard, ed. *Studies in Japanese Folklore.* Bloomington, 1963.

Dowden, K. *Death and the Maiden.* London, 1989.

Durán, Fray Diego. *The Aztecs: The History of the Indies of New Spain,* trs. Doris Heyden. New York, 1964.

———. *Book of the Gods and Rites and the Ancient Calendar,* trs. Fernando Harecasitas and Doris Heyden. Norman, Oklahoma, 1971.

Edzard, Otto Dietz. *Mesopotamien: Die Mythologie der Sumerer und Akkader.* In *Wörterbuch der Mythologie* I, ed. Hans Haussig, pp. 19–139. Stuttgart, 1965.

Einhorn, Paul. "Von jhrer Ehe und Hochzeit." In *Historia Lettica; das ist Beschreibung der lettischen Nation in Liefland.* Dorpat, 1649.

———. *Wiederlegung der Abgötterey.* Riga, 1627.

Eisler, Riane. *The Chalice and the Blade: Our History, Our Future.* San Francisco, 1987.

Eliade, Mircea. *Le chamanism et les techniques archaiques de l'extase.* Paris, 1951.

———. *A History of Religious Ideas.* 3 vols. London, 1979–82.

———. "Recent Works on Shamanism." *History of Religions* 1 (1961):152–68.

Eliade, Mircea, et al., eds. *The Encyclopedia of Religion.* New York, 1987.

Ellwood, Robert. "The Saigū: Princess and Priestess." *History of Religions* 7 (1967–68):35–60.

Evans, Arthur E. *The Mycenaean Tree and Pillar Cult and its Mediterranean Relations.* London, 1905.

———. "The 'Tomb of the Double Axes' and Associated Group of Ritual Vessels of the 'Little Palace' at Knossos." *Archaeologia* 65 (1914):1–94.

Falkenstein, A., and W. von Soden. *Sumerische und akkadische Hymnen und Gebete.* Zürich, 1953.

Farnell, Lewis R. *The Cults of the Greek States.* 6 vols. Oxford, 1896–1909.

Faure, Paul. *Fonctions des cavernes crétoises.* Paris, 1964.

Findeisen, Hans. *Das Tier als Gott, Dämon und Ahne.* Stuttgart, 1956.

———. *Schamanentum.* Stuttgart, 1957.

Fischer, John F. "An Analysis of the Central Eskimo Sedna Myth." *Temenos* 11 (1975): 24–42.

Fitzhugh, William W., and Aron Crowell. *Crossroads of Continents: Cultures of Siberia and Alaska.* London, 1988.

Fitzhugh, William W., and Susan Kaplan. *Inua: Spirit World of the Bering Strait Eskimo.* Washington, 1982.

Fleming, Andrew. "The Myth of the Mother-Goddess." *World Archaeology* 1 (1969): 247–61.

Florenz, Karl. *Die historischen Quellen der Shinto Religion.* Göttingen, 1919.

Fontenrose, Joseph E. *Python: A Study of Delphic Myth and Its Origins*. Berkeley and Los Angeles, 1959.

Frankfort, Henri. *Cylinder Seals: A Documentary Essay on the Art and Religion of the Ancient Near East*. London, 1939.

————. *Kingship and the Gods*. Chicago, 1948.

————. "A Note on the Lady of Birth." *Journal of Near Eastern Studies* 3 (1944):198–200.

Frankfort, Henri, John A. Wilson, and Thorkild Jacobsen, eds. *The Intellectual Adventure of Ancient Man*. Chicago, 1946.

Frazer, Sir James. *The Golden Bough: Spirits of the Corn and of the Wild*. Vols. 7 and 8. London, 1912.

Friedrich, Paul. *The Meaning of Aphrodite*. Chicago, 1978.

Gadon, Elinor. *The Once and Future Goddess: A Symbol of Our Time*. San Francisco, 1989.

García, Icazbalceta J. *Nueva Colección para la Historia de Mexico*. 5 vols. Mexico City, 1886–92.

Garth, Thomas. "Magna Mater and Attis." *Aufstieg und Niedergang der römischen Welt* 2,17,3 (1984):1500–25.

Gaster, T. H. *Thespis: Ritual, Myth and Drama in the Ancient Near East*. Garden City, 1950.

Gelling, Peter, and Hilda Ellis Davidson. *The Chariot of the Sun and Other Myths and Rites of the Bronze Age*. London, 1969.

de Genouillac, Henri. *Textes religieux sumériens du Louvre*. Paris, 1930.

Gerard, J. "Légende et politique autour de la mère des dieux." *Revue des études latines* 58 (1980):153–75.

Gimbutas, Marija. *The Balts*. London, 1963.

————. *The Civilization of the Goddess*. San Francisco, 1993.

————. *The Gods and Goddesses of Old Europe. 7000–3500 B.C. Myths and Cult Images*. London, 1974.

————. *The Language of the Goddess*. London, 1987.

Ginzberg, Louis. *The Legends of the Jews*. 8 vols., trs. H. Szold and P. Radin. Philadelphia, 1909–38.

Gjessing, Gutorm. *Arktiske helleristningar i nord-norge*. Oslo, 1932.

————. *Nordenfjelske ristningar og malingar av den arktiske gruppe*. Oslo, 1936.

Glahn, Henrik Christoffer. *Tagebücher*. Schriften der grönländischen Gesellschaft 4, 1771. Reprint, Copenhagen, 1921.

Goetze, Albrecht. "The Myth of Illuyankas." In ANET, pp. 125–26. Princeton, 1969.

————. "The Telipinu Myth." In ANET, pp. 126–28. Princeton, 1969.

Graf, Fritz. *Eleusis und die orphische Dichtung Athens in vorhellenistischer Zeit*. Berlin and New York, 1974.

Gragg, Gene R. "The Keš Temple Hymn." In *The Collection of Sumerian Temple Hymns* by A. Sjöberg and E. Bergmann, pp. 157–88. Locust Valley, 1969.

Graillot, Henri. *Le culte de Cybèle: mère des dieux, à Rome et dans l'Empire romain*. Paris, 1912.

Grapard, Allan. "Flying Mountains and Walkers of Emptiness: Towards a Definition of Sacred Space in Japanese Religions." *History of Religions* 21 (1981–82):195–221.

————. "Japan's Ignored Cultural Revolution." *History of Religions* 23 (1983–84):240–65.

Gressmann, Hugo. *Altorientalische Texte und Bilder zum alten Testament.* Tübingen, 1909.

Güterbock, H. G. *Kumarbi: Mythen vom churritischen Kronos.* Zürich, 1946.

———. "The Song of Ullikummi." *Journal of Cuneiform Studies* 5 (1951):135–61.

Guthrie, W. K. C. *Early Greek Religion in the Light of the Decipherment of Linear B.* London, 1959.

Haas, Volkert. *Hethitische Berggötter und hurritische Steindämonen. Riten, Kulte und Mythen.* Mainz, 1982.

———. *Der Kult von Nerik.* Rome, 1970.

Hall, H. R., and C. L. Woolley. *Ur Excavations I: Al-'Ubaid.* Oxford, 1927.

Hančar, Franz. "Zum Problem der Venusstatuetten im eurasischen Jungpaläolithikum." *Prähistorische Zeitschrift* 30–31 (1939):85–156.

Harada, Toshiaki. "The Village Tutelary Deity and the Use of Holy Rods." In *Studies in Japanese Folklore,* ed. M. R. Dorson, pp. 215–20. Bloomington, 1963.

Harrison, Jane Ellen. *Prolegomena to the Study of Greek Religion.* Cambridge, 1903.

Harva, Uno. (Holmberg) *Finno-Ugric. Siberian.* In The Mythology of All Races, vol. 4, ed. J. A. MacCulloch. New York, 1964.

———. *Die Religion der Tscheremissen. Folklore Fellows Communications* 61 (1926).

———. *Die religiösen Vorstellungen der altaischen Völker. Folklore Fellows Communications* 152, No. 125 Helsinki (1938).

———. *Die religiösen Vorstellungen der Mordwinen. Folklore Fellows Communications* 142 (1952).

———. *Die Wassergottheiten der finnisch-ugrischen Völker.* Suomalais-ugrilaisen seuran. Toimituksia 32 (1913). Helsingfors.

Haspels, Caroline Henrietta Emilie *The Highlands of Phrygia: Sites and Monuments.* 2 vols. Princeton, 1971.

Hastings, James. *Encyclopedia of Religion and Ethics.* Edinburgh, 1908–26.

Hatt, Gudmund. "The Corn Mother in America and Indonesia." *Anthropos* 46 (1951): 853–914.

Haussig, Hans William. *Wörterbuch der Mythologie I. Götter und Mythen im vorderen Orient.* Stuttgart, 1965.

———. *Wörterbuch der Mythologie II. Götter und Mythen im alten Europa.* Stuttgart, 1973.

Hawkes, E. W. *The Labrador Eskimo.* Memoirs of the Canadian Department of Mines, vol. 91. Ottawa (1916).

Head, Barclay C. *Historia Numinorum.* Oxford, 1911.

Helck, Wolfgang. *Betrachtungen zur grossen Göttin und den ihr verbundenen Gottheiten.* Munich and Vienna, 1971.

Hepding, Hugo. *Attis: seine Mythen und sein Kult.* Giessen, 1903.

Hirayama, Toshijiro. "Seasonal Rituals Connected with Rice Culture." In *Studies in Japanese Folklore,* ed. M. R. Dorson, pp. 57–75. Bloomington, 1963.

Historia de los Mexicanos por sus pinturas. Icazbalceta García, ed. *Nueva colección de documentos para la historia de México.* Vol. III. Mexico City, 1891.

Histoire Mexicaine. Manuscript of the Aubin-Goupil collection. Bibliothèque Nationale. Paris, 1891.

Historia Tolteca-Chichimeca. T. Preuss and E. Mengin, eds. Berlin, 1937–38.

Högström, P. *Beskriftning öfver de til Sveriges Krona lydende Lapmarker.* Stockholm, 1723.

Hoenn, Karl. *Artemis.* Zürich, 1946.

Holmberg—see Harva.

Holtved, E. "The Eskimo Myth About the Sea Woman: A Folklore Sketch." *Folk* 8/9 (1966–67):145–53.

Homeric Hymn to Delian Apollo. In *The Homeric Hymns,* trs. John Edgar. Edinburgh, 1891.

Hook, Arthur Darby. 1925. "Eunuchen ím Orient." *Archiv für Religionswissenschaft* 23 (1925):25–33.

Hoppál, Mihály, and Otto von Sadovski, eds. *Shamanism: Past and Present.* Los Angeles, 1989.

Hori, Ichirō. "Japanese Folk Beliefs." *American Anthropologist* 61 (1959):405–24.

———. "Mountains and Their Importance for the Idea of the Other-World in Japanese Folk Religion." *History of Religions* 6 (1966–67):1–23.

———. "Mysterious Visitors from the Harvest to the New Year." In *Studies in Japanese Folklore,* ed. M. R. Dorson, pp. 76–103. Bloomington, 1963.

Hosoi, Y. T. "The Sacred Tree in Japanese Pre-History." *History of Religions* 16 (1976–77):95–119.

Hultkrantz, Åke. "Arctic Religions." In *The Encyclopedia of Religion,* eds. M. Eliade et al. New York, 1987.

———. "Reindeer Nomadism and the Religion of the Saamis." *Arv* 39 (1983):11–28.

———. *Die Religion der Amerikanischen Arktis.* In *Die Religionen Nordeurasiens und der Amerikanischen Arktis,* eds. Hultkrantz, Paulson, and Jettmar, pp. 359–414. Stuttgart, 1962.

———. *Die Religion der Lappen.* In *Die Religionen Nordeurasiens und der Amerikanischen Arktis,* eds. Hultkrantz, Paulson, and Jettmar, pp. 283–303. Stuttgart, 1962.

———. *The Religions of the American Indians,* trs. Monica Setterwall. Berkeley, Los Angeles, and London, 1979.

———. "Types of Religion in the Arctic Hunting Cultures: A Religious-Ecological Approach." In *Hunting and Fishing,* ed. H. Hvarfner, pp. 265–318. Luleå, 1965.

———. "Water Spirits: The Elder of Fish in Aboriginal North America." *American Indian Quarterly* (Summer 1983):1–22.

———, ed. *The Supernatural Owners of Nature.* Stockholm, 1961.

Hultkrantz, Åke, Ivar Paulson, and Karl Jettmar, eds. *Die Religionen Nordeurasiens und der amerikanischen Arktis.* Stuttgart, 1962.

Ikeda, Hiroko. *A Type and Motif Index of Japanese Folk Literature. Folklore Fellows Communications* 89 (209). 1971.

Inscriptiones Graecae. Editio Minor I–IX. Berlin, 1924–68.

Jacobsen, Thorkild. "The Concept of Divine Parentage of the Ruler in the Stele of Eannatum." *Journal of Near Eastern Studies* 2 (1943):119–21.

———. *The Harp That Once . . . Sumerian Poetry in Translation.* New Haven and London, 1987.

———. *Mesopotamia.* In Frankfort 1946, pp. 125–219.

———. "Notes on Nintur." *Orientalia,* n.s. 42 (1973):274–305.

———. *The Treasures of Darkness.* New Haven and London, 1976.

Jacobsen, Thorkild, and Samuel Kramer. "The Myth of Inanna and Bilulu." *Journal of Near Eastern Studies* 12 (1953):160–88.

James, E. O. *The Cult of the Mother Goddess.* London, 1959.

Jenness, D. *The Life of the Copper Eskimo.* (Report of the Canadian Arctic Expedition 1913–18). Ottawa, 1925.

Jensen, Adolf E. 1960. *Mythos und Kult bei den Naturvölkern.* Wiesbaden.

Jettmar, Karl. *Die Aussage der Archäologie zur Religionsgeschichte Nordeurasiens.* In *Die Religionen Nordeurasiens und der Amerikanischen Arktis,* eds. Hultkrantz, Paulson, and Jettmar, pp. 305–56. Stuttgart, 1962.

Jochelson, Waldemar. *The Koryak, I. Religion and Myths.* (Memoirs of the American Museum of Natural History 6, 1). New York, 1905.

Johansen, Prytz J. "The Thesmophoria as a Woman's Festival." *Temenos* 11 (1975):78–87.

Johansons, Andrejs. *Der Schirmherr des Hofes im Volksglauben der Letten.* [Stockholm Studies in Comparative Religion 5] Stockholm, 1964.

———. "Der Wassergeist bei Balten und Slaven." *Acta Baltica-Slavonica* 2 (1965):27–52.

———. *Der Wassergeist und der Sumpfgeist, Untersuchungen volkstümlicher Glaubensvorstellungen bei den Völkern des ostbaltischen Raumes und bei den Ostslaven.* [Stockholm Studies in Comparative Religion 8] Stockholm, 1968.

de Jonghe, Éduard. "Histoire du Méchique: Manuscrit Français inédit du XVIe siècle." *Journal de la Société des Américanistes de Paris* n.s. 2 (1905):1–41.

Jonval, Michel. *Les Chansons Mythologiques Lettones.* Paris, n.d.

Joyce, Norma. "Ritual Creating and Planning." In *The Goddess Celebrates,* ed. Diane Stein, pp. 39–65. Freedom, California, 1991.

Kaibel, G. *Epigrammata Graeca ex lapidum collecta.* Berlin, 1878.

Kammenhuber, A. "Die protohattische Bilingue vom Mond der vom Himmel gefallen ist." *Zeitschrift für Assyriologie und vorderasiatische Archäologie* n.s. 17 (1955):102–23.

Kannisto, Artturi. *Materialien zur Mythologie der Vogulen.* [Suomalais-ugrilaisen seuran. Toimituksia, 113] (1958). Helsinki.

Karjalainen, K. F. *Die Religion der Jugravölker* I–III. *Folklore Fellows Communications,* 41, 44, 63 (1921–27).

Keil, J. "Die Kulte Lydiens." In *Anatolian Studies Presented to Sir William Mitchell Ramsay,* eds. W. H. Buckler and W. W. Calder, pp. 239–66. Manchester, 1923.

Kerényi, Caroly. *Eleusis: Archetypal Image of Mother and Daughter,* trs. Ralph Mannheim. London, 1967.

Kern, Otto. *Orphicorum fragmenta.* Berlin, 1922.

Kilmer, A. D. "The Mesopotamian Concept of Overpopulation and Its Solution as Reflection in Mythology." *Orientalia* n.s. 41 (1972):160–77.

Kitagawa, Joseph M. "The Buddhist Transformation in Japan." *History of Religions* 4 (1965):319–36.

———. "The Japanese Kokutai (National Community): History and Mythology." *History of Religions* 13 (1973):209–26.

———. "A Past of Things Present. Notes on Major Motifs in Japanese Religion." *History of Religions* 20 (1980–81):27–42.

———. "Prehistoric Background of Japanese Religion." *History of Religions* 2 (1962–63):292–328.

———. *Religion in Japanese History.* London, 1966.

Klein, Jacob. *Three Šulgi Hymns.* Bar-Ilam, 1981.

Kleivan, Inge. "Sedna." In *The Encyclopedia of Religion,* eds. M. Eliade et al. New York, 1987.

Kramer, Samuel. *Gilgamesh and the Huluppu Tree.* AS 10. Oriental Institute of Chicago, 1938.

————. "The Herder Wedding Text." *Proceedings of the American Philosophical Society for the Promotion of Useful Knowledge* 107 (1963):505–8.

————. "Inanna's Descent to the Netherworld." In ANET, pp. 52–57. Princeton, 1969.

————. *Lamentation over the Destruction of Ur.* AS 12. Chicago, 1940.

————. *The Sacred Marriage Rite.* Bloomington, 1969.

————. *Sumerian Mythology.* Philadelphia, 1944.

Krickeberg, Walter, ed. *Märchen der Azteken und Inkaperuaner, Maya und Muiska.* [Märchen der Weltliteratur] Jena, 1928.

Krickeberg, Walter, Hermann Trimborn, Werner Müller, and Otto Zerries, eds. *Die Religionen des alten Amerika.* Stuttgart, 1961.

Kroeber, A. L. 1899. "Tales of the Smith Sound Eskimo." *Journal of American Folklore* 12 (1899):166–82.

Kühn, Herbert. *Die Felsbilder Europas.* Stuttgart, 1952.

Kühne, Helmut. "Das Motiv der nährenden Frau oder Göttin in Vorderasien." In *Studien zur Religion und Kultur Kleinasiens. Festschrift für F. K. Dörner,"* eds. Sehin, Wagner, and Schwertheim, pp. 504–15. Leiden, 1978.

Kukubayashi, Fumio. "Amaterasu Ōmikami." In *The Encyclopedia of Religion,* eds. M. Eliade et al. New York, 1987.

Labat, René. *Le caractère religieux de la royauté Assyro-Babylonienne.* Paris, 1939.

Lafaye, Jacques. *Quetzalcoatl and Guadalupe. The Formation of Mexican National Consciousness* 1531–1813, trs. Benjamin Klein. Chicago and London, 1976.

Lambert, W. G., and A. R. Millard. *Atra-hasīs.* Oxford, 1969.

Langdon, Stephen. "A Hymn to Ishtar as the Planet Venus and to Iddin-Dagan as Tammuz." *The Journal of the Royal Asiatic Society* (1926):15–24.

————. *Die neubabylonischen Königsinschriften,* trs. Rudolf Zehnpfund. Leipzig, 1912.

Lantis, Margaret. "The Mythology of Kodiak Island, Alaska." *Journal of American Folklore* 51 (1938):123–72.

Laroche, Emmanuel. *Recherches sur les nommes des dieux Hittites.* Paris, 1947.

Larrington, Carolyne. *The Feminist Companion to Mythology.* London, 1992.

Leach, Edmund. *Lévi-Strauss.* London, 1970.

Lefkowitz, Mary R. "The New Cults of the Mother Goddess." *The American Scholar* 62 (1993):261–68.

————. *Women in Greek Myth.* London, 1985.

Lehmann, Walter. *Die Geschichte der Königreiche von Colhuacan und Mexico.* (Quellenwerke zur älteren Geschichte Amerikas. Ibero-Amerikanisches Institut). Berlin, 1938.

————. "Traditions des anciens Mexicains." Texte inédit et original au langue nahuatl avec traduction au latin *(Anales de Quauhtitlan). Journal de la Société des Américanistes de Paris* n.s. 3 (1906):239–97.

Lehmann, Walter, Gerdt Kutscher, and Günter Vollmer. *Geschichte der Azteken. Codex Aubin und verwandte Dokumente.* Berlin, 1981.

Lehtisalo, Toivo V. *Entwurf einer Mythologie der Jurak-Samoyeden.* Suomalais-ugrilaisen seuran. Toimituksia 53 (1924). Helsinki.

Léon-Portilla, M. *The Aztec Image of Self and Society.* Salt Lake City, 1992.

————. "These Made Worthy of the Divine Sacrifice: The Faith of Ancient Mexico." In *South and Meso-American Native Spirituality from the Cult of the Feathered Serpent to the Theology of Liberation,* eds. Gary H. Gossen and M. Léon-Portilla, pp. 41–64. New York, 1993.

Levy, Gertrude R. *The Gate of Horn: A Study of the Religious Conceptions of the Stone Age.* London, 1948.

Lévy-Strauss, Claude. "La vie familiale et sociale des Indiens Nambikwara." *Journal de la Société des Américanistes de Paris* 37 (1948):1–189.

Lincoln, Bruce. *Priests, Warriors, Cattle.* Berkeley, 1981.

Lloyd, Seton. *Early Anatolia.* 1956. Harmondsworth.

Lommel, Andreas. *The World of the Early Hunters,* trs. Michael Bullock. London, 1967.

Luckenbill, Daniel. *The Annals of Sennacherib.* Chicago, 1924.

Ludwig, Theodore. "The Way of Tea." *History of Religions* 14 (1974):28–50.

Lurker, Manfred. *The Gods and Symbols of Ancient Egypt.* London, 1974.

Maldonis, Wold. "Dievs, der Gott der lettischen Volkstradition." *Studia Theologica* 1 (1935):119–56.

Mallowan, M.E.L., and Rose Cruikshank. "Excavation at Tall Arpachiyah, 1933." *Iraq* 2 (1935):1–178.

Malten, L. "Der Raub der Kore." *Archiv für Religionswissenschaft* 12 (1909):285–312.

Mannhardt, F. W. "Die lettischen Sonnenmythen." *Zeitschrift für Ethnologie* 7 (1875): 73–104, 201–44, 281–320.

———. *Letto-preussische Götterlehre.* (Lettisch-literarische Gesellschaft) Riga, 1936.

———. "Die Mater Deum der Aestier." *Zeitschrift für deutsches Alterthum und deutsche Litteratur* 12 (1880):159–68.

———. *Mythologische Forschungen.* Strassburg, 1884.

Marshack, Alexander. *The Roots of Civilization, the Cognitive Beginnings of Man's First Art, Symbol and Notation.* London, 1972.

Mathews, Caithlín, ed. *Voices of the Goddess: A Chorus of Sibyls.* Wellingborough, Northhamptonshire, 1990.

Matsudaira, Narimitsu. "The Concept of Tamashii in Japan." In *Studies in Japanese Folklore,* ed. M. R. Dorson, pp. 181–97. Bloomington, 1963.

Mellaart, James. *Çatal Hüyük: A Neolithic Town in Anatolia.* London, 1967.

———. *Earliest Civilizations of the Near East.* London, 1965.

———. *Excavations at Hacilar.* 2 vols. Edinburgh, 1970.

de Mendieta, Fray Gerónimo. *Historia ecclesiástica Indiana.* J. Icazbalceta García, ed. Mexico City, 1870.

Merkur, Daniel. *Becoming Half-hidden: Shamanism and Initiation Among the Inuit.* [Stockholm Studies in Comparative Religion 24] Stockholm, 1985.

Meuli, Karl. "Griechische Opferbräuche." In *Phyllobia: Festschrift D. von der Mühl,* pp. 185–288. Basel, 1946. Reprint, *Gesammelte Schriften.* 2 vols. Basel, 1975.

———. "Ein altpersischer Kriegsbrauch." In *Festschrift für Rudolf Tschudi.* Wiesbaden, 1954. Reprint *Gesammelte Schriften.* 2 vols. Basel, 1975.

Michael, Henry N., ed. *Studies in Siberian Shamanism.* Toronto, 1963.

Miller, Alan. "Ame-No Miso-Ori Me (the Heavenly Weaving Maiden): The Cosmic Weaver in Early Shinto Myth and Ritual." *History of Religions* 24 (1984–85):27–48.

———. "Ritsuryō Japan. The State as Liturgical Community." *History of Religions* 11 (1971–72):98–121.

Mollard-Besques, S. *Catalogue raisonné des figurines et reliefs en terre-cuite grecs, etrusques, romains* IV, 1. Musée national de Louvre. Paris, 1954–63.

Monigliano, Arnold. "Cybele." In *The Encyclopedia of Religion,* eds. M. Eliade et al. New York, 1987.

Motz, Lotte. *The Beauty and the Hag: Female Figures of Germanic Faith and Myth.* Vienna, 1993.

————. "Ódinn and the Giants: A Study in Ethno-Cultural Origins." *The Mankind Quarterly* 25 (1985):387–418.

Müller, Werner. *Die Religionen der Indianervölker Nordamerikas.* In *Die Religionen des alten Amerika,* eds. Krickeberg, Müller, Trimborn, and Zerries, pp. 171–267. Stuttgart, 1961.

Muñoz, Camargo Diego. *Historia de Tlazcala.* Alfred Chavero, ed. Mexico City, 1892.

Murray, Margaret. *The God of the Witches.* Oxford, 1933.

Mylonas, George E. *The Hymn to Demeter and Her Sanctuary at Eleusis.* St. Louis, 1942.

Nahodil, O. "Mother Cult in Siberia." In *Popular Beliefs and Folklore Tradition in Siberia,* ed. Vilmos Diószegi, pp. 459–77. Budapest, 1968.

Naoe, Hiroji. "A Study of Yashiki-gami." In *Studies in Japanese Folklore,* ed. R. M. Dorson, pp. 198–214. Bloomington, 1963.

Narr, Karl P. 1959. "Bärenzeremoniell und Schamanismus in der älteren Steinzeit Europas." *Saeculum* 10 (1959):233–78.

Neckel G., and H. Kuhn, eds. *Edda. Die Lieder des Codex Regius nebst verwandten Denkmälern.* Heidelberg, 1983.

Neuland, Lena. *Jumis: die Fruchtbarkeitsgottheit der alten Letten.* Stockholm Studies in Comparative Religion 15. Stockholm, 1977.

Neumann, Erich. *The Great Mother,* trs. Ralph Mannheim. Princeton, 1955.

Neumann, Franke J. "The Flayed God and His Rattlestick: A Shamanic Element in Prehispanic Mesoamerican Religion." *History of Religions* 15 (1975):251–63.

Neumann, Günther. "Die Begleiter der phrygischen Muttergöttin von Boğazköy." In *Nachrichten der Akademie der Wissenschaften in Göttingen,* Phil.-hist. Klasse pp. 101–6. Göttingen, 1959.

Niels and Keiser. *Historical, Religious and Economic Texts and Antiquities.* New Haven, 1920.

Nihongi. Chronicles of Japan from the Earliest Times to A.D. 697, trs. William George Aston. London, 1896.

Nilsson, Martin P. "Die eleusinischen Gottheiten." *Archiv für Religionswissenschaft* 12 (1935):79–141.

————. *Geschichte der griechischen Religion.* 2 vols. Munich, 1967.

————. *Griechische Feste von religiöser Bedeutung mit Ausschluss der attischen.* Leipzig, 1906.

————. *A History of Greek Religion,* trs. F. J. Fielden. Oxford, 1925.

————. *The Minoan-Mycenaean Religion and Its Survival in Greek Religion.* Lund, 1950.

————. *The Mycenaean Origin of Greek Mythology.* Berkeley and Los Angeles, 1933.

Norlander-Unsgaard, S. "On Gesture, Posture, Movement and Motion in the Saami Bear Ceremonial." In *Saami pre-Christian Religion* by L. Bäckman and Å. Hultkrantz, pp. 187–99. Stockholm, 1985.

Numismatische Zeitschrift. vol. I. Vienna, 1870.

Obayashi, Taryo. "Die Amaterasu-Mythe im alten Japan und die Sonnenfinsternismythe in Südostsasien." *Ethnos* 25 (1960):20–43.

Ogibenin, B. L. "Baltic Evidence and the Indo-European Prayer." *Journal of Indo-European Studies* 2 (1974):23–45.

Ogura, Manabu. "Drifted Deities in the Noto Peninsula." In *Studies in Japanese Folklore,* ed. M. R. Dorson, pp. 133–44. Bloomington, 1963.

Öhlemütz, Erwin. *Die Kulte und Heiligtümer der Götter in Pergamon.* Darmstadt, 1968.

Ohnefalsch-Richter, M. *The Ancient Places of Worship in Cyprus.* Berlin, 1891.

Otto, Rdolf. *The Idea of the Holy,* trs. J. W. Harvey. Oxford, 1950.

Parrot, André. "Les fouilles de Mari, la sixième campagne (Automne 1938)." *Syria* 21 (1940):1–28.

———. *Sumer,* trs. T. S. Gilbert and J. Emmers. London, 1960.

Paulson, Ivar. *Himmel und Erde in der Agrarreligion der finnischen Völker.* Stockholm, 1963.

———. *The Old Estonian Folk Religion.* Bloomington, 1971.

———. *Die primitiven Seelenvorstellungen der nordeurasischen Völker. Eine religionsethnographische und religions-phänomenologische Untersuchung.* Stockholm, 1958.

———. *Die Religionen der finnischen Völker.* In *Die Religionen Nordeurasiens und der Amerikanischen Arktis,* eds. Hultkrantz, Paulson, and Jettmar, pp. 147–282. Stuttgart, 1962.

———. *Die Religionen der nordasiatischen (sibirischen) Völker.* In *Die Religionen Nordeurasiens und der Amerikanischen Arktis,* eds. Hultkrantz, Paulson, and Jettmar, pp. 1–144. Stuttgart, 1962.

———. *Schutzgeister und Gottheiten des Wildes (der Jagdtiere und Fische) in Nordeurasien.* In *The Supernatural Owners of Nature,* ed. Åke Hultkrantz, Stockholm, 1961.

Der Kleine Pauly. Lexikon der Antike. Stuttgart, 1964.

Pauly-Wissowa. *Paulys Realenzyklopädie der classischen Altertumswissenschaft begonnen von George Wissowa.* Stuttgart, 1893–.

Pettazzoni, R. *The Allknowing God,* trs. H. J. Rose. London, 1956.

Petterson, Olof. *Jabmek and Jabmeaimo.* Lund, 1957.

———. *Mother Earth.* Lund, 1967.

Philippi, Donald L. P. *Kojiki.* Tokyo, 1969.

Piggott, Stuart. *Prehistoric India.* Harmondsworth, 1950.

Poebel, A. "The Genesis of Enkidu." *AS* 11:58–60. Chicago, 1939.

Pope, Marvin, and Wolfgang Röllig. *Syrien. Die Mythologie der Ugariter und Phönizier.* In Hans William Haussig, *Wörterbuch der Mythologie* I, pp. 217–312. Stuttgart, 1965.

Porada, E. *Corpus of Ancient Near Eastern Seals in North American Collections,* Vol. 1. Washington, 1948.

Potanin, G. N. *Ocherki Severo-Zapadn.* Mongolii IV. St. Petersburg, 1883.

Preston, James J. "Conclusion: New Perspectives on Mother Worship." In *Mother Worship: Theme and Variation,* ed. James Preston, pp. 325–43. Chapel Hill, 1982.

———. "The Goddess Chandi as an Agent of Change." In *Mother Worship: Theme and Variation,* ed. James Preston, pp. 210–26. Chapel Hill, 1982.

———. "Goddess Worship." In *The Encyclopedia of Religion,* eds. M. Eliade et al. New York, 1987.

Preuss, Theodor K. *Mexikanische Religion.* In *Bilderatlas zur Religionsgeschichte,* ed. Hans Haas, et al. Leipzig, 1930.

Preuss, Theodor K., and E. Mengin. *Die historische Bilderhandschrift Tolteca-Chichimeca,* Pt. 1. In *Bässler Archiv,* Beiheft 9. Berlin, 1937.

———. *Die mexikanische Bilderhandschrift Tolteca-Chichimeca,* Pt. 2. In *Bässler Archiv* 21. Berlin, 1938.

Price, Theodora H. *Kourotrophos: Cults and Representations of the Greek Nursing Deities.* Leiden, 1978.

Pritchard, J. B., ed. *Ancient Near Eastern Texts Relating to the Old Testament.* Princeton, 1969.

Prokovyeva, Ye. D. "The Costume of the Enets Shaman." In *Studies in Siberian Shamanism,* ed. Henry Michael, pp. 124–56. Toronto, 1963.

Qvigstad, J. *Kildeskrifter til den Lappisk Mytologi I.* [*Det Kongl. Norske Videnskabers Selskabs Skr.*] Trondhjem, 1903.

Ränk, Gustav. *Die heilige Hinterecke im Hauskult der Völker Nordosteuropas und Nordasiens. Folklore Fellows Communications* 137 (1949). Helsinki.

———. *Lapp Female Deities of the Madder Akka Group. Studia Septentrionalia* 6 (1955).

———. "The Symbolic Bow in the Birth Rites of the North-Eurasian Peoples." *History of Religions* 1 (1961): 281–90.

Ranson, Jay Ellis. "Aleut Religious Beliefs: Veniaminov's Account." *Journal of American Folklore* 58 (1945): 346–49.

Rasmussen, Knud. *Across Arctic America.* London, 1927.

———. *Eskimo Folktales,* trs. W. Worster. London, 1921.

———. *Rasmussens Thulefahrt.* Frankfurt am Main, 1926.

Reischauer, Edwin O. *Japan: Past and Present.* London, 1947.

Reissner, G. A. *Sumerisch-babylonische Hymnen nach Thontafeln griechischer Zeit.* Berlin, 1896.

Reuterskiöld, E. *Källeskrifter till lapparnas mytologi.* Stockholm, 1910.

Rink, Henrik. *Tales and Traditions of the Eskimo.* 1875. Reprint, London, 1974.

Robertson, Charles M. *The History of Greek Art.* London, 1975.

Róheim, Géza. *Hungarian and Vogul Mythology.* Seattle and London, 1954.

———. "Die Sedna Sage." *Imago* 10 (1924): 159–77.

Roller, Lynn E. "The Great Mother at Gordion." *Journal of Hellenic Studies* 111 (1991): 124–33.

Rosaldo, Michelle, and Louise Lampere. *Women, Culture and Society.* Stanford, 1974.

Roscher, W. H. *Ausführliches Lexikon der griechischen und römischen Mythologie.* Leipzig, 1890–94.

de Sahagún, Fray Bernardino. *Florentine Codex. General History of the Things of New Spain,* trs. Arthur J. O. Anderson and Charles E. Dibble. Santa Fe, 1950–82.

Sakurada, Katsunori. "The Ebisu-gami in Fishing Villages." In *Studies in Japanese Folklore,* ed. M. R. Dorson, pp. 122–32. Bloomington, 1963.

Sanday, Peggy. 1974. "Female Status in the Public Domain." In *Women, Culture and Society,* eds. M. Rosaldo and L. Lampere, pp. 189–206. Stanford, 1974.

Schmidt, P. *Die Letten.* Riga, 1930.

Die Schöpfungsmythen. Ägypter, Sumerer, Hurriter, Hethiter, Kanaaiter und Israeliten. Zürich, 1964.

Schott, Albert, and Wolfram von Soden. *Das Gilgamesch-Epos.* Stuttgart, 1958.

Schrader, E. *Keilinschriftliche Bibliothek.* Vols. 1–4. Berlin, 1889.

Schröder, Dominik. "Zur Struktur des Schamanismus (mit besonderer Berücksichtigung des lamaistischen Gurtum)." *Anthropos* 50 (1955): 848–81.

von Schuler, Einar. *Kleinasien: die Mythologie der Hethiter und Hurriter.* In *Wörterbuch der Mythologie I,* ed. Hans W. Haussig, pp. 143–215. Stuttgart, 1965.

Scott, George R. *Phallic Worship.* London, 1966.

Seler, George, E. *Codex Borgia. Eine altmexikanische Bilderschrift der Bibliothek der Congregacion de Propaganda Fide.* 3 vols. Berlin, 1904–09.

———. *Codex Féjerváry-Mayer. Eine altmexikanische Bilderhandschrift der Free Public Museums in Liverpool.* Berlin, 1901.

———. *Codex Vaticanus 3773 B. Eine altmexikanische Bilderschrift der vatikanischen Bibliothek.* Berlin, 1902.

———. *Gesammelte Abhandlungen zur amerikanischen Sprach-und Altertumskunde.* 5 vols. Berlin, 1902–23.

———. *Das Tonalamatl der Aubinschen Sammlung.* Berlin, 1900.

Seroshevski, V. L. *Yakuty.* St. Petersburg, 1896.

Shetelig, Haakon, and Hjalmar Falk. *Scandinavian Archaeology,* trs. E. V. Gordon. Oxford, 1937.

Shirokogoroff, S. M. *Psychomental Complex of the Tungus.* London, 1935.

———. *Social Organization of the Northern Tungus.* Shanghai, 1929.

———. *Versuch einer Erforschung der Grundlagen des Schamanismus bei den Tungusen,* trs. W. Ukrig. Berlin, 1935.

Simčenko Ju. B. "Mother Cult among the North Eurasian People." In *Shamanism in Siberia,* eds. V. Diószegi and M. Hoppál, pp. 503–12. Budapest, 1978.

Simon, Erika. *Die Götter der Griechen. Aufnahmen von Max Hirmer.* Munich, 1985.

Sjöberg, Åke. *Der Mondgott Nanna in der sumerischen Überlieferung.* Stockholm, 1960.

Sjöberg, Åke, and E. Bergmann. *The Collection of Sumerian Temple Hymns.* Locust Valley, 1969.

Sjöö, Monica, and Barbara Moor. *The Great Cosmic Mother.* San Francisco, 1991.

Smith, Barbara. "Greece." In *The Feminist Companion to Mythology* by C. Larrington, pp. 65–101. London, 1992.

Snorri Sturluson. Edda, trs. Anthony Faulkes. London, 1987.

Sokolova, A. P. "The Representation of a Female Spirit from the Kazym River." In *Shamanism in Siberia,* eds. V. Diószegi and M. Hoppál, pp. 491–501. Budapest, 1978.

Solomutina, S. N. "The Role of the Altaic Shaman in the Symbolic Protection of Childbirth." In *Shamanism: Past and Present,* eds. M. Hoppál and O. von Sadovszki, pp. 191–97. Los Angeles, 1989.

Sonne, Birgitte. "Mythology of the Eskimos." In *The Feminist Companion to Mythology,* ed. C. Larrington, pp. 137–61. London, 1992.

Sonne, Birgitte, and Inge Kleivan. *Eskimos: Greenland and Canada.* Leiden, 1985.

Sourvinou-Inwood, Christiane. "Erotic Pursuit and Abduction as Paradigms of Greek Marriage." Women in Antiquity: Discussion Group. Oxford, 1987.

———. "Persephone and Aphrodite at Locri: A Model for Personality Definition in Greek Religion." *Journal of Hellenic Studies* 98 (1978):101–21.

Spekke, Arnold. *History of Latvia.* Stockholm, 1951.

Spence, Lewis. *The Gods of Mexico.* London, 1923.

Stein, Diane, ed. *The Goddess Celebrates: An Anthology of Women's Rituals.* Freedom, California, 1991.

Stender, Gotthard Friedrich. *Lettisches Lexikon.* Mitau, 1789.

Sternberg, Leo. "Der Adlerkult bei den Völkern Sibiriens." *Archiv für Religionswissenschaft* 28 (1930):125–53.

———. "Die Religion der Giljaken." *Archiv für Religionswissenschaft* 8 (1905):244–74.

Steward, Julian H. *Native Peoples of South America*. New York, 1959.

Stillwell, A. N. *Corinth (vol. 15): The Potters' Quarter*. Princeton, 1948–52.

Stone, Merlin. "Goddess Worship in the Ancient Near East." In *The Encyclopedia of Religion*, eds. M. Eliade et al. New York, 1987.

——. *When God Was a Woman*. London, 1976.

Thalbitzer, William. "Die kultischen Gottheiten der Eskimos." *Archiv für Religionswissenschaft* 26 (1928):364–430.

——. *Légendes et chants esquimaux du Groenland*, trs. Hollat-Bretagne. Paris, 1929.

Thureau-Dangin, F. *Les cylindres de Goudéa découverts par Ernest de Sarzec à Tello*. Paris, 1925.

——. *Les inscriptions de Sumer et d' Akkad*. Paris, 1905.

Torquemada, Juan de. *Los veinte y un libros rituales y monarchia Indiana*. 3 vols. Madrid, 1723.

Tscherneijtzow, V. N. "Bärenfest bei den Obugriern." *Acta Ethnographica* 23 (1975): 285–319.

Ucko, Peter. *Anthropomorphic Figurines of Predynastic Egypt and Neolithic Crete with Comparative Material from the Prehistoric Near East and Mainland Greece*. London, 1968.

Vaillant, G. C. *The Aztecs of Mexico: Origin, Rise and Fall of the Aztec Nation*. Harmondsworth, 1944.

Vermaseren, Maarten J. *Corpus cultus Cybelae Attidisque*. 7 vols. Leiden, 1987.

——. *Cybele and Attis: The Myth and the Cult*. London, 1989.

Waida, Manabu. "Sacred Kingship in Japan." *History of Religions* 15 (1975–76):319–42.

——. "Symbolism of the Moon and the Waters of Immortality." *History of Religions* 16 (1976–77):407–23.

Wardle, Newell S. "The Sedna Cycle: A Study in Myth Evaluation." *American Anthropologist* n.s. 2 (1900):568–80.

Warner, Langdon. *The Enduring Art of Japan*. Cambridge, 1952.

Wehrli, Fritz. "Die Mysterien von Eleusis." *Archiv für Religionswissenschaft* 31 (1934): 77–104.

Winter, E. *Die Typen der figürlichen Terrakotten*. Berlin, 1903.

Winter, Urs. *Frau und Göttin: exegetische und ikonographische Studien zum weiblichen Gottesbild im alten Israel und dessen Umwelt*. Freiburg, 1983.

Witzel, Maurus. *Tammuzlieder und Verwandtes*. Rom, 1935.

Wolkstein, Diane, and Samuel Kramer. *Inanna, Queen of Heaven and Earth*. New York, 1983.

Yonov, V. M. *K voprosu ob izuchonii dokhristyamanskh verovandi*. Petrograd, 1918.

Zanker, P. *Der Wandel der Hermesgestalt in der attischen Vasenmalerei*. Bonn, 1965.

Zicāns, Ed. "Die Hochzeit der Sonne und des Mondes in der lettischen Mythologie." *Studia Theologica* 1 (1935):171–200.

Zimmern, A. H. *Sumerische Kultlieder aus altbabylonischer Zeit* 1, 2. Vorderasiatische Schriftdenkmäler der königlichen Museen zu Berlin 2. Leipzig, 1912–13.

——. *König Lipit-Ištars Vergöttlichung*. In *Berichte über die Verhandlungen der Kgl. Sächsischen Gesellschaft der Wissenschaften*, Phil.-hist. Klasse 68 (1916): 1–143.

Picture Credits

We gratefully acknowledge the following persons and institutions for the photographs and illustrations in this book.

Figure 1, Photograph from Naturhistorisches Museum, Vienna; 2, Reprinted from Franz Hančar, "Zum Problem de Venusstatuetten im eurasischen Jungpaläolithikum." *Prähistorische Zeitschrift* 30–31 (Berlin: Walter de Gruyter & Co., 1939), pl. 10; 3, Reprinted from Arthur E. Evans, "The 'Tomb of the Double Axes' and Associated Group of Ritual Vessels of 'Little Palace' at Knossos," *Archaeologia* 65 (1914), fig. 16; 4, 5, 19, 20, and 21, Reprinted, by permission, from Peter Gelling and Hilda Ellis Davidson, *The Chariot of the Sun* (London: Orion, 1969), figs, 33, 31, 35, 23, and 25; 6, Reprinted from Gutorm Gjessing, *Arktiske helleristningar i nord-norge* (Oslo, 1932), pl. XI; 7, 8, and 9, Neumann, Erich, *The Great Mother*. Figs. 23, 24, and 25. Copyright 1955 by PUP. Copyright renewed 1983. Reproduced by permission of Princeton University Press; 10, Reprinted, by permission, from Manfred Lurker, *The Gods and Symbols of Ancient Egypt* (London, 1974), entry: birth brick; 11, 12, 13, and 36, Reprinted, by permission, from James Mellaart, *Excavations at Hacilar*, 2 vols. (Edinburgh: Edinburgh University Press, 1970), pls. VI, CLII and figs. 227 and 228; 14, 15 and 16, Reprinted from Margaret Murray, *The God of the Witches* (Oxford: Oxford University Press, 1933), figs. 2, 3, and 11; 16, Photograph from The National Museum, Copenhagen; 17, Reprinted from Gutorm Gjessing, *Nordenfjelske ristningar og malingar av den arktiske gruppe* (Oslo, 1936), pl. LI; 18, Reprinted, by permission, from Herbert Kühn, *Die Felsbilder Europas* (Stuttgart: W. Kohlhammer Verlag, 1952), fig. 140; 22, Reprinted from Arthur E. Evans, *The Mycenaean Tree and Pillar Cult and its Mediterranean Relations* (London, 1905), fig. 3; 23, Reprinted from Frank Brommer, *Satyroi* (Würzburg, 1937), Pl. 5; 25, 26, and 27, Reprinted from Gustav Ränk, *Lapp Female Deities of the Madder Akka Group. Studia Septentrionalia* Vol. 6 (1955), figs. 7, 2, and 8; 28 and 29, Reprinted from Knud Rasmussen, *Rasmussens Thulefahrt* (Frankfurt am Main, 1926), pp. 253 and 239; 30, 31, 32, and 38, Reprinted, by permission, from Urs Winter, *Frau und Göttin: exegetische und ikonographische Studien zum weiblichen Gottesbild im alten Israel und dessen Umwelt* (Freiburg: Éditions Universitaires, 1983), fig. 419, 390, 393, 281–83; 33 and 34, Reprinted, by permission, from Wolfgang Helck, *Betrachtungen zur grossen Göttin und den ihr verbundenen Gottheiten* (Munich: Oldenbourg Verlag, 1971), figs. 176 and 182; 35 and 37, Reprinted, by permission, from James Mellaart, *Çatal Hüyük: A Neolithic Town in Anatolia* (London, 1967), fig. 67 and p. 24; 39, Reprinted, by permission, from the Ankara Museum; 40, Reprinted, by permission, from Lynn E. Roller, "The Great Mother at Gordion," *Journal of Hellenic Studies* 111 (1991), pl. 3a; 41, Reprinted, by permission, from Maarten Vermaseren, *Corpus cultus Cybelae Attidisque* Vol. III (Leiden: Brill, 1987), pl. CCXCVIII; 42, 44, 45, and 46, Photographs from Hirmer Verlag, Munich; 43, Photograph from Antikensammlung, Staatliche Museen zu Berlin-Preussischer Kulturbesitz; 47, Photograph from The National Gallery, London; 48, Reprinted from George E. Seler, *Gesammelte Abhandlungen zur amerikanischen Sprach- und Altertumskunde* 5 vols. (Berlin, 1902–23), fig. 31, p. 480; 49, Reprinted from George E. Seler, *Codex Vaticanus 3773 B. Eine altmexikanische Bilderschrift der vatikanischen Bibliothek* (Berlin, 1902), fig. 529; 50 and 51, Reprinted from George E. Seler, *Codex Borgia. Eine altmexikanische Bilderschrift der Bibliothek der Congregacion de Propaganda Fide* 3 vols. (Berlin, 1904–09), figs. 345 and 256; 52, Reprinted from Codex Florentino. *Illustrations for Sahagún's Historia de las Cosas de Nueva España*. Edited by Arthur J. C. Anderson and Charles E. Dibble (Santa Fe, 1950–82), FL.

Index